Trade Liberalization and Indian Agriculture

Trade Liberalization and Indian Agriculture

SEEMA BATHLA

RAWAT PUBLICATIONS
Jaipur • New Delhi • Bangalore • Hyderabad • Guwahati

ISBN 978-81-316-0393-2

The publication of this book was financially supported by the ICSSR. The responsibility for the facts stated, opinions expressed, or conclusions reached, is entirely that of the author and that the ICSSR accepts no responsibility for them.

ICSSR Consultant: Professor V.R. Panchamukhi, Managing Editor, *Indian Economic Journal*, The Indian Economic Association, New Delhi.

Published by
Prem Rawat for **Rawat Publications**
Satyam Apts, Sector 3, Jawahar Nagar, Jaipur 302 004 (India)
Phone: 0141 265 1748 / 7006 Fax: 0141 265 1748
E-mail: info@rawatbooks.com
Website: www.rawatbooks.com

New Delhi Office
4858/24, Ansari Road, Daryaganj, New Delhi 110 002
Phone: 011 2326 3290

Also at *Bangalore, Hyderabad* and *Guwahati*

Typeset by Rawat Computers, Jaipur
Printed at Nice Printing Press, New Delhi

In loving memory of my sister,
Renu, who always inspired me to do my
best – personally and professionally

Contents

Foreword

Ever since India introduced economic reforms under the Structural Adjustment Programme in 1991, the impact of structural change and macroeconomic policies on agriculture has led to a critical debate in academic as well as policy making circles. Implementation of the World Trade Organization (WTO) Agreement on Agriculture further sparked an intense discussion in the country, especially on agricultural pricing and subsidy. The proponents of trade liberalization strongly believed that liberal policies would correct the 'neglect of agriculture', long over due, which in turn, would augment capital formation, competitiveness at the global level, higher output and growth. Those who opposed the new policies expressed concerns about the future of India's agriculture under the pressure of liberalization and multilateral trading rules, and their adverse impact on farmers' income, employment, poverty, prices and food security.

This study has analysed the impact of economic reforms and other globalization measures on the performance of agriculture. The author has developed a structural econometric model within a partial equilibrium framework, based on a priori theoretical linkages between agriculture, world price, macroeconomic and sector-specific policies and other factors to evaluate the degree of response palpable in agricultural pricing and output. An important concern, especially of the developing countries including India is to deal with untoward situations that may arise in a freer trade regime. A comprehensive assessment of the likely shocks and quantification of their impacts on prices, exports, imports and output for policy interventions is the strength of this book.

Among many important findings, the most striking is that Indian agriculture is increasingly being driven by an incentive structure arising out of policy reforms and initiatives in irrigation and technology. However, the volatility in world prices and exchange rates, non-tariff barriers, import surge, weak marketing system, non-alignment of external and internal trade policies, are some of the factors delineated in this book, that are holding back the expected gains. There are many more challenges that Indian agriculture faces today, as for example global recession, WTO trade negotiations, hike in oil price and fertilizer subsidies, which can form the subject matter for further research. The important policy implication is that agriculture needs appropriate and timely interventions in trade, price and marketing policies in tandem with other complementary measures not only to maintain a favourable price structure but also to accelerate competitiveness, output and growth.

Given the sparse literature on issues concerning trade and agriculture, the contribution of this book to public debate on the positive and negative impacts of trade on this sector will be to provide rich insights into appropriate macro- and sector-specific interventions within a broader mandate of trade negotiations. It will be of immense use to researchers interested in agricultural economics, trade and econometric modelling, and to policy makers for appraising the changing dynamics of agriculture in a globalizing world.

B.B. Bhattacharya
Former Vice-Chancellor, Jawaharlal Nehru University,
New Delhi

Preface

With the inception of Structural Adjustment Programme, the agricultural sector in many developing countries has begun to be viewed in a larger macroeconomic policy framework and is being looked upon as a source of income growth in its own right. The programme, based on an open economy model of the neo-classical, supported a greater integration of domestic economy with the world economy for higher output, economic growth and technological advancements. Thus, the 'anti-agriculture bias' manifested through overvalued exchange rate, restrictive trade policy and high industrial protection identified in the classical 'industry-led growth' model was to be obliterated by currency devaluation, reduction in tariffs, elimination of trade restrictions and initiation of liberal farm policies. Implementation of the Agreement on Agriculture (AoA) during 1994 along with establishment of the WTO further delineated the broad contours of agricultural trade policies and commitments to abide by the developed and the developing member countries.

This study taken up in the Indian context aims to examine the impact of trade liberalization, macroeconomic and sector-specific policy measures and factors on agriculture through price transmission, changes in the cropping pattern, exports, imports and acreage response. The analysis is carried out during the pre-and post-liberalization periods using time series cointegration and error correction techniques and a structural econometric model within a partial equilibrium framework. In view of the diversity and regional variations in crop choices and dominations, a disaggregate state and crop-level analysis has been carried out.

The findings reveal that trade in agriculture was firmly brought within the multilateral trading system only after the Uruguay Round negotiations established the WTO and formulated an Agreement on Agriculture. As a result, while the agricultural sector in India has certainly opened up relative to its past but this openness remains partial due to imposition of Non-tariff Barriers (NTBs) and various restrictions on both external and internal trade. Due to this and some other factors, price transmission across the state-level agricultural markets and also between the world and domestic ones is not perfect as expected. Though the long-run integration across spatial markets has improved in the post-liberalization period, commodity prices considerably drift apart in the short-run, compelling a strong need to speed up reforms, bridge information and other gaps for achieving greater market efficiency.

The study further divulges that cropping pattern changes are certainly transpiring across many states but the magnitude of diversification has been gradual. Results obtained from the structural econometric model confirm that the producers respond positively to price incentives arising out of liberal exchange rate, trade and price policies together with non-price technological, infrastructure and natural factors. It clearly indicates that had India been more open to world trade during the eighties, average exports would have been much higher. However, the acreage response is not very high in many cases, which again goes against the expectations. The study attempts to give reasons responsible for a not-so-significant upturn in the agricultural sector following the reforms, some of which relate to situations within the country while others to global conditions.

Finally, the simulation results reveal that the performance of agriculture in a free trade regime is quite sensitive to exogenous impulses, captured through maximum and minimum variations in the exchange rate, rainfall, world price, tariffs and minimum support price. Commodity prices and output tend to be more resilient to various shocks compared to the exports and imports. Also, commercial crops are more vulnerable to shocks as compared to cereals. An important finding that emerges from the 'best and worst' scenarios of change is that the macro-economic and sectoral policies that are in place have made Indian agriculture fairly resilient to shocks. Nevertheless, several pertinent issues and challenges exist for the agricultural sector in a globalized economy that require policy interventions.

This book is a revised and updated version of the author's Ph.D. thesis submitted to Jawaharlal Nehru University (JNU), New Delhi for award of the doctoral degree. The research was carried out under the joint supervision of Professor S.K. Thorat, Centre for the Study of Regional Development (CSRD), JNU and Professor B.B. Bhattacharya,

Director, Institute of Economic Growth (IEG), Delhi University. I am very thankful to Professor S.K. Thorat for his keen interest in the work and useful suggestions despite being busy as Chairman of the University Grants Commission (UGC). Professor B.B. Bhattacharya has been very generous in giving direction to the study and has continued to take interest even after taking charge as Vice-Chancellor of JNU. I have benefited immensely from the stimulating discussions with him on the work for which I will always be very grateful.

My sincere thanks are due to Professors G.S. Bhalla, G.K. Chadha and Ravi S. Srivastava for providing useful inputs at the initial stages of work. Professor Ramesh Chand has been kind enough to go through some of the chapters despite his busy schedule and offered many valuable suggestions on the findings. I shall always be grateful for his help. I gratefully acknowledge the valuable comments and suggestions given by Professors R.K. Sharma and R.S. Deshpande. I also owe my gratitude to Professor Ashok Gulati for generating my interest in agricultural economics and enabling me to delve into various issues that confront Indian agriculture while working with him at IEG. Professor B.D. Dhawan's encouragement was of immense help in pursuing the work. Many thanks to Professor Kanchan Chopra for awarding me the ICSSR doctoral fellowship and extending support during the course of work. I would like to place on record my thanks to Professor V.R. Panchamukhi for recommending its publication. I gratefully acknowledge the financial support provided by the Indian Council of Social Science Research (ICSSR) that enabled me to work first as a full time researcher at IEG, and subsequently to publish this book.

Sincere thanks are due to my friends Dr Pramod Kumar, Mr Devendra Pratap, Dr Sabhyasachi Kar and other colleagues at the institute, with whom I shared my academic experiences. I am grateful to Dr Pramod for discussion and providing useful comments on the findings. I am thankful to the staff of the library and the computer unit at IEG and to the staff of CSRD, JNU for their cooperation.

Last but not the least, I owe my gratitude to my family members who have always stood by me. I have no words to express my thanks to Sanjeev, Sanya and Shourya for their constant support, encouragement and patience. My sister Renu (Sonia) has always been and will remain a source of inspiration for me. I am highly indebted to my parents and parents-in-law for their blessings and cooperation, and to my sisters and brothers-in-law for their continuous support.

Seema Bathla

List of Tables and Figures

Tables

Figures

Annexures

Annexure Figure

Abbreviations

ADF	Augmented Dickey Fuller Test
AIC	Akaike Information Criterion
AMS	Aggregate Measure of Support
AOA	Agreement on Agriculture
APEDA	Agriculture and Processed Food Products Export Development Authority
APMC	Agricultural Produce Market Committee Act
ARCH	Auto Regressive Conditional Hetroscedasticity Models
ARIMA	Auto Regressive Integrated Moving Average Process
BOP	Balance of Payment
C	Canalized
CACP	Commission on Agriculture Cost and Prices
CCI	Cotton Corporation of India
CGEM	Computable General Equilibrium Models
CIF	Cost Insurance and Freight
CSO	Central Statistical Organization
DGCI&S	Directorate General of Commercial Intelligence and Statistics
DP	Domestic Price (Wholesale)
EAS	Employment Assurance Scheme
ECA	Essential Commodity Act
ECM	Error Correction Model

EXIM	Export Import
FAO	Food and Agriculture Organization
FOB	Freight on Board
FCI	Food Corporation of India
FPE	Final Prediction Error
GATT	General Agreement on Trade and Tariff
GCA	Gross Cropped Area
GDP	Gross Domestic Product
GIA	Gross Irrigated Area
GOI	Government of India
HS	Harmonized System
HVOC	Hindustan Vegetable Oil Corporation
HYV	High Yielding Variety
IMF	International Monetary Fund
IPR	Import Penetration Ratio
JCI	Jute Corporation of India
LDCs	Less Developed Countries
LM	Lagrange Multiplier Test
LR	Likelihood Ratio
MEP	Minimum Export Price
MIS	Market Intervention Scheme
MMTC	Minerals and Metals Trading Corporation
MSCGCMF	Maharashtra State Cotton Growers Cooperative Marketing Federation
MSP	Minimum Support Price
NAFED	National Agricultural Cooperative Marketing Federation for India Ltd.
NAS	National Accounts Statistics
NDDB	National Dairy Development Board
NDP	Net Domestic Product
NDPA	Net Domestic Product Agriculture
NPC	Net Protection Coefficient
NPK	Nitrogen Phosphorus Potash

NTBs	Non-tariff Barriers
OGL	Open General License
OLS	Ordinary Least Squares
PDS	Public Distribution System
QR	Quantitative Restriction
R	Restricted
RBI	Reserve Bank of India
REH	Rational Expectation Hypothesis
RER	Real Exchange Rate
RPDS	Revamped Public Distribution System
SMP	Statutory Minimum Price
SAP	Structural Adjustment Programme
SCC	Selective Credit Control
SIL	Special Import License
SSA	Sub Saharan African Countries
SSM	Special Safeguard Mechanism
STC	State Trading Corporation
STEs	State Trading Enterprises
TOT	Terms of Trade
TPDS	Targeted Public Distribution System
TRIFED	Tribal Cooperative Marketing Development Federation of India Ltd.
TRQ	Tariff Rate Quota
UR	Uruguay Round
UR AOA	Uruguay Round Agreement on Agriculture
USA	United States of America
UT	Union Territory
VAR	Vector Auto Regression
VECM	Vector Error Correction Model
WP	World Price
WTO	World Trade Organization

1

Economic Reforms and Indian Agriculture

A Contextual Framework

Place of Agriculture in the Growth Process

Many countries in the early stages of their economic development had followed the classical dual-economy growth model. The model envisages industry as the 'engine of growth' so that a significant transfer of investable resources, mainly labour and raw material takes place from agriculture with active support of the government. It also presumes that as long as there is disguised unemployment in agriculture, surplus labour exists in agriculture with zero marginal productivity and also that the real wage which is institutionally determined is fixed. Following Kuznet's analysis (1955), a rise in productivity in agriculture is assumed to be a precondition for economic growth and structural change, for it is only then that agriculture generates surplus and is in a position to release labour and raw material for industrial development (Lewis, 1955; Fei and Ranis, 1964; Preobrazhensky, 1965; Chakravarty, 1973). Accordingly, countries where this approach had gained wider acceptance such as in Latin America and many Asian countries including India, import substitution-led industrialization through favourable intersectoral terms of trade for manufacturing was promoted.[1]

Neo-classical economists such as Jorgenson (1961) viewed this vision of development to be inappropriate as it depresses the growth prospects of agriculture. Hirschman (1958) and Johnston (1970) argued that a preoccupation with surplus labour often seems to have encouraged neglect of the sector. The 'neglect thesis' is reinforced on grounds that terms of trade turn against countries that export primary products and import manufactures and also that agriculture provides no stimulus to the setting up of new activities through a linkage effect. Among others, Krueger (1984), Schiff and Valdes (1992 and 1998) maintained that the doctrine of a supportive role of agriculture in the process of economic growth meant that agriculture was not looked upon as a source of income growth in its own right. The approach was based on a distrust of the private sector and the market along with the belief that government should play a leading role in the development. It was also pessimistic about the responsiveness of agricultural output to price incentives or that exports from developing countries could grow. According to these authors, implementation of such a policy meant a protection of industry at the expense of agriculture through provision of subsidies and foreign exchange thereby levying an implicit or explicit tax on agriculture, directly or through pricing policies.

Based on a strong presumption that agriculture makes important contributions to economic growth through provision of labour, capital, foreign exchange and food to the industrial sector, Johnston and Mellor (1961), and Mellor (1966) laid emphasis on the inter-dependence of the two sectors. They advocated an agricultural development strategy that favoured development of the smallholder sector and markets for domestically produced industrial goods through increase in their productivity and technological innovations. Nevertheless, a decline in the relative share of agriculture in gross national income and labour force was considered to be the natural outcome of structural transformation following Clark (1951) and Kuznets (1966).[2] This changed orientation of economic growth implied a much more significant role for agriculture in the development process and hence expansions in the micro-level research. The research focused on studying sector-specific policies and constraints on employment, income and equity goals. While advocating a more complete vision of the agricultural development process, the extent of government intervention in promoting industry and repressing agriculture had remained an important discussion point. Another related concern had been the extent to which farm incomes can be reduced by pricing and taxation mechanisms so that agriculture output does not stagnate for lack of profitability (Norton, 2004).

The approach of assigning a greater role to agriculture in the development process and looking at it as a source of growth in its own right, had gained momentum. This happened after the global economic crisis and rise in the real interest rates, following the United States' monetary policy change after the oil shock of 1979, took place. Besides, many developing countries experienced severe economic crisis and a relatively sustained agricultural growth for a period of two to three decades. These factors were considered to have adverse repercussions for the Third World agrarian economies in terms of exports, foreign exchange and balance of payment. Concomitantly, the priority of industry vis-à-vis agriculture and a long-term policy of export-led industrialization became highly debatable and discussed in numerous studies (Krueger, Schiff and Valdes, 1988; Gulati and Pursell, 1992). It was argued that the macroeconomic trade, exchange rate and agricultural policies had failed to acknowledge the role of agriculture in the growth process and in fact, introduced a bias against it in most of the developing countries including India. In many studies, a strong negative relationship between a policy of taxing agriculture and an economy's overall growth rate was found. This relationship was studied through low real exchange rate, high industrial protection and low domestic prices compared to that in the international markets (Schiff and Valdes, 1992; Teyers and Anderson, 1992; Meerman, 1997).

Initiation of Economic Reforms and Agriculture

In the face of sluggish economic growth and balance of payment problem, many Latin American, Sub-Saharan African and South Asian countries had to resort to economic assistance and balance of payment support from the mid-or late eighties. The assistance was taken from the International Monetary Fund (IMF) and the World Bank and was conditional on adoption of short-term and medium to long-term World Bank Structural Adjustment Programme (SAP). The programme advocated reform in the monetary and fiscal policies, capital and financial market reform and sector-specific liberal policies. The Indian government also introduced a new economic policy similar to the SAP during this period. The policy emphasized liberalization of the domestic markets and imports for faster growth of industry and an overall higher rate of economic growth. However, a slow down in the industrial output, deceleration in the foodgrain production along with critical problems of balance of payments and deficits led the country to adopt SAP.

The broad objective of SAP was to correct disequilibrium in the foreign exchange market and fuel up economic growth through technological advancement and expansion in external trade in industrial and agricultural commodities. An increased level of exports from the developing nations was expected to accelerate foreign exchange earnings and reduce current account deficits, thereby contributing to macroeconomic stabilization in these economies. Accordingly, the programme favoured an open economy model of the neo-classical, which supported more openness in external trade and a higher integration of domestic economies with the world economy (Goldin and Knudsen, 1990; Giles, Brown, Milward, Williams, 2000). Within agriculture, the anticipation was that removal of trade barriers and exchange rate adjustments would increase the domestic price of exportables relative to their world price, and also reduce the domestic price of importables relative to the world price. A favourable price structure for agriculture along with the emergence of well-functioning markets would provide better production incentives, accelerate private investment and enable primary exports to grow. And an increased agricultural export growth would lead to higher rates of economic growth in the long run (Bautista and Valdes, 1993; Mckay, Morrissey and Vaillant, 1997 and 1998). It was envisaged that the agricultural sector in the developing countries would increasingly face world markets and would take land allocation and production decisions in view of competitiveness of crops. In the process, world price would become the reference point in the measurement of relative price structure, domestic resource cost and allocation of scarce resources within the domestic economy. This also implied a free market economy and a complete withdrawal of government intervention in all aspects of price determination (Gulati and Kelly, 1999).

Given this, the developing countries that attempted stabilization and SAP started viewing agriculture in a larger macro policy framework. Elimination of the relative 'neglect of agriculture' and a need to 'get prices right' i.e., raising real agricultural prices in accord with world prices and turning the Terms of Trade (TOT) in favour of agriculture for more production and hence exports became the central objectives. Accordingly, both macroeconomic and sector-specific policies were identified for implementation as these are considered to have a bearing on producers' incentives through change in the relative prices.[3] Initiation of SAP was perhaps the turning point in the growth strategy of the developing countries. It raised the following questions: How do macroeconomic and sector-level policies affect relative commodity prices and hence producers' incentives? Which policy reforms were to be implemented under the SAP? What is the likely response of agriculture to changing policy measures?

Macroeconomic Policy Links to Agriculture

A large body of literature has analysed the theoretical and empirical linkages between macroeconomic policies and the agricultural sector. While the macroeconomic policies that affect agriculture are seen as namely: trade, exchange rate, and fiscal policy, the sector-specific policies include price and marketing. The analyses indicate that though macroeconomic and sectoral policies are interlinked, the effect of the former on producers' incentives is indirect and that of the latter is direct. Further, apart from these policies, there are other key factors such as interest rates, monetary policy, income and demand effects that may have a direct or indirect bearing on agriculture. The impact of these policies and factors on agriculture is captured mainly through their effect on price incentives. There are some important studies on this subject[4] while the theoretical underpinnings of these policies and their likely impacts on agriculture are briefly explained below.

Trade Policy

Trade policy influences production through change effected in prices and by the quantities of competing products that are imported into the country and by effects on domestic prices received for exports. The main instruments of trade policy are namely: (i) import tariffs and quotas or a combination of both called tariff-rate quotas that make tariffs rise when imports exceed a specified limit; (ii) trade restrictions through non-tariff barriers; and (iii) export incentives through subsidies and direct income support. Trade policy that is pursued under the conventional development strategy promotes industrialization through imposition of import tariffs and quantitative restrictions. This shifts resources out of agriculture by reducing its profitability in relation to industry and hence turning the domestic terms of trade against agriculture. In other words, prices of import-competing industrial goods are increased relative to prices of import-competing and exports agriculture and the cost of agricultural inputs is also increased. This makes import substitution more profitable than exports through change in relative demand and competitiveness of exports. In case, import duties (tariffs) are reduced, the prices of imported goods become lower in the country and bring gains to agriculture through purchase of cheap industrial inputs, such as fertilizers and pesticides. The net effect is favourable terms of trade to agriculture, which induces changes in the cropping pattern and accelerates private investment, technology, output and finally, exports.

Trade restrictions are imposed through import quotas, export bans, subsidies and licensing requirements for imports, phytosanitary requirements apart from many more. All these restrictions are subject to great variations and adversely affect imports and exports and generate inefficiencies in a country's own productive structure. For example, an imposition of import control on a scarce commodity can raise its domestic price and conversely an export ban may lead to repression in the domestic price. The price effects of export incentives through subsidies are again mixed. High prices for exports raise domestic prices of commodities and provide incentives to growers to increase output. On the contrary, export subsidies, for instance given by the developed nations have effects of lowering the level of international prices and hence reducing prices for farmers in not so rich countries (Norton, 2004).

In view of these outcomes of trade policy, SAP placed an increased emphasis on adopting a liberal trade policy, both by developed and developing countries. Some of the important trade policy reforms include the following: (i) improvement in market access in exporting countries; (ii) reduction in tariffs; (iii) removal of non-tariff barriers such as quantitative restrictions, licensing, quotas, etc., to be replaced with tariffs; (iv) reduction in domestic support to agriculture through input subsidy and direct income support to farmers. These policies are considered to have a more stable effect on prices compared to one by trade controls (Giles, Brown, Milward, Williams, 2000).

Exchange Rate Policy

Exchange rate is the price of foreign exchange, which reflects its supply of and demand for foreign exchange. While supply arises primarily from exports and capital inflows, demand originates from the need to import goods and services. A distinction between nominal and real exchange rate is necessary at this juncture. Whereas nominal exchange rate is a monetary concept that measures the relative price of two moneys, real exchange rate (RER) is a real concept that measures the relative price of two goods. It is defined as prices of tradable with respect to non-tradable goods written as EPt*/Pn, where E is the nominal exchange rate, Pt* is the world price of tradables and Pn is the domestic price of non-tradables (Edward, 1988).

It is important to note that a decline in RER or a real exchange rate appreciation indicates an increase in the domestic cost of producing tradable goods. If there are no changes in relative prices in the rest of the world, this decline in RER represents a deterioration of country's degree of international competitiveness: the country now produces tradable goods in a relatively less efficient way than before (i.e., in relation to rest of the world). In other words, an overvalued exchange rate raises price of product in terms of foreign currency, which reduces the quantity demanded. With reduced foreign demand, price declines, supply decreases and quantity demanded increases domestically, exports are reduced and a decline in the gross income takes place. However, the extent of reduction in exchange earnings and gross income depends upon the respective elasticities of demand and supply and the amount of overvaluation. In sum, when agricultural commodities are important tradables in a country, an overvalued currency erodes their competitiveness in the world markets with little incentives to expand output. On the other hand, an increase in RER or real exchange rate depreciation likewise indicates an improvement in country's international competitiveness. Devaluation, i.e., undervaluation of exchange rate tends to raise farm prices in foreign currency, which shifts product demand and turns terms of trade in favour of agriculture. In case agriculture produces a substantial amount of tradable goods, then exporters of agricultural commodities gain through an increase in prices on account of devaluation (Oyejide, 1993; Wobst, 2001).

Since most of the developing nations had followed a policy of an overvalued exchange rate, which was recognized to have taxed agriculture and adversely impacted the country's economic growth, devaluation of currency was made mandatory under SAP. The impact of a liberal exchange rate on relative price movements and trade of commodities was expected to be favourable in countries that opted for economic reforms.

Fiscal Policy

Fiscal policy can affect farm prices through provision of key elements of infrastructure such as port facilities that allow better access to export markets, storage depots, roads that reduce the transportation cost, irrigation facilities and so on. Public expenditure on such investments increases producers' prices by increasing market supplies, providing access to new markets and reducing marketing and transaction costs. Fiscal policy also affects prices through imposition of taxes. Often marketing agencies implicitly tax commodity through a low price to producers in order to finance subsidies on imported items. This suppresses producers' prices for the domestic commodity as well as the item that is imported. Such taxes are considered to be harmful as they affect economic efficiency and hence growth prospects (Norton, 2004). Fiscal policy under SAP is suggested in a way such that it enables countries to upgrade infrastructural farm investment which further induces private investment.

Sector-Specific Policies

Price and Marketing

The sector-specific policies that have a bearing on real market prices and producers' incentives are the fixation of support price (administered price), and marketing. Administered price for commodities is set up to counterbalance a decline in the terms of trade being imposed by an overvalued exchange rate. The loss arising from a deliberate lower level of domestic output prices relative to their border price is often compensated by the provision of input subsidies. Further, in many countries, a policy of pan-territorial pricing or support prices is being followed. This policy attempts to control prices in the downward direction and allows them to rise without any restriction. The underlying rationale behind such a policy is that it provides incentives to growers as well as makes commodity prices free from fluctuations and hence brings price stability across spatial regions[5]. This policy has long been in place in many developing countries. In India, government fixes the minimum support price for essential commodities and procures wheat, paddy and sugar at that price to boost production, ensure price stability and food security and maintain equity in the distribution of food to the low-income population.

The positive contentions of price policy have been countered on grounds that frequently in a scenario of fixed commodity prices their quantities fluctuate in response to variations in harvest or decline in aggregate demand in the economy. This results in occasional problems of surplus or shortages in the domestic markets, which are difficult to monitor. Also, the demand and supply imbalances may not get equilibrated. Further, sustenance of fixed prices of commodities requires considerable interventions in their trade and hence, controls and regulations to avert an emergence of black markets and corruption (Chand, 2001 and 2009; Deshpande, 2008). Support prices are also stated to be costly to the government budget as they are fixed above the market clearing level for producers and below the level for consumers. Grain procurement and its storage by government agencies is again flawed with weaknesses that often distort market prices and act as disincentives to producers (Gulati, Kahkonen and Sharma, 2000; Ganesh-Kumar, Gulati and Cummings, 2009).

In this context, the primary focus of economic reforms has been to reorient price policy so that it does not distort free market price, benefits producers and increases private sector participation in the marketing and storage of produce. Implicitly, it implies a complete withdrawal of government intervention in all aspects of price determination. Minimal government intervention through state control boards in storage, procurement and distribution activities is also recommended. Commodity price bands, crop insurance and futures markets are suggested as the effective ways to tackle price instability that may arise in a situation of surplus or deficiency of commodities.

Compared to the above theoretical arguments and discussion in favour of implementation of liberalized policies under SAP and their positive impact on agriculture, it has been argued that any perceived gains from reforms may not materialize an account the following: (i) highly volatile nature of world prices, (ii) variations in the exchange rate, (iii) surge in imports due to reduction in tariffs, (iv) misallocation of resources and large inefficiencies, and (v) fiscal constraints and hence lower infrastructural public investment (Bhalla, 1994; Nayyar and Sen, 1994; Rao and Linneman, 1996). Other related concerns are the impact of free trade on the low-income population through reduction in prices of importable food items relative to domestic production along with changes in wages and employment, which have wider implications for food security and self-sufficiency goals (Patnaik, 1996; Chandrasekhar and Ghosh, 2002). Apprehensions have also been aired about the future of agriculture in the developing countries under the pressure of liberalization, setting up of the WTO and multilateral trading rules and trade negotiations under the UR Agreement on Agriculture (Grimwade, 2004; Bhalla, 2004). Many are of the opinion that the developed countries would gain the most by increase in their exports to the developing countries. It is likely that these nations refuse to withdraw subsidies and reduce tariffs in accordance with the WTO bound rates. Further, the world prices of several commodities have also been ruling at a lower level from the late nineties and hence a favourable incentive structure does not seem to exist for developing countries' agriculture.

Clearly, there has been lot of uninformed and ideological opposition to economic reforms and liberalization of agricultural trade and of late to the setting up of multilateral trading rules under the WTO. The arguments are well entrenched on methodological fronts also. The real impact of trade liberalization and globalization on agriculture can be ascertained only by an empirical investigation into various aspects of this sector, which are directly or indirectly influenced by liberalization.

Impact of Macroeconomic and Sectoral Policies on Agriculture

Empirical resolution of the impact of liberal trade and macroeconomic policies on agriculture rests on the movement of domestic and world commodity prices and the response of output and trade (export-import) to changes in relative prices. Though literature points towards a positive response of agriculture to reform measures in both developed and developing countries, but the magnitude of the effect on output and growth differs across these. For instance, in the case of Canada, Lassaad and Womack (1998) found the aggregate supply elasticity to be highly responsive to price incentives at 1.76 during 1960–92. The authors maintained that had Canada been more integrated with the world economy, its volume of trade would have been three per cent higher than its actual level. In a similar vein, Bond (1983) estimated a positive production response in nine Sub-Saharan African countries. The own price elasticity estimates showed very little difference in the short-run (between 0.05–0.54) and long-run (between 0.07–0.54). However, the aggregate supply response was low for all these countries showing long-run estimates to be slightly higher (0.21) than the short-run (0.18). The author reasoned that a mere increase in the producer price would not be sufficient to provide output incentive to farmers. It should go hand in hand with a package of policy changes that include improvement in extension, infrastructure, inputs, credit services and a depreciation of the exchange rate. Cleaver (1988) compared the growth performance of 16 adjusting countries with that of non-adjusting countries in Africa. Results revealed that the reforming countries experienced a higher annual growth rate by 0.9 percentage points during 1980–85 and 2.6 percentage points in 1987. Most of the increased growth was found to be occurring for exportables rather than for food crops. Balassa (1986) found the elasticity of share of exports in total output with respect to the real exchange rate to be 0.68 for LDCs as a whole and about 1.35 for the Sub-Saharan African countries.

Compared to these findings, Mckay, Morrissey and Vaillant (1997 and 1998) found that the exchange rate and liberalization programme had little direct impact on agriculture in the Cote d' Ivoire and Tanzania. Trade liberalization measures initiated in these countries since 1986 made it easier to import and did little to encourage exports. The auguries for supply response were observed to be favourable as agricultural growth was quite high at five per cent per annum. The aggregate own price elasticity for food was estimated to be 0.34 and cross price elasticity of food with respect to export crops was found to be minus unity. Kaabia and Gil (2000) showed that in the long-run, changes in agricultural variables did not have significant impact on macroeconomic variables in Spain. Input and output price reactions were of the same magnitude. In the short run, output prices appeared to be more flexible and reacted more quickly than the input prices. Farmers would benefit from increase in money supply and general prices, whereas over longer time periods the terms of trade for agriculture should deteriorate. Also, agricultural exports were more sensitive to farm prices than to any other macroeconomic variable.

In the Indian context, the extant literature though sparse reveals a positive response of agricultural growth to changes in exchange rate and trade policies. Studies based on CGE and macroeconometric models indicate that the agricultural sector has responded favourably to the terms of trade due to high cross elasticity of demand and a move away from non-agricultural goods towards agricultural goods (Storm, 1997). Simulations revealed that adoption of liberalization policies would have positive and significant implications for agricultural prices, output and growth. In a recent study, Kalirajan and Bhide (2003), found that depreciation in the exchange rate would accelerate output and increase the share of non-food grain output relative to foodgrain. While a 10 per cent reduction in import tariff on manufacturing can increase crop output by 0.21 per cent, an increase in farm prices by 10 per cent may raise output by 3.2 per cent. As a result of increase in crop prices relative to other prices, higher private investment in agriculture is expected, which in turn may lead to an increase in irrigated area and change in the crop mix. Results obtained by Bhattacharya and Kar (2007) showed considerable interlinkages of farm investment and prices with other sectors. Broadly, the findings suggest that capital output ratio in agriculture is quite sensitive to changes in rainfall, fertilizer use, and relative price. Private investment in agriculture is also significantly influenced by farm income, public investment, relative price and the lending rate in a liberalized regime. However, the authors suggested no major effects of trade liberalization on the rate of agricultural growth during 1978 to 1998, which is explained by the fact that significant reforms have not been undertaken in this sector.

Studies based on partial analysis project a likely shift in the cropping pattern from coarse grains towards wheat and rice, oilseeds and other commercial crops across various regions following the reforms (Naik and Jain, 1999; Gulati and Kelly, 1999). Estimates on acreage price elasticity in these studies though varied across the regions, showed a positive response of food and commercial crops to absolute and relative crop prices along with non-price factors. In the semi-arid regions, the expected output elasticity in response to change in prices in a free trade regime ranged from 0.16 to 0.47 for rice; 0.26–0.59 for wheat; 0.05–0.59 for oilseeds; 0.19–0.62 for sugarcane and 0.20–0.70 for cotton, respectively. It is important to note that these studies have not incorporated the effect of macroeconomic variables while capturing the impact of liberalization on commodity prices. Results of another study (Misra and Rao, 2003) show terms of trade to be positively influenced by foreign terms of trade from 1967–1997. These along with world prices, procurement price, tariff level and per capita output are found to have positive and significant impact on private investment and aggregate farm output.

An overall picture provides evidence in favour of significant interlinkages between macro- and sector-specific variables, which together influence the performance of agriculture and also the overall economic growth. In the case of low supply response, a combined policy of higher price for agriculture is suggested together with other policies such as provision of public goods, infrastructure, credit and the setting up of institutions. It is also pointed out that the linkages in the chain from trade liberalization to export and output response are not simple. Diaz-Bonilla and Robinson (2010) stated that while analysing the links of world and domestic macroeconomic changes to agriculture, it is important to note that not all agricultural products function as tradables. The export-oriented and import competing products may be affected differently by the broader policies. Further, apart from policies that make terms of trade favourable to agriculture, there are factors within and outside the economy, whose effect on prices may not be direct but they affect production. Some of these can include the following: (i) government intervention in external trade; (ii) heterogeneity of structures in developing countries; (iii) constraints in capital, infrastructure and technology; (iv) distortions in the world trade due to subsidies or export incentives given to farmers in the developed countries; (v) high fluctuations in world commodity prices; and (vi) low market access of developing countries' exports in other countries. Besides, agricultural policies in most of the developing countries are designed to address specific sectoral issues related to food security, price instability, import surge, input subsidies, rural poverty and regional inequalities. In such situations, agriculture and trade policies that are being followed internally come in direct conflict with the external trade policy. All this may not only impede a quicker and higher transmission of world prices to domestic producers but also adversely affect production incentives and growth.

Treatment of Agriculture under the GATT/WTO: Issues Therein

Recognizing many of the above issues that confront the agricultural sector in many developing economies, attempts have been made to discipline key aspects of trade within the regulatory framework of General Agreement on Trade and Tariffs (GATT). The measures initiated during the eighties and early nineties were considered to be largely ineffective due to a dominance of export and domestic subsidies in the world agricultural trade. It was only after the Uruguay Round negotiations (1986–1994) established WTO and formulated an Agreement on Agriculture on April 15, 1994, that trade in agriculture was firmly brought within the multilateral trading system. As per the UR AOA, the member countries were committed to reduce export subsidies, domestic support and import duties on farm products and replace non-tariff barriers with tariffs by the end of 1999 as part of the overall agreement on streamlining farm production and trading policies. Accordingly, the broad contours of domestic agricultural trade, marketing and other policies were delineated and the commitments under the AOA were categorized under three pillars namely, (a) market access and tariffication, (b) domestic support, and (c) export subsidies/ competition.[6]

While negotiating market access and tariffication, developing countries raised concerns for food and livelihood security, poverty, income growth, rural development and environmental degradation. They proposed certain exemptions such as exclusion of domestic support to farmers from any tariff reduction commitments and demanded placement of subsidies under amber, blue and green boxes. During the Doha Ministerial Declaration in November 2001, these proposals along with other prominent trade issues concerning substantial reductions in tariffs, readjustment of bound tariffs for developing countries, elimination of domestic support and export subsidy in developed nations were taken into consideration. Attention was also given to non-trade issues (see Chand and Bathla, 2005) such as imposition of NTBs on exportable items by developed nations on grounds of food safety, special and differential treatment to be given to agriculture of the developing countries along with establishment of special safeguard mechanism (SSM), formation of the food security box, and trade through State Trading Enterprises (STEs).

Proposals on these aspects and the modalities required in the commitments were subsequently submitted and discussed in the Cancun Ministerial conference in September 2003. Some of these suggestions were pushed and agreed upon in the July Package of 2004 and in the Hong Kong declaration (2006). But agreement on other proposals of the developing countries, which aimed at providing them a level playing field and reducing farm subsidies by developed countries failed to reach a consensus, leading to a breakdown of trade talks by 2006. In the third week of July 2008, WTO had called a mini-ministerial meeting to finalize the modalities for concluding the round. The draft contained formulas for cutting tariffs and trade-distorting subsidies along with provisions for special and differential (S&D) treatment under each stipulation of AOA and a separate S&D clause for developing countries' members. After passing through several rounds of negotiations and meetings held by different members, positions could not converge, primarily on the issue of SSM and the high level of support to cotton in USA. Finally on July 29, 2008 negotiations collapsed.

So far, the gains accrued from trade liberalization in the developing countries are mixed, as many of these nations have not been able to benefit as much as they had expected through the Uruguay Round Agreement an Agriculture (UR AOA). There has been variation in the market access rules being implemented and the opportunities have been affected by the increased protection and subsidies given to agriculture in the developed countries (Ingco and Kandiero, 2003). Further, world prices of most of the commodities after reaching a peak around 1997–98 have been falling since then with significant spikes and troughs. This has negated a better pricing environment for products of interest to developing countries and has resulted in a decline in their exports and a surge in imports.[7] Meanwhile, several realignments have taken place among member countries culminating in various positions.[8] It has been contended that the commitments made in the WTO AOA represented a frail effort at agricultural liberalization. The developing countries should aim at a fundamental reform of world agriculture in the multilateral trade negotiations (Hoda and Gulati, 2007). One positive outcome is the emergence of bilateral and regional trade agreements that might help countries to gain from trade.

Clearly, such outcomes have not only exposed the agriculture sector of the developing countries to greater openness but have also made apparent that any change in the macroeconomic policies and situations will significantly influence their domestic economic and agricultural policies. Some important questions have been raised in the context of trade liberalization, UR AOA and agricultural growth in the developing countries. Thus, to what extent have trade liberalization and macroeconomic policy changes improved price transmission between world and domestic agricultural commodity markets? Do movements in the relative world and domestic prices influence commodity trade and output? What kind of trade negotiations under the AOA can sustain price incentives to agriculture and enable higher exports from the developing countries? Can a uniform tariff policy over farm product help in aligning domestic prices with international prices? Is the exchange rate a more powerful policy measure than tariffs and price policy in influencing agricultural prices? How should internal trade and price policies be reformulated to keep the relative price structure in favour of agriculture without adversely affecting the broader objectives of food security, employment, poverty reduction and growth? To what extent and in what form can private sector participation be increased in agriculture? What kind of strategy should be developed and adopted in trade negotiations that suit the interest of developing countries? The present study is an attempt to examine some of these issues in the Indian context. It is undertaken with the following objectives and hypotheses.

Objectives of the Study

1. To delineate reforms in trade of major agricultural commodities, price and marketing policies and measure the extent of openness of agriculture during the nineties and early 2000 relative to its own past;
2. To empirically analyse the magnitude of price transmission across state-level agricultural markets and from international markets towards the domestic ones during the pre- and post-liberalization periods;
3. To examine the temporal and spatial changes in cropping pattern and estimate the extent of crop diversification at the national and state level;
4. To estimate acreage response function for major crops with respect to price (world price, individual and competing crop price, input price), policy (tariffs, exchange rate, support price) and non-price factors (irrigation, weather, technology);
5. To evaluate the resilience of agricultural prices, trade, acreage and hence production to extreme divergences in the exogenous macro-economic policies and factors, viz., tariffs, exchange rate, world price, minimum support price and rainfall;
6. To analyse the relative importance of macro policies and factors impacting agriculture and policy options that may neutralize the adverse effects of shocks arising in an open economy so as to maintain an incentive structure.

Hypotheses Tested

The hypotheses tested in the study are namely:

H1: Indian agriculture has become more open following an implementation of economic reforms in the early nineties;

H2: Trade liberalization has led to a higher transmission of price signals from world to domestic markets and hence improved market efficiency in a spatial system;

H3: A greater integration of agricultural markets has influenced cropping pattern changes and crop diversification in the years following the reforms;

H4: Crop area shifts are relatively more responsive to price factors than to the non-price factors in a liberalized regime;

H5: Acreage response is positive and high in the case of those crops where prices are well integrated with world prices;

H6: Sensitivity of area shifts to price factors varies as per the competitiveness of crops and regional conditions.

Database Used and Methodological Aspects

Geographically, the investigations are carried out at the all-India and state level, separately for six important tradable commodities, viz., wheat, rice, cotton, sugar, groundnut and soyabean seeds. The choice of these crops is determined by their increasing share in external trade and likely changes in their prices and output in due course. The analysis covers a time span of more than two decades from 1980–81 to 2002–03, broadly representing the pre-reform period from 1980–91 and post-reform period from 1992–2002.

Data is collected from secondary sources. An inventory of trade reforms (external and internal) from 1980–81 onwards is prepared on the basis of information given in the following: EXIM policy documents; Economic Survey; reports published by various ministries; and WTO website on the agreements signed and negotiations made by India. Information on legislative and institutional measures that have been initiated for specific commodities was taken from the Ministry of Agriculture and Ministry of Consumer Affairs, Food and Public Distribution. Time series data on exchange rate, tariffs, non-tariff barriers, exports and imports was collected from the Report on Currency and Finance, RBI, FAO data base and EXIM Policy. Data on annual and monthly wholesale prices of crops in global markets was collected from International Financial Statistics while at the state level from the Report of Commission on Agricultural Costs and Prices. All-India and state level data on area under high yielding varieties, area, yield and production of crops, rainfall, fertilizer consumption and prices, state domestic product, actual and normal rainfall, and road density are collected from various sources, namely: Statistical Abstract of India,

Agricultural Statistics at a Glance, Fertilizer Statistics and National Accounts Statistics. Data on commodity prices, fertilizer price, income, etc., given in nominal terms is converted into real prices at base 1993–94 using the appropriate price index and deflators.

Both descriptive statistics and empirical models have been employed to test the proposed hypotheses. At the outset, an inventory of policy reforms in the external and internal trade of important agricultural commodities is prepared and then the magnitude of openness of Indian agriculture to world trade is examined. The openness of agriculture is looked at relative to its own past experience by estimating the level of protection accorded to this sector through tariffs and NTBs, quantification of NTBs and compatibility of trade reforms with the commitments stipulated in the UR AOA of WTO. To address the analytical interests of the study, the impact of reforms on agriculture is first examined through an analysis of price transmission across the state-level wholesale markets and subsequently, between world and domestic markets. The empirical exercises are carried out for each of the selected commodities, separately in the pre-and post-reform periods based on monthly wholesale prices of selected commodities in each state from 1980–81 to 2002–03. Bifurcation of monthly data on prices into pre- and post-reform periods is based on the structural break test using Chow and CUSUM of Squares tests. In case structural break is not present, the year 1991 is taken as break-up period for decomposition of data into pre- and post-liberalization periods. The degree of price transmission is measured on the basis of cointegration and error-correction models based on Johansen Maximum Likelihood techniques in a multivariate framework.

The test of spatial price integration is followed by an evaluation of the temporal behaviour of cropping pattern changes at the national and state levels and the magnitude of diversification. Based on the Entropy Index, inter-crop diversification is analysed for major crops and categories at the all-India level from 1971–72 to 2002–03 and at the state level from 1981–82 to 2002–03. The response of crop acreage to changes in the world price, macro- and sector- specific variables is examined by developing a structural econometric model. The model consists of a set of four behavioural equations and a few identities. The behavioural equations are formulated on the basis of a priori theoretical linkages between agriculture and external price, macro variables (tariffs, non-tariff barriers, and exchange rate), support price, procurement and other factors. The variables used in the model are categorized into three broad groups namely: (i) endogenous or impact variables; (ii) exogenous and/or policy variables, and (iii) exogenous and/or supply side factors. The model is applied to individual commodities, separately under the exportable and importable scenarios. The analysis is carried out from 1980–81 to 2002–03 using OLS and simultaneous equation methods.

Finally, the estimates obtained are used to calibrate a simulation over the observed time period in order to examine the individual impact of exogenous policies and factors on endogenous variables, and to evaluate the resilience of agriculture to the 'best and worst' scenarios of unexpected change in each factor. The interactive exercise also points towards counter shock measures that can be opted for to maintain an incentive structure in a freer trade regime. For example, if tariffs are more than the ceiling, it enables a simulation to test whether a change in exchange rate policy shall be apt to arrive at optimal production. For the purpose, five counterfactual simulation experiments are undertaken based on the maximum and minimum change in the exogenous variables, i.e., exchange rate, tariffs, world price, minimum support price and rainfall and their impact is seen on endogenous variables, i.e., domestic price, export, import, area/output. The analysis is done for each commodity from 2000–01 to 2002–03. At the outset, the model is validated by looking into the errors based on the difference between the actual (historical) and forecasted values of endogenous variables, which should be as low as possible. The validated model is then used to perform simulations using the Gauss-Seidel method to generate the predicted values of endogenous variables. The method is based on Newtons's iterative procedure and a stopping rule which specifies that the percentage change in each solved variable during an iteration is less than 0.0001.

Plan of the Study

The study is organized into eight chapters. Chapter 1 presents contextual framework of interactions between macroeconomic and sectoral policies and the agricultural sector under the SAP and sets out the main objectives and hypotheses to be tested. It also briefly outlines the sources of data and methodology used to test various hypotheses. Chapter 2 reviews literature on price transmission in agricultural commodities along with acreage/supply response to changes in the incentive structure, policies and non-price factors in the pre- and post-liberalization periods. It also highlights important developments in the methodologies that have been used to measure price integration and acreage response over time. Chapter 3 maps the principal features of trade policy reforms as they relate to agriculture along with sector-level price, marketing and other policy changes. It then examines the extent of openness of Indian agriculture, first, by quantifying the level of protection given to farm commodities through tariffs and NTBs in the nineties and early 2000 relative to the eighties, and second by juxtaposing external and internal trade and farm policies against various stipulations advanced under the AOA.

Chapter 4 begins with a brief background on world and domestic price relationships and then provides empirical findings on the magnitude of price transmission within the domestic commodity markets and between the world and state-level markets. For the purpose, cointegration and error correction approach is applied to monthly wholesale prices of selected commodities, separately in the pre- and post-reform periods. Chapter 5 analyses temporal changes in the cropping pattern and measures the extent of crop diversification for major crops and crop groups at all-India over the period from 1971–72 to 2002–03 and at state level from 1981–82 to 2002–03.

The findings obtained in chapters 3 to 5 set the stage for evaluating various objectives proposed in chapters 6 and 7. The main objectives are namely, whether macroeconomic and sector-specific policies impact agriculture through change in the incentive structure? If it does, then, what is the magnitude of the response of key variables, viz., commodity price, export, import, acreage and output, broadly taken to judge the performance of agriculture, to such incentives? To what extent is the agricultural sector resilient to changes in macro (exchange rate, tariffs, world price) and other variables (minimum support price and rainfall)? What policy measures can be initiated to neutralize the effects of unexpected disturbances or shocks in these policy, price and natural factors so as to maintain price and production incentives in an open economy? For this, a structural econometric model is developed and is applied to individual crops, separately under the exportable and importable scenarios from 1980–81 to 2002–03. Chapter 6 begins with an analytical framework for analysing macroeconomic and agricultural sector linkages and specification of important variables in the model. This is followed by statistical procedures and presentation of empirical results for each commodity.

The actual estimates obtained from behavioural equations and identities are finally simulated in chapter 7. This is to estimate the impact of each of the important policy, price and natural factors on the performance of agriculture and policy options to neutralize their adverse effects, if any, in a free trade regime. The model is validated in order to test whether it can accurately explain various performance indicators considered in the study. Subsequently, simulations are carried out for each commodity under alternate assumptions of optimistic and pessimistic scenarios in the relevant exogenous variables. The base run values of endogenous variables are compared with their respective simulated values to analyse the degree of resilience of agriculture to unexpected changes. Chapter 7 concludes by presenting the main findings and their policy implications.

Notes

1. Classical economists were aware that terms of trade against agriculture would negatively affect marketed surplus to the extent that the wage goods constraint on industrial investment becomes operative. In this context, it was suggested to follow a balanced growth through technological change and capital accumulation in both sectors that sustain investment incentives, leaving terms of trade unchanged and ensuring that agriculture supplies labour for industrial expansion at a constant real wage.
2. The main reasons responsible for the relative declining share of agriculture were seen as namely: (a) Engle's Law that proposes a decline in the income elasticity of demand for agricultural output with higher incomes, and (b) technical change, a growing agricultural productivity, an increased supply of farm products relative to demand and hence a fall in prices that pressurizes farmers to move out of agriculture (Eicher and Staaz, 1984).
3. Besides economic policies, agricultural prices are stated to be influenced by other important structural factors, such as domestic supply and demand, secular or long-run trends in international prices and presence of subsidized exports in world markets (Norton, 2004).
4. See among others Schuh (1974); Chambers and Just (1981); Rausser et al. (1986); Krueger, Schiff and Valdes (1988); Bautista and Valdes (1993); In and Mount (1994); Mamingi (1996), Lassaad and Womack (1998); Norton (2004) and Diaz-Bonilla and Robinson (2010).
5. One of the implicit assumptions behind price policy is that crop adjustment and production decisions respond to changes in prices through their effect on

relative profitability (see among others Krishna Raj, 1963; Schultz, 1964; Askari and Cummings, 1976).

6. Along with these provisions, sanitary and phytosanitary measures and trade related aspects of intellectual property rights formed part of negotiations.
7. In any untoward situation, while developed countries are able to safeguard their agriculture and farming community through huge support, farmers in the developing countries are the most vulnerable owing to lack of resources and mechanism.
8. These are represented by G20 and G33 groups of developing countries, G10 group of developed countries, the African group, African-Caribbean-Pacific group, G90 comprising small countries and African group, USA and European Union.

2

Price Transmission in Agricultural Markets and Supply Response

Review of the Pre- and Post-liberalization Periods

With implementation of economic reforms and trade liberalization, the agricultural sector came to be seen in the wider context of an open economy environment. It is, therefore, likely to respond positively to an incentive structure, supposedly arising out of liberal macroeconomic policies and measures. Several attempts have been made to evaluate such impacts through an analysis of movement of commodity prices, terms of trade and market efficiency, changes in the cropping pattern, direction and volume of trade, food security, poverty, price volatility, output growth and welfare gains/losses. In this chapter, appraisal is made of studies that have been undertaken on two important aspects namely: (i) level of price integration of commodity markets within the domestic economy and from international markets to domestic markets, and (ii) cropping pattern changes and acreage (supply) response to changing price structure and other factors. The review covers literature spanning a period of more than four decades with an aim to first, capture the impact of polices and other factors prior to and after reforms in achieving better price and supply response and second, to understand the methodological developments in measuring the response. Broadly, the literature relates to the Indian context.

Price Transmission: Analysis based on Market Integration Approach

Price transmission provides insights into the relationship of interdependency between commodity prices in two related markets or between producer and consumer prices of consumption goods. The movement of commodity prices across separated markets and their level of association have been studied through the market integration approach. The approach has its roots in the 'Law of One Price', which has a primary rationale that in perfectly competitive and spatially well-integrated markets, the differences in prices in different markets for the same commodity reflect only transport and processing cost (Ardeni, 1989; Ravallion, 1986; Baffes, 1991). Therefore, a co-movement of commodity prices across markets would imply efficient transmission of price signals from consumers to producers and hence perfect integration. The speed at which prices in markets adjust to departures from their equilibrium relationship is taken as an indicator of market efficiency. Existence of efficient markets is one among many factors, that provides incentives to producers to expand their production base and reap the benefits of market liberalization. It also helps to determine the geographical level at which price policy should be targeted, at least in the short run to assure regular availability of food and price stability (Jha et al., 1997; Jayasuriya, Kim and Kumar, 2007).

Quite often, the spatial movement of commodity prices is influenced by government policies, which have a positive or negative bearing on the efficiency of markets. Farm price policy is a typical example that aims at achieving price stability and removing market imperfections, whereby the producer gets the maximum while the consumer pays the minimum for the produce. Similarly, trade policy presumes that provision of export incentives and reduction in commodity tariffs would equate world and domestic prices, which in turn may alter cropping pattern, accelerate output and exports and hence agricultural growth. That is why, a greater integration of world and domestic agricultural markets is expected after initiation of economic reforms under the SAP along with sector-specific liberal measures.

Spatial Integration of Agricultural Markets during Pre-liberalization Period

Cummings (1967) in his pioneering work examined the role of prices and private trade in the functioning of wholesale trade in 27 wheat markets in northern India based on time series data on wheat prices, arrivals and stocks in the markets from 1956 to 1974. The correlation coefficients between the wholesale price of wheat in different markets were estimated to be 0.85 during the period of free trade and 0.65 during government intervention. According to the author, if prices were at the perfectly competitive equilibrium level, then differences in the prices between markets would have reflected only transport and processing cost. In this situation, the bivariate correlation coefficient in two spatial markets will be equal to 1, which signifies full integration of markets. He concluded that although the private wheat trading system suffered from certain market imperfections such as transaction cost, lack of homogeneity in the produce, yet it was efficient and did not require replacement by government. The producers, consumers and the marketing firms responded well to economic incentives and there was hardly any evidence to prove that spatial and seasonal price differences were due to collusion. The author concluded that government through its well-designed policy could remove some of the weaknesses in foodgrain markets that aim primarily at supplementing private trade.

Lele (1967 and 1971) while studying the private marketing system for sorghum, wheat, rice, and jowar in selected markets in Punjab, West Bengal, Tamil Nadu and Maharashtra argued that temporal and spatial price differences were largely explained by storage and transportation costs and difference in varieties of foodgrains. Prices of these commodities across markets moved in unison, which implies a perfect system of signals as per market forces. The higher price differentials observed in the case of paddy-rice in West Bengal were not attributable to differences in the milling equipment and hence higher incidental costs but to controls exercised by the government. Further, inter-year variations in prices were such that traders would not have benefited by carrying over stocks from one year to the next to earn out of this activity. The price correlation between Delhi and five wholesale wheat markets in Punjab exceeded 0.90 during 1955 to 1965. The results were not significant for paddy and rice markets. In Tamil Nadu, correlation coefficients in the wholesale prices of paddy-rice and wheat exceeded 0.80 only in 3 cases out of 507 cases, which could be attributed to diverse patterns of market flow in the state. Harris (1979) however, argued that data used in the study was the primary cause for such diverse results.

Gupta (1973) also found that the rice, wheat, jowar and groundnut markets in Madhya Pradesh were well associated with each other as the average correlation coefficient was found to be 0.79 for rice, 0.71 for wheat, 0.85 for jowar and 0.91 for groundnut respectively from 1961–62 to 1965–66. Naik and Arora (1986) studied price efficiency of the arecanut market based on primary data of a random sample of 50 growers from Sisri market in Karnataka and the wholesale price data of secondary markets from all over the country. Correlation coefficients were on the higher side in the primary markets as well as in the distant secondary markets. In some cases such as in Kanpur, retail and wholesale prices in primary markets were not integrated due to long distances between the markets.

A parallel line of research has focused on the methodological aspects of testing market integration. Since a wide range of studies used the bivariate correlation coefficient to test integration of spatial markets, it was argued that this technique suffers from various shortcomings. The two price series can differ by a large margin and yet they move together in the same direction and show a correlation coefficient of one. Also, in many studies, correlation was found to be high between markets having no physical contact. Blyn (1973) further pointed out that there might be common underlying trends in the price series that provide an upward bias to results. At times, inflation or population growth might give rise to linear trends in the series as a result of which perfect correlation is shown even if markets are not remotely integrated. Heytens (1986) also pointed out that two functionally isolated markets often appear to be synchronized if prices in each are influenced by the third market or by a common factor. In some situations, spurious correlation could also emerge.

To overcome such problems, Blyn (1973) suggested that trend and season free data be used and correlated to find the extent of market integration. Based on this, he estimated the correlation coefficient using data given in the study by Cummings and found it to be 0.68, which was much below the figure found by Cummings at 0.85. Subbarao (1978) also estimated the correlation coefficient between the de-trended and de-seasonalized wholesale monthly price data of rice in six selected markets in Andhra Pradesh from April 1968 to December 1971. The results showed only four out of fifteen correlation coefficients to have exceeded the value of 0.80. Overall, the coefficients estimated were lower than those obtained by others using data without detrending it. Timmer (1974) while studying marketing margins in Indonesian rice observed that integration methodology in time and space was based on unidirectional model of price formation. He suggested the use of a two-way model of price formation between the rural producer market and urban consumer market. Under this, during the lean season, the rural hinterland prices may rise above the urban prices. And if rural demand is significant, it is possible to reverse the flow from urban to rural areas. According to the author, the marketing margin between rural and urban trade under this situation could be positive, zero or negative. If two-way trade is allowed, the correlation coefficient would yield unsatisfactory results on market integration and degree of correlation. It is, therefore, essential to carefully draw inferences about the nature of competition from indices of market integration. Harris (1979) also criticized the correlation technique on grounds that high correlation could just as easily indicate stable margins and monopolistic imperfections in the marketing system as competitive conditions and efficiency. In the same way, low correlation does not provide any indication that markets are not well integrated.

In order to find new techniques that overcome the shortcomings present in the correlation coefficient, Monke and Petzel (1984) used bivariate regression for testing vertical integration between qualities of cotton. Based on the time series of prices for different qualities, he used a regression to get an indication of constancy of discounts for the prices of differentiated products. Besides, a hedonic index estimation of the form $P = a + b_1 + D_1 + b_2D_2 + b_3D_3 +$ ....was used, where P is price and D_1, D_2 and D_3 are dummy variables that signify different quality characteristics. However, this approach failed to take into account error term that is usually auto correlated and might lead to inconsistent estimates. Ravallion (1986) improved the simple bivariate model by introducing a dynamic model of spatial price differentials. His model assumed a radical market configuration where regional markets are linked to the main central market. The specification of the equation is:

$$P_{it} = \sum_{k=1}^{n} a_{ik} P_{it-k} + \sum_{k=0}^{n} b_{ik} P_{jt-k} + X_{it} C_i + e_{it}$$

Where P_{jt} is the price of a central market that is taken to determine movements of price in the local market P_{it}. X_{it} is a vector of other influences on the local market, e_{it} is the error term. Using this model, Ravallion examined segmentation, long-run and short-run integration based on the following tests:

Test for market segmentation – $[b_{ik} = 0 \ (k=0,.....,n)]$

Long-run integration- $[\sum_{k=1}^{n} a_{ik} + \sum_{k=0}^{n} b_{ik} = 1]$

and, short-run integration-$[b_{io}=1,\ a_{ik} = b_{ik} = 0 \ (k = 1, 2, \ldots n)]$.

Since this model gives sufficient lags in the dependent variable that makes disturbance term white noise, it carries an advantage over the previous bivariate regression model. In case the lags are of relatively high order, the OLS estimates of coefficients will be imprecise, may be due to the presence of multicollinearity between lagged values of the explanatory variables. As pointed out by Granger and Newbold (1974), specification of the above equation may raise the problem of spurious regression of trending variables. In view of certain weaknesses in these methods, procedures have been evolved to study market integration within the framework of Ravallion, Augmented Dickey Fuller (ADF) and cointegration and error correction approaches. The procedures to evaluate market linkages using time series models are explained in Engle and Granger (1987) and Engle and Yoo (1987). The cointegration approach is based on the rationale that if commodity price series in the markets have long-run equilibrium relationships (despite short-run divergences) then these markets are integrated in the long run. In other words, if two price series are cointegrated, there exists a long-run equilibrium relationship between them, which signifies markets to be integrated.

The approach was used by Goodwin and Schroeder (1991) in testing the integration of 11 regional cattle markets in the USA from 1980 to 1987 using weekly price series and seven cointegration tests of Engle and Granger (1987). They concluded that most of the markets were not integrated during this period. A lower degree of integration was found among markets that were located far off than those located in close proximity. However, divergence of price over long distance could be warranted by market conditions. It was not large enough to allow profitable trade through regional movements of cattle. The study also analysed the factors that have a bearing on the cointegration relationship between markets such as distance, market volumes, market types and industry concentration ratio. Palaskas and Harriss-White (1993) also used the cointegration and error correction mechanism to examine the dynamic relationship in the prices of three commodities, viz., rice, potato and mustard in West Bengal, India from 1988 to 1990. Based on weekly spot prices, the study rejected full market integration and negated the results of many previous studies as done by Lele (1967). The study also examined statistical adequacy of the estimated equation by using the LM test that determines whether residuals are serially correlated, the ARCH test for conditional heteroscedasticity of residual and other explanatory variables, and the Chow test for parameter stability. The authors concluded that markets were indeed integrated but there was a lower degree of integration of rice and mustard. Structural and institutional factors were reported to be the main factors that affect market performance.

Carol and Wyeth (1994) reported that the Ravallion model was widely applied and could be taken as a special case within a more general framework of cointegration. Based on the reduced form of error correction mechanism that allows the test for exogeneity as well as indicates the direction and strength of causality in price formation between markets, the authors tested integration of rice markets in

Indonesia. Out of seven markets, the results based on monthly data showed five markets to be integrated. The study confirmed that supply sources were more important in driving prices compared to the demand sources. Jha, Bhanumurthy, Nagarajan and Seth (1997) tested market integration for 44 centres for rice and 47 centres for wheat in India for the period January 1980 to December 1990 using the Goletti-Ravallion test. They used bilateral as well as multilateral cointegration tests and found a high degree of market integration in these markets in India. The authors argued for the removal of barriers to internal trade in foodgrains so as to make price policy more effective. In a subsequent study, Jha, Bhanumurthy and Sharma (2005) tested market integration for 55 wholesale rice markets in India using monthly data during the period from January 1970 to December 1999. The authors identified common factors and found integration to be far from complete due to excessive interference by government agencies. They maintained that as a result of intervention, it is hard for scarcity conditions in isolated markets to be picked up by markets having abundant supply. These results are contrary to the ones obtained in the earlier study where they found a high degree of market integration in cereals.

Spatial Integration of Agricultural Markets during Post-liberalization Period

Following economic reforms, the prices of several farm commodities are expected to converge across domestic markets and also with prices in the international markets. Due to trade liberalization, the process of price transmission is expected not only to be complete but also to be symmetric. While numerous studies have examined the level of inter-state price convergence during the pre- and post-reform periods, only a few have analysed price linkages between domestic and international markets over time.

Acharya (2001) used the bivariate correlation approach to estimate integration of wholesale commodity markets in India during the eighties and the nineties. The results revealed that markets, which showed a high degree of interaction in the past for many commodities have become more integrated since the initiation of liberal reforms in the early nineties. The results were slightly different for coarse cereals like jowar that revealed a lower degree of interaction. Based on full information maximum likelihood and VAR procedure, Wilson (2001) formulated an analytical framework, which explicitly incorporated simultaneous inter-dependencies between market prices. Using monthly wholesale price data in selected state-level markets in India, he found an increasing degree of market integration for wheat, rice, rapeseed and mustard in contrast to jowar and groundnut from January 1992 to June 1998 to that from January 1982 to June 1988.

Kumar and Sharma (2003) studied spatial price integration and pricing efficiency at the farm level for paddy in four markets in one Indian state, viz., Haryana. Using the Johansen maximum likelihood and error correction representation and identifying n–1 cointegrating relations, the authors found the selected markets to be well integrated in the long run both in the pre-liberalization period, i.e., from 1978–79 to 1989–90 as well in the post-liberalization periods, viz., 1990–91 to 2001–03. However, in the short run, there was no price adjustment among the markets. Notably, the adjustment process was found to be quicker in the post-liberalization period compared to that in the pre-liberalization period. The analysis done for nine wheat, six mustard seed and four gram markets in the same state in Kumar (2007) showed slightly different results. While wheat markets exhibited a long-run relationship during both periods, inter-linkages in mustard seed and gram markets were relatively less efficient in the period following reforms. In all commodity cases, price transmission was found to be lacking in the short run, indicating adjustment time among the markets to be around 2–3 weeks.

As far as price integration between domestic and world agricultural markets is concerned, the extant literature indicates mixed results distinct from the trends seen in the domestic markets in which a higher integration has been observed during the years following economic reforms.

A review of some important studies and observations on refinements in the methodologies used to test integration follows below.

Hazell et al. (1990) did not find evidence of a greater integration between domestic and export prices of most of the commodities in the developing countries from 1961 to 1987. The authors also tested whether price instability has increased and fluctuations in the domestic markets of developing countries have followed variability of the world prices. The estimations revealed that world prices became more volatile and fluctuations were passing to countries' export unit values and not to producers' prices due to interventionist policies of the government and adjustments in the exchange rate.

Contrary to these results, Mundlak and Larson (1992) examined the relationship between domestic agriculture prices and world prices in 58 countries from 1968–78, and in countries of the European community from 1961–85. Using a simple logarithmic OLS specification to regress domestic prices on world prices and taking into account the possible effects of exchange rate and inflation, they found most of the variations in world prices to get transmitted to domestic prices. A lower price transmission is estimated when price relationships were examined separately for selected commodities, viz., wheat, coffee and cocoa. Cardenas (1994) while focusing on the role of stabilization funds in managing coffee price fluctuations also found that in Costa Rica and Kenya where government hardly intervenes, fluctuations in world prices are fully transmitted to producers.

Golleti and Babu (1994) studied the behaviour of monthly retail prices of maize at eight locations in Malawi over the period January 1984 to December 1991. Results showed almost all the markets to be integrated, which suggests the presence of causal relationship between them. The number of markets that were integrated was more after liberalization took place in 1987. Nevertheless, the degree of integration was not perfect, as adjustment of price changes to stock originating elsewhere was not 100 per cent and was below 50 per cent for most of the markets. It was observed that supply (and demand) shocks were transmitted equally, both when they tend to increase prices and when they put a downward pressure on prices. This was contrary to the general belief that price increase is transmitted to consumers and traders are the main beneficiaries of price decrease. The authors concluded that market liberalization could not achievė structural change in market integration, unless investment in marketing infrastructure gets initiated.

Sinharoy and Nair (1994) studied variations in international trade in pepper. They found that prices for pepper in India and Indonesia have moved synchronously in the long run and hence were integrated. This was despite the fact that short-run drifts existed in the series. It was pointed out that there could be a kind of tacit collusion among exporters on market sharing and price parity. However, these results may not vary even if stock adjustment and forward trading in pepper is considered. Baffes and Gardener (2003) estimated price transmission for 10 commodities for the selected countries that opted for the SAP. Based on an error correction model from the mid-seventies to mid-nineties and while introducing structural breaks, the authors concluded that in most of the developing countries, world prices had a very limited effect on price transmission after the reforms. Out of 31 country-commodity cases, only six countries were integrated with world markets. Also, changes in world prices accounted for only a small share of the variation in domestic prices. Similarly, Krivonos (2004) examined price transmission from the world coffee market to local markets in the main producing countries before and after coffee sector reforms. The results show that the share of producers' prices in world price increased substantially in all countries except one. Price integration between domestic and world markets improved after reforms.

Jayasuriya, Kim and Kumar (2007) tested whether prices of rice in different locations in India were convergent over time. The study used monthly data for rice prices from April 1980 to December 2002 (273 observations) for 23 cities in India and the world price (5% broken rice Thailand). Broad findings based on panel unit root tests and the method of half-life estimation suggest that after the major reforms of 1994, liberalized rice exports appear to have significantly improved market integration. However, foreign trade liberalization is not symmetric in the way it deals with exports and imports, and this has implications for the spatial patterns of price convergence. Reflecting the dominance of producer interests in policy formation, exports have been made significantly more liberal than imports. As a result, surplus locations converge faster towards international prices. Also as expected, better infrastructure facilitates faster price convergence.

As regards methodology, most of the studies have considered the Johansen cointegration and vector error correction model to be the best as it estimates the dynamic nature of price adjustment to equilibrium. It also takes into account the properties of the error term (et) like the problem of auto correlation and checks for non-stationarity of the time series variables. Although the ADF/Engle and Granger approach is relatively simple and intuitive, literature indicates that it suffers from several limitations, such as follows: (i) the distribution of test statistics is not invariant with respect to the nuisance parameter and therefore the critical values given in Engle and Granger (1987) can be considered as a rough guide; (ii) when a pair of markets is considered, the procedure ignores linkages that can operate through a third market; (iii) the approach considers only one long-run relationship between the price series and hence fails to reflect on the existence of more than one relationship. Johansen's maximum likelihood procedure overcomes many of these problems and is particularly useful when cointegration is to be tested among more than two variables/price series. However, in recent studies, it is pointed out that the Johansen multivariate test may not be applicable if transaction costs are non-stationary and there are reversals in the trade flows across markets (Barret and Li, 2002). Rashid (2004) found that the conclusions of available cointegration-based studies go largely against this contention. A few studies have tried to incorporate changes in the procedure by finding common factors across markets as suggested by Rivera-Gonzalez and Helfand (2001).

Cropping Pattern Changes and Supply Response in Indian Agriculture

Based on the presumption that trade liberalization would result in a quick transmission of world price signals to domestic producers, the next step in assessing agricultural performance is to gauge farmers' land allocation decisions and supply response to economic incentives attributable to liberal macroeconomic and sectoral policies and factors. The acreage (supply) response is expected to be high and to vary across crops and regions depending upon the movement of world and domestic prices, supply situation in a particular state, extent of market efficiency, government policies, infrastructure, domestic consumption and export demand. These factors can conveniently be categorized as price and non-price factors. In this section, a discussion on the response of Indian agriculture to various factors is presented. The review covers both pre- and post-liberalization periods in order to assess the impact of agricultural policies and trade reforms on output and to track the methodological advancements in the subject over a longer period of time.

At the outset, it is important to recall the debate on supply response that arose during the sixties and the seventies in India which queried: To what extent and under what conditions do farmers decide to put land under the cultivation of a particular crop and hence determine the crop output? Based on the theoretical premise that farm firms seek to maximize expected profits or minimize expected loses if acting under uncertain conditions, Schultz (1964), Mellor (1966), Krishna (1963), Narain (1965), Herdt (1970), Cummings (1975) strongly held the view that Indian farmers respond to changes in relative prices of individual crops. In other words, crop adjustments and production decisions are made in response to changes in commodity prices through their effect on relative profitability. Those who did not support the hypothesis of price responsiveness of agriculture include among others Epstein (1962), Gupta and Majid (1965), Mydral (1968). These authors maintained that along with prices, other factors like irrigation, technology, market access, weather and risk-related factors, also called supply shifters and broadly termed as non-price factors are equally important in adjusting crop acreage and output. Despite that, literature contemplates the profit motive factor, be it determined by individual or competing crop prices, input prices, yield level or at aggregate sectoral level by relative prices (terms of trade) to be the guiding force in land allocation decisions.

The empirical investigations to support these theoretical underpinnings necessarily hinged on the estimation of area or supply response of aggregate agriculture and also of individual crops to various price and non-price factors. A plethora of studies estimated supply response within a partial equilibrium framework and only a few applied the computable general equilibrium model. Under the latter, output response is studied through the effects of changes in inputs produced or provided by the non-agricultural sectors along with economy wide changes in savings and investments. The partial approach which is widely used is based on the partial adjustment model developed by Nerlove (1958). The model hypothesized farmer reactions in terms of price expectations and/or partial area (production) adjustments. It assumes that technological and institutional constraints that operate in agriculture do not permit immediate full adjustment in output or marketed surplus in response to price expectation. It is further assumed that a one-year-lagged price represents farmer's expected price.

Over the period, several refinements have taken place in this basic model. The modifications are noted with respect to price expectation and inclusion of variables other than price, risk-related factors, and capital stock effects. Some of the important developments include for example, (i) improvements in the expectation models as to price, yield and returns, (ii) treatment of risk, (iii) inclusion of government policy variables, and (iv) estimation procedures in the econometric analysis. Along with the Nerlovian dynamic supply response model of adaptive expectations (or distributed lags) and further extensions in it through the rational and quasi-rational expectation hypotheses, several other dynamic response models have also got evolved. Some of the partial approaches are production function, profit function, multinomial logit models, time series cross section models, normative approaches such as mathematical programming and dynamic supply-demand models based on variants of the theory of distributed lag models.

Based on these, the responsiveness of supply to economic stimuli has been estimated in several studies. These can be classified into two broad categories. The first category relates to the crop-specific supply response functions that consider individual crop area or output and its responsiveness to price, the relevant variable being absolute or relative price of the crop under consideration.[1] In case of exportable item, export price or price prevalent in the world markets can also be tested. The second category of studies focus on the response of aggregate output where the impact of broader policies such as price, fiscal, devaluation and export-import policies is taken into account. The relative price variable is then represented by barter/income terms of trade or a change in the aggregate agricultural price index. For exportable crops, the impact on domestic terms of trade is studied through movements in the foreign terms of trade. Chibber (1988) and Binswanger (1989) maintained that both kinds of studies hold importance depending upon the region-specific or wider economic goals. For instance, estimates on crop-specific (area or output) response to own price or price of substitutable crop is deemed crucial in finding the implications at the household level, sustainability of land and water resources and inter-crop resource shifts. On the other hand, farmer's response of aggregate production to changes in the TOT is essential for determining the feasibility of agricultural pricing and other support policies and then formulating economy-wide adjustment programmes, food security, self-sufficiency, export growth objectives.

Whether it is an analysis of crop-specific response or aggregate-supply response, studies have focused primarily on exploring the extent to which price and non-price factors stimulate expansion of crop area and output. While there is no dearth of literature on crop-specific supply response of agriculture in India, studies on aggregate supply response are limited in number. Some widely referred to studies are by Herdt (1970), Bapna et al. (1981), Chibber (1988), Binswanger, Khandekar and Rosenzweig (1989), and Misra and Rao (2003). The focus in the present review is on documenting the supply response at the commodity level in India in the pre- and post-liberalization periods. Empirical evidence on supply response in other countries is provided in Askari and Cummings (1977) and Narayana and Shah (1984). The main findings of studies carried out in the context of economic reforms in countries other than India have already been discussed in Chapter 1.

Crop Supply Response during Pre-liberalization Period

Literature abounds an area/supply response for several crops at the all India, state and district level[2]. While most of the studies have been undertaken using partial analysis, a few have applied the CGE model. A discussion on selected studies that were done before initiation of the economic reforms programme in the country follows in an attempt to review the response of agriculture to price incentives and supply side factors.

Maji, Jha and Venkataramanan (1971) derived supply (area) and demand elasticities for wheat, maize and rice in Punjab from 1948 to 1965 using variants of the theory of distributed lags based on the Nerlovian model. For all three crops, both absolute and relative harvest prices were taken along with relative yield, total irrigated area and risk variable (price variability). The acreage response of all crops with respect to price was positive in the range of 0.02 to 0.66. Madhavan (1972) used an optimization technique to estimate the acreage response of rice in Tamil Nadu from 1947 to 1965. The estimated area elasticity varied between 0.03 to 0.34 in the short run and between 0.04 to 0.65 in the long run.

Narayana and Parikh (1981) found results based on the Nerlovian model to be unsatisfactory in the Indian case. They applied the Auto Regressive Integrated Moving Average Process (ARIMA) on grounds that expectations of price or revenue should account for the process of its movement over time and the occasional random shocks. Results based on 16 major crops indicated a positive response to relative revenue at the individual level. Krishna and Chibber (1983) developed an econometric model for wheat in India with an objective to ensure supply to the masses, at least possible cost to the government. Accordingly, the model included equations for supply, demand, imports, government purchases and sales based on time series data from 1961–78. Reduced form equations estimated from the model elicited the wheat supply system to be highly sensitive to changes in prices. The demand for wheat also responded more to prices which is unusual for subsistence crops. Similar was the case with imports, concessional sales and government purchases. Simulations were carried out using different scenarios of supply and demand conditions and the necessity of imports or exports. The model developed in the study was found to very useful in analysing the optimum values for the main variables involved in government purchases, viz., sales, imports and stocks.

Chand (1991) studied supply response in the context of price policy for major crops, viz., wheat, gram, paddy and cotton in the Punjab region. Using a normalized quadratic profit function, the author simultaneously estimated output supply and factor demand equations based on farm-level cross sectional data for the period 1977–79. Results indicated that factor prices negatively affect output supply, i.e., output decreases with increase in normalized prices of variable inputs. Further, output price has a positive effect on supply and the highest response was observed in the case of wheat at 0.18, followed by paddy at 0.13. The supply of cotton and gram did not respond to changes in their prices, perhaps due to technological ceilings and low profitability.

Aradhyula (1987) and Ghosh and Neogi (1995) studied India's foodgrain market using the Rational Expectation Hypothesis. By taking different factors from the demand as well as supply side, such as income levels and public foodgrain policy measures that influence commodity prices, the authors arrived at supply elasticities for rice and wheat. Ghosh and Neogi found elasticity of rice supply to lagged price at 0.36 while for lagged rationed distribution to be at 0.092 for the period 1964 to 1989. A high response to procurement price at 0.852 and irrigation at 2.13 was found. In the case of wheat, price elasticity was positive but relatively on the lower side than that of rice at 0.26 and for procurement price it was 0.52. The authors concluded that both price policy and technological advances have favoured wheat more than rice.

Kumar (1998) used a dynamic supply response model based on the multinomial logit function for estimation of area response of rice, sorghum, pearl millet and maize and Nerlovian Adaptive Response Model for wheat. The all-India estimates were arrived at from 1970–71 to 1988–89 using time series cross sectional input and output data based on four blocks of supply system (quasi-fixed inputs, area allocation, choice of techniques and yield and input determination) in block recursive mode. The area share of the crop system was made a function of expected crop revenue, normalized returns to maize, irrigated and rainfed area in the crop system, lagged dependent variable and dummy variables for regions. Zellner's generalized least squares technique corrected for correlation and heteroscedasticity in the disturbance terms was applied in the model. The own price area elasticity was estimated to be in the range of 0.02–0.25 in the short run and from 0.08 to 1.04 in the long run for selected crops.

Compared to partial analysis, only a few studies have used CGE model. As mentioned in Narayana (1989), the first attempt on the CGE model was carried out by Quizon and Binswanger (1986) who tried to examine the impact of agricultural growth and government policy on income distribution in India. The authors distinguished farm sector by four commodity groups, viz., rice, wheat, coarse cereals and other crops. Other crops were examined at the aggregate level. The outputs of these were estimated jointly with three inputs, viz., labour, draft power and fertilizer. The exogenous technology-related variables used were land, rainfall, irrigation, HYV, roads, farm capital, markets and technological change. The non-agricultural production is also taken exogenously. The commodity-wise supply response did not figure at all and hence aggregate supply response was estimated except for wheat and rice. The dynamic general equilibrium responses at the aggregate level were responsive to prices as most of the relevant variables – non-agriculture and trade were treated exogenously.

De Janvry and Subbarao (1986) in their CGE model distinguished agriculture into five commodity sectors, viz., rice; wheat; other food, i.e., cereals, grains, pulses, groundnut, fruits and vegetables; dairy products; and all other agricultural commodities. Other sectors taken in the economy were industry and services. The authors specified output of selected commodities in an input-output relation involving input-output technical coefficients, final demands as functions of prices, government's demand, investment, stock changes and trade. The outputs were taken exogenously with their prices as being endogenous. In some of the policy exercises carried out with a focus on price policy and income distribution, the authors considered both prices and quantities in the supply response function exogenously. In the absence of endogenous supply responses, the scope of the detailed supply response to policy analysis was found to be limited.

Narayana, Parikh and Srinivasan (1987) categorized agriculture into nine sectors, viz., wheat, rice, coarse grains, bovine and ovine meats, dairy products, other animal products, protein foods (oil cakes), other food (sugar, coffee), and non-food (jute, tobacco). The non-agriculture sector was treated as a single sector in their model. The acreage and yield functions were estimated separately for 25 crops and outputs obtained were aggregated to the above-required level only before exchange. Crop acreage and yield were modelled as functions of irrigation, expected prices (as ARIMA models) and other variables. Irrigation, an endogenous variable like prices, trade flows and stocks, was made a function of investment. Rates of HYV adoption for various crops were taken exogenously. The supply responses, thus obtained and projections carried out under various policy simulations were the result of dynamic general equilibrium effects.

Storm (1993) examined the impact of agriculture on other sectors in the economy during 1985–90 and the economy-wide effects on removal of the fertilizer subsidy. The CGE model considered nine sectors of which five were agricultural (rice, wheat, other food crops, commercial crops and other agriculture), another sector is a supplier of fertilizer, a couple of sectors were industrial (consumer and basic industries) and the ninth being the service sector. Both static (one period) and inter-temporal (multiperiod) simulations were generated. In the case of multiperiod, inter-temporal adjustment took place through non-agricultural investment, investment in irrigation, adaptive (Nerlovian) adjustment of area allocation among crops and indexation of non-agricultural wages. The model distinguished three income categories, viz., agricultural income, non-agricultural wage income, and non-agricultural mark up income, respectively to the three economic actors, viz., farmers, non-agricultural wage earners and non-agricultural profit earners having different saving and other patterns. The author specified separate private investment demand functions for agriculture and manufacturing. Public investment and its allocation were treated as policy variables. Results on acreage response function, separately for irrigated and unirrigated area, with respect to relative price reveal elasticities to differ considerably between crops. Price responsiveness in both short run and long run is fairly high for wheat (0.79) and for commercial crops (0.35). It is low for unirrigated other food crops and for irrigated rice cultivation.

Crop Supply Response during Post-liberalization Period

Bhalla and Singh (1996) estimated supply response in Punjab based on likely changes in prices as a result of the opening up of external trade in agriculture. The response of various crops, viz., wheat, paddy, maize, cotton, sugarcane was studied with respect to three main policy variables, viz., output prices (absolute and relative prices and profits), technology and input prices. The results based on the Nerlovian approach showed supply elasticity to be responsive to price variables except in the case of maize, which had a negative response to absolute and relative crop prices. However, for all the crops the impact of technology embodied in the form of modern varieties of crops was found to be relatively high and significant in determining output than own price and competing crop prices.

Storm (1997) used a CGE model to examine the impact of trade reforms on Indian agriculture. Both exports and competitive imports were considered exogenous. Among many aspects, the model was directed to analyse the implications of fertilizer subsidy for output pricing, response of model to policy changes (the most important being public expenditure policy and its impact on investment), fertilizer and food subsidy and public procurement. Simulations based on close integration were carried out on the basis of full liberalization of India's foreign trade and removal of input subsidies (fertilizer). The strategic simulations were based on two assumptions, viz., first, markets for rice, wheat and commercial crops were guided by government intervention and support prices were raised to the level of market prices; second, there could be no free trade in these crops. The results had significant implications for growth, output and prices under close and strategic integration. Among many aspects, results showed favourable response of terms of trade to agriculture due to high cross elasticities of demand and a move away from non-agricultural goods towards agricultural goods.

Naik and Jain (1999) applied the Nerlovian adjustment model to estimate the extent of influence of price (own and competing) and non-price factors, viz., yield and risk on crop acreage of major cash crops at the national and state levels from 1975–76 to 1995–96 and at the district level from 1975–76 to 1992–93. The study also examined changes in these factors and hence area under a crop as a result of the WTO agreement on agriculture. The results revealed short- and long-term own price elasticities of area under cotton, jute, soyabean, oilseeds, pepper, coffee and castor seeds to be positive but low in most of the states (range 0.08 to 2.39 and 0.32 to 9.96). These were not very high for foodgrains except for jowar and bajra. Oilseed responded favourably to its own and competing prices. The authors found a decline in area under oilseeds, as world prices were lower for edible oils than for domestic prices. The extent of change in acreage would vary from state to state depending on the direction and magnitude of changes in factors, trade opportunities that India has in world markets, productivity and competitiveness of crops. Expected changes in crop area in a WTO regime were estimated. Results indicated that the area under wheat, cotton, groundnut, jute and sugarcane would increase while that under jowar, rapeseed and mustard, sunflower and soyabean would decline. However, the impact would vary in a situation of technological change.

Gulati and Kelly (1999) tested various hypotheses relating to farmers' behaviour in allocating land across different crops under profit maximizing and subsistence-oriented conditions. A fixed effects model of time series cross-section models was employed to analyse cropping pattern changes in 23 crop zones in the semi-arid regions of India from 1970 to 1990 through formulation of crop-specific equations. Both price and non-price variables were included in estimating the elasticity of area changes. The empirical results indicated a positive but low supply response to own price (profit-related factors) as well as to competing crop price. However, the importance of price factors along with non-price factors varied from crop to crop and from zone to zone. Wheat and maize were found to have a marginal effect compared to paddy, coarse cereals and groundnut. The authors expected economic stimuli, i.e., price changes due to shifts in trade to become more important in the coming years. Subsequently, they analysed the likely impact of change in prices on production, consumption, government revenues, foreign exchange earnings, welfare of producers and consumers on the basis of demand and supply estimates of cereals and cash crops. A multi-market model that incorporated the supply and demand system was developed. While indicating the probable direction and extent of change in cropping pattern that might emerge following trade liberalization, the model estimated a range of supply elasticities under alternate scenarios and an imposition of vector of world commodity prices on domestic prices. These ranged from 0.16 to 0.47 for rice; for wheat 0.26 to 0.59; for oilseeds 0.05 to 0.59, and for sugarcane and cotton 0.19 to 0.62, and 0.20 and 0.70, respectively.

Based on a time series model as developed by Krishna and Chibber (1983), Sharma, Ghosh and Kumar (2001) applied a policy model for open market operations of wheat at the all-India level from 1973–1997. The authors studied interactions between production, demand, imports, procurement and PDS issues and solved the behavioural equations using an iterative method. The results reveal both acreage and yield to be responsive to price, weather, irrigation and their own past values. But the supply elasticity to prices was found to be low at 0.13 (short run) and 0.30 (long run) and high at 0.73 for irrigation. Important variables that explained the rising demand were level of income and prices and availability of substitutes. The procurement responded to prices fixed by government.

Kalirajan and Bhide (2003) formulated a macroeconometric model at the national and regional level. The model incorporated the frontier production function approach to model agriculture and manufacturing production and simulated the impact of alternative policy scenarios on agriculture, in particular on overall prices, output and national income. The results based on data from 1970–92 show that exchange rate depreciation would accelerate agriculture output and increase the share of non-food grain output relative to foodgrain output. A 10 per cent reduction in import tariff on manufacturing would increase output by 0.21 per cent. Further, an increase in crop prices by 5 per cent would raise agriculture output by 1.6 per cent. As a result of rise in crop prices relative to other prices, higher private investment in agriculture would take place, which would accelerate irrigated area and induce changes in crop mix in favour of foodgrains. Other factors that may significantly influence output are production efficiency, rural literacy, fertilizer price and infrastructure. At the regional level, the impact of policies that affect production efficiency was greater in regions having a lower level of efficiency. The impact of increasing production efficiency, rural literacy, irrigation, fertilizer price, human and physical infrastructure on output and prices varied across the states as per the production, weather and other regional conditions.

Bhattacharya and Kar (2007) developed a structural macroeconometric model for the Indian economy based on several behavioural equations and identities in agriculture, manufacturing and tertiary sectors and in the external sector. Agricultural capital output ratio is assumed to be determined by changes in rainfall, fertilizer use and relative price. Real private investment is taken to be a function of agricultural income, public investment, relative price and lending rate. Further, agricultural prices are seen as being determined by disposable income growth, representing demand and growth in farm output–present and lagged rate, representing supply side variables. Another variable, growth rate of procurement price index is also included in the model as a policy variable. The results obtained from the estimation of the model from 1970–71 to 1998–99 show agriculture capital output ratio, private investment and prices to be responsive to the factors taken. For instance, an increase in real public investment by 4 per cent of GDP is shown to accelerate the agricultural growth rate from 2.9 to 3.4 per cent. However, there have been no significant effects of liberalization on agriculture, which according to the authors can be explained by the fact that significant reforms have not been undertaken in this sector.

In short, the following key observations can be made with respect to empirical testing of the hypothesis of responsiveness of individual crops to price and non-price factors. First, the Nerlovian model has continued to dominate literature on supply response despite econometric and data problems encountered in its application. Realizing such limitations, a parallel line of research has evolved over time which has brought certain refinements and developments in the original model with respect to process of price expectation, treatment of risk and inclusion of policy variables. Consequent upon these, several variants of the distributed lag model such as rational expectation hypothesis, the ARIMA model and quasi-rational hypothesis have been applied in the research work. Researchers have also used other partial equilibrium approaches to study crop shift decisions of farmers. Only in a few studies, CGE and macroeconometric models have been used, with a focus on aggregate crops, foodgrain and non-foodgrain segments only. There is no doubt that these macro models are important in the formulation of national-level policies but it may not be easy to capture the impact of changes in price and other policies on output at the regional level by mean of these.

Second, results based on both traditional and new approaches though not comparable from crop to crop and from region to region have found acreage/output of food and non-food crops to be responsive to economic stimuli, except in some regions which lack irrigation, technology and marketing facilities. While considerable shifts in area have taken place from coarse cereals to cereals, oilseeds and cash crops over the period, estimates on area price elasticity for these commodities are low, thus indicating the importance of non-price factors. With expansion in irrigation, technology, markets and infrastructure, a fairly stronger and increasing influence of market incentives on farmers' area allocation decision is likely to emerge. This is expected to increase further due to a changing economic environment under the era of globalization and liberalization. Third, there are only a few studies that have attempted to examine the impact of economic reforms and trade liberalization on Indian agriculture. These studies are partial as the impact is seen only through changes in domestic prices as a result of greater opening of markets to free trade. The individual effect of other factors that have a bearing on prices, namely trade (tariffs and non-tariff barriers) and exchange rate, fiscal and sector-specific policy changes, global recession, hike in oil prices and subsidies, etc., on crop shifts and output decisions have not been investigated in greater details.

Summing up

This chapter has presented a review of studies on two interrelated aspects of Indian agriculture namely, price transmission from world to domestic markets, and supply (acreage) response of individual crops to price incentives and supply side factors. Literature survey of these two subjects covers a period of nearly four decades. It captures the impact of policies on agriculture prior to and after economic reforms and also one to understand the methodological developments that have taken place on these subjects. The main findings are summed up as follows.

Price Transmission based on Market Integration Approach

The discussion provides evidence in favour of an improvement in price transmission in many farm commodities in the post-reform period over the pre-reform period. However, full price transmission across the state-level markets has been refuted on grounds of high transportation costs, stringent controls and barriers such as varied rates of sales tax, octroi and infrastructural bottlenecks. The same holds true for transmission between domestic and world markets due to the restrictive policies being followed by many countries such as trade quotas, quantitative restrictions, high tariffs, strict quality controls and other NTBs whereby government intervention in trade occurs through fixation of prices, etc. Consequently, it may be difficult for world price signals to perfectly reach domestic producers and hence establish long-run equilibrium relationship. Some of these factors may also lead to asymmetric price transmission between world and domestic markets. On methodological aspects, the hypothesis of no cointegration of markets, which was tested using correlation coefficient, is taken over by ADF, regression technique and Johansen procedures with considerable refinements in these over time. Even though the ADF approach is relatively simple and intuitive, it suffers from limitations as are faced in the correlation coefficient method. Since the estimates based on correlation and regression techniques are limited to two markets only, the Johansen maximum likelihood approach is preferred over these. Besides allowing analysis in a multivariate framework, the approach takes care of endogeniety and simultaneity problems that are associated with other cointegration tests. However, recent studies have pointed to a limited application of the Johansen test in situations of non-stationary transaction costs and reversals in trade flows across markets. Accordingly, a few attempts have been made to bring refinements in this method based on finding common factors across markets.

Cropping Pattern Changes and Acreage (Supply) Response

For estimating the response of agriculture to price and non-price factors, literature has relied more on partial analysis than on the computable general equilibrium framework. Within partial analysis, the Nerlovian partial adjustment model based on the concept of adaptive expectations is found to have a wider application. In many studies, some variants of the original model such as the ARIMA model, rational expectation hypotheses, quasi-rational hypothesis have also been employed. Broad results elicit a shift in acreage from coarse cereals and traditional crops during the seventies towards rice, wheat and oilseeds during the eighties. The expectation in the nineties and 2000 has been towards an increased commercialization and diversification of agriculture in view of greater openness of domestic economy to world markets. The crop area and output response to price incentives is found to be positive in both the pre- and post-reform periods in most of the developing countries that opted for liberal reforms. However, the relative importance of price, policy and non-price factors has differed across crops and regions due to different time periods considered, regional differences, specification of variables and econometric models. This would essentially imply that cropping pattern changes in a free trade regime may vary across regions and also the factors that influence such crop shifts will not be the same. For instance, coastal areas may be gaining more from external trade than other regions due to their close proximity to ports. Furthermore, price convergence between border and domestic prices may be faster in areas near delivery points, which may further influence acreage decisions. However, a regional dimension of agricultural performance with respect to changes in domestic and world prices, crop area shifts and their response to free market prices and broader policies and conditions is yet to be explored. Another important aspect is that a positive supply response is accompanied with an increasing sensitivity of agriculture to high fluctuations in global prices and other exogenous impulses, perhaps induced by exchange rate and tariffs. This needs to be probed in detail.

The present study aims to fill some of these research gaps by testing the extent of world and domestic price transmission for important tradable commodities, separately in the pre- and post-liberalization periods using the Johansen multivariate cointegration and error correction model. This is followed by a detailed analysis of inter-crop area shifts and inter-linkages between agriculture, macroeconomic policies, relative prices and non-price factors. The magnitude of the response of acreage, output and trade to these factors is estimated using a structural econometric model. Simulation experiments are then carried out to assess the resilience of agriculture to hypothetical changes and shocks in macroeconomic policies, price and natural factors and its performance in a market-driven economy.

Notes

1. In most of the crop-specific studies, area price elasticity is taken to be a good estimate of price elasticity of crop output. The estimates may not be accurate as yield is assumed to be constant.
2. Among the initial studies made on the individual area/supply response, the following: Krishna (1963); Krishna and Rao (1967); Madhavan (1972); Askari and Cummings (1976 and 1977); Maji, Jha and Venkataramanan (1971) are frequently referred to in the literature.

3

Trade Policy Reforms and Openness of Indian Agriculture

Analysis at the Commodity Level

Before evaluating world and domestic price linkages and acreage response to liberal macroeconomic and sector-specific measures, it is pertinent to explore what have been the salient features of trade policy reforms and to what extent has Indian agriculture opened up to world markets? These issues are important as India has committed to incorporate an open and liberal policy framework for her farm sector following the Uruguay Round Agreement on Agriculture of the General Agreement on Trade and Tariff (GATT), now vested in WTO. This necessitates introducing trade reforms not only on the external front, essentially in accordance with the stipulations contemplated in the AOA but also transforming internal (domestic) agriculture towards a decentralized market mechanism. This transition implies a notable departure from the protectionist policies being followed in the past and a gradual move towards a freer agricultural economy that integrates aptly with the world economy. As Indian agriculture cannot remain unconstrained by multilateral trading rules, an assessment of the policy changes initiated so far and the magnitude of openness would help determine the exact position of this sector and challenges ahead. The analysis will also provide a context for testing various hypotheses in the chapters that follow. Accordingly, a delineation of the principal features of external and internal trade, price and marketing policies and reforms as they relate to major commodities is here followed by an analysis of the magnitude of the openness of Indian agriculture. The analysis is done by quantifying the level of protection accorded to agriculture through tariffs and non-tariff barriers during the nineties and early 2000 relative to its own past, and then juxtaposing trade reforms against the commitments advanced in the Uruguay Round Agreement on Agriculture (UR AOA).

Agricultural Trade Policy and Reform Measures

Economic reforms began in 1991 with the agricultural sector witnessing a modest attempt at relaxation of trade controls for select commodities. The process of reform initiatives actually began from 1994–95 when India became part of the multilateral trading system under the auspices of the WTO. Since then, considerable changes have been made in the export-import policy in consonance with the provisions of the WTO. Tariff rates and NTBs have been reduced for several commodities and provision made to revise these in view of movement of global prices and other concerns such as import surge, food security and self-sufficiency. Export promotion measures have been initiated through notification of agri-export zones in major states along with a removal of restrictions with respect to licensing and other regulations. Attempts have also been made to reform domestic trade by abolishing and simplifying physical and regulatory measures on private trade under the aegis of price, legislative and institutional measures. In the following section the external (export-import) and internal trade and other policies for important commodities, viz., foodgrains (rice, wheat and pulses), oilseeds and edible oils, sugar and raw cotton are discussed. Table 3.1a and b presents a matrix of changes in the import and export status of farm commodities during the pre-reform (1990–91) and post-reform (2006–07) periods.

Foodgrains

Foodgrains comprise rice, wheat, coarse cereals and pulses. Export-import policy for these commodities is influenced by their demand and supply situations in the domestic markets. Before executing the liberalized measures, a restrictive trade policy was followed for these commodities. Though most of the restrictions on trade in cereals have been removed in the post-Uruguay Round period, trade in these commodities continues to operate under the purview of government regulation. While import of wheat and rice is canalized through Food Corporation of India (FCI), export of rice (both basmati and

TABLE 3.1a *Status of Import Policy of Agricultural Commodities during the Pre- and Post-liberalization Periods*

Commodity	*Import Policy: 1991*				*Import Policy: 2006*					
	Canalizing/ Agency	*OGL*	*Quanti-tative restri-ctions*	*Lice-nsing*	*Canalizing/ Agency*	*OGL*	*Quantitative restrictions*	*Licensing/ce rtificate*	*Within Tariffs-bound rate*	*Remarks*
A. Foodgrains Wheat	Yes/FCI	Yes	Yes	Yes	C/FCI	Yes	R-BoP*	Yes	Yes	Products of milling industry free; seeds of cereals through SIL
Rice (Non-basmati)	Yes/FCI	Yes	Yes	Yes	C/FCI	Yes	R-BoP*	Yes	Yes	Products of milling industry free
Rice (Basmati)	Yes	Yes	Yes	No	C/FCI	Yes	No	No	Yes	
Pulses and Coarse Cereals	Yes/NAFED ; Pulses No	Yes	Yes		C/FCI//NA FED	Yes	Subject to TRQ allocation	Import contracts to be registered with APEDA	Yes	

Cont'd...

Cont'd…

B. Sugarcane/Sugar	Yes/STC	Yes	Yes	Yes	Free	Yes	Quantitative ceilings	Certificate by APEDA	Yes	Additional duty is imposed; sugar imports delicensed
C. Raw Cotton	Yes/CCI	Yes	–		Free	Yes	No	Registration with textile commi-ssioner	Yes	
D. Oilseeds/Oils Groundnut seed and Oil, Rapeseed/mustard and Mustard Oil	Yes/ NAFED/ STC/ HVOC	Yes	Yes		Free/in shell R/seeds-R	Yes	SIL for seeds: Subject to quarantine restrictions	Certificate from exporting agency	Yes	Oils free to import

Source: GOI Import-Export Policy and Customs Tariffs, Arun Goyal (various issues).

TABLE 3.1b *Status of Export Policy of Agricultural Commodities during the Pre- and Post-liberalization Periods*

Commodity	*Exports: 1991*					*Exports: 2006*						
	Canalizing	*OGL*	*MEP*	*Licensing/ Quota*	*Remarks*	*OGL*	*MEP*	*Licensing/ Quota/ Registration*	*Quantative Ceilings*	*Export Tariff*	*Export Cess*	*Remarks*
A. Foodgrains Wheat	No	Yes	No	Yes/APEDA	From 1993 onwards, private sector was allowed to export durum wheat s.t. quantitative ceilings and MEP; removed in 1994	Free	No	Registration of certificate by APEDA	May be imposed	No	Yes	
Rice (Non-basmati and Basmati)	No	Yes	Yes	Yes/APEDA		Free	No	Registration of contracts with APEDA	May be imposed	No	Yes	Paddy in husk-R; license; millers exporting rice is subject to levy

Cont'd...

Cont'd…

Pulses and Coarse Cereals	No	Yes; No for pulses	Yes/ No for Pulses	Yes APEDA/ No for Pulses	For pulses, NAFED makes purchases; exports not allowed	Pulses restricted	No	License for pulses;for others registration with APEDA	No; pulses free upto 5 kg pack others require license	No	Yes	Hybrid jowar and processed pulses from export processing zones or duty exemption scheme free
B. Sugarcane/ Sugar	Yes/STC	No	No	No	Yes on quantity to be exported	Free	No	Registra-tion cum allocation certificate by APEDA	May be imposed; quanti-tative ceilings	No	No	Private individuals can export
C. Raw Cotton	No	Yes	Yes	Yes (textile commissioner)		Free	No	Certificate from textile boards	–	No	Yes	
D. Oilseeds/Oils Groundnut seed and Oil, Rapeseed/mustard and Mustard Oil	No	No	No	Yes	Export banned except hand picked select groundnut which is under OGL	Restricted	No	Permitted under license for oilseeds and groundnut oil	–	No	Yes; mustard and ground nut	Tariff is on deoiled groundnut cake and meals; for some seeds exports are canalized through TRIFED; vege-table oil other than ground nut is free

Source: Same as in Table 3.1a.

non-basmati) is allowed freely subject to minimum export price (MEP) and registration of contracts with Agricultural and Processed Food Products Export Development Authority (APEDA). Export controls on all varieties of rice were abolished in October 1994. From 2001, high tariff walls were raised to counter the fear of dumping. Export of rice in husk is permitted under license. From October 2007, export of non-basmati rice was banned and MEP was fixed subject to revision from time to time. From April 2008, non-basmati export has been prohibited on private account. In the case of wheat, exports were restricted on balance of payment grounds and were subject to a quantitative ceiling fixed by the government, licensing, export quotas and MEP. In 1993–94, exports of durum wheat were allowed by private agencies subject to a quantitative ceiling and MEP. The condition of MEP was abolished in 1994. The ceilings get revised every year in view of stock position and level of procurement. During 2001–02, the Government of India allowed roller flourmills to import for actual use with zero per cent duty. Further, from April 2002, export restrictions have been removed on wheat and wheat products, rice and pulses. Import of coarse cereals is restricted on Balance of Payment (BOP) grounds, canalized through FCI and is subject to Open General License (OGL). Exports of these items are free but subject to minimum export price, quantitative ceiling/registration-cum-allocation certificate and quota specified by the APEDA. In the case of pulses, exports are restricted through license (except in consumer packs upto 5 kg allowed freely) and imports are placed at zero per cent duty under OGL. The import tariff was reduced from 10 per cent to 5 per cent in 1995 and was completely abolished in 1998. An overall scenario on foodgrains reveals imposition of tariffs on rice and wheat from the early 2000 and relaxation in NTBs to a great extent. From early 2000, the Ministry of Agriculture controls import of cereals through issue of agriculture permits.

Oilseeds and Edible Oils

As for foodgrains, the export-import policy for oilseeds and edible oils is also influenced by their availability in the domestic markets. For long, import of seeds as well as oils were restricted and canalized through State Trading Corporation (STC) and Hindustan Vegetable Oils Corporation (HVOC). Import of palm oil was regulated to maintain domestic prices of oilseeds/oils. In 1994–95, palmolein oil was brought under OGL at 65 per cent import duty for private traders and at a concessional duty of 20 per cent by the state agencies, viz., National Dairy Development Board (NDDB) and STC. Significant changes have taken place from 1995 when all edible oils except coconut oil were placed under OGL at an import duty of 30 per cent. However, oilseeds import remained in the government's domain. Import duty got reduced to 15 per cent in 1996. In 1998, government allowed import of sunflower seed and soybean in cracked and split form at a duty of 40 per cent. It was perceived that cheap imports made production of oilseeds less competitive. A high import duty and a few restrictions were placed in order to prevent excessive imports. Futures trading in oilseeds got reintroduced from the year 1999. From 2002, import of groundnut oil and mustard oil has been made free and their effective duties are within the Uruguay Round (UR) bound rates. It is interesting to find that to promote oilseed production, government provides support to growers by keeping domestic prices above the world prices. Yet domestic production of oilseeds is on a decline and there has been a surge in the edible oil imports. Nearly 50 per cent of the demand for edible oils is met through imports, which will continue unless some technological breakthrough happens that improves the yield of oilseeds (Singh and Asokan, 2001). Edible oils (mainly palmolein) are allowed import through State Trading Enterprises (STEs) and distributed through the Public Distribution System (PDS) by HVOC at a price higher than the import price but lower than the market price. At times, imports are subject to quarantine checks also, which is a kind of NTB. Some other NTBs that have been imposed lately on oilseeds include obtaining an agriculture permit as well as phyto-sanitary and Bureau of Indian Standards' quality certificates on edible oils. The duty structure is revised to regulate the import of edible oils and harmonize the interests of various stakeholders.

As far as reforms in oilseeds and edible oils exports are concerned, exports were banned before 1994–95 except for hand picked select groundnut, which was placed under OGL. Oil meals were exported without any condition of license but exporters were required to take/register export contracts. This registration rule was abolished in 1995 along with export controls/quantitative ceilings on sunflower seed and rapeseed-mustard. However, export of other oilseeds continued to be controlled and permitted against license and a registration-cum-allocation certificate issued by APEDA. Export of oilseeds for consumption purposes is free except for niger seed, which is canalized through state agencies. Rapeseed/mustard seed exports are also free but subject to quarantine restrictions. From April 2001, export restrictions have been removed on many edible oils such as groundnut oil, but they are permitted only against a license. From April 2008, export restrictions have been lifted on coconut oil and certain oils produced from minor forest. Export of edible oil in branded consumer packs is allowed.

Sugar

External trade in sugar has also been in the government's domain. In 1991, export of sugar and molasses were canalized by the STC. Export of molasses was restricted to keep the domestic price below world prices so as to protect the interests of the alcohol industry. This restriction was removed with the reform process till 1994. From 1994, exports have been restricted primarily to protect the sugar alcohol industry. After de-canalization of sugar, exports were regulated under the Sugar Export Promotion Act by the Indian Sugar and General Industry Export Import Corporation. Exports were subject to approval of the Ministry of Food and Civil Supplies. Accordingly, export quotas were allocated to sugar mills. As in the case of export, import of sugar and raw sugar was also restricted before liberalization. Import of molasses was unrestricted but subject to high import duty. Significant relaxations were given for import of sugar at zero duty only from March 1994 until April 1998. Imports were de-licensed and import duty got reduced to zero. This policy continued for two years and subsequently a basic duty of 5 per cent and an additional import duty of 5 per cent were introduced from 1998. In 1999, the Sugar Control Order 1966, was amended to bring importers and imported sugar under its purview. As of now, sugar import is under OGL and government has imposed a 5 per cent custom duty along with a countervailing duty of Rs 850 per tonne to provide protection to domestic producers. A levy obligation was also imposed on importers of sugar from February 2000. Custom duty was raised to 40 per cent from December 1999 and further to 60 per cent in 2000 and then to 100 per cent in 2003 with an existing countervailing duty at Rs 850 per tonne. From 2008, customs duty has been fixed at 60 per cent with a countervailing duty at Rs 950 per tonne. All import contracts are to be registered with APEDA. From 2003, imports are subject to one barrier, viz., the Essential Commodity Act (ECA). Under this Act, levy obligations and release system is applicable on imported sugar on the same lines as for domestic sugar. Exports are allowed to liquidate surplus stocks. From 2008, an export assistance scheme has been initiated for sugar mills, which covers payment of internal transport and freight charges including ocean freight and handling and marketing charges. Sugar factories are allowed to export raw sugar along with milled white sugar.

Raw Cotton

Government allocates quotas of raw cotton for export with the bulk going to the state agencies like Cotton Corporation of India (CCI) and the rest going to state-level marketing federations and private traders. Frequently, the state agencies contract out these quotas to private traders for a commission. Import of cotton was allowed for exporting units directly after 1994. Also, import of raw cotton was made free till 1999 (with no import duty) to ensure its easy availability at competitive prices to the textile industry. From March 1999, a duty of 5 per cent plus a surcharge of 10 per cent has been imposed. Regarding NTBs, the import contracts are to be registered with the textile commissioner and an agriculture permit has to be obtained.

Internal Agricultural Trade Policy and Reform Measures

Compared to external trade, internal (domestic) trade in agricultural commodities is well developed and is not physically restricted within the country. Private and regulated markets operate in most of the states and goods are traded despite transport and infrastructure bottlenecks. The communication network is well developed due to effective mobile services and a dissemination of commodity prices through print media and the radio. However, in spite of the smooth functioning of wholesale regulated markets across the country, private trade faces many physical and regulatory constraints. These are imposed by the Central and State governments under the aegis of price, legislative and institutional measures. The government/state agencies like FCI for cereals and CCI for cotton often enforce physical controls and regulations on private trade through entry barriers (licensing/permits), restrictions on the movement of goods without permits, stock limits, futures trading, credit controls, price fixation, multiple tax structure, compulsory procurement, levy on rice and sugar and several other marketing regulations. The main legislative instruments through which most of these controls operate include the following: the Essential Commodity Act, 1955 (ECA); State Agricultural Produce Market Act, 1966 and 2003; Agriculture Produce (Grading and Marking) Act, 1937 and 1986; Prevention of Food Adulteration Act, 1954, 1964, 1976, 1986; Fruits Product Order, 1955 and 1997; Milk and Milk Products Order, 1992 and several other commodities specific Acts.

Some of the controls and regulations implemented under various Acts are considered to have outlived their time and are also considered to distort prices, impede the functioning of markets and market intermediaries and hence go against the principles of free trade. It was, therefore, suggested to amend and do away with these regulations

(Gulati, 1998; World Bank, 1999). There was no liberalization in these policy instruments till the middle of the nineties. Subsequently, towards the end of the nineties and in early 2000, certain amendments were made to the Acts and several measures were proposed and implemented in the output price, trade and marketing operations so as to promote private trade. For brevity, we have categorized various policy measures into two groups, namely: (a) trade, marketing, legislative and developmental measures; and (b) price, buffer stock and PDS policies. Needless to say that there is considerable overlapping of many policy instruments and reform measures under these two categories. Effort is made to place them appropriately under each of the defined groups. Table 3.2 summarizes the present status of reforms in agricultural trade and other policies within the domestic markets.

Agricultural Trade, Marketing and Legislative Measures

As part of the reform process, the central government has decided to treat the entire country as one zone for inter-state and intra-state movement of foodgrains from March 1993. Information gathered from the department of food, Ministry of Agriculture reveals that the states and Union Territory (UTs) are advised to take necessary action in this direction. All the states with only exception of West Bengal, Tamil Nadu, Jammu & Kashmir have removed all statutory restrictions on free movement of grain within the country. At times, informal controls such as non-availability of railway wagons for shipment of wheat by traders during procurement period and restrictions on movement of rice in some states are imposed. Those states, which are continuing restrictions on free movement of grains outside their state boundary, view their policy as facilitative of procurement within the state and as a preventive step to control smuggling of foodgrains across the international borders. Of late in November 2000 and then in January 2001, the central government has again requested the states/UTs to do away with all types of restrictions on trade and industry dealing with wheat, wheat products and rice and also informal movement restrictions, if any, imposed on their own. The overall comfortable food situation, storage constraints faced by FCI and promotion of free trade justify this. In response, the states have argued for a case of movement restrictions on certain local conditions. Tamil Nadu, which has long followed a monopoly procurement system, has already made a beginning by removing movement restrictions and levy on all varieties of paddy and rice, and also has withdrawn an increase in sales tax on flour of pulses (*Business Line:* September 14, 2001). Along with these measures, a national policy

TABLE 3.2 *Domestic (Internal) Trade and Other Policies for Major Farm Commodities (as on 2006–07)*

Commodity	*ECA*	*Levy*	*Procure-ment/Price Support*	*Movement Restrictions*	*Licence/ Permits for private trade*	*Stock Limits*	*Future Trading*	*Selective Credit Control*	*Other Interventions/Remarks*
A. Foodgrains 1. Wheat	Yes	No	Yes (FCI)	No (Occasional)	Yes	Yes	No	Yes	Movements informal except in West Bengal, Tamil Nadu and Jammu-Kashmir; restrictions imposed at times in surplus states; Less availability of wagons for private shipment; Stock limits removed/relaxed in many states.
2. Rice (Non-basmati)	Yes	Yes (25 –75%)	Yes (FCI)	No (Occasional)	Yes	Yes	No	Yes	Monopoly procurement in Tamil Nadu, informal movement restrictions elsewhere; Stock limits removed/relaxed in many states; Removal of levy under consideration by the Central govt.
2a. Rice (Basmati)	Yes	No	No	No	Yes	Yes	No	–	Procurement through levy in some years; finally withdrawn.
3. Pulses and Coarse Cereals	Yes	No	Yes (No PDS) (NAFED)	No	Yes for transpor-tation	Yes	No/Yes for pulses	–	Direct sales not allowed outside Andhra Pradesh, Hyderabad and Tamil Nadu without permits.
B. Sugarcane/ Sugar	Yes	Yes (15%)	Yes (No PDS)(FCI)	No	Yes	Yes	Yes	–	Movement restricted – direct sales allowed only with permits; monthly release controlled; Registration on installation of new units through license.

Cont'd...

Cont'd…

C. Raw cotton	Yes	No	Yes (No PDS)(CCI and Maharashtra Federation)	Regulated through CCI	Regulated through CCI	Yes	Yes	–	Withdrawal of monopoly procurement in Maharashtra is recommended
D. Oilseeds/ Oils Groundnut seed and Oil, Rapeseed/mustard and Oil	Yes	Yes	Yes (No PDS)(NAFED /NDDB)	No	Removed in 1991 but do exist in some states	Yes	Yes; Re-introduced in 1999	Yes	Small quantities procured and distributed through PDS; Central state tax is imposed on inter state trade

Source: Agricultural Statistics at a Glance, Ministry of Agriculture, and Economic Survey, Ministry of Finance, GOI (various issues).

on handling and storage of foodgrains at the farm and commercial level was announced in 2000. The policy proposes to involve the private sector in building storage capacities for keeping government's stock and for bulk handling and transportation. As a precondition, this would necessitate amendments in the existing levy order, licensing order, movement restrictions, maximum stock hoarding limits and other bans on trading.

The licensing requirements and stocking limits that form part of the ECA, 1955 and other state orders and Acts vary from state to state. A simplification in their procedure is witnessed from 1994. Many states except Punjab and Orissa have removed these restrictions and licensing requirements. Stocking limits on traders were reimposed in 1996 when wheat prices shot up. While coarse grains have no stocking limits, other commodities such as pulses, oilseeds, edible oils and sugar continue to face limits. Elimination of levy and licensing on domestic trade are still on the offer. As a reform measure, levy to the free sale ratio of sugar has been reduced from 40:60 to 30:70 from January 2000, and to 15:85 from February 2001. From March 1, 2002, levy obligation of domestic sugar factories were reduced to 10 per cent to enable them to sell more in the open market. There also exists release of free sale sugar quotas and distribution and pricing of molasses. There has been a little change in the levy on rice, which varies from 25 per cent to 75 per cent in most of the states. Some changes were identified in the selective credit control policy, which has long been followed to regulate institutional credit to control trader's holding of commodity stocks. The policy is operational in the case of foodgrains, sugar/*gur*/*khandsari*, oilseeds, vegetable oils and *vanaspati* and cotton. In 1996, liberalized measures under the policy were introduced in case of sugar, *gur, khandsari, kapas* and cotton. A policy of Selective Credit Control (SCC) was continued for advances against buffer stock and unreleased stocks of sugar. The margin in the latter case was reduced from 20 per cent to 15 per cent. Reforms in futures trading were identified from the year 1997. The 1997–98 Union Budget allowed resumption of futures trading in ginned and baled cotton and jute. A proposal to set up international castor oil future exchange in Mumbai has been placed. In 1998–99, a renewed focus was placed on resumption of futures trading in oilseeds, oilcakes and edible oils. From 2002, many more items have been allowed under futures trading such as sugar. Trading in wheat and rice was allowed for a few years and was banned due to an increase in their prices, which was considered to have occurred due to speculation. As mentioned above, as a prerequisite this policy initiative requires liberalization of ECA, which inhibits traders to stock goods beyond a certain limit. As of now, there are differential tax rates and standards in agri-commodities across the country, which prevent rational and uniform pricing strategies

As far as reforms in legislation are concerned, amendments of far reaching nature have been introduced in the ECA. A fairly large number of new control orders have been issued, while several others have been repealed by the central as well as the state governments. For instance, the central government has taken a lead in repealing some of the restrictive legislations such as: (i) Rice milling industries (Regulation) Act, 1958; (ii) Ginning and Pressing Factories Act, 1925, (iii) Licensing, Price Control and Requisitioning under Cold Storage Order, 1965 (as amended in 1980) and so on. Domestic policies related to production, supply, and distribution of various agricultural commodities under the state Agricultural Produce Market Committee Act, 1966 (APMC) have also been brought under review for appropriate modifications. The Central government has proposed several amendments in the Act. The Ministry of Agriculture in 2003 has prepared a new Model Act for agricultural produce marketing, which can be used by the state governments to prepare their individual Acts. The Model Act allows participation by the private sector in direct marketing and contract farming. Though the states are willing to replace the existing APMC Act with the new one, progress has been uneven so far. Karnataka has already made headway by permitting establishment of an 'Integrated Produce Market' to be owned and managed by the National Dairy Development Board (NDDB) for marketing of fruits, flowers and vegetables in the state. Punjab also proposes to reduce bureaucratic controls in the agriculture markets. Issues with respect to price policy, food security and self-sufficiency are on high priority in the committees constituted to examine foodgrain policies (GOI, 2002).

Reforms in Price, Buffer Stock and PDS Policies

Under price policy, government regulates prices and movement of essential commodities through fixation of support price, procurement and open market sales. Farm prices have always been kept low on social and equity grounds. As part of the reform process, substantial increase in the minimum support price of cereals and hence their issue price was made during 1993–94 to remove the existing policy bias against agriculture. An excessive rise in the market price of these commodities was checked through open market sales operations. At that time, some suggestions were put forward on liberalization of the price fixation procedures as followed by the Commission on Agricultural Costs and

Prices (CACP). The existing principle of price fixation, which is based on the criterion of cost of production of each crop, was suggested to include other factors such as domestic demand and supply conditions, stock position, international price and a balanced view with respect to the interests of industry versus farmers and consumers versus farmers. A change in the procedure is expected to transcend earlier inflexibilities and benefit all the stakeholders involved in the agricultural marketing chain.

For commodities other than foodgrains such as vegetables, fruits and spices, price policy has not been put in place. Government announced the Market Intervention Scheme (MIS) in 1991–92 to promote domestic private trade for the reason that this sector suffers from technological and infrastructural constraints. The scheme is not part of the minimum support price. Under MIS, farmers are extended support at a price mutually agreed to by the centre and state governments for a specific area during a predefined period. Losses on account of distress sale are to be shared on an equal basis between the central and the respective state governments. The scheme continued during the nineties and efforts have been made to strengthen it in many states.

In order to increase private sector participation, several steps have been taken to liberalize the procurement operations of wheat, rice, sugar and other commodities in the latter half of the nineties and during 2000. Revisions in the minimum buffer stocking levels for wheat and rice prescribed in 1995–96 were further revised in 1998–99. Several state governments have initiated their own procurement operations, which aim to reduce the cost of FCI. The latter also proposes to undertake open market operations within a prescribed price band through release of stocks at the time of shortages in the market. This decentralized procurement system has been adopted in a proactive manner in Madhya Pradesh, Uttar Pradesh and West Bengal. These states retain a part of grain in the state pool for operating PDS and the rest is surrendered for the central pool. Now, commodity-specific controls and state implemented movement bans will no longer be required. This also implies that it is not essential to continue with the ECA any more. Many state governments such as Punjab and Karnataka are in the process of introducing liberal changes in the Market Regulation Acts that aim to reduce the role of government with a lawful role for the private sector in market development. Further, as part of reforms, the CACP has recommended withdrawal of the monopoly procurement scheme. The Maharashtra government, however, has opposed this view. The scheme was expected to be terminated by July 2000 and the accumulated stocks were suggested to be handled by the CCI.

Significant changes have been observed in the public distribution system (PDS) during the nineties. A beginning was made in 1991–92 when subsidy on sugar distributed through PDS was abolished. Suggestions were proposed at that time to revamp PDS on the basis of area approach, increase in allocation of commodities during lean periods and elimination of leakage and dismal practices. In 1993–94, under the revamped PDS, availability of foodgrains was increased and the scheme was extended to more areas. In 1995–96, the mid-day meal scheme was launched for school students in the RPDS/EAS blocks. The PDS was further strengthened in 1996–97 by a policy of supplementing supplies of sugar, edible oils, skimmed milk powder and pulses through imports. A new scheme based on Targeted PDS was introduced in 1997–98 and implemented in Haryana and Tripura and other states except in Delhi, Goa, Punjab and UT of Lakshadweep. In 2000–01, the *Antyodaya Anna Yozna* scheme was launched to make TPDS more focussed and targeted towards the poor. Lately in 2008, the government introduced a scheme for distribution of up to 10 lakh tonnes of imported edible oils at a subsidized rate of Rs15 per kg to the poorer sections of the society. Four public sector undertakings have been asked to import, refine, pack and distribute subsidized oil to the states.

Magnitude of Openness of Indian Agriculture

It is evident from the preceding section that trade in agricultural commodities has got liberalized but it is still subject to trade barriers of one or the other kind. Quantification of these barriers is done to understand the extent to which the protection level has decreased following economic reforms and whether Indian agriculture has opened up, to world markets. This aspect is studied by computing the level of protection accorded to agriculture through tariffs and non-tariff barriers and comparing it relative to its own past. Besides quantification of tariffs and non-tariff barriers, the openness of agriculture is also explored by analysing compatibility of external and internal trade reforms with WTO stipulations.

Measurement of Level of Protection through Tariffs and NTBs

Tariffs and non-tariff barriers are the two main instruments that are applied to protect external commodity trade. Literature in the context of agriculture elicits a greater focus on the measurement of protection through tariff-based methods, viz., net protection coefficients and effective rate of protection (Gulati and Kelly, 1999; Bhalla, 2004). Only in a few studies, viz., Gulati, Mehta and Narayanan (1999), Pandey (1999) and Mehta (1997), the level of protection is estimated on the basis of NTBs. Some NTBs measures that have been employed are for example: (i) frequency-type measures, i.e., frequency ratio and import coverage ratio that indicate the frequency of occurrence of NTBs (The first measure is unweighted and the second is weighted by production or imports); (ii) price differential measure based on price relatives or tariff equivalents of NTBs; and (iii) quantity impact measures such as import penetration ratio and trade flows. While the first two methods enable the quantification of changes in the NTBs, the third method captures the joint effect of protection given to commodities using both tariffs and non-tariff measures.

Based on these measures of tariffs and NTBs, the broad results obtained from these studies indicate a decline in the level of protection given to agriculture over a period of time. In case of NTBs, Mehta (1997) reported an average decline in the incidence of NTBs in the manufacturing sector (based on frequency ratio) from 50 per cent in 1995 to 42 per cent by 1998. In contrast, agriculture showed a marginal decline by 2 per cent from 74.43 to 72.01 per cent during this period. The tariff equivalents of the NTBs, measured as percentage excess of domestic price over international price, were found to be fairly low for rice, maize, soyabean, barley and potatoes from 1991–97. Cereals and rubber had tariff equivalents of almost 20 per cent; sugar 40 per cent and groundnut oil cake 42.5 per cent in the early nineties. It was high for spices, milk products and potatoes exceeding 100 per cent in most cases. Since these estimates of NTBs pertain to some years (1993–98) during the nineties, they do not provide substantial evidence for the magnitude of decline in the level of protection. Also, now that India has reduced/eliminated quantitative restrictions on many commodities as per the WTO mandate and has agreed to replace them with tariffs from the year 2000 onwards, a longer series on changes in commodity tariffs and NTBs would be more meaningful. The magnitude of protection to selected commodities is estimated from 1980–81 to 2002–03. Changes in the level of protection during the nineties and early 2000 are judged relative to that in the eighties. The results across major food and non-food commodities that are obtained by analysing the average rate of tariffs and quantifying NTBs using the above listed measures are discussed as follows.

Change in the Tariff Rates

There are two rates of duty on imports, viz., standard rate of duty and preferential rate of duty. The latter wherever applicable is generally 10 percentage points lower than the former and is applicable to import of some commodities from a few countries. Table 3.3 gives tariff rates of

TABLE 3.3 *Standard Rates of Duty on Import of Selected Agricultural Commodities in India during 1980–81 to 2003–04*

Years	*Rice (non-basmati)*	*Wheat*	*Pulses*	*Raw Cotton*	*Sugar*	*Oilseeds*	*Soyabean Oil*	*Groundnut Oil*
1980–81	0	0	0	40	60	60	60	60
1981–82	0	0	0	40	100	60	50	50
1982–83	0	0	0	40	100	60	195	195
1983–84	0	0	0	40	60	60	200	200
1984–85	0	0	0	40	100	60	190	190
1985–86	0	0	0	40	100	60	190	190
1986–87	0	0	0	40	100	60	190	190
1987–88	0	0	0	40	100	50	45	125
1988–89	0	0	0	40	100	50	200	200
1989–90	0	0	0	40	100	50	200	200
1990–91	0	0	10	35	35	55	45	125
1991–92	0	0	10	35	35	55	45	45
1992–93	0	0	10	40	40	60	45	65
1993–94	0	0	10	85	85	85	45	85
1994–95	0	0	10	65	65	65	35	65
1995–96	0	0	10	50	0	50	30	30
1996–97	0	0	5	50	50	50	30	40
1997–98	0	0	5	40	40	40	30	30
1998–99	0	0	5	40	40	40	15	15
1999–00	0	0	5	40	40	35	30	30
2000–01	92	108	5	25	100	35	100	100
2001–02	70–80	100	5	5	100	35–40	25–45	25–100
2002–03	70–80	100	10	5	100	35	45	100
2003–04	70–80	100	10	5–10	100	35	45	35
Bound rate	70–80	100	100	150	150	100	45,300	45,300

Note: There are two types of duty rates on imports; standard and preferential. Preferential duty rate is generally 10 percentage points lower and is applicable to import of some commodities from a few countries.

Source: *GOI Exim Policy* (various issues), and *Customs Tariffs*, Arun Goyal (various issues).

selected farm commodities at the four-digit level from 1980–81 to 2003–04. It is evident that there was not much change in the tariff rates of commodities during the eighties. Alterations took place only from 1991 when India opened her markets to world trade. For cereals, the tariff rate was zero in most of the years and imports were checked primarily through quantitative restrictions, agriculture permits, canalization and other NTBs. From 1999–2000, when most of the NTBs were removed, varying rates of tariffs were levied to provide protection against import. In the case of oilseeds, a high and uniform duty was imposed till 1994–95, which gradually came down to a lower level of 35 per cent in 1999 signifying a move towards liberalization of agriculture. Import duty for groundnut oil was highest at 200 per cent in 1988–89, which came down to its lowest at 15 per cent in 1998–99 and again reached a high level at 75 per cent in 2002–03 and then fell to 30 per cent in 2003–04. The tariff rates were increased mainly to dissuade a sudden inflow of imports into the domestic market due to a low level of global prices. Palm oil and refined vegetable oil continue to have higher rates of import duty varying between 75 to 100 per cent. In case of other commercial crops like cotton, the import duty has varied between 35–50 per cent. Similarly in the case of sugar, tariff rates witnessed changes between 35 to 100 per cent except in 1995–96 when it was nil. Tariff on raw cotton in 2003–04 is also stable between 5–10 per cent. Exports of cotton and groundnut are subject to certain notifications on tariff exemptions. A cess at the rate of 0.50 per cent is charged on the tariff value of agricultural exports.

On the whole, tariffication of farm commodities has changed in the post-liberalization period as compared to the pre-liberalization period, in that a significant decrease has occurred in the level of protection and hence a move towards greater openness. However, despite a decline in the rate of import tariffs, some of the commodities continue to enjoy protection through imposition of quantitative restrictions, canalization and license system as explained in the preceding sections. Literature also confirms a pervasive use of NTBs in many developing countries. India was asked by the WTO to remove all kinds of restrictions from April 2001 and replace these by tariffs, but it has continued with some of the NTBs, for example the obtaining of agriculture permits, registration with state agencies such as APEDA and canalization of foodgrains through FCI. What has been the degree of import protection given to domestic commodities through these NTBs? The answer necessarily requires a quantification of non-tariff barriers, which appear to have a more crucial and dominant role in Indian trade policy rather than tariffs in providing protection to domestic production against imports. The exercise is attempted as follows.

Quantification of Non-Tariff Barriers

Non-tariff barriers consist of all barriers to trade that are not tariffs. The measures range from narrowly-conceived ones affecting particular products to more general ones that are rooted in national level measures, institutions and policies (Greenaway and Milner, 1993). It is, therefore, difficult to quantify many of the NTBs. Also one should be aware of the various characteristics of NTBs even though it may be difficult to capture them empirically.[1] The NTBs are quantified from 1980–81 to 2003–04 for selected commodities at a six-digit level based on import coverage ratio, price differentials, import penetration rate, and trade flows methods.

Import Coverage Ratio

The import coverage ratio is a frequency-based method and is defined as:

$$C_j = \sum D_i M_i / \sum Mi,$$

where Di is a dummy variable defined as $Di = 1$, if the product is listed under R (banned/restricted, limited permissible, canalized),

=0, if the product is listed under F (OGL list).

j stands for a particular industry/group and i represents a product line within that particular industry/group. Di is a dummy variable and each product category at 4-digit HS codes is given either a number 1 or 0 depending on whether the product is affected by NTBs or not. The items were treated as affected by NTBs if they fall under the category: restricted (R), which covers all of the restrictive lists (banned/restricted, limited permissible, permit and canalized) and hence given a weight 1. The items under OGL are treated as free (F) and given a weight of 0. M is the value of imports of the ith product category, which is subject to NTBs (R in the study) and $\sum Mi$ is the sum of the value of imports of all the product lines within the industry/group. This method is useful as it serves as an important indicator of NTBs but it does not capture the price advantage, which domestic producers get. This can be gauged by computing tariff-equivalents of NTBs.

Quantification of NTBs based on the import coverage ratio reveals that all the six commodities selected for estimation have 100 per cent protection from 1980 to 2003. As mentioned earlier, even though most of the quantitative restrictions have been removed on import of cereals, sugar and raw cotton from the mid-nineties and subsequently from April 2001, some of the restrictions such as obtaining agriculture permit, import contracts to be registered with APEDA/textile commissioner and trade through state agencies are still in place. Rice and wheat continue to have import restrictions during the nineties and 2000 through the agricultural permit system and also enjoy protection against imports.

Price Differentials or Tariff Equivalents of NTBs

Price differentials of a commodity can be measured in terms of price relatives, i.e., ratio of domestic and international reference price or in terms of tariff equivalents of NTBs estimated as percentage excess of domestic commodity price over international reference price, i.e., [(DP-WP/WP)*100]. A price ratio greater than unity or a positive number in the latter case indicates the presence of NTBs and enables an estimation of its impact on changes in imports. The tariff equivalents of NTBs also suggest a tariff rate that can be applied in a situation of removal of all restrictions while imports remain unchanged. The tariff equivalents of NTBs are estimated only for those commodities whose time series data on domestic and international price are available. The domestic prices of farm commodities represent average wholesale prices available for state-level markets weighted by production. The international prices relate to wholesale price in the major trading centres of the world and are converted into rupees using the nominal exchange rate. All price series are specified in Rs ton and are deflated by the wholesale price index of all commodities to convert them into base 1993–94.

Table 3.4 provides estimates on tariff equivalents of NTBs for selected commodities from 1980 to 2003. It is clear that the tariff equivalents of NTBs are not relevant in the case of groundnut seed and raw cotton as world reference prices of these commodities have always been higher than their domestic prices. For other commodities, the picture is mixed with some years showing a positive estimate and some a negative estimate of tariff equivalents. The tariff equivalents lie within a positive minimum and maximum range of 2.59 to 44.33 per cent for wheat; 2.02 to 27.17 per cent for rice; 2.35 to 87.06 per cent for sugar and 2.93 to 99.14 per cent for soyabean seed respectively. As expected, the dispersion of tariff equivalents has reduced in the nineties and early 2000 compared to that in the eighties. From the estimates one can also find the maximum rate of tariff that can be applied in lieu of NTBs to keep imports at the same level. In recent years, it is the highest for raw sugar and wheat at more than 40 per cent followed by soyabean seed and rice at almost 26 and 15 per cent, respectively.

TABLE 3.4 *Tariff Equivalents of Non-tariff Barriers for Selected Farm Commodities during 1980–81 to 2002–03*

Years	*Wheat*	*Rice*	*Sugar*	*Cotton*	*Groundnut Seed*	*Soyabean Seed*
1980–81	3.97	-49.25	-23.75	-55.00	-66.13	-25.14
1981–82	2.59	-23.33	-5.68	-31.06	-46.34	2.93
1982–83	21.74	3.57	22.51	-35.43	-49.37	21.80
1983–84	10.65	-3.61	21.55	-31.06	-48.05	8.54
1984–85	-5.04	2.02	87.06	-19.14	-40.95	-0.31
1985–86	16.98	12.57	50.00	-3.73	-48.37	31.59
1986–87	44.33	27.17	70.48	-31.10	-25.13	99.14
1987–88	39.88	-5.92	81.62	-3.76	-44.20	38.54
1988–89	11.03	-23.13	2.35	-24.09	-50.73	20.38
1989–90	-16.14	-24.35	-8.69	-49.79	-54.75	16.96
1990–91	22.5	-32.90	-17.24	-47.51	-62.90	17.25
1991–92	-5.03	-29.38	-28.78	-31.03	-44.83	34.78
1992–93	-8.15	-21.69	13.11	-29.17	-66.36	14.18
1993–94	-13.64	-44.95	-0.76	-16.73	-63.20	4.59
1994–95	-14.69	-31.71	-10.78	-20.00	-51.21	27.21
1995–96	-38.06	-45.67	-26.34	-54.16	-60.09	-2.94
1996–97	-19.62	-34.42	-10.06	-53.59	-58.55	16.37
1997–98	-0.61	-33.74	12.65	-29.72	-64.81	4.73
1998–99	17.90	-17.00	32.52	-16.79	-58.53	-0.34
1999–00	41.38	2.93	56.15	-22.61	-56.81	1.46
2000–01	8.18	14.76	18.68	-32.56	-66.43	6.37
2001–02	4.35	3.12	86.25	-19.00	-52.95	26.22
2002–03	-12.60	3.66	75.98	-37.08	-53.16	10.36

Note: Calculations based on domestic and world wholesale prices (real) of commodities.

Import Penetration Ratio

The third method, i.e., import penetration ratio (IPR) is measured as:

IPRj = Mj/(Pj+Mj-Xj),

where *j* stands for the group/product and *P*, *M* and *X* are production, imports and exports. The method has an advantage over the import coverage method as it captures the combined effect of both tariffs and non-tariff barriers of trade policy. An increase in imports is expected with a lowering of tariffs as well as shifting of commodities from the restricted/banned list to OGL. The denominator estimates the net availability of commodities in the domestic market. The estimates based on the import penetration ratio in Table 3.5 show a decline in the rate of protection to raw cotton, pulses and edible oils such as soyabean oil as import penetration rate has increased for these commodities from 1980–81 to 2002–03. The evidence on rice, wheat, sugar (raw and refined) is mixed. The ratio for these commodities increased in the early eighties and early nineties and then during 1996–98, and finally fell in the subsequent years.

TABLE 3.5 *Import Penetration Ratio in India: 1980–81 to 2002–03*

Years	*Rice*	*Wheat*	*Cotton*	*Ground-nut*	*Soya-bean*	*Oil-seeds*	*Sugar*	*Refined Sugar*	*Pulses*	*Edible Oils*
1980–81	0.008	1.10	0.001	0.00	1.62	0.20	0.73	0.67	0.68	27.92
1981–82	0.09	1.57	0.29	0.00	0.07	0.21	1.13	1.04	1.94	22.01
1982–83	0.04	3.70	0.34	0.00	0.00	0.04	0.07	0.06	0.68	20.12
1983–84	0.35	6.55	0.006	0.00	0.00	0.08	0.00	0.00	1.41	16.23
1984–85	0.86	2.98	0.00	0.00	0.00	0.03	2.03	1.87	1.94	20.73
1985–86	0.09	0.30	0.61	0.00	0.00	0.07	9.47	8.78	2.24	19.30
1986–87	0.03	0.35	0.22	0.00	0.00	0.10	5.15	4.76	4.92	14.38
1987–88	0.009	0.05	0.03	0.00	0.00	0.24	3.35	2.54	6.26	20.83
1988–89	0.99	3.20	3.08	0.00	0.00	0.08	0.002	0.002	5.84	9.25
1989–90	0.63	0.50	0.21	0.00	0.00	0.05	0.64	0.59	4.01	1.09
1990–91	0.08	0.11	0.01	0.00	0.00	0.02	0.05	0.05	5.69	0.86
1991–92	0.01	0.00	0.06	0.00	0.00	0.06	0.01	0.00	2.96	0.77
1992–93	0.14	2.33	2.73	0.00	0.00	0.07	0.006	0.00	2.95	1.67
1993–94	0.09	0.40	0.23	0.00	0.00	0.04	0.002	0.001	4.67	0.82
1994–95	0.009	0.001	3.88	0.00	0.00	0.04	6.54	5.72	3.99	1.25
1995–96	0.00	0.01	3.11	0.00	0.57	0.17	0.58	0.53	3.93	4.23
1996–97	0.00	0.91	0.13	0.00	0.00	0.01	0.008	0.004	4.65	5.41
1997–98	0.00	2.19	0.51	0.001	0.002	0.01	1.27	0.45	7.75	3.97
1998–99	0.008	2.48	2.63	0.001	0.47	0.18	3.11	1.81	4.10	14.26
1999–00	0.03	1.76	10.47	0.00	0.00	0.07	3.98	2.28	2.00	20.97
2000–01	0.01	0.01	11.45	0.00	0.003	0.04	0.10	0.009	3.27	21.68
2001–02	0.00	0.005	13.26	0.00	0.001	0.02	0.10	0.09	15.12	23.61
2002–03	0.001	0.001	9.87	0.00	0.00	0.11	0.16	0.13	16.45	25.82

Notes: Data on production of raw sugar, sugar and oils is based on conversion factors from sugarcane/oilseeds given in Agricultural Statistics at a Glance, Ministry of Agriculture.

Trade Flows

Table 3.6 furnishes commodity-wise changes in the value of share of agricultural exports and imports in net domestic product in agriculture and allied activities (NDPA) from 1980–81 to 2001–02 based on five-year averages. It is important to mention that of the total imports and exports in the country, the share of agricultural imports and exports has fluctuated over the years. There has also been a change in the composition of export and import items over time. At present, the import basket includes pulses, wheat, other cereals, sugar, edible oils, raw cotton and raw jute and cashew nuts. The export items, include rice (basmati and non-basmati), wheat (occasionally), tea, coffee, tobacco, spices, oilseeds, oil meals, sugar, molasses, fruits-vegetables, dairy products and marine products. The share of exports and imports of some of these commodities in the net domestic product of the agricultural sector is explained below.

TABLE 3.6 *Percentage Share of Value of Trade in NDP Agriculture and Allied activities at 1993–94 Prices: Five Years Averages during 1980–81 to 2002–03*

Commodities	*Trade*	*1980–84*	*1985–89*	*1990–94*	*1995–99*	*2000–02*
Rice	Exports	0.37	0.28	0.46	1.25	1.02
	Imports	0.06	0.08	0.02	0.00	0.00
	Total	0.43	0.35	0.48	1.25	1.02
Wheat	Exports	0.02	0.03	0.03	0.13	0.35
	Imports	0.50	0.10	0.09	0.19	0.00
	Total	0.51	0.13	0.12	0.32	0.35
Pulses	Exports	0.00	0.01	0.03	0.07	0.11
	Imports	0.08	0.24	0.24	0.25	0.57
	Total	0.09	0.25	0.26	0.33	0.68
Cotton Lint	Exports	0.19	0.08	0.22	0.16	0.01
	Imports	0.00	0.02	0.07	0.13	0.38
	Total	0.20	0.10	0.29	0.29	0.39
Raw Sugar	Exports	0.11	0.01	0.07	0.10	0.33
	Imports	0.08	0.19	0.18	0.17	0.01
	Total	0.19	0.20	0.25	0.26	0.34
Sugar Refined	Exports	0.11	0.01	0.06	0.06	0.25
	Imports	0.08	0.18	0.17	0.10	0.01
	Total	0.18	0.19	0.22	0.15	0.26

Cont'd...

Cont'd...

Groundnut Seed	Exports	0.05	0.02	0.03	0.10	0.06
	Imports	0.00	0.00	0.00	0.00	0.00
	Total	0.05	0.02	0.03	0.10	0.06
Soyabean Seed	Exports	0.00	0.00	0.00	0.00	0.01
	Imports	0.00	0.00	0.00	0.00	0.00
	Total	0.00	0.00	0.00	0.01	0.01
Oilseeds Total	Exports	0.07	0.05	0.09	0.21	0.24
	Imports	0.01	0.01	0.01	0.01	0.01
	Total	0.08	0.06	0.10	0.22	0.24
Fixed Veg. Ed. Oil	Exports	0.12	0.08	0.12	0.21	0.19
	Imports	0.72	0.34	0.05	0.44	0.66
	Total	0.83	0.42	0.17	0.65	0.85
All Agriculture Commodities	Exports	3.94	3.04	4.01	6.12	6.21
	Imports	2.57	1.97	1.66	3.38	4.27
	Total	6.51	5.01	5.66	9.50	10.48
All Agriculture Commodities in NDP Economy	Exports	1.61	1.11	1.34	1.76	1.54
	Imports	1.05	0.72	0.55	0.96	1.06
	Total	2.67	1.83	1.90	2.72	2.60

Statistics based on five year averages reveal an increase in the export of farm commodities in NDPA from 3.94 per cent in the early eighties to 6.21 per cent in early 2000. The share of imports almost doubled during this period from 2.57 to 4.27 per cent with the total share of trade (imports + exports) in NDPA rising from 6.51 to 10.48 per cent, respectively. Among the selected exportable commodities, rice and fruits-vegetables have a maximum share in NDPA followed by oilseeds. On the import side, fixed vegetable oils and fruits-vegetables occupy the maximum share in NDPA followed by pulses. Commodity-wise details show that rice exports as percentage of NDPA increased from 0.37 per cent in 1980–84 to 1.02 per cent in 2000–02. The share of wheat exports was stable till the mid-nineties and increased in the subsequent years from 0.13 to 0.35 per cent. In the case of imports the share has declined for rice and shows fluctuations for wheat over the last two decades. Wheat and rice exports did show a declining trend from 1996 but a reversed trend was noticeable in the recent years from the early 2000.[2] Import of pulses has witnessed an increase over the years due to declining levels of domestic production. Its share in NDPA has increased from 0.08 per cent in the early eighties to 0.57 per cent in the early 2000.

The export-import position of cotton (raw/lint) indicates imports have increased their share in NDPA from 0.02 per cent in 1985–89 to 0.38 per cent in 2000–02. However, the share of exports in total NDPA has shown an increasing trend from 1980 to 1994 and then a declining trend from the mid-nineties to early 2000. A hike in import of raw cotton is the result of crop failure and increased demand from the industrial sector. As mentioned above, for exports, the government allocates quotas of raw cotton with the bulk going to the state agencies and the left over to state-level marketing federations and private traders. Import of cotton has been allowed for exporting units directly after 1994. Also, import of raw cotton was made free till 1999 (with no import duty) to ensure easy availability of cotton at competitive prices to the textile industry. As far as the export-import position of sugar (raw and refined) is concerned, while the share of sugar exports in NDPA has declined from 0.11 per cent (averaged 1980–84) to 0.06 per cent (averaged 1995–99), the share of imports has increased to 0.17 per cent during this period. From 1999 onwards, the share of sugar exports in NDPA has increased and that of imports has declined. An increase in imports till the mid-nineties took place due to the inability of the government to cope with a situation of low price of sugar in the world markets relative to that in the domestic markets. Some reforms in the domestic policies are, therefore, required to deal with mounting stocks and variability in prices that have emanated from greater international exposure.

Among oilseeds and edible oils, India has been exporting seeds – groundnut, niger, soyabean, castor oil, the share of which has been increasing over time. The share of total oilseeds exports in NDPA stands at 0.24 per cent in 2000–02. India's dependence on import of edible oils–groundnut, rapeseed-mustard, soyabean and palm oil has increased manifold during the last two decades. Some vegetable oils are exported but the share of imports has been higher than that of exports. Statistics reveal that during the eighties, import of fixed vegetable oils (that includes palm oil as well) as a percentage of NDPA was high at about 1.14 per cent, which then declined to 0.18 per cent during early nineties due to imposition of restrictions. However, from 1995 when imports of these were placed under OGL subject to quarantine checks, there was a sudden spurt in their imports. This exceeded more than 1 per cent of the share in NDPA and 50 per cent of domestic production during 2000. Of all the edible oils, imports of palm oil constituted a significant 40 per cent share. Though restrictions on export of edible oils have been removed from early 2000, there has not been a significant increase in the share of exports due to a lower production base, higher cost of production and higher domestic prices relative to international prices. One may see considerable acceleration in the export of rice, fruits-vegetables and dairy products.

Trade Reforms and their Compatibility with the WTO Regime

The extent to which external trade policy is in compliance with the obligations advanced under WTO can also be considered as an important indicator to determine the extent of openness of Indian agriculture.[3] As mentioned earlier, agricultural exports and imports operate in accordance with the guidelines and commitments given in the AOA within the ambit of GATT, 1994, now WTO. The commitments fall under three main categories, namely, (a) market access and tarrification, (b) domestic support, and (c) export competition.[4] The trade rules formulated under each of these provisions aim at disciplining world production, trade and hence prices that often get distorted due to large-scale subsidies extended to agriculture along with complex protective measures adopted by most of the countries in the world. In this section, India's external and internal trade reforms with respect to tariffs and NTBs are juxtaposed against the three main provisions stipulated in the UR AOA. This is done to evaluate India's accomplishments for each of the WTO provisions across selected commodities and progress in the liberalization of internal trade and policies and tasks yet to be completed.

Commitments under the AOA and India's Position

(a) Market Access and Tariffication: The agreement under market access and tariffication covers rules and concessions, contained in the country schedules, governing protection against import competition. There were four components of this provision: (i) reduction in the base tariffs by an average of 36 per cent and 24 per cent over six years for developed and developing countries, (ii) tariff binding and conversion of all non-tariff trade (import) barriers to its equivalent in ordinary tariffs, also called tariffication, (iii) market access opportunities, and (iv) special treatment, safeguards and exemptions. Minimum market access commitments are envisaged at a level of 5 per cent of the base period (1986–88) consumption for developed countries and at 3 per cent for developing countries. Accordingly, tariff quotas are established at reduced tariff rates wherein for the minimum or current access levels of imports, a country imposes a low bound tariff. And imports above the minimum commitment envisage a higher tariff on a tariff line-by-line basis (Gulati and Naryanan, 2003; Results of the Uruguay Round: Legal Texts).

Before analysing the commitments with respect to the market access provision, it is essential to know that the WTO Agreement on Agriculture refers to 686 commodities at the 6-digit level under the Harmonized Tariff System (HS). These are divided into four sections under the HS classification, covering chapters 1 to 24. Around 72 agricultural tariff lines are contained in other chapters (from 29 to 53). For each commodity, bound rates are specified and vary considerably. In 2001–02, they varied from a lower level of 15 per cent to a maximum level of 300 per cent, averaging to 114.97 per cent for all the 686 commodities that fall under agriculture. The concentration of tariff bindings is the highest at bound tariff of 100 per cent for 330 lines followed by 150 per cent for 219 lines. About 26 and 25 lines are bound at 300 per cent and 55 per cent, respectively (Gulati, Mehta and Narayanan, 1999; GOI Exim Policy).

A comparison of bound rates and actual import duty of major commodities/groups at 4-digit HS level in Table 3.3 reveals that for commodities such as rice, wheat, oilseeds and edible oils, fruits and vegetables, milk and milk products, the concentration of tariff bindings is on the lower side (less than 75%) except in the case of edible oils. In almost all commodity cases, applied tariff rates are less than the corresponding UR final bound rates and at times show a very low or 0 per cent level (in the case of cereals during mid-nineties). This implies that India has maintained UR bound rates and has also reduced basic custom duties over the period. However, quantitative restrictions (QRs) manifested in licensing requirements and canalization are still in place for a few commodities. These have been maintained primarily on two counts: (i) import restrictions for reasons relating to health, food security, and livelihood needs, and (ii) balance of payment (BOP) reasons. Quantitative Restrictions (QRs) on these accounts are permitted under the GATT. With greater ease on BOP grounds, QRs were removed in 2000 on several commodities. For the remaining commodities, such as in the case of cereals and milk products, QRs placed on BOP and other grounds are considered to be GATT compliant. Trade in these essential and hence sensitive commodities is done largely through the State Trading Corporation, NAFED, NDDB, CCI and HVOC.

A review of commitments under 'market access provision' further reveals that import of many commodities – particularly cereals and some edible oils is restricted, canalized, subject to quality and packaging-labelling conditions as well as registration with government agencies in addition to the agriculture permit system. NTBs are imposed mainly to protect domestic agriculture from an import surge and maintain food self-sufficiency. Many countries have followed special safeguard measures to protect their domestic agriculture. Since India has no recourse to this measure, she has resorted to other NTBs as stated above (Gulati, Mehta and Narayanan, 1999). Of all the NTB's, trade through government agencies, also called State Trading Enterprises (STEs) is of particular concern. STEs everywhere, especially in the Asian countries have an influential presence in agriculture trade. Ackerman and Dixit (1999) have argued that these STEs may distort world trade. In India, efforts were taken to minimize controls and regulations by these parastatals on trade in sugar and cotton during the nineties, but trade is largely encouraged through them. As a part of the GATT, 1994 requirement under Article XVII:4(a), India has notified the major STEs that are permitted to operate in trade of commodities (GOI EXIM policy 2002–03).

(b) Domestic Support: Provisions under domestic support include rules and concessions, contained in the country schedules, relating to the use and the level of 'non-border' measures implemented to support agricultural production. Estimation of aggregate measure of support (AMS) was proposed, which covered expenditures on domestic subsidies and market price support policies that affect trade. It excluded expenditures on programmes that support agriculture and direct transfers (payments) to the growers. Accordingly, support to agriculture is grouped into three categories: (i) amber box, (ii) green box, and (iii) blue box. Out of these three, the WTO agreement requires reduction only in the amber box, whereas support under all other heads is exempted. The AMS is estimated as per the product specific and non-product specific support and member countries are required to keep it at *de minimis* level. It should not exceed 10 per cent of the total value of agricultural product for developing countries and 5 per cent for developed countries relative to the 1986–88 base period.

Gulati and Narayanan (2003) and the Trade Policy Review of India by WTO (1998) have calculated AMS for 19 agriculture commodities. The estimates reveal a negative figure, which indicates that domestic support requirements are in accord with GATT obligations. While AMS on non-product specific support (input subsidy) at the 1986–87 base period amounted to 4.5 per cent of the value of agriculture output, product-specific support (through price intervention) was negative at 21.6 per cent of the total value under the importable hypothesis. This implies that agriculture in India was discriminated against and hence implicitly taxed despite the provision of input subsidies. From 1996 onwards, domestic support prices have been higher than border prices in commodities like wheat and rice. The difference between the two might have exceeded the GATT stipulation of maintaining a certain level of AMS besides having implications for a greater flow of cheap imports and domestic price instability.

(c) Export Competition: Export competition constitutes the third objective of UR AOA. It aims at rules and concessions, contained in the country schedules, in connection with reduction in export subsidy, both in terms of budgetary outlays and volume of subsidized exports. Accordingly, AOA stipulates a reduction of 36 per cent below the 1986–88 level in the case of developed countries and by 24 per cent in the case of developing countries. The quantity of subsidized exports was to be reduced by 21 per cent for developed and 14 per cent for developing countries over a period of 6 and 10 years. While estimating export subsidy, the agreement excludes in its calculations, policy tools such as export credits and guarantee, differential export taxes, export market promotion expenditure and monopoly exporting agencies in a single seller system. The public funding programmes to be reduced include direct government subsidies, including non-cash benefits to companies, producers of agricultural goods, sale of products for export from public warehouses at prices below regular market prices, government funded payments for export of agricultural commodities and coverage of transport and freight costs for exported products at home and abroad. Certain exemptions are given to the developing countries for reducing subsidies.

India's position where export competition is concerned, is fully in tune with the AOA stipulations because agricultural exporters in India do not enjoy any direct export subsidy. As part of an interventionist policy, the government supports exporters through income tax exemptions from profits of agriculture exports and provision of subsidies on cost of freight on export shipments. However, all these payments are exempt from reduction commitments but are subject to notification to the WTO. At the same time the government applies controls and regulatory measures on export of several commodities through the minimum export price, quotas and quantitative ceilings, etc. Export quotas are specified for wheat and other cereals, sugar, cotton and dairy products. In the case of sugar, government had enacted a Sugar Export Promotion Act for compulsory export of sugar, which was repealed by an ordinance. Exports have now been made voluntary and de-canalized though quantitative ceilings and registration with APEDA is still in place. STEs continue to hold place in exporting cereals, oils and onions through permits given to individuals and corporate agencies.

Suffice to say that on all the three grounds of market access and tariffication, domestic support and export competition, India aligns itself with the WTO provisions. The rules, however, prohibit usage of quantitative restrictions but they have been adopted not only by India but also by other member countries. The objective here is primarily to protect domestic agriculture from import surges and maintain food self-sufficiency. And this may be a cause of concern for the WTO. Domestic support and export subsidies continue to be within the stipulated limits in India, while they exceed these limits in developed countries through provision of direct income support and export subsidies. The Fourth Ministerial meeting of the WTO, which was held in 2001 at Doha and the subsequent ministerial meetings also witnessed a concerted effort made by the developed countries to initiate a new round of negotiations related to competition rules, regulations on government procurement and foreign investment. The developing countries also raised issues concerning the elimination of export subsidies and discipline on other types of support for exports. The WTO General Council reached some broad agreement on July 31, 2004 on a framework for further negotiations. The framework, also called the 'July Package', permitted developing countries to designate a list of 'special products' that would not be subject to market access commitments. The package also retains a special safeguard mechanism for 'sensitive products' for all the WTO members that allows developed countries to deny market access in their countries to the products defined as sensitive. Given these developments, India may be required to reformulate its policies related to market access.

One important factor that may act as a barrier to trade under the market access and export competition objectives is the active participation of STEs in the export and import of agricultural commodities in the world market. Despite the fact that trade through STEs is permissible within the GATT framework, it has not been properly attended to in the GATT.[5] This policy issue may invoke questions on grounds of functioning, transparency and lucidity of the STEs as well as in the context of emergence of competition policy in the markets in the coming years. It is generally argued that STEs can subsidize exports especially when these agencies regulate procurement and sale of products, discriminate among trading partners and engage in cross subsidization activities that distort competition (Hoekman and Kostecki, 2001 and Ackerman and Dixit, 1999). Creation of STE's in developing countries is basically to ensure food security and offset malpractices that prevail in the trade of foodgrain and other essential commodities. The United States and Canada however raised objections in the WTO regarding India's wheat exports at subsidized rates in 2000 (*Hindu* "India dragged to WTO on wheat exports", March 29, 2001). Given this situation, India may be asked to review her domestic policies in which involvement of STEs can become an issue of priority.

India has already proposed that special and differential treatment to be given to agriculture in developing countries and that STEs be formed to serve goals of poverty alleviation, food security and livelihood needs without exercising monopoly in international trade. These measures may be clubbed under a 'food security box' exclusively for developing countries so that they can protect their primary commodities from import threats and enhance productive capacity through domestic support and other measures. However, there has been a deadlock in talks since July 2008 with no major progress further on any of these issues.

Compatibility of External and Internal Agricultural Policies

As noted above, India has been somewhat liberal in pursuing its trade (export-import) policy in accord once with the WTO obligations but agricultural trade and other policies that are being followed internally appear to be stringent. Table 3.7 provides a comparative picture of

TABLE 3.7 *External vs Internal Agricultural Policies (as on 2006–07)*

	Controls/Regulations	*External Markets*	*Internal Markets*
A.	**Legislation (ECA/ Agricultural Produce Market Act)**	No	Yes
B.	**Physical Controls/QRs/NTBs**		
(i)	License/permits/canalized	Yes	Yes
(ii)	Quota	Yes	Yes
(iii)	Movement restrictions	No	Partial
(iv)	Market fees and other charges	No	Yes
(v)	Stock limits	No	Partial
(vi)	Monopoly procurement	No	Yes (with relaxations)
(vii)	Controls on trade/traders	Partial	Yes
(viii)	State trading enterprises/Boards	Yes	Yes
(ix)	Standards and other Technical Requirements	Yes	No
C.	**Price Measures**		
(i)	Price fixation	No (in some cases MEP is fixed)	Yes
(ii)	Levy	No	Yes
(iii)	Subsidy	No	Yes
(iv)	Procurement (for food security)	No (considered important under non-trade concerns)	Yes
(v)	Buffer stock (for price stability)	Partial	Yes

external and internal policies that have been in place for agricultural commodities. The interventions are categorized in terms of legislation, physical controls and price measures. The legislative measures include imposition of restrictions within the domain of ECA, 1955 and APMC, 1966 and APMC (Model Act) 2003. Physical controls cover quantitative restrictions, non-tariff barriers, stock limits and other controls on private trade. Under price measures are included policies related to fixation of commodity price, levy, procurement and buffer stock.

An overall comparative picture reveals that there is not much in common between the domestic internal and external policies under legislative and price measures. Physical controls exist in varying degree both in external and internal markets. External markets witness the imposition of some quantitative restrictions on the export-import of commodities and in some cases fixation of minimum export price whereas internal markets continue to be intruded upon by legislative orders, administered prices and levy. These QRs or non-trade barriers imposed in external trade are activated on certain protective grounds mentioned above. Nonetheless, private trade in external markets is not bound to operate under a legislative framework and is not liable to follow price policy, as is the case in domestic markets. A partial buffer stock policy and NTBs are followed for export-import of wheat and rice, which is considered essential to serve the livelihood needs of the population below the poverty line. Relatively lesser controls are envisaged in trade of commodities other than wheat and rice. It is mandatory to follow international standards and other technical requirements in external trade. One characteristic that seems mutual in both external and internal markets is the continuation of trade, particularly of cereals and edible oils through state agencies.

To sum up, the analysis reveals that external trade reforms initiated from the early nineties have gained momentum only after implementation of the AOA during 1994–95. Since then a substantial reduction in tariff rates of commodities along with the removal of many NTBs has been observed. From 2001, tariffs do not exceed the bound rates and are sufficiently high to restrain imports. For some commodities such as pulses, cotton and edible oils, applied tariffs are fixed below the bound rate to encourage their imports. A quantification of NTBs based on various measures indicates that protection is still given in many cases, which is somewhat permissible under the WTO provisions. It is also considered to be desirable in view of food security concerns, world price volatility, import surge, poverty alleviation and livelihood needs. Tariff equivalents of NTBs, that can be applied to maintain the same level of imports fall within a range from 2 to 55 per cent across commodities. The import penetration rate of select commodities has increased and so has the share of agri-trade in NDPA, which got doubled from 5.01 per cent during the early nineties to 10.48 per cent during early 2000. However, the share of exports in NDPA, which showed a remarkable increase during the nineties, has become stable in the recent period and the share of imports has continued to accelerate. This can be a major cause of concern more so when area, production and yield of principal crops grown in the country have also shown a deceleration in their rates of growth during the last two decades. Compared to external trade in agriculture, internal trade continues to be inflicted by stringent regulations under a price, institutional and legislative set-up and also fails to comply with external trade reforms. The compliance though not mandatory under the WTO provisions can be effective for avoiding any constraining factors reforming external trade and progressing towards integration of domestic agriculture with the world agriculture. On the whole, the analysis indicates that Indian agriculture has certainly opened up relative to its own past but the progress may be considered partial due to continuation of protection given to some essential commodities.

Notes

1. Deardorff and Stern (1999) explained some of these characteristics as: (i) reduction in quantity of imports, (ii) increase in price of imports, (iii) change in the elasticity of demand for imports, (iv) variability of NTBs, (v) uncertainty of imports, (vi) welfare and resource costs of NTBs.
2. A slowdown in the growth of exports after 1996 can be attributed to fall in the international trade due to East Asian crisis and deceleration in the world commodity prices. The downfall in the commodity prices and a concomitant rise in the administrative prices might have made Indian exports less competitive (Chand, 2001).
3. This section is drawn from Bathla (2004).
4. Apart from these, there are other important issues such as sanitary and phyto-sanitary measures, food security, state trading enterprises, government procurement and special and differential treatment that do not fall directly under the AOA but have implications for trade in agriculture.
5. GATT provisions have given a working definition of state trading enterprises under Article XVII and have framed notification procedures that are designed to ensure transparency in their working.

4

World and Domestic Price Transmission in Agricultural Commodities

Analysis at the State Level

The agricultural sector in India is gradually opening up to external trade leading to an interdependency between commodity prices across spatial markets. This chapter aims to examine first, whether changes in prices of agricultural commodities respond to changes in their respective international prices, or does price transmission exist between domestic and world markets? Second, the extent to which price transmission has improved from world to domestic markets and across the state-level markets following economic reforms. It is hypothesized that price integration from world to domestic markets and within the domestic ones has improved in the post-reform period compared to the pre-reform period. In what follows, the theoretical and empirical literature on world and domestic price relationships is examined first. Next, the sources of data and econometric models employed for testing the hypothesis are elaborated upon. Thereafter, the results obtained from empirical exercises are followed by an appraisal of the main findings and the conclusion.

World and Domestic Price Relationships: Theory and Evidence

The relationship between world and domestic prices of agricultural commodities and changes therein depend upon many factors in accordance with the demand and supply conditions. The main factors that affect commodity demand and hence its price at the global level are downfall in the purchasing power, interventionist policies such as taxation or subsidy being followed by the trading countries and unforeseen factors, viz., East Asian crisis. In contrast, changes in farm prices at the national level are influenced by demand and supply conditions in the world and domestic markets, tariffs and non-tariff barriers, exchange rate that may change independently because of changes in factors like recession in the world markets, infrastructure and government policies. Consequent upon these factors and the diverse policy set up, international and domestic commodity prices do not necessarily converge. That is why, efforts are being made under the economic reform programme to bring significant changes in some of these factors and policies, major among which being currency devaluation, reduction in tariffs, removal of non-tariff barriers, price deregulation and other controls. Trade and exchange rate liberalization is expected to affect domestic prices, partly due to globalization of the economy and partly due to removal of administered pricing and trade restrictions. These policies along with the emergence of well-functioning markets enable agricultural prices to move closer to their international prices. A greater interdependency between commodity prices across spatial markets is an indicator of market efficiency. A perfect price transmission, among many factors provides signals to producers for good allocation of resources, to expand production base and become globally competitive.

The theoretical underpinning of this outcome is based on the fourth major theorem that arises out of the Heckscher-Ohlin model, known as the factor-price equalization theorem. Simply stated, it proposes that when prices of goods are equalized between the countries, as countries move to free trade, then the prices of the factors (capital and labour) will also be equalized between the countries. This implies that free trade will even out wages of the workers and rentals earned on capital across the trading countries in the world. In other words, since the trading countries share same marginal productivity relationships it follows that only one set of wage and rental rates can satisfy these relationships for a given set of output prices. Thus, free trade will equalize commodity prices, wage and rental rates, which signifies that an increased level of market integration is a must for achieving free mobility of factors of production. Furthermore, since two countries face the same wage and rental rates, they will also produce each good using the same capital-labour ratio. However, because countries continue to have different quantities of factor endowments, they will produce different quantities of the two goods. The theorem derives from assumptions of the model, the most critical being that the two countries share the same production technology and markets are perfectly competitive, which may not exist in reality.

Evidence on commodity price transmission across separated markets and the extent to which they have synchronized or diverged before and after initiation of reforms is found to be diverse. As apparent from Chapter 2, one set of studies could not find a greater integration between domestic and international prices of most of the commodities in the developing countries that opted for reforms. It is argued that price fluctuations, on account of high world price were passing to countries' export unit values and not to producers' price due to interventionist policies and adjustments in the exchange rate (Hazell et al., 1990; Baffes and Gardener, 2003). Another set of studies presented results to the contrary by highlighting a perfect price transmission to have taken place for agricultural commodities in the years following reforms (Cardenas, 1994; Krivonos, 2004).

In the Indian context, while numerous studies have revealed a higher and improved integration of wheat, rice, jowar, and oilseeds markets in the post-reform period as compared to the pre-reform period (Wilson, 2001; Acharya, 2001; Kumar 2007; Bathla, 2009), evidence on the same between the international and domestic markets is limited. Among the studies carried out, one on pepper and other on rice have shown domestic prices and supply to be responsive to international market conditions (Sinharoy and Nair, 1994). However, it is argued that foreign trade liberalization is not symmetric in the way it deals with exports and imports, which has implications for spatial patterns of price convergence. For instance, rice exports have been made more liberal than its imports due to which surplus locations have converged faster towards international prices (Jayasuriya, Kim and Kumar, 2007). Concerns have also been raised about the likely adverse effects of high volatility of international prices on developing countries' markets (Nayyar and Sen, 1994; Chand and Jha, 2001).

For the most part, literature points out that in the developing countries, implementation of liberal macroeconomic polices may not be sufficient to ensure a higher responsiveness of their domestic prices to the world prices. To date, in many countries, policies such as trade quotas, quantitative restrictions and other non-tariff barriers, viz., licensing, strict quality controls and high tariffs that often exceed bound rate, etc., are constantly being followed, which may distort prices. Trade is also not free of government intervention as the central and state agencies continue to monitor imports of essential commodities by adjusting tariffs, often permitting trade through state trading agencies, fixing pan-seasonal/pan-territorial prices and providing subsidies on grounds of food security and livelihood needs. In many situations, transaction costs are disproportionate and the 'Law of One Price' cannot hold (Zanias, 1993). Knowing that world trade in agriculture is still in a transitional phase as negotiations concerning some of these issues and many more, have not been settled so far, the expected full transmission of world price signals to domestic producers may not transpire.

Empirical Model to Test Price Transmission and Data Set

Literature draws heavily on the market integration approach to understand the nature of price linkages in two or more related markets and measure the extent to which they synchronize or diverge. The approach deals with the subject under the notion of 'Law of One Price' (Ravallion, 1986; Ardeni, 1989; Baffes, 1991; Asche et al., 1999). Market integration is said to exist when prices of homogeneous commodities in perfectly competitive and spatially separated markets move mutually in response to the forces of demand and supply and difference in their prices reflect only the transport and processing cost.

The methodological approaches for estimating the degree of competitiveness of markets are wide and are based on time series data on commodity prices. The bivariate correlation coefficient and regression techniques, which were used in earlier studies, were taken over by the cointegration and error correction approach as developed by Granger (1986), and Engle and Granger (1987). Though considerable refinements have been observed in each of these approaches over a period based on time series properties, stationarity of the variables and multivariate analysis, the cointegration tests are found to have wider application.

The cointegration approach is based on the notion that economic forces may not allow persistent long-run deviations from equilibrium conditions even if short-run deviations take place, i.e., individual prices may diverge but certain pairs of prices must move together in the long run. A long run stable equilibrium relationship between two or more time series variables is captured through co-movement of prices and is tested by the Granger representation theorem. The theorem states that if a set of variables is cointegrated, then there exists a valid error correction representation of the data (Engle and Granger, 1987). Recent literature has extensively applied the Johansen Full Information Maximum Likelihood test as developed by Johansen (1988) and Johansen and

Juselius (1990). This test is carried out in a vector auto-regressive (VAR) mode and is a reduced form method. The Johansen test has an advantage over all other techniques as it can be carried out in a multivariate framework, it estimates the dynamic nature of price adjustment to equilibrium, and also takes care of the endogeniety and simultaneity problems associated with other cointegration tests. Of late a few studies have pointed out a limited application of this test in situations of non-stationary transaction costs and reversals in the trade flows across markets (Barret and Li, 2002; Rashid, 2004). Despite this, the approach has drawn considerable attention in analysing price relationships under different policy regimes.

In brief, cointegration among price series is tested based on error correction representation in a VAR framework:

$$Y_t = A_1 y_{t-1} + ...A_p\, y_{t-p} + Cx_t + \varepsilon_t$$

where y_t is a column vector of current values of non-stationary I(1) variables, x_t is a matrix of deterministic variables such as intercept and time trend, and e_t is a vector of innovations. To rewrite VAR in first difference:

$$\Delta y_t = \prod y_{t-1} + \sum^{p-1} T_1 \Delta y_{t-1} + Cx_t + \varepsilon t_t$$

where, $\prod = \sum_{i=1}^{p} Aj - I, \Gamma_t = \sum_{ji+1}^{p} Aj$

As per Granger's representation theorem, if the coefficient matrix Π has reduced rank r<k, then there are k*r matrices α & β each with rank r such that $\Pi = \alpha\,\beta'$ and $\beta' y_t$ is stationary, i.e., I(0) even though y_t itself is I(1). r is the number of cointegrating relations and each column of β is the cointegrating vector. The cointegration matrix described the long run relationships in the model. The elements of α are known as adjustment parameters, which explain the speed of adjustment of specific variables on account of deviations from the long-run relationships. Johansen's method is to estimate the Π matrix in an unrestricted form, and then test whether the restrictions implied by the reduced rank of Π can be rejected. It is tested by likelihood ratio test statistics for the number of cointegrating vectors 'r' namely, the maximum eigenvalue (λ-max) statistics of the stochastic matrix. According to Rivera and Helfand (2001), for establishing a long-run relationship between variables/prices in a multivariate framework, the number of cointegrating vectors should be r=N−1, where N represents the total number of variables cointegrating. For example, in a system of five

non-stationary variables, the Johansen test estimates five different stochastic trends. The rank of Π should be (n–1) cointegrating vectors, i.e., there should be at least four cointegrating vectors for markets to be truly integrated. This is because the system must contain at least one stochastic trend for the price series to be non-stationary by themselves.

To begin with, the variables are checked for stationarity along with their order of integration. The cointegration test is applied on variables that are integrated of the same order. The cointegrating vectors or relations that are obtained in the analysis are normalized. Normalization is done in such a way that the first r series in the vector is normalized to an identity matrix. Since cointegration tests are not based on a structural model, it is difficult to interpret long-run elasticities in terms of signs and magnitudes given by these cointegration equations. The only inference one can draw from the results of the cointegrating equations is the presence of a long-run relationship between the variables under consideration. Once the variables are found to be cointegrated, a vector error correction model (ECM) is estimated by taking the respective variables in their first difference, their lagged values and lagged residual from cointegrating equations. The error term of variables/prices indicates the magnitude and time path of reactions of variables/prices to deviations from a long-run relationship shown by cointegration. In other words, ECM captures the short-run dynamics and indicates the speed of adjustment of prices or convergence towards equilibrium. The value of this parameter must be negative and should be as close as possible to –1 to indicate immediate adjustment to deviations from the equilibrium.

In the present study, the Johansen test is applied to a cyclical index of nominal monthly world and domestic wholesale prices of six tradable commodities from 1980–81 to 2002–03, separately in the pre- and post-liberalization periods. The bifurcation of this period is based on a structural break identified in the price series estimated using the Chow Test and Cusum of Squares Test developed by Brown, Durbin and Evans (1975). In case, the structural break is not present in the time series, 1991 is taken as the break-up period for decomposition of data into pre- and post- liberalization periods. The statistical adequacy of the estimated error-correction equations is examined using the LM test and ARCH statistics. The Ramsey reset specification test is also used to check stability of the parameters and right specification of the ECM. Since the estimates are based on monthly data, it is possible that serial correlation may occur upto the 12th order. An application of these tests has rejected the presence of serial correlation with a few exceptions as in the case of soyabean seed. Further, the presence of homoscedasticity is not rejected except in a few cases where heteroscedasticity is found.

The main sources of data on monthly wholesale prices are the Agriculture Prices in India and CACP reports, Ministry of Agriculture, GOI. For each crop, a wholesale market is chosen from each state for which monthly price data is available from 1980–81 to 2002–03. The international prices of selected commodities are monthly reference prices at the major global trading centres given in International Financial Statistics, IMF. Annexure 4.1 provides the names of the state and district where the wholesale market is located along with the name of the global trading centre. Price differences on account of the quality and variety of a commodity such as cotton is ignored in the analyses. The monthly price data are adjusted as per the crop year. World prices are available in dollar terms and are converted into domestic currency using appropriate exchange rate given in the Report on Currency and Finance, RBI. The empirical results derived from the model are as discussed below.

Empirical Results on Price Transmission in the Pre- and Post-reform Periods

An evaluation of the extent of price signals that have been transmitted across spatial markets is done in two steps, first across the state-level wholesale markets and then between world and state-level markets. Both exercises are done separately for pre- and post-reform periods. As mentioned above, the cointegration test has to be preceded by a test of non-stationarity for individual price series using DF and ADF tests. The estimates are obtained on natural logs of price series as their first differences reflect the rate of change of the variable. While testing stationarity, the regression is run with a trend factor as well as without time trend. The order of lag is determined by the minimum value of Akaike's Final Prediction Error criterion. Annexure Tables 4.1A-F present the results of the ADF test for unit root for all the six selected commodities during the pre- and post-liberalization periods. It reveals world and most of the state level wholesale prices to be integrated of order 1, i.e., I(1). The only exceptions are a few domestic groundnut seed and sugar price series where the ADF test does not reject the null hypothesis that prices follow a unit root process. The Johansen test is applied on a series that are integrated of the same order. The test assumption is taken to be no deterministic trend in the data. In a few cases, the assumption considered is linear deterministic trend in data. The order of VAR (lag interval) is determined by the minimum AIC and SBC.

Based on Johansen multivariate cointegration procedure the commodity-wise results on inter-market price transmission are as follows: Tables 4.1A-F provide results on long-run integration within the domestic markets and between domestic and world markets. The normalized cointegrating coefficients obtained from cointegration are provided in Annexure Table 4.2. These are used to estimate the long-run path of price adjustments. The short-run dynamics based on error correction model in two time periods are given in Annexure Tables 4.3A-F. Table 4.2 summarizes estimates of the error term for each commodity based on the average values obtained for selected states and world markets. The maximum number of cointegrating vectors and error correction estimates obtained during the pre- and post-liberalization periods are compared to see the magnitude of impact of reforms on market integration.

Wheat

The structural break test when applied on relative monthly domestic and world prices of wheat accepts the null hypothesis of structural stability from 1980–81 to 2002–03. Therefore, cointegration analysis for wheat is carried out from 1980 April to 1991 March and from 1991 April to 2003 March, the period before and after initiations of reforms. The ADF unit root test (see Annexure Table 4.1A) confirms wheat prices during the eighties to be integrated of order one, i.e., I(1) in levels but integrated of order zero (i.e. stationary) in the first difference except in Gujarat and Delhi. In the second period, the same results hold except for Gujarat, Madhya Pradesh and Delhi. In these states, the null hypothesis of non-stationarity in levels is rejected.

The Johansen test is applied on price series that are integrated of the same order, i.e., I(1) to determine the rank of Π or number of cointegrating vectors present. Cointegration is tested for five sets of price series in the domestic markets and six price series when the world price of wheat is also taken. From the LR statistics, one can reject the null hypothesis $r=0$, $r \leq 1$, $r \leq 2$ and $r \leq 3$ (no cointegration) against the alternative hypothesis $r=4$ at the 5 per cent level of significance. Results confirm the presence of 4 cointegrating vectors among prices in Punjab, Haryana, Karnataka, Rajasthan and Uttar Pradesh and hence suggest a long-run cointegrating or equilibrium relationship among the state-level prices of wheat, both in the pre- and post-liberalization periods. Prices in three state-level markets, viz., Madhya Pradesh, Delhi and Bihar are not integrated with other state-level markets. When the world price series is taken along with the domestic prices, the analysis shows only two cointegrating vectors in the eighties, which indicates that only in a few states prices were integrated with the world price. The long-run relationship gets improved in the post-liberalization period because the number of cointegrating vectors is found to be at the maximum at five.

The analysis is followed by an estimation of the error correction model. While estimating ECM in the first difference, the price of wheat in Gujarat, which was found to follow a unit root process in the nineties, is also included. The results present estimates of coefficients of error-correction with their t-values and explanatory variables (state-level prices) in first difference. The coefficients of state-level prices indicate change in price in a particular state on its own as well as change in price of other states in the system. It is clear that most of the coefficients of explanatory variables in the short-run model are statistically significant in the first lag. As far as estimates of error term are concerned, results ensure that the coefficients are negative and vary between 0 and 1 in both domestic markets (Annexure Table 4.3A.1–A.2) and domestic and world markets (Annexure Table 4.3A.3–A.4). This implies stable short-run price movements along the long-run equilibrium path. For instance, a value of –0.38, –0.26 and –0.16 for Haryana, Rajasthan and Gujarat indicates that the system corrects its previous period's disequilibrium by 38 per cent, 26 per cent and 16 per cent in a month's time period.

The averages of the estimated error term during the pre and post-liberalization periods are given in Table 4.2. In the first period, the estimated coefficients in domestic markets are negative and statistically significant (average –0.23). Since the estimates are not in close proximity to 1, they indicate a slow speed of adjustment in state-level prices to a shock in their own price in a year. The average speed of adjustment for wheat has improved in the post-reform period from 23 per cent to 37 per cent. The error-term estimates between the world and domestic wheat prices in the pre-reform period are again negative and significant with a few exceptions, viz., Rajasthan and Uttar Pradesh. This could be explained by the fact that domestic and world markets were not integrated during this period. A statistically insignificant and negative coefficient value at 0.02 and 0.13 implies that wheat prices in these two states may or may not return to an equilibrium path. Results in the post-reform period are comparatively better with an average speed of adjustment to be 0.33. However, in both time periods the speed of adjustment of prices towards equilibrium is found to be slow. The

TABLE 4.1A *Wheat: Johansen's Maximum Eigenvalue and Trace Test for the Number of Cointegrating Vectors in the Pre- and Post-reform Periods*

Series in Log	*Null Hypothesis*	*Alternate Hypothesis*	*Eigen Value*	*Likelihood Ratio*	*5 Per cent Critical Value*	*1 Per cent Critical Value*	*Hypothesized No. of CE(s)*	*Lag Interval*
				Sample: 1980 April to 1991 March				
				Domestic Markets				
Punjab	r = 0	r =1	0.173	70.32	59.46	66.52	None **	2
Haryana	r ≤ 1	r =2	0.131	45.77	39.89	45.58	At most 1 **	
Karnataka	r ≤ 2	r =3	0.107	27.54	24.31	29.75	At most 2 *	
Rajasthan	r ≤ 3	r =4	0.09	12.88	12.53	16.31	At most 3 *	
Uttar Pr.	r ≤ 4	r =5	0.003	0.45	3.84	6.51	At most 4	
				Domestic and World Markets				
Punjab	r = 0	r =1	0.229	97.45	82.49	90.45	None **	2
Haryana	r ≤ 1	r =2	0.171	63.80	59.46	66.52	At most 1 *	
Karnataka	r ≤ 2	r =3	0.138	39.55	39.89	45.58	At most 2	
Rajasthan	r ≤ 3	r =4	0.111	20.25	24.31	29.75	At most 3	
Uttar Pr.	r ≤ 4	r =5	0.035	4.93	12.53	16.31	At most 4	
World	r ≤ 5	r =6	0.002	0.30	3.84	6.51	At most 5	
				Sample: 1991 April to 2003 March				
				Domestic Markets				
Punjab	r = 0	r =1	0.33	45.34	76.07	84.45	None **	1
Haryana	r ≤ 1	r =2	0.274	86.84	53.12	60.16	At most 1 **	
Karnataka	r ≤ 2	r =3	0.136	41.18	34.91	41.07	At most 2 **	
Rajasthan	r ≤ 3	r =4	0.083	20.37	19.96	24.60	At most 3 *	
Uttar Pr.	r ≤ 4	r =5	0.055	8.06	9.24	12.97	At most 4	
				Domestic and World Markets				
Punjab	r = 0	r =1	0.34	169.09	102.14	111.01	None **	1
Haryana	r ≤ 1	r =2	0.289	108.90	76.07	84.45	At most 1 **	
Karnataka	r ≤ 2	r =3	0.139	60.38	53.12	60.16	At most 2 **	
Rajasthan	r ≤ 3	r =4	0.123	38.99	34.91	41.07	At most 3 *	
Uttar Pr.	r ≤ 4	r =5	0.0916	20.25	19.96	24.60	At most 4 *	
World	r ≤ 5	r =6	0.045	6.59	9.24	12.97	At most 5	

Notes: *(**) denotes rejection of the hypothesis at 5 per cent (1%) significance level. L.R. test indicates 4 cointegrating equation(s) at 5 per cent significance level in domestic markets in two time periods. With inclusion of world prices, the number of cointegrating equations are 2 in the eighties and 5 in the nineties.

FIGURE 4.1A *Wheat: Long-term Price Adjustment Path during Pre- and Post-liberalization Periods*

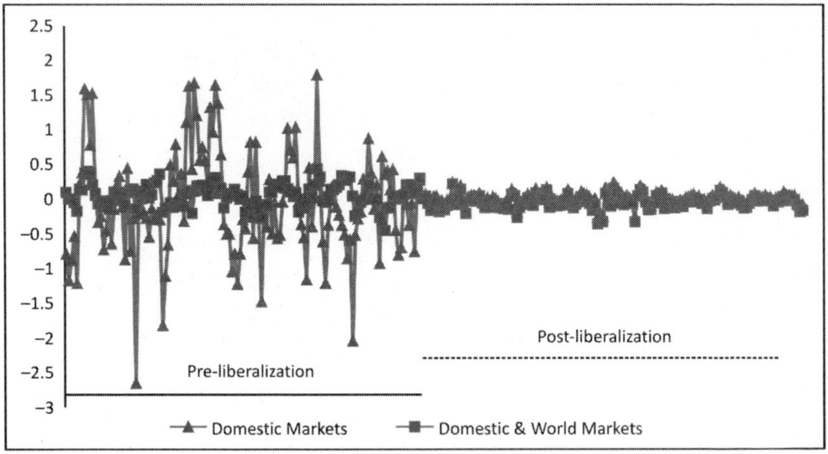

long-run path of price adjustments based on normalized cointegration relations also shows deviations to be more stable in the post-reform period compared to that in the pre-reform period (Figure 4.1A). Overall analysis indicates an improvement in the long-run relationship between all the markets in the post-reform period, which is consistent with expectations. However, the average speed of price adjustment though improved from 12 to 33 per cent over the period shows a weak association among these markets in the short run. It may take around 2–3 weeks time in a month for transmission of information about prices from one market to another.

Rice

As in the case of wheat, the relative price series of rice reveals absence of a structural break from 1980–81 to 2002–03. The bifurcation of this period is, therefore, done as per the initiation of SAP in 1991. The unit root test carried out during the pre- and post-liberalization periods rejects the null hypothesis of unit root problem (non-stationarity) in all the state-level markets and world price in both time periods. Only in one state, viz., Maharashtra, the hypothesis of unit root is accepted and hence is excluded from the long-run cointegration analysis (Annexure Table 4.1B). One may find most of the states to be integrated of order one at varying lag intervals in both pre- and post-liberalization periods, which implies the presence of similar long-run characteristics amongst domestic and world rice prices. Nonetheless, of all the states taken in the analysis, integration is found between Andhra Pradesh, Karnataka, Kerala, Orissa, Tamil Nadu and West Bengal during the eighties. In the post-reform period, Kerala and Orissa have failed to show any association with these states. Instead, rice prices in the Haryana and Uttar Pradesh markets have shown greater integration with other domestic markets in the nineties. The states, which have hardly shown any association with other state-level market prices, are Gujarat and Bihar.

As far as the long-run relationship of state-level prices with world price is concerned, one can reject the null hypothesis $r \leq 3$ (no cointegration) against the alternative hypothesis $r = 4$ at the 5 per cent level of significance. The results confirm the presence of 4 cointegrating vectors among the rice prices in Andhra Pradesh, Karnataka, Kerala and Tamil Nadu and the world trading centre during the eighties. The same result occurs during the nineties but it shows a strong association of world price with prices only in the important crop producing states, viz., Andhra Pradesh, Tamil Nadu, Haryana and Uttar Pradesh. Though West Bengal is the largest producer of rice, it lacks integration with world markets, which could be due to varietal differences. It is interesting to find that in major paddy producing states, the government agencies mediate the most through procurement at support price and also the state-level prices positively respond to MSP. Despite this fact, a co-movement of state-level and world prices is witnessed during the nineties. An increased integration of prices in some of the states with world reference price explains a narrowing of gap between the domestic and world markets as well as a growing competitiveness and demand for exports (Table 4.1B).

The estimates of long-run co-integrating equations are normalized around prices in Andhra Pradesh and bear the expected signs. Based on these estimates, diversions across the stable long-run path within the domestic markets and between world and domestic ones are plotted, which appear to be more or less of the same amplitude in two time periods, wit h a few exceptions (Figure 4.1B).

The short-run dynamics captured through VECM during the two time periods across domestic markets and between domestic and world markets show robust results (Annexure Tables 4.3B.1–B.4). Estimates of error term show coefficients to be negative and significant for all the selected markets in the eighties. The coefficients vary between a minimum value of 0.20 to a maximum of 0.37 (averaged 0.27), which

TABLE 4.1B *Rice: Johansen's Maximum Eigenvalue and Trace Test for the Number of Cointegrating Vectors in the Pre and Post-reform Periods*

Series in Log	*Null Hypothesis*	*Alternate Hypothesis*	*Eigen Value*	*Likelihood Ratio*	*5 Per cent Critical Value*	*1 Per cent Critical Value*	*Hypothesized No. of CE(s)*	*Lag Interval*
Sample: 1980 October to 1991 December Domestic Markets								
Andhra Pr.	r = 0	r =1	0.234	112.76	82.49	90.45	None **	1
Karnataka	r ≤ 1	r =2	0.193	78.01	59.46	66.52	At most 1 **	
Kerala	r ≤ 2	r =3	0.155	50.13	39.89	45.58	At most 2 **	
Orissa	r ≤ 3	r =4	0.112	28.22	24.31	29.75	At most 3 *	
Tamil Nadu	r ≤ 4	r =5	0.090	12.71	12.53	16.31	At most 4 *	
West Bengal	r ≤ 5	r =6	0.002	0.31	3.84	6.51	At most 5	
Domestic and World Markets								
Andhra Pr.	r = 0	r =1	0.310	109.06	68.52	76.07	None **	2
Karnataka	r ≤ 1	r =2	0.202	61.18	47.21	54.46	At most 1 **	
Kerala	r ≤ 2	r =3	0.115	31.95	29.68	35.65	At most 2 *	
Tamil Nadu	r ≤ 3	r =4	0.098	16.13	15.41	20.04	At most 3 *	
World	r ≤ 4	r =5	0.020	2.6911	3.76	6.65	At most 4	
Sample: 1991 October to 2002 September Domestic Markets								
Andhra Pr.	r = 0	r =1	0.285	139.67	102.14	111.01	None **	1
Karnataka	r ≤ 1	r =2	0.217	96.029	76.07	84.45	At most 1 **	
Tamil Nadu	r ≤ 2	r =3	0.180	64.225	53.12	60.16	At most 2 **	
West Bengal	r ≤ 3	r =4	0.119	38.41	34.91	41.07	At most 3 *	
Haryana	r ≤ 4	r =5	0.114	21.85	19.96	24.60	At most 4 *	
Uttar Pr.	r ≤ 5	r =6	0.045	6.039	9.24	12.97	At most 5	
Domestic and World Markets								
Andhra Pr.	r = 0	r =1	0.26	103.40	76.07	84.45	None **	1
Tamil Nadu	r ≤ 1	r =2	0.16	63.32	53.12	60.16	At most 1 **	
Haryana	r ≤ 2	r =3	0.12	39.11	34.91	41.07	At most 2 *	
Uttar Pr.	r ≤ 3	r =4	0.11	21.79	19.96	24.60	At most 3 *	
World	r ≤ 4	r =5	0.04	5.44	9.24	12.97	At most 4	

Notes: *(**) denotes rejection of the hypothesis at 5 per cent (1%) significance level. L.R. test indicates 5 cointegrating equation(s) at 5 per cent significance level in domestic markets and 4 cointegrating equations in the domestic and world markets together in two time periods.

FIGURE 4.1B *Rice Long-term Price Adjustment Path during Pre and Post-liberalization Periods*

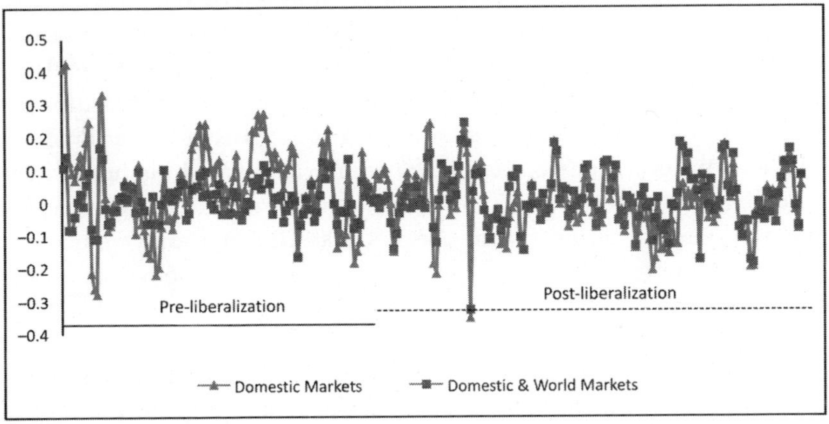

indicates a slow speed of adjustment towards equilibrium. Notably, the average speed of price adjustment in the two time periods is more or less the same at around 28 per cent, which indicates an insignificant improvement in price transmission following the economic reforms. The inclusion of world price series along with domestic prices again shows the error term to be low and negatively significant except in the world and Maharashtra markets. The same between domestic and world markets again shows a slow adjustment with an average speed at 31.25 per cent during the pre-reform period which fell to 26.16 per cent in the subsequent period. This indicates a weak networking of markets in the short run with a lag of 3–4 weeks. The situation was comparatively better in the pre-reform period as the time period of shock absorption and error correction was 2–3 weeks in a month's time. The overall results for rice suggest that markets share a common path in the long-run while in the short run inter-market prices drift apart.

Sugar

Cusum of squares test carried out on sugar prices reveals no structural break. The results estimated separately for the eighties (1980 October to 1991 September) and the nineties (1991 October to 2001 September) show the unit root problem to be present in most of the states during the eighties (Annexure Table 4.1C). Of all the states, the prices in Uttar Pradesh, Punjab and Karnataka are I(1). Cointegration results carried out for these three states indicate the presence of long run or equilibrium relationship between prices. As shown in Table 4.1C, these three state-level markets are also integrated with the world market as LR statistics accept the number of cointegrating vectors to be equal to three. Results during the nineties suggest sugar prices to be integrated across the domestic markets with only the exception of Maharashtra. The null hypothesis of no cointegration $r \leq 4$ against the alternative hypothesis $r=5$ is rejected at the 5 per cent level of significance and it confirms the presence of 5 cointegrating vectors among sugar prices of Uttar Pradesh, Punjab, Andhra Pradesh, Karnataka, Bihar and Tamil Nadu markets. The domestic prices of sugar are not integrated with world sugar price in the post-reform period. From the LR statistics, one may notice the presence of only 4 cointegrating relationships, which implies that prices in only a few selected states such as Uttar Pradesh are integrated with the world market.

As expected, the short-run error correction model reveals negative and statistically significant values of the error term during the pre-reform period (Annexure Table 4.2 C1–C3). It is negative and insignificant only in Punjab and Karnataka. When the international reference price is included in the analysis, the error term is found to be insignificant in Tamil Nadu and the world markets. As in the case of wheat and rice, the ECM of sugar prices is also on the lower side thereby indicating a slow speed of reconciliation of short-run behaviour with the long run with a lag of 2–3 weeks in a month. Compared to pre-reform estimates, the coefficients of error term in the post-reform era show significant improvement. The ECM in all the state-level markets is negative and significant and varies between 0.14 in Punjab to 0.43 in Bihar. The error term of world sugar price is positive and insignificant. This implies that

FIGURE 4.1C *Sugar: Long-term Price Adjustment Path during Pre- and Post-liberalization Periods*

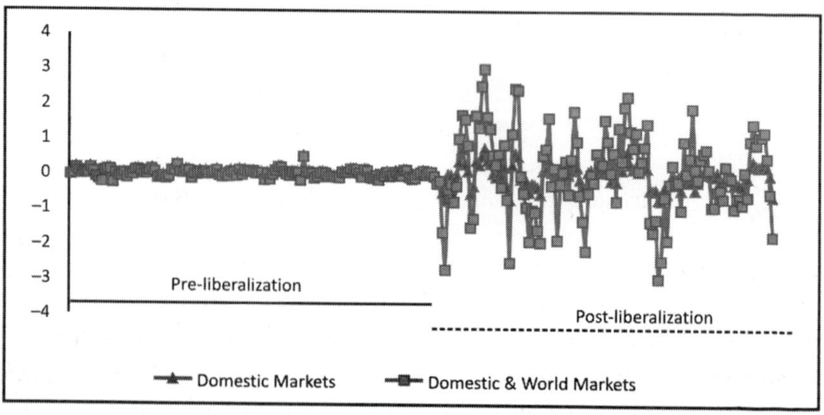

TABLE 4.1C *Sugar: Johansen's Maximum Eigenvalue and Trace Test for the Number of Cointegrating Vectors in the Pre and Post-reform Periods*

Series in Log	*Null Hypothesis*	*Alternate Hypothesis*	*Eigen Value*	*Likelihood Ratio*	*5 Per cent Critical Value*	*1 Per cent Critical Value*	*Hypothesized No. of CE(s)*	*Lag Interval*
				Sample: 1980 October to 1991 September Domestic Markets				
Uttar Pr.	r = 0	r =1	0.296	70.561	34.91	41.07	None **	1
Punjab	r ≤ 1	r =2	0.115	24.77	19.96	24.60	At most 1 **	
Karnataka	r ≤ 2	r =3	0.065	8.866	9.24	12.97	At most 2	
				Domestic and World Markets				
Uttar Pr.	r = 0	r =1	0.305	88.43	53.12	60.16	None **	1
Punjab	r ≤ 1	r =2	0.126	41.12	34.91	41.07	At most 1 **	
Karnataka	r ≤ 2	r =3	0.112	23.57	19.96	24.60	At most 2 *	
World	r ≤ 3	r =4	0.060	8.11	9.24	12.97	At most 3	
				Sample: 1991 October to 2001 September Domestic Markets				
Uttar Pr.	r = 0	r =1	0.343	163.78	102.14	111.01	None **	1
Punjab	r ≤ 1	r =2	0.280	114.09	76.07	84.45	At most 1 **	
Karnataka	r ≤ 2	r =3	0.217	75.32	53.12	60.16	At most 2 **	
Tamil Nadu	r ≤ 3	r =4	0.155	46.38	34.91	41.07	At most 3**	
Bihar	r ≤ 4	r =5	0.138	26.41	19.96	24.60	At most 4**	
Andhra Pr.	r ≤ 5	r =6	0.072	8.81	9.24	12.97	At most 5	
				Domestic and World Markets				
Uttar Pr.	r = 0	r =1	0.366	185.40	131.70	143.09	None **	1
Punjab	r ≤ 1	r =2	0.306	131.47	102.14	111.01	At most 1 **	
Karnataka	r ≤ 2	r =3	0.244	88.27	76.07	84.45	At most 2 **	
Tamil Nadu	r ≤ 3	r =4	0.163	55.11	53.12	60.16	At most 3*	
Bihar	r ≤ 4	r =5	0.142	34.10	34.91	41.07	At most 4	
Andhra Pr.	r ≤ 5	r =6	0.087	16.02	19.96	24.60	At most 5	
World	r ≤ 6	r =7	0.043	5.24	9.24	12.97	At most 6	

Notes: *(**) denotes rejection of the hypothesis at 5 per cent (1%) significance level. L.R. test indicates 2 and 5 cointegrating equation(s) at 5 per cent significance level in domestic markets in two time periods. When world price series is included, the number of cointegrating equations are 3 in the eighties and 4 in the nineties.

the world price may or may not return to the equilibrium path. For all the state-level markets together, the average speed of the error term has become faster from 19.7 to 33.8 per cent. However, the speed of price transmission between the domestic and world markets shows slight improvement. In both cases, the analysis indicates weak linkages among spatial markets in the short run. This is also evident from Figure 4.1C which depicts a higher magnitude of price fluctuations in the post-liberalization period compared to the pre-liberalization period in domestic as well as between domestic and world markets.

Cotton

Time series data on wholesale prices of cotton lint is available only for two markets, viz., Maharashtra and Tamil Nadu that too from 1982 to 1998. The structural break test carried out on domestic and world prices show the break to have occurred first in January 1991 and then in January 1995. Therefore, the time series data is bifurcated into pre- and post-reform period as 1982 October to 1990 September and 1994 October to 1998 September. The ADF test of unit root performed on each price series in two time periods reject the null hypothesis of unit root in levels. As shown in Annexure Table 4.1D, all the three price series are integrated of order one, both in the pre- and post liberalization periods with the number of lags at 1. From the estimates of Eigen values and maximum likelihood ratio and their critical values, one may notice the presence of only one cointegrating vector during the eighties but none during the nineties (Table 4.1D). This suggests that prices in these two domestic markets were integrated during the eighties and lacked linkage during the subsequent decade. Further, in both time periods, the results do not provide evidence in favour of full integration of domestic markets with the world market. Long-run cointegration results between world, Maharashtra and Tamil Nadu markets reveal only one cointegrating relationship in two time periods. This would imply co-movement of world and domestic lint price only in one market in the pre- and in the post-reform period. Investigative exercise shows the Tamil Nadu market to be closely associated with the international market of cotton. The estimates of long-run cointegrating equations are normalized around prices in Maharashtra. The coefficient of Tamil Nadu market bears a positive sign in the equation.

The error term is negative and significant for Maharashtra and world in the pre-reform period. The same, however, is significant only

FIGURE 4.1D *Cotton: Long-term Price Adjustment Path during Pre- and Post-Liberalization Periods*

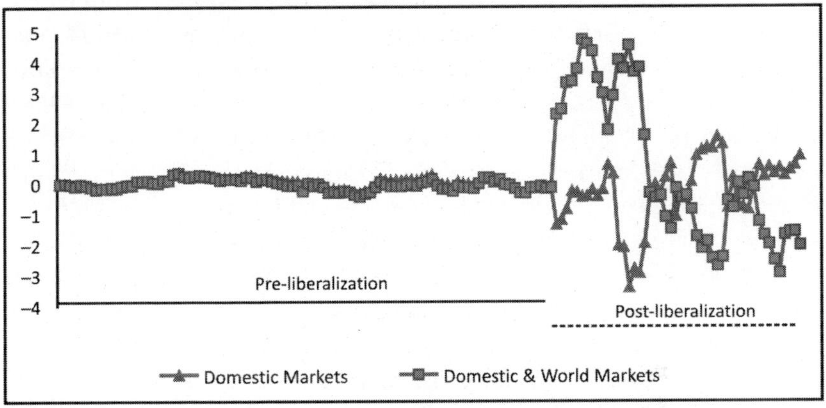

TABLE 4.1D *Cotton: Johansen's Maximum Eigenvalue and Trace Test for the Number of Cointegrating Vectors in the Pre and Post-reform Periods*

Series in Log	*Null Hypothesis*	*Alternate Hypothesis*	*Eigen Value*	*Likelihood Ratio*	*5 Per cent Critical Value*	*1 Per cent Critical Value*	*Hypothesized No. of CE(s)*	*Lag Interval*
			Sample: 1982 October to 1990 September Domestic Markets					
Maharashtra	r = 0	r =1	0.14	21.43	19.96	24.60	None *	2
Tamil Nadu	r ≤ 1	r =2	0.073	7.06	9.24	12.97	At most 1	
			Domestic and World Markets					
Maharashtra	r = 0	r =1	0.213	25.95	24.31	29.75	None *	2
Tamil Nadu	r ≤ 1	r =2	0.037	3.671	12.53	16.31	At most 1	
World	r ≤ 2	r =3	0.0015	0.146	3.84	6.51	At most 2	
			Sample: 1994 October to 1998 September Domestic Markets					
Maharashtra	r = 0	r =1	0.160	10.46	19.96	24.60	None	2
Tamil Nadu	r ≤ 1	r =2	0.051	2.41	9.24	12.97	At most 1	
			Domestic and World Markets					
Maharashtra	r = 0	r =1	0.369	43.019	42.44	48.45	None *	3
Tamil Nadu	r ≤ 1	r =2	0.313	22.751	25.32	30.45	At most 1	
World	r ≤ 2	r =3	0.131	6.186	12.25	16.26	At most 2	

Notes: *(**) denotes rejection of the hypothesis at 5 per cent (1%) significance level. L.R. test indicates 1 cointegrating equation(s) at 5 per cent significance level in the Domestic during eighties and none during the nineties. With inclusion of world price, the number of cointegrating equations is again 1 in both time periods.

for world markets in the post-reform period. The speed of adjustment in domestic and world markets is very low as has been observed for cereals and sugar too. It is somewhat faster in the post-reform period from 6.6 to 20.6 per cent, which implies a time lag of 3–4 weeks for prices to adjust among spatial markets. Further, the coefficients of explanatory variables in the short-run model in the first lag are not statistically significant in any of the three markets (Annexure Tables 4.3D.1–D.3). Fluctuations around the long-run path have also been much higher in the post-reform period compared to the pre-reform period (Figure 4.1D). Large drifts in prices in the short run could be explained by either lack of information or slow dissemination of available information. The overall results for cotton show the inter-market price transmission to be inefficient over a period of time both in the long-run as well as in the short-run. Price transmission is somewhat better between the domestic and world markets compared to that across state-level wholesale markets.

Oilseeds

Of the two oilseeds taken, viz., groundnut and soyabean, world price of groundnut is found to have the unit root problem in the eighties. Therefore, the cointegration test is performed for domestic markets of groundnut during the eighties and the nineties and between domestic and world markets during the nineties only. For soyabean seed, price integration is tested across the domestic as well as between world and domestic markets. Analysis of groundnut shows the structural break to have occurred during 1992–93 in many states and that is why the time series price data from 1980–81 to 2002–03 is divided into two periods – 1980 November to 1992 October and 1992 November to 2003 October, representing the pre- and post-liberalization periods. The ADF test of unit root reveals prices in Gujarat and world markets in the eighties and the prices in Gujarat and Tamil Nadu in the nineties to be I(0) (Annexure Table 4.1E). the Johansen test employed on wholesale prices indicates groundnut prices in three states, viz. Andhra Pradesh, Tamil Nadu and Uttar Pradesh to be integrated during the pre-reform period. As the cointegration test is applied to a series that are integrated of the same order, Tamil Nadu is excluded from the analysis during the nineties due to a different order of integration. The results confirm an equilibrium relationship between Andhra Pradesh and Uttar Pradesh as the LR statistics rejects the null hypothesis of $r=0$ against $r=1$ and indicates one cointegrating relationship (Table 4.1E).

For estimating the speed of adjustment of groundnut prices to equilibrium, prices in Gujarat and world are also included in the ECM. Results reveal the statistically significant negative value of the error term for Andhra Pradesh, Uttar Pradesh and Gujarat markets during the eighties with values estimated at 0.21 to 0.23 (averaged 0.28), respectively. There is not significant improvement in the error term in the subsequent decade. The coefficients are statistically significant with negative signs varying between 0.04 to 0.21 in select states (averaged 0.14). The error term estimates are on the lower side in both time periods suggesting 3–4 weeks for prices to adjust. When the analysis is made between domestic and world markets during the nineties, estimates for the two states show higher values (–0.32 and –0.55). The short-run association though weak is found to have improved on an average from 16 to 23 per cent. The price adjustment path in Figure 4.1E shows large fluctuations in the two time periods with different amplitudes of deviations. Thus, the domestic and world groundnut markets are found to be integrated in the long run during the post-reform period. But the adjustment process in the short run has been weak as has been identified for other commodities as well. The domestic markets have become more inefficient over time, which suggests that producers/traders may not be transferring their produce from one market to another as per changes in price.

FIGURE 4.1E *Groundnut Seed: Long-term Price Adjustment Path during Pre and Post-liberalization Periods*

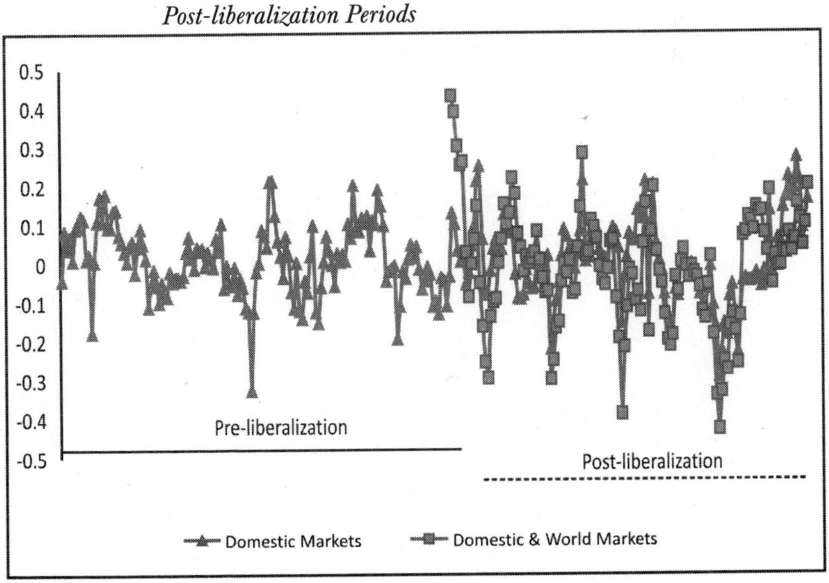

For soyabean seed, the structural break appears to have taken place in 1996 January. Therefore, bifurcation of time series data from 1982–83 to 1998–99 is done into two periods, 1982 November to 1991 October and 1995 November to 1999 October. Wholesale price data is available for only two markets, one in Madhya Pradesh and other in Uttar Pradesh. In both cases, the ADF test of unit root does not reject the null hypothesis that the price time series follow the unit root process. However, the hypothesis in the first difference enables the rejection of unit root at the 1 per cent level of significance in all the three markets (Annexure Table 4.1F). This implies that price differentials can be used in the ECM. Long-term cointegration in domestic prices and between domestic and world prices in the pre-and post-reform periods are presented in Table 4.1F which reveals that while we can reject the hypothesis of no cointegration in domestic markets in the pre-reform period, the same cannot be rejected in the post-reform period. Turning to cointegration between domestic and world prices, the results appear to be same in both periods and show only one cointegrating relationship in three price series against two expected relationships. Out of the two states, the price in Uttar Pradesh is likely to be integrated with world price both in the pre- and post-reform periods as prices series in this state tags along the world price.

Since long-run integration is not detected in domestic markets in the post-reform period, no error correction model is estimated. In the pre-reform period, the estimate of error term in Madhya Pradesh is negative and insignificant, and that of Uttar Pradesh is negatively significant (0.29) at the 1 per cent level of significance (Annexure Tables 4.3 F.1–F.3). Results of the ECM between domestic and world prices in two time periods are not very encouraging. Though the average speed of adjustment in the two markets improved from 15 per cent to 28 per cent it shows a weak association in the short run. The time period of price adjustment could be 3–4 weeks in a month. Individually, the estimate of error term for the world market is negatively significant only in the nineties and shows a faster speed of adjustment towards equilibrium at 72 per cent. Madhya Pradesh shows a positive and significant value of the error term, which implies that in a situation of any external shock, the variable will move to a different equilibrium path. Results indicate that despite being integrated in the long-run, soyabean prices have drifted apart in the short-run. The long-run price adjustment path has been fairly stable in the pre-liberalization period compared to the post-liberalization period (Figure 4.1F).

FIGURE 4.1F *Soyabean Seed: Long-term Price Adjustment Path during Pre- and Post-liberalization Periods*

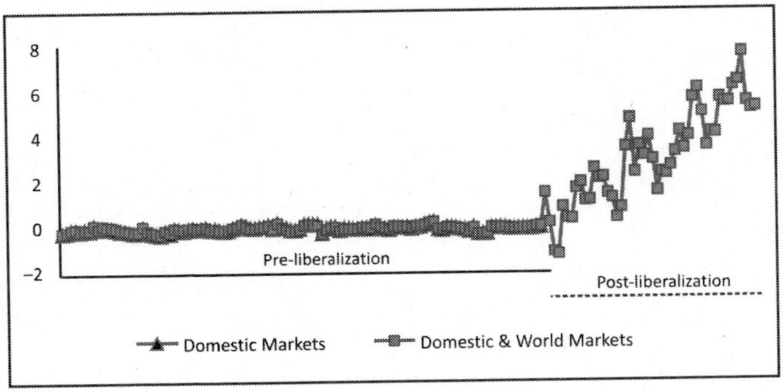

TABLE 4.1E *Groundnut Seed: Johansen's Maximum Eigenvalue and Trace Test for the Number of Cointegrating Vectors in the Pre and Post-reform Periods*

Series in Log	*Null Hypothesis*	*Alternate Hypothesis*	*Eigen Value*	*Likelihood Ratio*	*5 Per cent Critical Value*	*1 Per cent Critical Value*	*Hypothesized No. of CE(s)*	*Lag Interval*
				Sample: 1980 November to 1992 October Domestic Markets				
Andhra Pr.	r = 0	r =1	0.195	57.35	34.91	41.07	None **	1
Tamil Nadu	r ≤ 1	r =2	0.127	26.40	19.96	24.60	At most 1**	
Uttar Pr.	r ≤ 2	r =3	0.048	7.00	9.24	12.97	At most 2	
				Sample: 1992 November to 2003 October Domestic Markets				
Andhra Pr.	r = 0	r =1	0.119	23.36	19.96	24.60	None *	1
Uttar Pr.	r ≤ 1	r =2	0.050	6.80	9.24	12.97	At most 1	
				Domestic and World Markets				
Andhra Pr.	r = 0	r =1	0.152	42.03	34.91	41.07	None **	1
Uttar Pr.	r ≤ 1	r =2	0.091	20.51	19.96	24.60	At most 1*	
World	r ≤ 2	r =3	0.060	8.08	9.24	12.97	At most 2	

Notes: *(**) denotes rejection of the hypothesis at 5 per cent (1%) significance level. L.R. test indicates 2 cointegrating equation(s) at 5 per cent significance level in the domestic markets during the eighties and 1 during the nineties. With inclusion of world price, the number of cointegrating equations are 2 in the nineties. World price series is stationary during 1980–92.

TABLE 4.1F *Soyabean Seed: Johansen's Maximum Eigenvalue and Trace Test for the Number of Cointegrating Vectors in the Pre and Post-reform Periods*

Series in Log	*Null Hypothesis*	*Alternate Hypothesis*	*Eigen Value*	*Likelihood Ratio*	*5 Per cent Critical Value*	*1 Per cent Critical Value*	*Hypothesized No. of CE(s)*	*Lag Interval*
			Sample: 1982 November to 1991 October Domestic Markets					
Madhya Pr.	r = 0	r = 1	0.202	28.48	19.96	24.60	None **	1
Uttar Pr.	r ≤ 1	r = 2	0.041	4.44	9.24	12.97	At most 1	
			Domestic and World Markets					
Madhya Pr.	r = 0	r = 1	0.216	40.99	34.91	41.07	None *	1
Uttar Pr.	r ≤ 1	r = 2	0.095	15.12	19.96	24.60	At most 1	
World	r ≤ 2	r = 3	0.041	4.47	9.24	12.97	At most 2	
			Sample: 1995 November to 1999 October Domestic Markets					
Madhya Pr.	r = 0	r = 1	0.145	8.53	19.96	24.60	None	1
Uttar Pr.	r ≤ 1	r = 2	0.028	1.33	9.24	12.97	At most 1	
			Domestic and World Markets					
Madhya Pr.	r = 0	r = 1	0.422	43.20	42.44	48.45	None *	1
Uttar Pr.	r ≤ 1	r = 2	0.247	17.95	25.32	30.45	At most 1	
World	r ≤ 2	r = 3	0.100	4.85	12.25	16.26	At most 2	

Notes: *(**) denotes rejection of the hypothesis at 5 per cent (1%) significance level. L.R. test indicates 1 cointegrating equation(s) at 5 per cent significance level in the domestic markets during eighties and none during the nineties. With inclusion of world price, the number of cointegrating equations is again 1 in both time periods.

TABLE 4.2 *Estimates of Error Correction in Domestic and World Markets during Pre- and Post-reform Periods (Averages based on World and State-Level Estimates)*

Markets	*Domestic Markets*		*Domestic and World Markets*	
	Pre-reform	*Post-reform*	*Pre-reform*	*Post-reform*
Wheat	–0.23	–0.37	–0.12	–0.33
Rice	–0.275	–0.284	–0.31	–0.26
Sugar	–0.197	–0.34	–0.25	–0.26
Cotton	–0.08	–	–0.066	–0.21
Groundnut Seed	–0.28	–0.15	–0.16	–0.23
Soyabean Seed	–0.20	–	–0.15	–0.28

Appraisal of Findings and Remarks

The empirical analysis provides evidence of an improvement in the long-run transmission of prices of wheat, rice, sugar and groundnut seed in the post-reform period with a larger set of state-level wholesale markets in India to be integrated with each other. For cotton and soyabean seed, price integration is non-existent in the post-reform period. Results are not satisfactory for states other than the major producing states for the selected commodities. The short-run dynamics are negatively significant and vary between 0 and 1. But the coefficients are not in close proximity to 1, which indicates that the previous period's disequilibrium in commodity prices is corrected at a slower pace with a time lag of 2–3 weeks in a month. For all the chosen commodities, the speed of convergence towards a long-run path resulting from price shocks is fairly quicker in the post-reform period except in groundnut seed. Thus, the hypothesis that price transmission across wholesale markets in India has improved in the post-reform period is accepted for wheat, rice, sugar and groundnut seed but only in the major crop-producing states. Results suggest that the produce is transferred from one market to another in accordance with price changes and that arbitrage through trade bind their prices together. However, in the short run, price transmission among the domestic markets is absent for all the chosen commodities both in the pre- and post-liberalization periods.

The results further indicate that there exist fewer variations along the long-run adjustment path for wheat and rice and to some extent for sugar as compared to cotton and oilseeds. Price variability tested by using the coefficient of variation also reveals wholesale prices in most of the states, particularly for wheat and rice to be less compared to those prevailing in several other states and in the global markets. This phenomenon could be attributed to price policy, which helps absorb price shocks and bring stability, particularly in those states that make a significant contribution to the central pool (Jha et al., 1997; Chand and Jha, 2001).

The findings obtained in this study validate this point as a higher degree of integration of wheat and rice prices is identified mainly among the wholesale markets in Andhra Pradesh, Haryana, Punjab, Tamil Nadu and Karnataka where the central/state agencies actively undertake procurement operations as per their support price. A co-movement of wholesale and MSP of wheat and rice found in these states apparently sets the trend in markets for prices to wander and stabilize. However, it creates complexity in terms of comprehending price transmission in an empirical model. By comparison, in states like Bihar, Orissa and Kerala, where procurement of cereals is not effective, their prices tend to follow the forces of demand and supply and often fall when the produce reaches the market. Empirical results confirm absence of price convergence in these states. This, in a way indicates that price policy has not been effective in appropriately targeting the geographical locations for regular supply of food and protecting consumers from volatility in prices.

Besides regional bias in the price policy, large diversions in commodity prices could also be attributed to namely (i) concentration of production in a particular region, like wheat in north, (ii) delay in dissemination of information, (iii) transport and infrastructural bottlenecks, (iv) low production and marketable surplus, (v) time lag in their imports, (vi) controls and regulations on private trade under the ECA, 1955, differential tax rates on oil meals, oil cakes and seeds across states, and (vii) partial amendments in the APMC and marketing reforms. A greater magnitude of diversion in oilseed prices might have occurred due to an exceptional increase in its prices during 1998–99. Also, unlike cereals, the MSP for oilseeds though announced every year does not seem to be successful in inducing price stability. The movement of oilseed prices depends entirely on the market situation. Needless to say that these factors may lead to a fragmentation of markets and an extended period of adjustment to a long-run equilibrium path resulting from shocks in prices. This may happen even though prices move in unison in the long run.

Results on price transmission between the world and state-level markets are again mixed and partial. The hypothesis of structural break is rejected for wheat, rice and sugar, which suggests that the economic reforms that began in 1991 were not forceful enough to show up in the empirical tests. Estimates in the pre-reform period show a strong association between world price and state-level price in selected markets of only rice and sugar. This could be explained by imports of these commodities during the eighties. The magnitude of price transmission is found to have improved in the post-reform period for all the selected commodities. It is better for wheat, rice and groundnut seed compared to sugar, cotton and soyabean seed. However, an improvement in market efficiency is identified only in those states which hold a higher share of crop output, which is expected as the major crop producing states can only generate surplus for exports. While the long-run analysis indicates that most of the markets share a common path, in none of these are the coefficients representing the short-run dynamics in close proximity to 1. A slower pace of correction of previous period's disequilibrium in the world and domestic prices indicates that prices have considerably drifted apart and hence were not integrated in the short run.

This result is somewhat similar to the findings of some other studies on price transmission analysed for agricultural commodities in many developing countries. A complete transmission of prices has not yet transpired in many cases due to various factors and policies. Some of the factors that may explain the partial or even lack of integration of India's agricultural markets with world markets could be as follows:

1. In many states, the price of a commodity rules above the world price, implying its lack of competitiveness in international markets. Some of the states may also not be benefiting from free trade due to a low marketable surplus, locational disadvantage, i.e., port/trading centre may not be near the production centre and other regional differences;
2. International commodity prices are subject to large fluctuations due to changing demand and supply conditions along with volatility in the exchange rate;
3. The structure of India's export-import market is such that it is dominated by a few players whose interest seems to lie more in the movement of domestic prices, and, are thus reluctant to import when the situation demands as it would reduce prices and hence their margin in country's market (Chand, Ramesh, *Financial Express*, December 19, 2009). It is also likely that the players/intermediaries may collectively decide to pass on a decrease in the world price to stakeholders in the chain and holdup transmission in case of an increase in price with an aim to gain an additional margin. Quite often, this results in asymmetric price transmission,[1] the evidence of which is well documented for several commodities in many countries (Peltzman, 2000; Meyer and Taubedel, 2004);
4. There is still no settlement on trade policy issues being raised by several developing countries concerning rules on market access, high subsidies and income support given by the developed nations to their farmers/exporters, and identification of subsidies into various boxes, viz., green, blue and amber. Also, external trade policy being followed in a country may not necessarily synchronize with multilateral trading rules adopted at the international level which creates a gap in commodity prices. In India, the trade reforms (delineated in Chapter 3) clearly indicate initiation of commodity-specific measures through reduction of tariffs as per the bound tariff rates and removal of many non-tariff barriers from

1991 in consonance with the WTO provisions. Nonetheless, NTBs were applicable to farm commodities till the year 1998. To date, adhocism in exports, high tariff walls and some of the quantitative restrictions are still in place in trade of several commodities such as wheat, rice, edible oils, and dairy products. Some of these measures though inconsistent with the WTO stipulations are acceptable on grounds of food security, protection from unstable world prices and import surge. Nevertheless, presence of these factors indicates that India does protect her agricultural markets and has partly opened up to external trade;

5. India's internal farm policies may not be fully compliant with the external trade regime, the most notable being price and legislative controls on essential commodities across the states, which are often not in place when goods are traded from a particular state to other countries. A dual pricing structure for commodities may also act as a barrier to full price transmission.

A little more deliberation on the last factor reveals that variations in the wholesale prices of wheat, rice and to some extent of sugar are explained more by their respective support prices than by their corresponding international prices. As elicited above, the co-movement of wholesale and administered prices is pronounced more in those states where parastatals intervene heavily for procurement, which eventually explains a higher degree of market integration among these states. This aspect along with the fact that domestic cereal markets are inflicted with many controls, which are important enough to restrain prices to move mutually across spatial markets and hence indicate weak or no integration with the global markets.

Thus, a higher and an improved integration between world and domestic markets of wheat and rice observed during the nineties and early 2000 is driven more by a policy of support price than by liberal trade policy or multilateral trading rules of the WTO. This point is verified by plotting the wholesale prices of wheat and rice in selected states along with their MSP and world reference prices. As expected, a unidirectional movement of MSP and wholesale price over the period from 1980–81 to 2002–03 is discernible mainly in states such as Punjab, Haryana, Andhra Pradesh and Tamil Nadu where procurement operations are carried out. Further, from 1991–92 to 2002–03, the MSP and international price show similar movements in an upward direction from 1991–92 to 1995–96 for wheat and from 1991–92 to 1994–95 for rice. From the mid-nineties, the world prices of both commodities showed a declining trend till 1999–2000 and then a recovery from 2000–01. In contrast, the MSP of wheat revealed an upward trend and that of rice remained unchanged till the year 1998–99 and then increased from 1999–2000. This indicates that following the reforms, the MSP of wheat and rice rose in accord with their respective world price till the middle of the nineties and so did domestic prices in many states. From the mid-nineties, world cereal prices fell but there was no roll back in MSP and domestic prices tend to follow the latter only.

An empirical verification of this finding is also done through the cointegration exercise by bifurcating monthly price series during the nineties into two time periods. The first period from 1991–92 to 1995–96 commensurate with a rising trend in MSP of both wheat and rice and the second period from 1996–97 to 2002–03 corresponds to an upward trend in MSP of wheat and an unchanged trend in the MSP of rice. The result furnished in Table 4.3 shows rejection of null hypothesis of no cointegration $r \leq 4$ against the alternative hypothesis $r=4$ at 5 per cent level of significance from 1991 to 1996 and then from 2000 to 2003. It confirms the presence of 5 cointegrating vectors among wheat prices of Punjab, Haryana, Karnataka, Rajasthan, Uttar Pradesh and world in these two time periods when the price series showed an increasing trend. No integration is identified between world and domestic prices from 1996 to 2000 when world price declined and domestic prices aligned with higher MSP. In the case of rice, the null hypothesis of $r \leq 3$ against $r=4$ is rejected from 1991 to 1994 and then from 1998 to 2001 thereby affirming a long-run relationship to be present among prices in Andhra Pradesh, Tamil Nadu, Haryana, Uttar Pradesh and world markets. The analysis, thus suggests that following reforms, the price policy has been successful in providing remunerative prices to growers in line with an increase in world price, supporting them in a situation of fall in world prices and achieving price stability. Nonetheless, it seems to have inhibited a free play of the market mechanism in providing signals to producers for good allocation of resources.

Summing up, the findings corroborate an improvement in integration across spatial commodity markets following liberal trade and sector-specific measures. However, the process of price transmission is far from complete and also appears to be asymmetric due to various factors and policies. In the case of wheat and rice, price policy backed by procurement, though it ensures price stability yet it appears to create a gap between the world and domestic prices. For commodities other than cereals, forces of demand and supply operate at large because their guaranteed prices are not backed by procurement. However, the prices of non-food grains tend to be more volatile as compared to those of

TABLE 4.3 *Wheat and Rice: Johansen's Maximum Eigenvalue and Trace Test for the Number of Cointegrating Vectors*

Series in Log	*Null Hypothesis*	*Alternate Hypothesis*	*Eigen Value*	*Likelihood Ratio*	*5 Per cent Critical Value*	*1 Per cent Critical Value*	*Hypothesized No. of CE(s)*	*Lag Interval*
				Wheat Sample: 1991 April to 1996 March				
Punjab	r = 0	r =1	0.589	150.44	94.15	103.18	None **	2
Haryana	r ≤ 1	r =2	0.506	99.72	68.52	76.07	At most 1 **	
Karnataka	r ≤ 2	r =3	0.367	59.45	47.21	54.46	At most 2**	
Rajasthan	r ≤ 3	r =4	0.258	33.30	29.68	35.65	At most 3*	
Uttar Pr.	r ≤ 4	r =5	0.219	16.23	15.41	20.04	At most 4*	
World	r ≤ 5	r =6	0.036	2.09	3.76	6.65	At most 5	
				Sample: 2000 April 2003 March				
Punjab	r = 0	r =1	0.809	157.08	94.15	103.18	None **	2
Haryana	r ≤ 1	r =2	0.689	102.40	68.52	76.07	At most 1 **	
Karnataka	r ≤ 2	r =3	0.544	63.86	47.21	54.46	At most 2 **	
Rajasthan	r ≤ 3	r =4	0.483	37.925	29.68	35.65	At most 3**	
Uttar Pr.	r ≤ 4	r =5	0.344	16.133	15.41	20.04	At most 4*	
World	r ≤ 5	r =6	0.064	2.183	3.76	6.65	At most 5	
				Rice Sample: 1991 October to 1994 September				
Andhra Pr.	r = 0	r =1	0.745	122.96	76.07	84.45	None **	3
Tamil Nadu	r ≤ 1	r =2	0.655	79.12	53.12	60.16	At most 1 **	
Haryana	r ≤ 2	r =3	0.479	44.81	34.91	41.07	At most 2 **	
Uttar Pr.	r ≤ 3	r =4	0.398	23.95	19.96	24.60	At most 3*	
World	r ≤ 4	r =5	0.212	7.66	9.24	12.97	At most 4	
				Sample: 1998 October to 2001 September				
Andhra Pr.	r = 0	r =1	0.648	111.26	76.07	84.45	None **	3
Tamil Nadu	r ≤ 1	r =2	0.572	73.58	53.12	60.16	At most 1 **	
Haryana	r ≤ 2	r =3	0.467	42.98	34.91	41.07	At most 2 **	
Uttar Pr.	r ≤ 3	r =4	0.359	20.28	19.96	24.60	At most 3	

Notes: *(**) denotes rejection of the hypothesis at 5 per cent (1%) significance level. L.R. test indicates 5 cointegrating equation(s) in wheat and 4 in rice at 5 per cent significance level. Test assumption – Linear deterministic trend in data in case of wheat and no deterministic trend in the data in case of rice.

cereals and little effort has been initiated to bring stability in these prices. At the broader level, the relationship between world and domestic prices of agricultural commodities may encounter either of the two situations: First, that of volatility when world prices are at an extreme high and a rising trend in prices is greater than the domestic prices, thus negating perfect convergence. This is because if domestic commodity price is higher than the corresponding support price, then there is some pressure to equate the two so that price fluctuations are not passed on to producers and consumers. Second, when world commodity prices are lower than the domestic prices then integration may not happen on its own, but may come through trade provided high tariffs are not imposed. In both these situations, protectionist policies such as price and trade, even though if these impede full price transmission, are generally followed, particularly for cereals, to ensure price stability and to offset the market power of intermediaries involved in trade.

Note

1. The term 'symmetry' implies if the price response to a variation in another price along the marketing chain is independent from the direction of the change of the latter. In other words, if price transmission is asymmetric then some group may not be benefiting from a price reduction (buyers) or increase (sellers) which, under conditions of symmetry, would have taken place sooner, and have been of a greater magnitude than observed. The presence of asymmetric price transmission is a manifestation of market failure, inefficiency and signals redistribution and net welfare losses.

5

Temporal and Spatial Changes in the Cropping Pattern and Magnitude of Crop Diversification

Cropping pattern changes are the outcome of many interactive factors. These can be grouped into four broad categories, namely: (i) natural factors, which include climatic, rainfall and soil conditions; (ii) technological factors; (iii) policy, institutional and infrastructural factors such as those related to government price support and subsidies, land reforms, tenancy rights, road network, markets and storage; and finally, (iv) price factors that include output and input prices, trade and other economic policies that influence the incentive structure and investment decisions. Recent studies have explained crop area shifts in favour of high-value and processed commodities by rising levels of income, increasing urbanization, changing consumption patterns and liberalization of trade.

The relative importance of each factor differs across the regions and farm groups and depends largely upon how it meets the multiple objectives of farm households in maximizing profit, minimizing risk and meeting the subsistence needs. Another noticeable aspect is that while both price and non-price factors influence changes in cropping pattern, the former along with the government policies that affect agricultural prices are stated to have acquired an increasing role over time in most of the regions. Two factors are explained behind an increasing influence of economic incentives over non-economic factors in crop area shifts. First, many regions have experienced development in irrigation, infrastructure, regulated markets and technological advancement. Second, due to economic reforms and the opening up of domestic markets to international markets, external trade in agriculture may have assumed considerable importance. Essentially, in a market-driven economy, liberal policies through their impact on changes in relative prices in international and domestic markets are presumed to be more influential in directing the crops that are to be grown in accordance with the demand and supply conditions.

Some recent studies that have examined the nature and direction of cropping pattern changes at the all-India level and in states have focused on the temporal pattern and regional variations in the sources of farm growth over different time periods.[1] A few have estimated the magnitude of agricultural diversification, its determinants and the likely response of acreage shift to prices in a free trade regime. Broad findings elicit a gradual change in the cropping pattern and diversification towards production and consumption of high-value crops and processed commodities. This emerging change is both demand and supply driven, mainly owing to rise in income and change in food habits, improvement in technology and infrastructure and implementation of liberal policies. Simulations/forecasts based on econometric models suggest that price factors are likely to play a more dominant role in inducing area shifts and diversification in due course.

An attempt is made in this chapter to examine this aspect by first, analysing the temporal and spatial changes in cropping pattern and the extent of inter-crop diversification at the all-India level and in major states. This is followed by an empirical examination of the acreage response of selected crops to price incentives, which are likely to have occurred following liberal macroeconomic trade and exchange rate policies. The first exercise is dealt with, in the present chapter and the second one is taken up in the chapters that follow.

Nature and Direction of Cropping Pattern Changes at All-India and Major States

Cropping pattern changes are assessed for six principal crops namely paddy/rice, wheat, groundnut seed, rapeseed-mustard, cotton, sugarcane and five crop groups, namely, 'other cereals', 'all cereals', 'all pulses', 'all oilseeds' and 'all principal crops'. These crops occupy more than eighty per cent of total area in almost all the major states of India. In all, 11 agriculturally important states are identified for the analysis and the states other than these are clubbed under 'other states' category. The exercise is based on five years averages of gross cropped area at the all-India level from 1971–72 to 2002–03 and at the state level from 1980–81 to 2002–03. The selected time period is marked by major policies and programmes in the agricultural sector as a result of which, area under various crops is considered to have undergone substantial changes. Crop area shifts during the seventies and early eighties represent the post-green revolution situation when wheat and paddy acreage expanded phenomenally in absolute and relative terms. The expansion was witnessed not only in the northern parts of India but also in the southern and eastern regions. The period from the mid-eighties is characterized by policy changes on oilseed crops under the Technology Mission Programme and hence expansion of area under several oilseeds. Finally, the period starting from the early nineties holds importance in terms of implementation of trade liberalization policies, signing up of the UR AOA and setting up of the WTO and consolidation of the phase of rural infrastructure.

Temporal Shifts in Area Share of Crops/Crop Groups: All-India 1971–72 to 2002–03

Table 5.1 presents the temporal behaviour of crop area shifts at the all-India level in relative terms based on five years averages from 1971–72 to 2002–03. It is evident that for major crops and crop groups, the area share of crops has changed in response to both shifts in area under competing crops/alternative crops as well as to fresh areas brought under cultivation. In both situations, significant changes are observed in the nature and direction of cropping pattern. Data indicate a marginal increase in the area share under paddy/rice as percentage of gross cropped area (GCA) from 22.83 per cent in 1971–75 to 23.26 per cent in 1996–00. However, in absolute numbers, acreage rose from 38.03 million ha to 42.89 million ha over this period. Compared to paddy, substantial increase in area under wheat is also witnessed over this period from 18.94 million ha to 25.6 million ha.

TABLE 5.1 *Area under Crops as Percentage of Gross Cropped Area in India: Five Years Averages during 1971–72 to 2002–03*

Crops/Years	*1971–75*	*1976–80*	*1981–85*	*1986–90*	*1991–95*	*1996–00*	*2001–02*
Paddy/Rice	22.83	23.17	22.91	23.03	22.89	23.26	23.41
Jowar	9.91	9.45	9.31	8.45	6.62	5.49	5.18
Bajra	7.38	6.50	6.37	6.06	5.43	5.13	4.67
Maize	3.50	3.42	3.29	3.27	3.25	3.35	3.45
Ragi	1.47	1.51	1.38	1.27	1.04	0.90	0.84
Wheat	11.37	12.67	13.23	13.15	13.31	14.04	13.97
Barley	1.59	1.13	0.82	0.60	0.48	0.41	0.37
Other Cereals	2.80	2.45	1.83	1.42	0.83	0.80	0.71
Total Cereals (1–8)	60.86	60.38	59.14	57.26	53.85	53.39	52.61

Cont'd...

Cont'd...

Gram	4.56	4.33	4.20	3.74	3.56	3.57	3.30
Tur/Arhar	1.53	1.58	1.75	1.91	1.88	1.84	1.83
Other Pulses	7.74	7.67	7.33	7.24	6.67	6.16	6.60
Total Pulses (1–3)	13.83	13.70	13.28	12.90	12.11	11.57	11.72
Total Foodgrains	74.69	74.08	72.42	70.16	65.96	64.96	64.33
Sugarcane	1.63	1.86	1.78	1.87	2.03	2.18	2.44
Condiments	1.07	1.22	1.24	1.34	1.47	1.51	1.56
Fruits-Vegetables	2.31	2.67	3.05	3.51	3.83	4.12	4.51
Other Food Crops	0.09	0.07	0.07	0.09	0.07	0.09	0.12
Condiments-Fruits -Vegetables (1–3)	3.46	3.96	4.35	4.94	5.38	5.71	6.18
Groundnut	4.30	4.15	4.13	4.39	4.36	3.76	3.32
Castor Seed	0.29	0.26	0.35	0.36	0.39	0.41	0.36
Sesame	1.38	1.39	1.28	1.30	1.16	0.90	0.85
Rape-seed Mustard	2.09	2.08	2.27	2.67	3.41	3.22	2.61
Linseed	1.20	1.09	0.85	0.64	0.49	0.38	0.28
Coconut	0.66	0.62	0.66	0.78	0.89	0.96	1.04
Other Oilseeds	0.85	1.07	1.68	2.64	4.11	4.61	4.56
Total Oilseeds (1–7)	10.77	10.66	11.21	12.77	14.81	14.24	13.01
Cotton	4.76	4.58	4.36	4.00	4.25	4.69	4.58
Jute	0.43	0.49	0.49	0.41	0.41	0.46	0.47
Other Fibres	0.31	0.30	0.24	0.19	0.16	0.15	0.15
Total Fibres (1–3)	5.49	5.36	5.04	4.63	4.88	5.40	5.48
Indigo	0.00	0.00	0.00	0.00	0.00	0.00	0.00
Opium	0.03	0.03	0.02	0.01	0.01	0.01	0.01
Coffee	0.11	0.12	0.15	0.16	0.16	0.17	0.19
Tea	0.22	0.22	0.23	0.24	0.24	0.23	0.28
Tobacco	0.25	0.28	0.26	0.23	0.23	0.22	0.18
Fodder Crops	4.29	4.53	4.58	4.45	4.45	4.72	5.39
Plantation and Fodder Crops (1–6)	4.89	5.18	5.23	5.08	5.09	5.36	6.06
Gross Cropped Area (million Ha)	166.54	17 1.32	17 6.77	17 9.36	18 5.75	18 9.90	18 3.24
All Major Crops/ GCA	99.30	99.24	98.26	97.58	96.12	95.66	95.07

Note: Area under fruits and vegetables and condiments from 1995 to 1998 is taken to be same as in 1994. Data for 2001–02 is two years average. The total adds to 95 per cent in the latest years due to non-availability of data for many crops.

The share of wheat acreage in GCA went up from 11.37 per cent in the early seventies to 13.97 per cent in the early 2000. Also, an initial acceleration in area under wheat-paddy took place only after the adoption of improved technology under the green revolution programme and implementation of agricultural price policy. Notably, both paddy and wheat replaced pulses, oilseeds, other cereals such as barley, sorghum (jowar) and coarse grains. However, cereals as a group gained a marginal increase in area from 101.35 million ha to 104.5 million ha in 1981–85 immediately after the green revolution and then continued to decline thereafter. Its relative share got reduced significantly from 60.86 per cent to almost 52.6 per cent during this time period. This decline is attributable primarily to an absolute fall in area under sorghum, barley and other coarse grains. Similarly, total pulses, which did not lose much area in absolute terms, indicated a relative decline in area share by 3 per cent over time. In all, cereals and pulses groups have lost absolute area marginally but have suffered the most in terms of relative area loss. Approximately 4.4 million ha of area was shifted from cereal to non-cereals crops during the last three decades and the gainers were oilseeds, cotton, sugarcane, plantation crops, fibres and fruits-vegetables.

Fresh area was also brought under cultivation of fibres, fruits and vegetables. The absolute and relative change towards oilseeds became pronounced only from the mid-eighties when the Technology Mission programme on oilseeds and favourable support price system were launched. The share of oilseeds as a group went up from 17.9 million ha to 27.0 million ha and accounted for almost 2 per cent shift. It fell to 23.8 million ha during 2001–03. Within the oilseeds category, groundnut, rapeseed-mustard, castor, sunflower and soyabean showed improvements in their area share during the eighties till the middle of the nineties. The relative share of area under oilseeds as a group increased from 10.8 per cent during the early seventies to 13.01 per cent during 2000. The relative share of groundnut fluctuated with a marginal decline after the middle of the nineties. Area under rapeseed-mustard, sunflower and soyabean increased and that of linseed, groundnut and sesamum either declined or fluctuated.

Along with area gains in oilseeds, area under other commercial crops, viz., plantation crops, cotton, sugarcane and fibres witnessed a remarkable increase in absolute terms. However, their relative share has more or less remained constant during the last three decades. Within this group, only sugarcane, spices-condiments, fruits-vegetables and 'other crops' showed a relative increase in their area shares, whereas cotton and jute experienced a gradual decline, particularly during the early years in the nineties. The area shift towards oilseeds as a group, which was quite remarkable from the mid-eighties till the mid-nineties began to decline gradually towards the end of the last decade and early 2000. Major beneficiaries of this declining relative acreage share of oilseeds have been fruits-vegetables, sugarcane, spices-condiments and other commercial crops. This development indicates an increasing tendency towards crop specialization and commercialization in the nineties, the period marked by globalization and liberalization of agriculture.

Temporal Shifts in Area Share of Crops/Crop Groups across States

Cropping pattern changes at the state level provide a closer look at inter-crop shifts that have occurred at various regional and crop group specific contexts in India. Within a particular region, area allocation to a crop largely depends on the resource endowments such as soil conditions, irrigation, agro-climatic conditions and infrastructural development. As noted already, such crop decisions are also the outcome of government policies on agricultural output and inputs as well as comparative advantage of crops. The crop area shifts at the state level are examined from 1981–82 to 2002–03. The choice of this period is based on the fact that crop diversification in the sixties and the seventies occurred within the cereal group in response to technological factors and support prices in favour of wheat and paddy. It was only during the eighties and the nineties, cropping pattern shifts became more prominent not only within the cereal group but also towards non-cereal and commercial crops. The analysis is based on five years averages of area from 1981–82 to 1985–86, 1986–87 to 1990–91, 1991–92 to 1995–96, 1996–97 to 2000–01 and two years averages from 2001–02 to 2002–03. These time periods are also selected to make a comparative analysis of area shifts to various crops during the pre- and post-liberalization situations. Evaluation is made for the principal crops and crop groups in each of the agriculturally important states in the country. Table 5.2 presents the broad results.

It is evident that in the early eighties, area under *all cereals* crop group captured more than 50 per cent of the GCA in most of the states. In the subsequent period, its share started declining in all the major states except in Haryana, Punjab and Madhya Pradesh. Uttar Pradesh revealed an upward trend in area share of cereals in the early nineties and showed a decline in the latter half of the nineties. This declining relative share of area under cereals in these states is attributed primarily

TABLE 5.2 *Temporal Changes in Area Share of Crops across States: 1981–82 to 2002–03 (Percentage)*

States	*Period*	*Paddy*	*Wheat*	*Other Cereal*	*All Cereals*	*Pulses*	*Groundnut*	*Rape/ Mustard*	*All-Oil seeds*	*Cotton*	*Sugarcane*	*All Major Crops*	*Other Crops*
Andhra	1981–85	29.24	0.13	27.33	56.70	11.15	12.54	–	17.12	4.04	1.30	90.31	9.69
Pradesh	1986–90	30.14	0.09	19.39	49.62	12.02	16.50	–	22.00	4.60	1.38	89.61	10.39
	1991–95	28.57	0.08	13.31	41.96	12.45	18.00	–	25.16	6.63	1.79	87.72	12.26
	1996–00	30.70	0.09	11.55	42.34	12.44	14.73	–	21.16	8.00	2.09	85.58	14.41
	2001–02	27.33	0.10	11.26	38.70	16.18	13.00	–	20.01	7.86	1.63	84.61	15.39
Gujarat	1981–85	5.32	5.89	26.77	37.99	7.44	19.09	1.84	24.32	13.37	1.10	84.16	15.84
	1986–90	5.24	5.09	22.26	32.59	7.30	16.10	2.56	22.36	10.07	1.04	73.39	26.61
	1991–95	5.51	5.24	18.60	29.36	8.31	18.12	3.63	27.47	11.27	1.28	77.69	22.32
	1996–00	5.88	5.06	14.52	25.47	7.41	17.13	2.83	26.21	14.49	1.67	75.26	24.74
	2001–02	5.56	4.39	15.57	25.53	6.90	19.02	1.98	27.28	16.43	1.79	77.97	22.02
Haryana	1981–85	9.65	30.33	19.11	59.10	13.72	0.14	4.43	4.57	6.35	2.31	86.03	13.95
	1986–90	10.73	32.40	15.91	59.04	10.95	0.07	6.79	6.86	7.85	2.45	87.15	12.84
	1991–95	12.76	33.32	12.78	58.86	7.90	0.04	10.06	10.94	9.89	2.31	89.90	10.10
	1996–00	16.18	35.65	11.33	63.17	5.19	0.02	8.18	8.98	9.65	2.26	89.31	10.69
	2001–02	15.68	36.97	11.61	64.27	2.40	0.02	9.25	9.40	9.23	2.69	88.20	11.79
Karnataka	1981–85	10.08	2.76	38.71	51.56	14.04	7.04	0.03	15.38	7.74	1.66	90.38	9.62
	1986–90	9.49	1.93	37.12	48.55	13.93	8.00	0.04	20.27	4.75	1.94	89.40	10.56
	1991–95	11.64	1.83	32.57	45.01	12.85	8.62	0.04	23.49	5.07	2.48	88.89	11.11
	1996–00	11.64	2.12	32.99	46.76	14.69	9.15	0.05	20.93	4.71	2.81	89.99	10.01
	2001–02	11.08	2.19	31.43	44.70	16.49	7.32	0.05	19.34	4.31	3.23	88.25	11.74

Cont'd...

Cont'd...

Maharashtra	1981–85	7.56	5.18	43.64	56.38	13.95	3.74	0.02	10.73	13.45	1.75	96.29	3.71
	1986–90	7.25	3.91	42.18	53.35	15.17	3.85	0.03	11.93	12.74	1.66	94.88	5.12
	1991–95	7.35	3.39	37.90	48.64	15.81	3.00	0.05	10.01	12.93	2.19	89.61	10.39
	1996–00	6.80	3.97	34.61	45.38	15.70	2.39	0.05	7.66	14.34	2.45	85.53	14.46
	2001–02	6.77	3.42	31.62	41.81	15.31	1.89	0.04	5.63	13.17	2.66	78.50	21.50
Madhya Pradesh	1981–85	6.76	15.19	17.05	38.99	10.92	1.22	1.40	7.80	1.91	0.27	59.89	40.11
	1986–90	6.49	15.25	21.08	42.81	10.92	1.19	1.72	12.87	2.10	0.29	69.00	31.00
	1991–95	8.16	20.16	20.12	48.44	14.11	1.23	3.19	25.33	2.68	0.25	90.77	9.22
	1996–00	8.19	21.52	17.04	46.76	13.40	1.14	3.05	29.04	2.53	0.25	91.96	8.04
	2001–02	9.28	18.21	18.35	45.86	13.56	1.09	2.35	28.76	2.95	0.25	91.38	8.61
Punjab	1981–85	21.24	43.70	5.91	70.85	3.30	0.90	1.63	2.74	8.83	1.27	86.99	13.01
	1986–90	25.02	43.42	3.93	72.37	2.27	0.33	1.46	2.09	9.18	1.37	87.28	12.72
	1991–95	28.29	42.97	2.98	74.18	1.40	0.13	1.14	2.49	8.59	1.39	88.05	11.95
	1996–00	30.74	41.93	2.67	75.38	0.98	0.08	0.86	1.99	7.43	1.52	87.45	12.55
	2001–02	31.82	43.09	2.35	77.27	0.68	0.06	0.74	1.21	6.69	1.81	87.74	12.26
Rajasthan	1981–85	0.79	10.40	38.50	49.69	19.92	1.12	4.35	8.56	2.04	0.18	80.39	19.60
	1986–90	0.67	9.88	40.33	50.92	16.73	1.35	7.56	12.06	2.17	0.12	82.05	17.99
	1991–95	0.74	10.83	33.35	44.90	17.19	1.27	12.12	17.76	2.62	0.13	82.60	17.39
	1996–00	0.79	12.51	30.14	43.47	17.14	1.34	12.04	17.80	2.95	0.10	81.46	18.54
	2001–02	0.58	10.07	27.62	38.25	14.35	1.19	8.07	13.48	2.21	0.07	68.33	31.66
Tamil Nadu	1981–85	34.55	–	21.71	56.25	9.51	13.02	–	17.37	3.30	2.69	89.05	10.95
	1986–90	29.17	–	19.69	48.85	12.10	14.90	–	20.60	3.65	3.22	88.43	11.57
	1991–95	31.27	–	14.18	45.45	10.13	15.83	–	21.83	3.68	3.93	85.01	14.98

Cont'd...

Cont'd...

	1996–00	33.40	–	13.38	47.08	10.27	12.57	–	19.61	3.22	4.51	84.74	15.26
	2001–02	28.78	–	12.59	43.92	10.78	10.2	–	18.62	2.10	4.63	80.51	19.49
Uttar Pradesh	1981–85	20.42	31.58	15.22	67.22	7.94	0.87	1.92	2.15	0.12	6.39	83.81	16.18
	1986–90	20.16	32.50	15.79	68.45	7.34	0.53	2.20	3.38	0.08	6.76	86.01	13.98
	1991–95	21.36	34.96	16.49	72.80	6.38	0.53	3.13	4.68	0.05	7.27	91.19	8.80
	1996–00	21.56	36.09	16.02	74.65	5.28	0.51	3.05	4.62	0.03	7.39	92.32	7.70
	2001–02	19.35	36.21	13.60	70.52	4.81	0.39	2.21	3.17	0.02	7.24	86.81	13.19
West Bengal	1981–85	68.03	3.83	1.46	73.32	5.26	0.07	2.64	4.17	–	0.27	83.03	16.96
	1986–90	65.57	3.97	2.06	71.59	3.99	0.21	4.27	5.93	–	0.16	81.67	18.32
	1991–95	66.76	3.43	0.84	70.84	2.88	0.26	4.34	6.11	–	0.16	80.01	19.99
	1996–00	63.20	4.06	0.57	67.76	2.70	0.34	3.84	5.70	–	0.26	76.43	23.57
	2001–02	64.11	4.35	0.52	66.62	2.56	0.35	4.40	6.15	–	0.22	75.56	24.44
Other States	1981–85	58.71	10.78	11.73	81.44	23.06	1.62	5.90	18.16	0.52	0.70	96.00	4.00
	1986–90	60.82	10.91	4.54	74.24	22.74	2.21	4.63	15.23	0.31	0.84	92.00	8.00 4
	1991–95	46.46	8.89	2.11	58.53	16.20	1.14	3.09	11.08	0.01	0.73	86.54	13.45
	1996–00	52.11	9.00	1.28	58.41	14.92	0.61	2.79	11.24	0.15	0.69	85.51	14.48
	2001–02	59.81	10.27	0.20	64.47	17.34	0.33	2.62	11.70	0.22	1.17	94.59	5.40
All-India	1981–85	22.91	13.23	23.00	59.14	13.28	4.13	2.27	11.21	4.36	1.78	89.77	10.23
	1986–90	23.02	13.15	21.06	57.22	12.89	4.39	2.67	12.77	4.00	1.87	88.80	11.19
	1991–95	22.86	13.31	17.63	53.85	12.11	4.36	3.40	14.81	4.24	2.03	87.05	12.96
	1996–00	23.24	14.04	16.09	53.38	11.56	3.76	3.22	14.24	4.70	2.18	86.07	13.92
	2001–02	22.70	13.97	15.23	52.62	11.72	3.22	2.61	13.01	4.58	2.34	84.37	15.63

Note: Figures are percentages of gross cropped area in each of the states.

to a dramatic fall in the cultivation of coarse grains and other cereal crops. The relative area shares of rice and wheat have remained constant at around 23 and 13 per cent of GCA at the all-India level. A similar pattern is observed at the regional level too. Acreage under paddy/rice has shown an upward trend in all states except Maharashtra, West Bengal and 'other states'. Similarly, wheat shows a decline in the relative area only in Gujarat, Punjab and 'other states'. In some states like Maharashtra, the relative share of area under wheat declined from 5.18 per cent in 1981–85 to 3.39 per cent in 1991–95 and rose to 3.97 per cent in the subsequent period.

Overall, wheat and paddy/rice together continue to occupy a prime share in GCA in each of the major crop producing states in India. The case of *pulses* is similar to 'other cereals' group that shows a declining trend in the area share in most of the states over time. Pulses accounted for 10–19 per cent of total area in many states in the early eighties, which fell by 3–5 percentage points by the year 2000. Significant reductions in area are found in all the Northern states, Rajasthan, West Bengal and other states category. In contrast, significant increases in acreage share of pulses have occurred in Maharashtra, Karnataka, Madhya Pradesh and Andhra Pradesh.

All Oilseeds group gained substantial increase in area since the middle of the eighties. The area share has increased significantly in Andhra Pradesh, Gujarat, Madhya Pradesh, Rajasthan and Tamil Nadu. In many states, viz., Haryana, Karnataka, Punjab and Uttar Pradesh, area under oilseeds increased after 1986 till the middle of the nineties and fell in the subsequent period, i.e., from 1996 onwards. Notably, in most of these states, area under cereals has also fallen – that indicates area expansion under oilseeds has taken place at the expense of cereals other than wheat and paddy and all pulses group. One may note that not all the decline in area under cereals is replaced by oilseeds; there are other crops that have also gained an increasing area share in GCA. Of all the oilseeds, groundnut has captured a relatively higher share than other seeds. The concentration of this crop is largely in Andhra Pradesh, Gujarat, Karnataka and Tamil Nadu. With only exception of Karnataka that shows an increase in the relative area share of groundnut over time, other states revealed a declining trend in it from 1996 onwards. Scenario is the same for rapeseed-mustard in Gujarat, Haryana, Madhya Pradesh, Rajasthan, West Bengal and Uttar Pradesh. Only exception is Punjab that shows a continuous decline in the area share of rapeseed-mustard over time. Overall, a slight decline in the area share of oilseeds is witnessed during 1996–2000 compared to earlier time period, which has picked up during 2001–03.

Cotton is another commercial crop that appears to have gained area in all the states over time, both in absolute and relative terms. Only in Punjab, Tamil Nadu, Uttar Pradesh and Karnataka did relative share of cotton in total cropped area decline. Punjab and Karnataka gained acreage in oilseeds and paddy. Amongst all the states, substantial area gains in cotton have occurred in Andhra Pradesh and Haryana from an initial 4.04 per cent and 6.35 per cent in 1981–85 to 7.86 per cent and 9.2 per cent in the early 2000. Like cotton, *sugarcane* also appears to have gained significantly both in absolute and relative terms. Sugarcane occupies only two per cent of GCA in India and an upward trend in its share is visible only in the nineties compared to that in the eighties. The increase has been concentrated more in Andhra Pradesh, Karnataka, Maharashtra, Tamil Nadu, Gujarat and Uttar Pradesh. In contrast, Madhya Pradesh and Rajasthan, which hardly dominate in sugarcane production witnessed a decline in its relative area. Notably, in a majority of states, an increasing area share of commercial crops, viz., cotton and sugarcane has taken place at the expense of cereals. In some states, fresh area has also been brought under cultivation of these crops.

For all the *principal crops* together that include cereals, pulses, oilseeds, cotton and sugarcane occupying more than eighty per cent of the total area in all the major states, one may observe a downward trend in their area share till the mid-nineties and an increasing trend thereafter in many states. Four states, viz., Haryana, Madhya Pradesh, Punjab, and Uttar Pradesh witnessed an increasing share of principal crops during the last two decades, which is primarily attributable to wheat, paddy and oilseeds. Of the entire principal crops group, cereals suffered the most in relative area loss mainly due to a decline in the share of coarse cereals and pulses. As a result, oilseeds, cotton and sugarcane gained advantage. In many states, the relative area share of principal crops suffered a loss particularly in coarse cereals growing states. It indicates a changing preference for new crops in the recent years. Andhra Pradesh, Gujarat, Karnataka, Maharashtra, West Bengal and 'other states' appear to be taking lead in putting more area under crops other than coarse cereals, pulses and oilseeds. There seems to be reversal in the trend from the latter half of the nineties. While pulses have gained area share in Andhra Pradesh, Karnataka and Maharashtra, coarse cereals are picking up in Madhya

Pradesh. It appears that almost all the major states as well as 'other states' have shown an increasing tendency towards crop diversification, specialization and commercialization in the nineties over the eighties.

Spatial Shifts in Area Share of Crops/Crop Groups: 1980–81 to 2002–03

Like significant cropping pattern changes that have taken place in each of the agriculturally dominant states over time, an analysis of locational shifts in area share of crops too reveals interesting results. As in the case of crop area share in each state, the analysis of area share of states in all-India area is presented for major crops and crop groups based on five years averages from 1981–82 to 1999–00 and average of two years – 2001–02 and 2002–03 in Table 5.3. The analysis of area share of each state in a particular crop reflects concentration of a crop in a particular region. For instance, area under cereals is comparatively more in the northern and southern states than in the eastern and western states. Similarly, area under oilseeds is concentrated largely in the southern and western states, viz., Andhra Pradesh, Madhya Pradesh, Karnataka, Gujarat and Rajasthan. Same is the case with sugarcane that is concentrated mainly in Uttar Pradesh and Maharashtra.

A detailed analysis of area share of states in major crops indicates a negligible change in the relative share of paddy, wheat, pulses and sugarcane grown in different states and a substantial shift in area under other cereals, oilseeds and cotton across the states. Relative area under paddy is gradually shifting from Maharashtra, Tamil Nadu and other states to Andhra Pradesh, Punjab, Haryana and Uttar Pradesh. Relative area share of wheat has marginally declined in Gujarat, Punjab and Uttar Pradesh and has increased in Haryana, Karnataka, Maharashtra, Rajasthan and Madhya Pradesh over the last twenty-two years. These states have also shifted area to coarse cereals, which used to be dominant in Andhra Pradesh and Gujarat during the eighties. As far as locational shift of crop group 'all cereals' is concerned, it is apparent that the cultivated area is shifting from Andhra Pradesh, Gujarat and Maharashtra to Haryana, Madhya Pradesh, Uttar Pradesh and West Bengal.

In the case of oilseeds, nine oilseeds are grown in different parts of India and the concentration is mostly in the southern states and in two western states, viz., Rajasthan and Gujarat. For all oilseeds crop group, Andhra Pradesh, Gujarat, Karnataka, Maharashtra, Punjab and other states have lost their share of area to Haryana, Madhya Pradesh, Gujarat

TABLE 5.3 Temporal Changes in the Crop Area Share of States at All-India: 1981–82 to 2002–03 (Percentage)

Crops	*Period*	*AP*	*GJ*	*HR*	*KAR*	*MH*	*MP*	*PB*	*RJ*	*TN*	*UP*	*WB*	*OTH*	*India*
Paddy/Rice	1981–85	9.17	1.43	1.33	2.82	3.74	3.74	3.67	0.36	5.77	12.57	12.70	42.70	100
	1986–90	9.26	1.33	1.45	2.74	3.64	3.58	4.46	0.30	4.68	12.27	13.33	42.96	100
	1991–95	8.66	1.39	1.75	3.06	3.65	3.60	5.07	0.34	5.07	12.22	13.65	41.54	100
	1996–00	9.14	1.44	2.25	3.20	3.38	3.67	5.51	0.38	4.96	12.64	13.22	40.21	100
	2001–02	7.75	1.33	2.26	3.00	3.54	4.03	5.85	0.27	4.17	12.23	13.88	41.70	100
Wheat	1981–85	0.07	2.74	7.25	1.34	4.45	14.55	13.08	8.11	–	33.66	1.24	13.52	100
	1986–90	0.05	2.27	7.67	0.98	3.44	14.73	13.56	7.30	–	34.63	1.41	13.96	100
	1991–95	0.04	2.27	7.86	0.91	2.89	15.27	13.25	8.54	–	34.40	1.21	13.36	100
	1996–00	0.05	2.06	8.21	0.97	3.27	15.95	12.45	9.66	–	33.51	1.41	12.46	100
	2001–02	0.05	1.77	8.92	0.99	3.00	13.25	13.27	7.98	–	35.84	1.64	13.29	100
Other Cereals	1981–85	8.54	7.15	2.63	10.79	21.53	9.40	1.02	17.27	3.61	9.33	0.27	8.46	100
	1986–90	6.51	6.17	2.35	11.74	23.13	12.71	0.77	18.58	3.45	10.50	0.46	3.63	100
	1991–95	5.23	6.07	2.28	12.16	24.40	11.49	0.68	19.85	2.98	12.23	0.22	2.39	100
	1996–00	4.97	5.15	2.28	13.12	24.89	11.02	0.70	20.31	2.85	12.99	0.17	1.55	100
	2001–02	4.91	5.75	2.57	13.07	25.37	12.24	0.66	20.09	2.57	12.35	0.18	0.24	100
All Cereals	1981–85	6.89	3.95	3.16	5.59	10.82	8.36	4.74	8.67	3.64	16.03	5.31	22.86	100
	1986–90	6.13	3.33	3.21	5.65	10.77	9.50	5.19	8.63	3.15	16.76	5.85	21.82	100
	1991–95	5.41	3.14	3.43	5.51	10.27	9.07	5.66	8.76	3.13	17.71	6.17	21.74	100
	1996–00	5.49	2.72	3.82	5.60	9.83	9.11	5.89	8.83	3.02	18.24	6.18	21.27	100
	2001–02	4.88	2.73	4.12	5.38	9.72	8.85	6.32	8.05	2.60	18.53	6.67	22.15	100
Pulses	1981–85	6.03	3.44	3.27	6.78	11.91	10.42	0.98	15.48	2.73	8.43	1.70	28.83	100
	1986–90	6.59	3.31	2.65	7.20	13.61	10.75	0.72	12.59	3.47	7.98	1.45	29.67	100

Cont'd...

Cont'd...

	1991–95	7.14	3.95	2.05	6.99	14.85	11.75	0.47	14.91	3.11	6.90	1.12	26.76	100
	1996–00	7.44	3.65	1.45	8.12	15.69	12.05	0.35	16.06	3.04	5.95	1.14	25.05	100
	2001–02	9.16	3.31	0.69	8.91	15.96	11.75	0.25	13.56	2.86	5.67	1.15	26.74	100
Groundnut Seed	1981–85	21.83	28.41	0.10	10.94	10.28	3.73	0.87	2.81	12.06	2.92	0.07	5.98	100
	1986–90	26.59	21.44	0.05	12.13	10.13	3.43	0.31	2.98	12.54	1.69	0.23	8.48	100
	1991–95	28.63	23.92	0.03	13.01	7.82	2.84	0.13	3.06	13.47	1.58	0.28	5.24	100
	1996–00	27.14	25.99	0.02	15.57	7.36	3.14	0.09	3.86	11.45	1.77	0.44	3.17	100
	2001–02	25.96	32.17	0.02	13.95	6.96	3.35	0.08	3.98	9.57	1.61	0.56	1.79	100
Rapeseed Mustard	1981–85	0.00	4.98	6.17	0.07	0.12	5.98	2.85	19.77	–	11.93	4.98	43.15	100
	1986–90	0.00	5.61	7.93	0.10	0.12	8.18	2.25	27.53	–	11.54	7.50	29.24	100
	1991–95	0.00	6.13	9.28	0.09	0.15	9.45	1.38	37.36	–	12.05	5.98	18.14	100
	1996–00	0.00	5.01	8.20	0.11	0.18	9.85	1.13	40.51	–	12.36	5.79	16.85	100
	2001–02	0.00	4.27	11.96	0.12	0.21	9.16	1.21	34.32	–	11.72	8.88	18.15	100
All Oilseeds	1981–85	10.97	13.32	1.29	8.79	10.86	8.82	0.97	7.88	5.92	2.71	1.59	26.88	100
	1986–90	12.18	10.23	1.67	10.57	10.79	12.80	0.67	9.17	5.96	3.71	2.17	20.06	100
	1991–95	11.79	10.68	2.32	10.45	7.68	17.25	0.69	12.60	5.47	4.14	1.94	14.97	100
	1996–00	10.28	10.49	2.04	9.40	6.22	21.21	0.58	13.55	4.71	4.23	1.95	15.34	100
	2001–02	10.20	11.78	2.43	9.41	5.29	22.45	0.40	11.48	4.46	3.37	2.49	16.25	100
Cotton	1981–85	6.66	18.82	4.59	11.37	34.97	5.56	8.01	4.82	2.84	0.38	–	1.99	100
	1986–90	8.13	14.72	6.11	7.91	36.80	6.70	9.42	5.29	3.37	0.27	–	1.30	100
	1991–95	10.51	15.29	7.32	7.86	34.62	6.27	8.31	6.50	3.22	0.15	–	–0.05	100
	1996–00	11.81	17.61	6.65	6.50	35.34	5.57	6.67	6.81	2.35	0.09	–	0.61	100
	2001–02	11.38	20.15	6.83	5.96	35.12	6.56	6.29	5.33	1.43	0.06	–	0.90	100

Cont'd...

Cont'd...

Sugarcane	1981–85	5.27	3.60	4.11	6.01	11.40	1.92	2.83	1.06	5.79	50.74	0.64	6.61	100
	1986–90	5.19	3.30	4.06	6.90	10.32	1.98	3.00	0.66	6.35	50.57	0.40	7.27	100
	1991–95	5.93	3.63	3.57	8.04	12.27	1.24	2.81	0.67	7.20	46.93	0.37	7.33	100
	1996–00	5.22	4.37	3.43	8.30	12.99	1.13	3.05	0.51	7.14	46.14	0.59	7.13	100
	2001–02	5.05	4.24	3.93	8.84	12.89	1.04	3.33	0.21	6.52	47.05	0.48	6.41	100
All Major Crops	1981–85	7.23	5.76	3.03	6.45	12.17	8.46	3.84	9.24	3.79	13.17	3.96	22.91	100
	1986–90	7.14	4.83	3.06	6.71	12.35	9.87	4.04	8.97	3.68	13.58	4.31	21.48	100
	1991–95	7.00	5.14	3.24	6.73	11.70	10.51	4.15	9.97	3.63	13.72	4.31	19.89	100
	1996–00	6.88	4.99	3.35	6.69	11.49	11.11	4.24	10.26	3.37	13.98	4.32	19.31	100
	2001–02	6.65	5.19	3.52	6.62	11.37	11.00	4.47	8.97	2.97	14.23	4.71	20.27	100

Notes: Figures are averages of five years from 1981–2000 and subsequently averages of two years from 2001–03.
Figures are percentages of gross cropped area under a crop in India.

Madhya Pradesh and Rajasthan. However, at the disaggregate crop level, Andhra Pradesh, Gujarat, Madhya Pradesh and Karnataka's share of groundnut area has increased over time and that of Haryana and West Bengal has increased in rapeseed-mustard. This indicates that within the oilseed group, substantial area shifts have taken place over time with the result that some states show concentration of castor, sesame and sunflower and others concentrate on groundnut, rapeseed-mustard and other oilseeds. For two selected oilseeds in this study, viz., groundnut and rapeseed-mustard, one may note that Andhra Pradesh and Gujarat dominate in groundnut cultivation with almost 26 and 32 per cent of area share under this crop. Rajasthan, Uttar Pradesh and Haryana hold prime position in cultivation of rapeseed-mustard with 34, 11.9 and 12 per cent of area share at all-India. During the last two decades, while the share of Rajasthan in rapeseed-mustard area has increased from 19.7 per cent to 34.3 per cent, the same for other states declined from 43.15 per cent to 18.15 per cent.

For other commercial crops, i.e., cotton, the analysis reveals area share of Andhra Pradesh, Gujarat Maharashtra and Rajasthan is increasing at the cost of decline in area in Karnataka, Punjab and Tamil Nadu. Similarly, in the case of sugarcane, the rise in the area share of Andhra Pradesh, Karnataka, Maharashtra and Tamil Nadu is taking place at the cost of decline in area share of leading sugarcane cultivation state, viz., Uttar Pradesh. Over a period of last two decades, the area share of 'all major crops' is declining in Andhra Pradesh, Gujarat, Tamil Nadu, and 'other states', increasing in Haryana, Madhya Pradesh, Punjab, Uttar Pradesh and West Bengal and fluctuating in Karnataka and Maharashtra respectively.

In short, the above analysis indicates the post-reform period to be marked by a changing preference of crops from cereals to non-cereals, and a locational shift of major crops with relatively high concentration in states located in the southern and western regions. These changes can lead to either crop diversification or specialization and may also accelerate output and alter the sources of growth.

Magnitude of Inter-Crop Diversification: All-India and States

The pattern of crop diversification and/or specialization can be studied by constructing a diversification index such as the Entropy, Ogive and Hirchman-Herfindahl index. In this study, the entropy index as given in Theil (1971) is used. It is defined as:

$$\text{Entropy Index (EI)} = \sum_{i=1}^{N}(P_i)[\text{Log}(1/P_i)]$$

where P_i is the area share or proportion of crop i in GCA and N is the number of crops that are analysed. EI is the weighted sum of proportions where weight is $\log(1/P_i)$. It varies inversely with proportions. The index varies between 0 and log (N) and a value of 0 imply a state of complete specialization and log (N) indicates a condition of perfect diversification.

The pattern of crop diversification at the all-India level is estimated for major crop groups from 1971–72 to 2002–03 based on five year averages and is presented in Table 5.4. It is clear that the overall index of 'all major crops' category has risen, suggesting an increase in crop diversification at the national level. A categorization of crops into different groups indicates an increase in specialization in cereals, sugarcane-fruits-vegetables and plantation-fodder crops groups. The index for cereals has declined from 1.72 to 1.49, which implies that cereals as a group have achieved specialization over the years. An increased specialization in cereals is primarily attributable to yield enhancing green revolution technologies adopted during 1966–67 and government price policy aiming at increase in the food production. Within cereals, an increasing share of wheat and rice and a declining share of coarse cereals indicate specialization that is credited only to wheat and rice. This also suggests an increase in the supply of wheat and paddy and a reduction in the supply of coarse cereals, which is possible because an increase in income is accompanied by a fall in the demand for coarse grains.

TABLE 5.4 *Crop Diversification by Major Crop Groups in India: 1971–72 to 2002–03*

Crops/Years	*1971 -75*	*1976 -80*	*1981 -85*	*1986 -90*	*1991 -95*	*1996 -00*	*2001 -02*
1. Cereals	1.72	1.69	1.65	1.61	1.55	1.52	1.49
2. Pulses	0.93	0.94	0.96	0.97	0.98	0.99	0.97
3. Sugarcane-Fruits-Vegetables and Other Food Crops	1.08	1.05	1.04	1.04	1.02	1.02	1.02
4. Oilseeds	1.66	1.67	1.69	1.67	1.63	1.61	1.60
5. Fibres	0.48	0.52	0.49	0.47	0.44	0.43	0.46
6. Plantation-Fodder Crops	0.52	0.52	0.52	0.52	0.52	0.50	0.48
7. All Major Crops (1–6)	1.24	1.25	1.27	1.29	1.34	1.36	1.38
8. Foodgrains (1–2)	0.47	0.47	0.48	0.48	0.48	0.47	0.48
9. Non-Foodgrains (3–6)	1.29	1.31	1.30	1.28	1.25	1.28	1.31

Specialization in sugarcane-fruits-vegetables group is evident from the early nineties, as area under these crops has increased significantly during the last decade. Compared to these crop groups, pulses have witnessed an increased diversification over the years due to rise in the area share of arhar and other pulses and fall in the area share of traditional ones like gram. Like pulses, oilseeds as a group have also witnessed diversification till the end of eighties and then specialization from 1991 onwards. This can be explained by the rising area share of soyabean, sunflower and other new categories of oilseeds along with traditional groundnut and rapeseed mustard oilseeds. Fibres that include cotton and jute also reveal an increase in diversification till the mid-eighties followed by an increase in specialization from mid-eighties and then diversification in the early 2000.

The state-level diversification index is constructed from 1981–82 to 2002–03 based on five years averages across major crop categories, viz., cereals, oilseeds, commercial crops, all major crops, foodgrains and non-foodgrains. Table 5.5 shows that within the *all major crops* category, the trend in most of the states has been towards diversification, except in Punjab, Haryana, Uttar Pradesh, and West Bengal. These are wheat-paddy dominant states and specialization is expected in these over the years due to adoption of yield enhancing technologies and increase in demand for cereals. As expected, diversification across various crop categories indicates a different pattern. Within the *cereal group*, a declining EI is observed in three major paddy cultivating states in the north and in Andhra Pradesh and Tamil Nadu. Another rice dominant state, i.e., West Bengal exhibits a mixed picture with an increase in the value of EI (i.e., increase in diversification) from the mid-nineties. In states other than these, diversification has been witnessed in cereals, which is expected due to cultivation of different crops.

In the case of *oilseeds*, almost all the states have experienced specialization as indicated by a falling value of EI. In some of the states like Gujarat and West Bengal, an increase in diversification in the eighties is followed by specialization in the late nineties. This could be due to rise in the area under oilseeds other than groundnut. Commercial crop group that includes area under sugarcane and cotton provides a mixed picture. Only three states, viz., Andhra Pradesh, Rajasthan and Uttar Pradesh show specialization during the last two decades while others reveal diversification. This could probably be due to a falling trend in area under cotton in most of the states in this period. Pulses show specialization only in two states, viz., Gujarat and Madhya Pradesh. The value of EI in the foodgrain category (cereal and pulses) has fallen in some of the states, viz., Haryana, Punjab, Uttar Pradesh, 'other states' and West Bengal. It has increased in almost all other states, which implies a trend towards diversification over the years. As mentioned above, *pulses* as a group has witnessed an increase in area towards arhar and other pulses during the last decade. An increased diversification is also witnessed in almost all the states in the non-foodgrain category mainly on account of cotton and to some extent due to change in area under oilseeds.

TABLE 5.5 *Crop Diversification by Major Crop Groups in the States: 1981–82 to 2002–03*

States/ Crop Groups	*Period*	*Cereals*	*Pulses*	*Oilseeds*	*Commercial Crops*	*All Major Crops*	*Food-grains*	*Non-foodgrains*
Andhra Pradesh	1981–85	0.708	0.623	0.228	0.555	1.033	0.447	0.549
	1986–90	0.681	0.679	0.216	0.540	1.122	0.493	0.519
	1991–95	0.638	0.714	0.240	0.517	1.209	0.538	0.557
	1996–00	0.601	0.841	0.252	0.457	1.220	0.536	0.622
	2001–02	0.621	0.934	0.280	0.487	1.264	0.606	0.632
Gujarat	1981–85	0.811	0.999	0.385	0.259	1.234	0.446	0.660
	1986–90	0.845	0.986	0.484	0.314	1.238	0.476	0.636
	1991–95	0.911	0.974	0.542	0.330	1.269	0.528	0.622
	1996–00	0.980	0.982	0.519	0.333	1.293	0.534	0.665
	2001–02	0.939	0.907	0.442	0.326	1.288	0.519	0.673
Haryana	1981–85	1.003	0.285	0.134	0.580	0.938	0.484	0.644
	1986–90	0.993	0.501	0.128	0.548	0.984	0.434	0.678
	1991–95	0.985	0.611	0.122	0.491	1.020	0.364	0.693
	1996–00	0.980	0.629	0.103	0.490	0.911	0.269	0.683
	2001–02	0.971	0.853	0.036	0.538	0.840	0.155	0.686
Karnataka	1981–85	0.691	0.865	0.358	0.467	1.136	0.519	0.673
	1986–90	0.659	0.940	0.378	0.602	1.150	0.531	0.566
	1991–95	0.717	0.985	0.380	0.633	1.184	0.530	0.559
	1996–00	0.722	1.006	0.367	0.661	1.168	0.544	0.597
	2001–02	0.677	1.047	0.376	0.689	1.136	0.549	0.626
Maharashtra	1981–85	0.687	0.976	0.381	0.361	1.129	0.498	0.678
	1986–90	0.649	1.009	0.377	0.359	1.168	0.529	0.690
	1991–95	0.666	1.023	0.366	0.416	1.204	0.557	0.688
	1996–00	0.704	1.055	0.344	0.416	1.232	0.570	0.680
	2001–02	0.677	1.053	0.325	0.455	1.211	0.565	0.677

Cont'd...

Cont'd...

Madhya Pradesh	1981–85	1.033	0.482	0.513	0.319	1.039	0.525	0.508
	1986–90	1.003	0.470	0.479	0.341	1.042	0.505	0.438
	1991–95	1.030	0.392	0.407	0.291	1.094	0.534	0.321
	1996–00	1.032	0.367	0.363	0.301	1.097	0.530	0.293
	2001–02	1.045	0.354	0.328	0.281	1.115	0.537	0.347
Punjab	1981–85	0.866	0.940	0.674	0.378	0.650	0.182	0.518
	1986–90	0.832	0.998	0.566	0.386	0.603	0.136	0.471
	1991–95	0.811	0.862	0.512	0.403	0.567	0.092	0.523
	1996–00	0.811	0.773	0.492	0.456	0.499	0.068	0.471
	2001–02	0.805	0.817	0.449	0.531	0.431	0.050	0.382
Rajasthan	1981–85	0.591	0.734	0.611	0.284	0.984	0.599	0.502
	1986–90	0.562	0.726	0.550	0.213	1.012	0.559	0.424
	1991–95	0.632	0.713	0.457	0.189	1.104	0.590	0.389
	1996–00	0.687	0.735	0.466	0.153	1.121	0.596	0.410
	2001–02	0.614	0.595	0.516	0.170	1.034	0.562	0.354
Tamil Nadu	1981–85	0.667	0.451	0.187	0.688	1.023	0.413	0.580
	1986–90	0.674	0.460	0.160	0.692	1.126	0.498	0.586
	1991–95	0.621	0.471	0.139	0.693	1.143	0.475	0.602
	1996–00	0.595	0.399	0.295	0.683	1.136	0.470	0.619
	2001–02	0.618	0.355	0.158	0.640	1.110	0.475	0.658
Uttar Pradesh	1981–85	1.053	0.573	0.520	0.090	0.878	0.337	0.664
	1986–90	1.052	0.579	0.507	0.061	0.808	0.318	0.693
	1991–95	1.048	0.633	0.450	0.039	0.771	0.280	0.693
	1996–00	1.044	0.640	0.461	0.028	0.735	0.243	0.689
	2001–02	1.026	0.608	0.440	0.023	0.704	0.237	0.665
West Bengal	1981–85	0.302	0.651	0.392	–	0.472	0.246	0.206
	1986–90	0.343	0.482	0.359	–	0.467	0.207	0.120
	1991–95	0.257	0.404	0.376	–	0.436	0.165	0.120
	1996–00	0.275	0.466	0.432	–	0.436	0.163	0.181
	2001–02	0.346	0.570	0.397	–	0.439	0.157	0.145
Other States	1981–85	0.781	0.395	0.728	0.361	0.737	0.528	0.382
	1986–90	0.636	0.397	0.731	0.288	0.782	0.545	0.375
	1991–95	0.584	0.419	0.710	0.349	0.737	0.523	0.482
	1996–00	0.503	0.390	0.671	0.515	0.706	0.507	0.512
	2001–02	0.736	0.467	0.533	0.436	0.716	0.496	0.543

Notes: Foodgrain includes cereals and pulses; Non-foodgrain includes oilseeds and commercial crops; Commercial crops include sugarcane and cotton.

Summing up and Implications of Crop Diversification/Specialization

A temporal and spatial analysis of cropping pattern reveals shifts in favour of high yielding crops, viz., wheat, paddy, oilseeds, cotton and sugarcane up to the eighties and towards paddy, sugarcane, fruits-vegetables, fibres, plantations, condiments and spices during the nineties and early 2000. While acreage under wheat and paddy has expanded solely at the cost of coarse cereals and pulses, commercial crops have benefited both from area shifts and fresh land brought under cultivation. A considerable change in the structure and composition of oilseeds is also observed at the national level. As a result, traditional oilseeds, notably groundnut, rapeseed-mustard, castor and coconut have been losing out their area share to new ones, viz., soyabean, safflower and sunflower. Another significant aspect in case of oilseeds is that an initial spurt in their acreage, in both absolute and relative terms has subsided over the period. The state-level picture provides mixed results. While a dominance of wheat-paddy in GCA is visible in all the states, cultivation of commercial crops has become more prominent in the western, central and southern parts than in the northern states. Further, slight locational shifts have also been identified during the nineties in the case of paddy to almost all the states, in the case of cotton from Punjab, Karnataka and Tamil Nadu to Andhra Pradesh, Gujarat, Maharashtra and Rajasthan and in case of sugarcane from Uttar Pradesh to Karnataka, Andhra Pradesh, Tamil Nadu and Maharashtra.

Consequent upon these trends, there has been an increased level of specialization towards cereals, sugarcane, fruits-vegetables, plantation and fodder crops and diversification within pulses and fibres over time. Oilseeds indicate an increasing trend towards diversification till the end of eighties and specialization during the nineties and early 2000. This could be explained by changes in the area and composition of oilseeds during the nineties, the period marked by globalization and liberalization of agriculture. Non-foodgrains as a whole have witnessed diversification from the mid-nineties. Across the states, Punjab, Haryana, Uttar Pradesh and West Bengal reveal an increasing specialization in foodgrains, oilseeds and 'all major crops' categories. In contrast, states other than these, which are expanding acreage under wheat, paddy, cotton, pulses, sugarcane and other commercial crops evince diversification. Three states, viz., Maharashtra, Punjab, Rajasthan and Uttar Pradesh have witnessed diversification in non-foodgrains till the mid-nineties and from then onwards specialization.

The most disquieting feature of specialization in cereals and also diversification towards non-food crops is that it has not led to any significant improvement in their rate of growth in area, output and productivity. Table 5.6 provides estimates on trend growth rates of area, production and yield of crops from 1980–81 to 1991–92 and then from 1991–92 to 2000–01. It shows a marginal decline in the annual rate of growth in area and output of rice, wheat, sugarcane and all oilseeds. Whereas, the same in the case of 'other cereals', pulses, rapeseed-mustard and cotton is significantly lower in the nineties than in the eighties. The annual rate of growth of yield in the post-reform period has almost been the same for foodgrains, marginally improved for oilseeds, sugarcane and lowered for cotton. With the exception of Tamil Nadu, West Bengal, Punjab, almost all the states have observed a deceleration in the rate of growth in crop production and productivity despite gains in acreage. This trend may have occurred because of an increasing degradation of land, less availability of surface and ground water, imbalance in the use of NPK and little technological innovations. This finding is somewhat contrary to what has been observed in the post-green revolution period, especially from 1981–82 to 1991–92 when the annual rate of growth of food and non-food output and productivity rose significantly to a higher level compared to that from 1968–69 to 1981–82 (Sawant and Achuthan, 1995). Since productivity has a greater contributory role in the expansion of crop output, a deceleration in its rate of growth may have serious implications for food security, increase in exports, oilseed production due to large import of edible oils and overall agricultural growth.

The upshot of above analysis is that the northern states have experienced a fall in diversity in the cropping pattern over time due to dominance of wheat-paddy rotation. The declining diversity, that occurred mainly due to price policy has far-reaching implications in terms of overuse of natural resources, ecological and income risks. In contrast, a good number of south-western states are gradually heading towards an increasing diversity. As stated in many studies, acreage shift towards non-food commodities is found to be taking place in several South Asian countries, primarily in response to rise in income and urbanization and improvements in infrastructure, relative profitability

TABLE 5.6 *Annual Rate of Growth and Sources of Growth of Principal Crops in India: 1980–81 to 2000–01*

Crops	*Periods*	*Per cent Growth Rate*			*Output Growth*	
		Output	*Area*	*Yield*	*Area (%)*	*Yield (%)*
Rice	1980–90	3.69**	0.58***	3.11	15.61	84.39
	1991–00	1.85**	0.72***	1.13	38.88	61.12
Wheat	1980–90	3.61*	0.51***	3.10*	14.09	85.91
	1991–00	3.06**	1.39**	1.67**	45.40	54.60
Other Cereals	1980–90	0.65	–1.36*	2.02**	–208.08	308.08
	1991–00	0.36	–1.45*	1.81	–401.83	501.83
Pulses	1980–90	1.85**	0.23	1.62*	12.42	87.58
	1991–00	0.04	–0.77	0.81	–1930.19	2030.19
Groundnut Seed	1980–90	3.48*	1.68**	1.80	48.22	51.78
	1991–00	–2.29**	–2.65	0.36	115.94	–15.94
Rapeseed-Mustard	1980–90	7.95*	2.94**	5.01*	36.94	63.05
	1991–00	–1.16	–1.82***	0.66	156.83	–56.83
All Oilseeds	1980–90	5.64*	2.83*	2.81*	50.17	49.83
	1991–00	1.03	–0.59	1.62	–57.23	157.23
Cotton	1980–90	3.10***	–0.96***	4.07*	–31.06	131.06
	1991–00	–1.36	2.16**	–1.92**	–158.89	140.85
Sugarcane	1980–90	2.41*	1.71***	0.70	70.85	29.14
	1991–00	2.77*	1.91***	0.87	68.75	31.24
All Major Crops	1980–90	2.78*	0.29	2.49*	10.53	89.47
	1991–00	2.26*	0.08	2.18**	3.69	96.31

Notes: *,** and *** significant at 1, 5 and 10 per cent levels of significance. Trend growth rate is estimated using equation: log (Y) = C + b(Time).

and risk in different commodities (Joshi, Gulati and Cummings, 2007). As analysed in the preceding chapters, liberalization in the trade policy, changing trends in commodity export-import and an improvement in price transmission may also be contributing to this change. However, the speed of diversification is found to be slow, which among many factors is explained by the following: (i) preference of government to maintain self-sufficiency in cereals, (ii) partial openness to external trade, (iii) high production risk and transaction costs, which dissuade small landholders to actively participate, (iv) inadequate infrastructure and marketing facilities, and (v) little private sector participation. Nevertheless, the importance of diversity in the cropping pattern is well recognized in increasing income, employment and lessening poverty. At the same time, it indicates the likely risk to producers in coping with market failure, volatilities in international prices, import surge in an open economy and a strong need for appropriate and timely policy interventions.

Note

1. See among others Bhatia (1991); Sawant and Achuthan (1995); Gulati and Kelly (1999); Naik and Jain (1999); Saleth (1999); Kumar (2001); and Joshi et al. (2007).

6

Macroeconomic Policies and Agriculture Supply Response

A Commodity-Level Analysis

Cropping pattern changes, which initially occurred in response to the support price system and technological developments, might have been precipitated by trade liberalization measures and the setting up of multilateral trading rules under the WTO. An increasing significance of the impact of globalization on producers' incentives through changes in the relative world and domestic prices leads to an analysis of the magnitude of response of commodity prices, trade, area and output to this impact in the context of this study. Accordingly, the main hypotheses that are put to test are: (i) trade and macroeconomic policy changes have positively influenced the agricultural sector in India, (ii) crop area shifts in a liberalized regime are more responsive to price factors than the non-price factors, and (iii) price elasticity of area is positive and high for those crops whose prices are well integrated with the world prices. For this, a structural econometric model is developed and applied to individual crops at the national level from 1980–81 to 2002–03. The chapter begins with an analytical framework for evaluating macroeconomic and the agricultural sector linkages and specification of key variables in the structural model. Next an analysis of commodity-wise results is obtained from empirical exercises followed by main findings and concluding remarks.

Analytical Framework for Macroeconomic Links to Agriculture: Choice of Empirical Model

As stated in Chapter 1, the theoretical and empirical literature has analysed macroeconomic links to the agricultural sector through various channels, focusing mainly on macroeconomic and sectoral policies,

Published earlier in the *Indian Economic Journal*, Vol. 57 (2), July-September 2009. Reproduced here with permission.

global factors and other conditions. As shown in the Flow Chart 6.1, the impact of macro and sector-specific policies and other variables on agricultural supply can be gauged through exchange rate, trade policy. world reference price, and external price (export/import) of commodities. Theoretically, implementation of liberal macro and sectoral policies would imply reduction in protection to the manufacturing sector and hence, an improvement in the terms of trade in favour of agriculture. Favourable terms of trade (price incentives) are expected to have a

Flow Chart 6.1

Trade, Exchange Rate and World Price Linkages to Agriculture

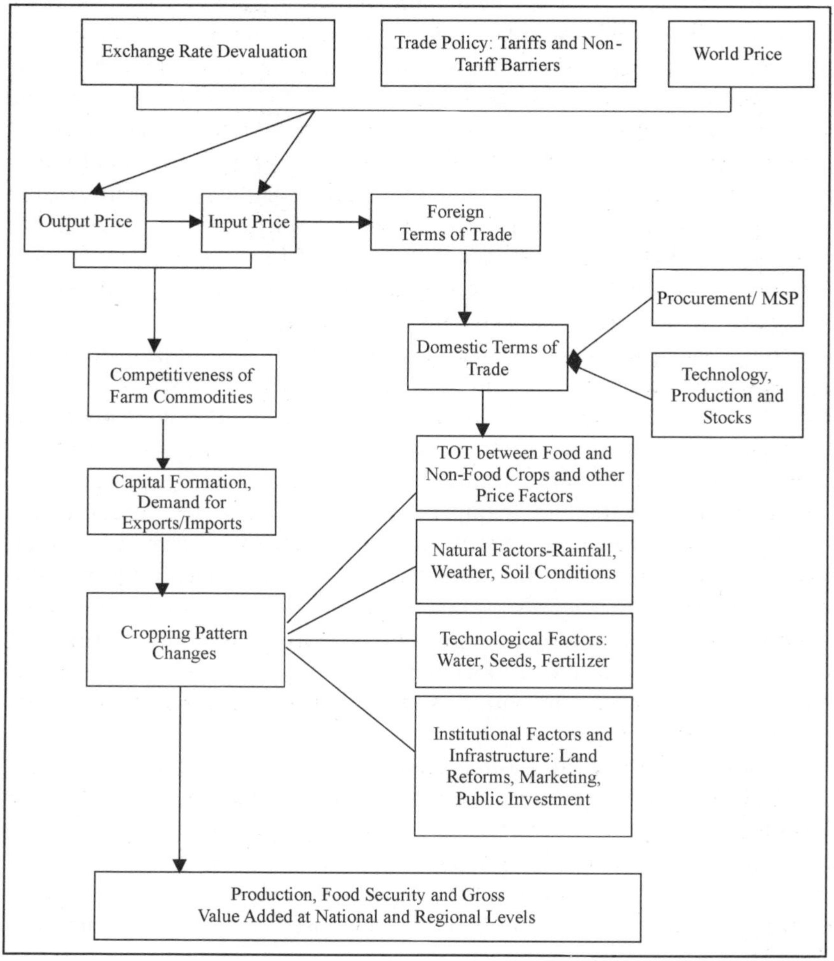

positive impact on agriculture in terms of an increase in private investment, change in crop area shifts, higher exports, production and growth. Along with price variables, technology, weather, irrigation and infrastructure or the non-price variables also influence land allocation decisions. All these variables put together change the incentive structure, which in turn determine the level of exports, imports, crop acreage and output. These interactions between macroeconomic and sector-specific factors, operating directly or indirectly on agriculture have provided a framework for the analysis.

Literature elicits a large number of econometric models that have been used to analyse the impact of broader policies and other factors on price incentives, exports and rate of growth in agriculture. These include namely CGE models, supply response models, structural econometric models, time series econometric models and multimarket model. Of all these, supply response models, which measure the response of aggregate as well as individual crop area/output to price/profit, have a larger application in the Indian context. Some of the supply response models used within the partial framework include Nerlove's adaptive expectation model and its variants, viz., rational expectation hypothesis and ARIMA model, profit function approach, multinomial logit model, time series and/or cross section econometric models, production function and normative programming approaches. Annexure 6.1 provides a comprehensive review of the salient features of each of these supply response models, issues unaddressed and their application in crop-specific studies in India. In brief, most of the supply response models rest on the theoretical premise that farmers act as profit maximizers and adjust their crop acreage and output to changes in crop prices/relative profitability. Along with price factors (captured through own price, input price, relative output to input price), non-price factors (studied through irrigation, weather, infrastructure, technology) that may influence the choice of crop grown are also specified. Their specification in the models is based on a priori theoretical grounds and in some cases on regional conditions. The relative importance of various factors in explaining changes in crop area and output is identified on the basis of parameter estimates and elasticities.

While choosing the model, many studies have reflected upon the application procedures and the usefulness of available models. For instance, CGE models are considered to be very data intensive and are difficult to apply at the disaggregate regional and crop levels. But these models assume importance as they capture the effects of changes on the entire economy and predict/simulate precise estimates for initiating policies in each sector. Compared to CGE models, partial models are simpler to estimate but they are confined to a particular economic sector. The results, thus, obtained may not contribute much towards suggesting concrete policies at the national level. Despite this limitation, the estimates arrived at using partial analysis are considered important as they indicate the direction and extent of changes, which may take place within a sector or in a particular region in response to policy changes. Furthermore, a partial model enables one to analyse crop-specific effects of macroeconomic and sectoral policies, such as on price and output which are considered important, as India possesses comparative advantage only in selected commodities.

Notwithstanding these broad arguments, each model is stated to have advantages as well as limitations associated with its use and application. For instance, the Nerlovian model is considered simple but it fails to address how expectations regarding prices get formulated and is also unable to capture the influence of factors other than price on output in a single equation approach. That is why modifications were made in the original model so as to examine the effects of non-price variables on output along with certain refinements related to formulation of expectations of returns, treatment of risk and policy variables. Supply models other than Nerlovian assume added significance. This is because models such as profit function, analyse interdependencies that exist between output supply and input demand and also enables evaluation of the impact of policies on input use. However, such models require a highly disaggregate data set. Further, the structural econometric model is preferred over the profit function and adaptive expectation as it for example, (i) can easily incorporate the Nerlovian framework, (ii) enables a study of inter-linkages between two or more sectors, and (iii) is suitable for forecasts/simulations under alternate policy scenarios. Nonetheless, the estimation methods in such models usually suffer from the problems of multicollinearity, auto correlated error term, omitted variables and spurious regression due to non-stationarity of data (Greene, 1990; Mamingi, 1996).

The choice of analytical model therefore, ultimately depends upon the issues and objectives at hand with a chosen degree of disaggregation and availability of data on the variables to be taken. Keeping in view the main objective, i.e., analysing the response of agriculture to price incentives caused by liberal macroeconomic and sectoral policies and its performance under alternate policy scenarios, this study draws on a structural econometric model in a partial framework. The model comprises a certain number of behavioural equations and identities and is applied to individual crops, separately under the exportable and importable scenarios. It measures the impact of exogenous factors on key endogenous variables from 1980–81 to 2002–03 based on ordinary least squares (OLS) and 3 Stage Least Squares (3SLS) procedures. It also allows simulation for unknown values of endogenous variables based on historical data on exogenous variables and actual parameter estimates. Care has been taken to minimize the problems encountered in time series analysis by taking the right specification of variables, lagged variables and improving estimation procedures. The statistical adequacy of the estimated coefficients is checked using the LM test for serial correlation of residuals and Ramsey reset specification test for stability of the parameters.

Specification of Structural Econometric Model

In all, four behavioural equations and a few identities are specified in the model, separately for exportable and importable commodities. Of all the principal crops grown, rice, wheat, sugarcane (sugar), cotton, groundnut and soyabean seeds are chosen for the purpose. The equations in order and explanation of each variable are given below.

Equations for Exportable Commodity

Pe = Pw * Exchange Rate ....(1)
Pd = f(Pe, MSP, Production, Procurement, Export) ....(2)
Export = f(Pe/Pd, Stock, Production, Procurement, World Income, Openness) .....(3)
Crop Area = f(Lagged Pd/Ip, Pc, Rainfall, Irrigation, Technology, Risk, Road Density, Lagged Crop Area) ....(4)
Yield = f(Rainfall, Fertilizer consumption/GCA, Irrigation, Technology) ....(5)
Production = Crop Area * Yield ....(6)

Equations for Importable Commodity

Pi = Pw * Exchange Rate ....(1)
Pit =Pi * (1+Tariff) ....(1a)
Pd = f(Pit, MSP, Production, Procurement, Import) ....(2)
Import = f(Pit/Pd, Stock, Procurement, PDI, Openness, Dummy) ....(3)
Crop Area = f(Lagged Pd/Ip, Pc, Rainfall, Irrigation, Technology, Risk, Road Density, Lagged Crop Area) ....(4)
Yield = f(Rainfall, Fertilizer consumption/GCA, Irrigation, Technology) ....(5)
Production = Crop Area * Yield ....(6)

Where,
Exchange rate is nominal exchange rate in Rs/Dollar;
Pw is the world reference commodity price in US dollars;
Pi and Pe are world reference price in Rs/ton and represents export (fob) price and import (cif) price of farm commodities;
Pd is wholesale commodity price in domestic markets (weighted average state level prices) in Rs/tonne;
Pc is price of competing crop in Rs/tonne;
Ip is input price represented by price of fertilizer (NPK) in Rs/tonne weighted by consumption of NPK;
Irrigation is represented by gross irrigated area under a crop (GIA) in 000' ha or irrigation ratio, i.e., GIA under a crop/Crop Area;
Technology is represented by own crop yield, yield of competing crop (yieldc) in kg/hectare or relative yield, i.e., ratio of own crop yield to competing crop yield (yieldc);
MSP is minimum support price as fixed by the government in Rs/tonne;
PDI is personal disposable income in India in Rs;
Dummy represents non-tariff barriers and other factors not captured by the specified variables;
Openness is represented by India's share in world trade and/or ratio of export + imports to GDP agriculture.

Equations 1 to 5 examine the effect of world price, exchange rate, tariffs, support price policies and other variables on four endogenous (impact) variables, viz., domestic wholesale price (incentive structure), trade, acreage and yield. To begin with, equation 1 shows external price (export/import) of a commodity to be influenced by exogenously given world reference price, exchange rate and tariffs in case of an importable item. These are taken to affect farmers' incentives through changes in domestic price as shown in equation 2. Domestic wholesale price is also taken to be governed by three other exogenous variables, viz., support price (MSP) as fixed by the government, procurement by the central and state agencies, production and absolute volume of trade (export/import).

It is possible to take real exchange rate as a separate variable in equation 2 with a theoretically negative sign, which implies that with a fall in currency appreciation, domestic price should rise and so does the level of exports and production. Since the effect of exchange rate is already captured through price, it is not taken as a separate variable. The impact of macroeconomic and sectoral policies on commodity trade is seen in equation 3, separately for exports and imports. Export of a commodity is determined by its relative price (export price/domestic price), stocks, procurement, world income (GDP), and openness of agriculture to world trade. Theoretically, all these variables are expected to have a positive sign. If external price is higher than domestic price, i.e., relative price ratio is greater than one and is increasing, it will positively influence the level of exports and hence, bears a positive sign. It also indicates competitiveness of a commodity in the world markets. On the contrary, if external world price is less than the domestic price, i.e., the relative price ratio is less than one, then there is no incentive to export and the variable may statistically be insignificant with positive or negative sign. Besides relative price movement, production can also explain exports because with an increase in output, more marketable surplus can be utilized for export purposes. Further, a greater openness of economy through reduction in export barriers, cess and quantitative restrictions is likely to create a positive environment for export growth. The effect of this variable is captured indirectly through one of these variables, viz. India's share of agriculture trade in total world agriculture trade and ratio of commodity trade to GDP agriculture.

In contrast to export function, import function for each crop is specified using price ratio, stocks, personal disposable income, openness and dummy (equation 3). Imports increase when domestic price of a commodity rises and its external (import) price falls. Accordingly, coefficient of domestic price variable will bear a positive sign and that of external price will have a negative sign. If external import price is higher than the domestic price (which generally is the case and price ratio is >1), then the variable will bear a negative sign, i.e., with an increase in relative price ratio, reduction in imports is expected. Similarly, if price ratio is less than 1, which implies that import price is less than the domestic price, then an increase in import demand is expected. And a decline in the price ratio will lead to an increase in import demand and the variable is again expected to bear a negative sign. The sign of the coefficient in the latter case will also depend upon demand for that commodity in the domestic markets, tariffs and NTBs imposed on that item.

Other variables that are taken to determine import demand are level of income and stocks. While an increase in PDI augments the capacity of the economy to import, an increase in stocks, procurement, tariffs and NTBs may exert a downward pressure. However, openness through liberal reforms and a greater integration of world and domestic markets is expected to have a positive impact on the level of imports. A dummy variable is specified to capture the effect of NTBs[1] and other factors, if any on imports. Since most of the restrictions on imports got removed only from 1999 when India was asked by the WTO to replace

QRs with tariffs, the value of dummy is taken as 1 from 1980–81 to 1998–99 and 0 from 1999–2000 to 2002–03. The expected sign of this variable is negative, which implies that external trade will get a boost with decrease in the QRs. As NTBs are to be replaced by tariffs, the tariff equivalents of NTBs were also estimated and tried as an explanatory variable in place of dummy. The results remained unchanged.

Turning to acreage response to incentive structure, equation 4 specifies absolute area to be determined by a host of factors, broadly termed as price and non-price factors. Price incentives are explained by profitability, defined as ratio of output price in domestic markets to input price. Assuming that farmers are profit maximizers and also trade, exchange rate and price policies have created a positive economic environment through increase in the output price and decrease in the input cost, this variable is expected to exert a positive influence on area under a crop. The variable is taken in both current and lagged form. Lag is preferably taken as it incorporates adaptive expectations in price formation. Besides profit, own price and price of competing crop are also taken as explanatory variables. An increase in price of competing crop is likely to yield a negative influence on crop acreage.

Along with price factors, producers are expected to grow a particular crop keeping in view weather conditions, irrigation, technological changes, infrastructure and area devoted to cultivation in the previous year. All these variables are explained from the supply side and are termed as 'non-price' factors or 'shifter' variables in the literature. The impact of weather is captured through rainfall index, estimated as percentage deviation from normal rainfall. While gross irrigated area or ratio of gross irrigated area to crop area represents the irrigation variable, road density represents infrastructure. Technology represents own crop yield and yield of competing crop or ratio of own yield to competing yield. Yield of competing crop will have a negative influence on crop area. The variable risk is measured by squared deviation of difference between actual and expected price as well as own crop yield. The expected crop price/yield is taken to be three years moving average and is expected to bear a negative sign. Lagged dependent variable as an explanatory variable represents partial adjustment, i.e., farmers respond slowly to changes in relative prices and other variables in the short run. However, in the long run, producers achieve certain desired levels of acreage and hence production. Finally, in equation 5, yield is taken to be determined by rainfall, irrigation, fertilizer consumption. Technology is represented by percentage of area under high yielding varieties to gross cropped area. Since most of the explanatory variables in area and yield equations overlap, the econometric exercise was tried without specification of the yield equation, i.e., assuming yield to be determined exogenously. The results, however, did not vary much.

In sum, the structural model that is developed incorporates both price effects, attributable to world price, macro and sectoral policies and non-price effects on four endogenous variables, viz., domestic price, trade, absolute crop area and yield. The key variables selected can be grouped into the following three broad categories:

1. *Endogenous or impact variables:* Own commodity price, export, import, acreage under the crop, and yield (productivity);
2. *Exogenous and/or policy variables:* Exchange rate, trade policy (tariffs and non-tariffs), world commodity price, minimum support price, commodity stocks and procurement by the central and state agencies;
3. *Exogenous and/or supply side variables:* World income, India's personal disposable income, own crop price, profitability (output price/input price), competing crop price, input (fertilizer) price, technology (own crop yield, competing crop yield or relative yield), gross irrigated area or irrigation ratio, yield or price risk, annual rainfall index, infrastructure represented by road density, dummy variable to account for NTBs, India's agri-trade share in world agri-trade and ratio of commodity exports+imports to GDP agriculture. The last three variables are taken to capture the openness of agriculture to world markets.

Data Sources

Annexure 6.2 describes in detail the selection of variables along with their sources of data. Data for the chosen variables is collected from 1980–81 to 2002–03 at the all-India level from Agriculture Statistics at a Glance, Economic Survey, FAO and Reports of Commission on Agricultural Costs and Prices. World prices are taken from International Financial Statistics published by the IMF. Price variables are specified in Rs/tonne and are converted into real prices at base 1993–94 using wholesale price index of all commodities. Since data on wholesale prices are available at the state (market) level, weighted average state-level prices are taken to represent price at the all-India level. The weight is taken to be production of crop under question. The external reference price of commodities represents price prevalent at major trading centres in the world. Price series given in US dollar are converted into Rupees using the appropriate exchange rate and are deflated for converting into real prices at base 1993–94. Export and import prices based on the value of exports/imports divided by quantity exported/imported were also tried in the model. In the final analysis, world reference price is taken so as to account for individual effects of tariffs and exchange rate on exportable and importable commodities. All data series except export and import relate to crop year.

Model Estimation and Empirical Results

For each commodity, the behavioural equations are estimated in double log form individually as well as simultaneously applying OLS and 3SLS methods. The simultaneous equation model satisfies the following two conditions namely: (i) number of endogenous variables is equal to number of equations and (ii) number of exogenous variables is less than the degrees of freedom. The estimates obtained from both OLS and 3SLS provide consistent results, which imply that the estimates from individual equations are not different from those obtained from system solution. Following conventions in economic literature, 3SLS estimates are presented as proxy for robustness of OLS. The interpretation of results is primarily based on OLS estimates. Preliminary tests carried out reveal high correlation between some of the variables, viz., road density, area under HYV, gross irrigated area and lagged area. This necessitates dropping of some variables in the equations. However, this sometimes results in omitted variable bias leading to serial correlation and poor Durbin Watson statistics. In this situation, behavioural equations are estimated with autoregressive process AR(1). In some cases, alternate equations are estimated to avoid the problem of multicollinearity among the explanatory variables. It is also important to mention that only those variables, which are statistically significant, are retained. In some cases, such as in the export and import functions, some of the specifications yield expected signs but show insignificant estimates.[2] These are included with an objective to understand their likely effects on the endogenous variables. Commodity-wise results under exportable and importable scenarios are presented below.

Wheat

Figure 6.1 depicts the movement of real wholesale price of wheat at the national level based on weighted average state level wholesale prices and world reference price from 1980–81 to 2002–03. The picture has been mixed showing domestic price to be higher than the world price for most of the years except from 1991 to 1996. Overall movements reveal that Indian wheat price has not followed trends in the world wheat price thereby implying a weak price transmission.

FIGURE 6.1 *Wheat: World and Domestic Prices, Exports, Imports, Area and Production*

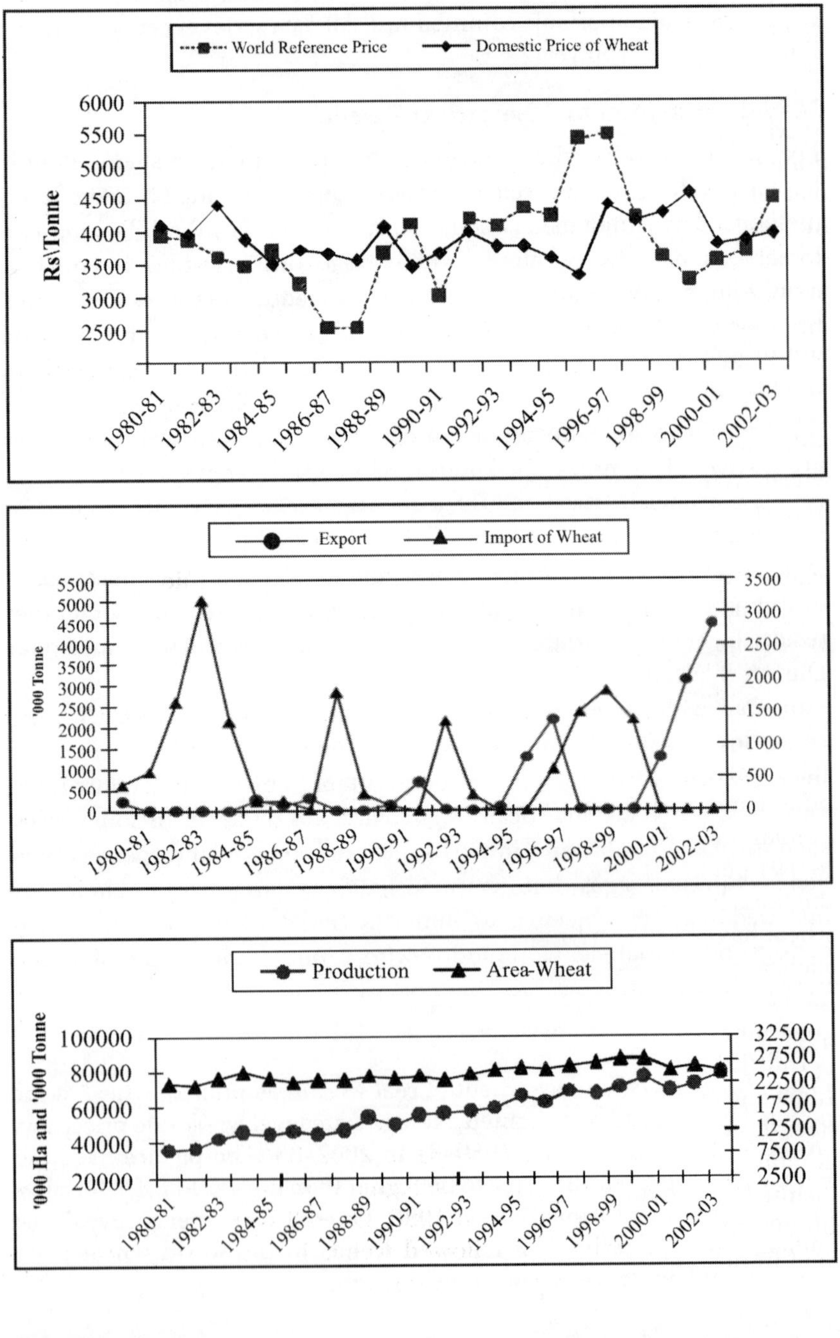

Empirical results furnished in Table 6.1 do not show any influence of external price of wheat on domestic price. This may have negative implications for wheat exports and may encourage its imports. Two policy variables, viz., MSP and procurement determine the domestic price of wheat, which is expected due to a greater dominance of price policy. The estimated coefficients bear the expected positive sign in case of MSP and negative sign in case of procurement. The elasticity of domestic price with respect to support price is estimated to be 0.64 and that of procurement to be – 0.17, which implies that a 10 per cent increase in MSP will bring about a 6.4 per cent change in price in domestic markets. Production has the expected negative sign and this along with time trend is significant in explaining the movement of price. The coefficients for exports and imports bear unexpected signs and are also insignificant in explaining variations in prices, which could be due to lagged relationship between production and exports. The overall fit explains 69 and 78 per cent of variation under two scenarios and indicates a dominant role of domestic policies in determining price of wheat. What implications do these results have for wheat exports and imports?

The graphical presentation shows that the absolute volume of total wheat exports have remained at a low level till the mid-nineties and picked up only towards the end of nineties. The share of exports in total production has increased from 0.33 per cent during mid-nineties (averaged 1990–95) to 2.12 per cent towards the end of nineties and early 2000 (averaged 1996–2003). Acceleration in exports took place only when world price started declining and also multilateral trading rules were being formulated under the WTO. Wheat imports, on the other hand, have seen ups and downs and average imports as percentage of total production have come down from 3.33 per cent in early eighties to 0.91 per cent in the latter half of eighties and have remained at almost the same level till 2002–03. This is despite the fact that domestic price of wheat has been higher than the world price in most of the years and in such a situation, inflow of imports is expected. A not so significant increase in imports could be due to increase in production as well as government intervention in the external trade through a system of permit/license to exporters/importers, trading by Food Corporation of India and other NTBs. Though in recent years, government has initiated liberal steps and has allowed imports by roller flourmills but trade continues to be highly governed. High tariffs could also be one of the factors for a not so high increase in imports. Tariffs on wheat were zero till the year 1999–2002 and were placed at high level at almost 100 per cent from early 2000 to check surge in imports.

TABLE 6.1 *Wheat: Results under Exportable and Importable Scenarios from 1980–81 to 2002–03 at 1993–94 Prices*

Dependent Variables/Independent Variables under Exportable Scenario									
Price	*World Price*	*Support Price (MSP)*	*Export*	*Procurement*	*Production*	*Trend*	*Constant*	*R2*	*D-W*
OLS	–0.063 (–0.86)	0.64* (3.86)	–0.007# (–1.21)	–0.17* (–2.69)	–0.56*# (–2.15)	0.02* (2.29)	10.97	0.69	2.6
3SLS	–0.07 (–1.49)	0.75* (6.7)	–0.003# (–0.90)	–0.13* (–3.07)	–0.31***# (–1.75)	0.011*** (1.67)	7.13	0.67	2.7
Export	Pe/Pd	Stock	World Income	–	–	–	Constant	R2	D-W
OLS	3.52*** (1.71)	3.57*# (3.66)	2.58* (2.64)	–	–	–	–64.94	0.66	2.04$
3SLS	2.32 (1.23)	3.31*# (3.63)	2.65* (2.92)	–	–	–	–63.57	0.65	1.99$
Area	LaggedPd/Ip	Rain Index	Yield/Yieldc	Pc Rape seed-Mustard	Yield Risk	Lagged Area	Constant	R2	D-W
OLS	0.10** (2.08)	0.20* (3.28)	0.15* (2.17)	–0.06 (–1.42)	–0.004 (–1.5)	0.35** (2.09)	6.09	0.83	2.2
3SLS:	0.11* (3.66)	0.18* (4.69)	0.16* (3.66)	–0.06* (–2.28)	–0.006* (–3.88)	0.35* (3.44)	6.23	0.87	2.24
Yield	Fert.con/GCA	Technology	Trend	–	–	–	Constant	R2	D-W
OLS	0.05* (2.15)	0.94* (3.72)	0.003 (0.51)	–	–	–	8.83	0.97	2.5
3SLS	0.05* (2.41)	1.50* (2.13)	0.01* (2.09)	–	–	–	7.21	0.96	2.3

Cont'd…

Cont'd...

Dependent Variables/Independent Variables under Importable Scenario									
Price	WorldPrice	Support Price	Import	Procurement	Production	Trend	Constant	R2	D-W
OLS	–0.06#	0.77*	0.0002#	–0.17*	–0.59*#	0.02*	10.19	0.78	2.8
	(–1.06)	(4.02)	(0.04)	(–2.85)	(–2.50)	(2.41)			
3SLS	–0.11*#	0.89*	–.002#	–0.12*	–0.44*#	0.02*	7.69	0.75	2.9
	(–5.34)	(11.95)	(–0.74)	(–5.37)	(–5.39)	(5.16)			
Import	Pit/Pd	Stock	Procurement	Openness (share)	Dummy (NTB)	Constant	–	R2	D-W
OLS	–3.05*	–2.28*	–3.93*	5.78*	–1.11	65.06	–	0.70	1.62
	(–2.26)	(–2.65)	(–2.33)	(2.32)	(–0.73)				
3SLS	–2.55*	–3.31*	–3.35*	8.08*	–0.06	68.86	–	0.68	1.43
	(–2.52)	(–5.34)	(–2.45)	(4.15)	(–0.06)				
Area	Lagged Pd/Ip	Rain Index	Yield/Yieldc	Pc Rapeseed-Mustard	Yield Risk	Lagged Area	Constant	R2	D-W
3SLS	0.09*	0.13*	0.08*	–0.09*	–0.007*	0.44*	5.97	0.81	2.3
	(3.87)	(5.04)	(2.13)	(–4.35)	(–6.19)	(4.37)			
Yield	Fert.con/GCA	Technology	Trend	–	–	–	Constant	R2	D-W
3SLS	0.05*	2.82*	0.001	–	–	–	6.85	0.96	2.3
	(2.58)	(4.52)	(0.29)						

Notes: Figures in parentheses are t-values. *,** and *** denote 1,5 and 10 per cent level of significance respectively. # denotes one year lag. $ specified using AR(1). The estimates are respective elasticities based on double log functional form. OLS estimates of area and yield equations would be same under the two scenarios.

The relative prices, i.e., ratio of external to domestic price have little role in influencing wheat exports. This is expected, as domestic price has been higher than the world price in most of the years during the last two decades. Compared to price, other variables, viz., stocks (elasticity 3.75) and world income (elasticity 2.58) play a greater role in influencing wheat exports. Unlike exports, imports are explained by both price and non-price factors. The coefficient of relative price is estimated to be –3.05, implying that a one per cent decline in relative price ratio (in this case ratio is < 1, i.e., external price < domestic price) would increase import demand significantly by 3 per cent. This, however, has not happened in India because of high tariffs and imposition of regulatory controls. Other variables that are crucial determinants of wheat import are its availability through stocks and procurement, which are highly significant and openness measured through share of agriculture trade in total world agriculture trade. The dummy variable representing NTBs, though bears a negative sign, is statistically insignificant. The extent to which price incentives, if any, have influenced area and yield of wheat is analysed next.

Both area and production of wheat have been rising in India as shown graphically. During the eighties, faster dissemination of technology through spread of HYV, assured irrigation and a favourable price structure backed by assured procurement have been the driving forces behind expansion of area, yield and output. During the nineties, area has become the major factor behind increasing level of output as productivity of wheat is found to be decelerating. The dynamics of acreage and its response to price and supply side non-price factors show absolute area under wheat to be determined by profitability, rainfall, ratio of crop yield to yield of competing crop, risk and lagged area. The elasticity of area with respect to one year lagged profitability is estimated to be 0.10, implying that a 10 per cent increase in price will bring about 1.0 per cent change in area. The same for rainfall, relative yield and lagged area are 0.20, 0.15 and 0.35 respectively. The price of competing crop, i.e., rapeseed-mustard, though bears the expected negative sign is insignificant in explaining acreage. Finally, yield equation, which is explained by selected inputs shows fertilizer consumption and technology to be significant having elasticity 0.05 and 0.94, respectively.

Rice

Figure 6.2 depicts the movement of real wholesale price of rice at the national level based on weighted average state level wholesale prices, and world price at the major trading centre. World price of rice has been higher than domestic price from 1980–81 to 1984–85 and then from

FIGURE 6.2 *Rice: World and Domestic Prices, Exports, Imports, Area and Production*

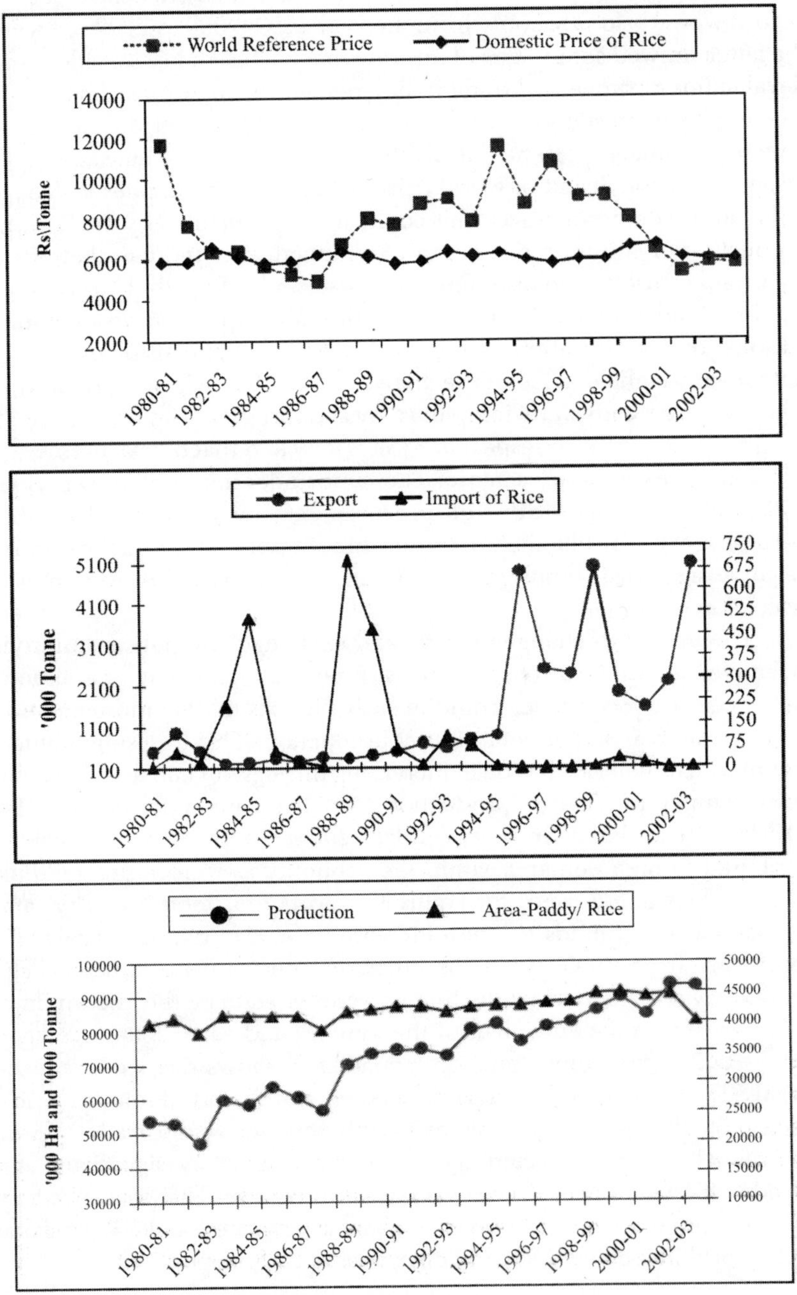

1987–88 to 1999–2000. Domestic price has followed neither the rising nor the falling trends in world prices. Variations in its price have been in accord with world price only from the year 1999–2000 to 2002–03 when the latter showed some signs of improvement. This makes it evident that devaluation of rupee and trade policy reforms were not instrumental in converging domestic rice price with the world price till the middle of nineties. Estimates presented in Table 6.2 show a positive but statistically insignificant coefficient of world price, which broadly implies its lack of influence on domestic price. This could also be explained by the fact that production of common rice is more dominant in India than that of the exportable variety, and also only a few states, viz., Punjab, Haryana and Andhra Pradesh have been growing rice for export purposes. Other reasons could be variations in the exchange rate and inclusion of average state level weighted price in the analysis. Also, like wheat, variations in rice price are significantly influenced by support price and procurement, the price elasticity with respect to MSP is 0.69 and that of procurement is –0.22 under exportable scenario. The same under importable scenario is 0.71 and 0.16 for MSP and procurement, respectively. All other variables, viz., production, exports and imports have the expected negative signs but are insignificant in explaining variations in domestic price of rice.

The impact of change in trade and exchange rate policies on price incentives is visible through exports. One may note that rice exports have been at a lower level from the early eighties till the mid-nineties at approximately 0.80 per cent of total production. This is despite the fact that production of rice has been increasing throughout and also India has been competitive in rice production, which is authenticated by NPC (DP/WP) to be less than unity (Gulati, 2004). Lower exports could be attributed to high demand within the economy as well as protectionist policies being followed to control exports on food security and self-sufficiency grounds through increase in stocks. Exports received a spurt only from 1995, when liberal trade policies were initiated. The share of exports in total production was estimated to be the maximum at 3.73 per cent in the latter half of the nineties and early 2000 (averaged 1996–2003). The export function (equation 3) shows rice exports to be positively influenced by lagged relative world and domestic price, lagged stocks, world income and openness to world trade. These variables bear the expected signs and are statistically significant and together explain 89 per cent of variations in exports. The price elasticity of world price relative to domestic price is estimated at 1.73, stocks at 0.62, world income at 0.93, and openness at 2.28, respectively.

TABLE 6.2 *Rice: Results under Exportable and Importable Scenarios from 1980–81 to 2002–03 at 1993–94 Prices*

Dependent Variables/Independent Variables under Exportable Scenario									
Price	*World Price*	*Support Price*	*Export*	*Procurement*	*Production*	*Trend*	*Constant*	*R2*	*D-W*
OLS	0.043 (0.76)	0.69** (1.92)	–0.05 (–1.25)	–0.22** (–2.18)	–0.19 (–1.13)	0.015 (1.55)	7.30	0.45	1.64$
3SLS	0.03 (0.63)	0.42*** (1.71)	0.05*# (3.61)	–0.12* (–2.06)	–0.28* (–2.79)		9.05	0.30	1.50$
Export	Pe/Pd	Stock	World Income	Openness (share)	–	–	Constant	R2	D-W
OLS	1.73*# (4.15)	0.62*# (2.15)	0.93* (3.25)	2.28* (4.21)	–	–	–11.56	0.89	1.78
3SLS	1.70*# (4.71)	0.58*# (2.33)	0.97* (3.89)	2.29* (4.90)	–	–	–11.76	0.89	1.77
Area	Lagged Pd/Ip	Rain Index	Yield/Yieldc	Pc Maize	Yield Risk	Lagged Area	Constant	R2	D-W
OLS	0.09*** (1.85)	0.19* (3.11)	–0.07 (–1.07)	–0.009 (–0.13)	–0.001 (–0.303)	0.38 (1.61)	5.76	0.81	2.15
3SLS	0.06 (1.49)	0.20* (4.25)	–0.08 (–1.56)	0.006 (0.11)	–0.0001 (–0.08)	0.50* (2.82)	4.31	0.80	2.2
Yield	Fert.cons/ GCA	GIA/ Area	Technology	–	–	–	Constant	R2	D-W
OLS	0.08** (2.20)	0.35 (1.65)	0.80*# (5.19)	–	–	–	8.75	0.94	1.68
3SLS	0.08* (2.68)	0.43* (2.32)	0.74*# (5.62)	–	–	–	8.76	0.94	1.66

Cont'd...

Cont'd...

Dependent Variables/Independent Variables under Importable Scenario									
Price	World Price	Support Price	Import	Procurement	Production	–	Constant	R2	D-W
OLS	0.02# (0.29)	0.71** (2.08)	0.001 (0.26)	–0.16** (–2.09)	–0.11 (–0.68)	–	5.59	0.30	1.71$
3SLS	–.08*# (–2.11)	0.54* (2.69)	–0.001 (–0.34)	–0.11*** (–1.71)	0.06 (0.62)	–	5.52	0.20	1.61
Import	Pit/Pd	Stock	Dummy (NTB)	Lagged Import	–	–	Constant	R2	D-W
OLS	–0.80 (–0.38)	–4.51* (–3.60)	–2.32*** (1.70)	0.36* (2.44)	–	–	44.5	0.72	1.81
3SLS	–1.31 (–0.81)	–4.84* (–5.12)	–3.04* (–2.96)	0.31* (2.92)	–	–	48.40	0.71	1.83
Area	Lagged Pd/Ip	Rain Index	Yield/Yieldc	Pc Maize	Yield Risk	Lagged Area	Constant	R2	D-W
3SLS	0.16* (3.95)	0.17* (3.55)	–0.08 (–1.59)	0.02 (0.39)	–0.002 (–1.24)	0.17 (0.91)	7.87	0.78	1.77
Yield	Rain Index	Fert.cons./GCA	GIA/ Area	Technology	–	–	Constant	R2	D-W
3SLS	–	0.77* (2.33)	0.31*** (1.70)	0.82*# (6.58)	–	–	8.72	0.94	1.66

Notes: Figures in parentheses are t-values. *,** and *** denote 1,5 and 10 per cent level of significance respectively. # denotes one year lag. $ specified using AR(1). The estimates are respective elasticities based on double log functional form. OLS estimates of area and yield equations would be same under the two scenarios.

Compared to an increasing trend in exports, import of rice has been declining over the period. As a percentage of production, imports have fallen from 0.28 per cent in the early eighties (averaged 1980–85) to 0.07 per cent during 1990–95 and 0.008 per cent during 1996–03. A high dependence on imports identified during the eighties got diminished in the subsequent decade due to an increase in domestic supply and attainment of near self-sufficiency. Like wheat, rice imports are also controlled by the government, despite the fact that some attempts have been made to deregulate trade in foodgrains. Government resorts to import only when food shortages occur within the domestic economy. The role played by market forces, through movement of relative world and domestic price is limited in determining import demand, which is evident from a higher level of external price of rice than the domestic price. For long, NTBs have been imposed to check import surge. From 1999 onwards, NTBs have been replaced by tariffs with a few exceptions such as obtaining permits. Given a controlled trade scenario, imports are influenced mainly by the availability of stock, lagged imports and NTBs. These variables bear the expected signs showing elasticity of imports to stock at –4.51, dummy at –2.32 and lagged imports at 0.36.

The impact of world price and external trade is analysed on acreage under rice and its yield. Due to the multicollinearity between gross irrigated area and lagged dependent variable, alternate equations were tried to estimate the acreage response function. The equation that is finally reported reveals acreage to be responsive to lagged profitability, weather and lagged area. The elasticity is estimated at 0.09, 0.19 and 0.38, respectively for these variables. The elasticity of the substitute crop, i.e., maize is –0.009 but is insignificant. A positive and significant coefficient of lagged dependent variable suggests partial adjustment in the short run due to changes in price and technological variables. However, in the long run, producers achieve certain desired levels of acreage and hence production. Another variable, viz., risk has the expected negative sign but is insignificant. Overall, irrigation has a more dominant role in influencing area under rice than price. Of all the variables, yield is not contributing towards expansion of area, which could be due to deceleration in the rate of growth of productivity during the last two decades. Variations in yield, in turn, are significantly determined by irrigation, fertilizer consumption and lagged technology, which together explains 94 per cent of variations.

Sugar

The wholesale price of sugar was higher than the world reference price from 1980–81 to 1988–89 and then from 1997–98 to 2002–03 as depicted in Figure 6.3. The results presented in Table 6.3 show that sugar price is significantly influenced by variations in the external price and the elasticity is nearly 0.14 under exportable and importable scenarios. Other variables that influence domestic price significantly are administered price, exports and imports with elasticity estimated at 0.98, 0.04 and –0.02, respectively. Production has the expected negative sign but is statistically insignificant. The estimate of NPC of sugar, measured as ratio of domestic price to its external reference price (CIF or FOB) adjusted for freight and marketing cost, reveals lack of price competitiveness of sugar in most of the years during the last two decades. And this is supported by actual trade flows that have taken place. It is evident from Figure 6.3 that sugar exports have always been at a lower level and became high only from the mid-nineties when export restrictions were removed and then from 1996–97 when both domestic and world price fell. Sugar exports as percentage of production increased from a low average level of 0.75 per cent during 1990–95 to 2.14 per cent during 1996–03. Imports, on the other hand, reached a peak during the mid-eighties at 4 per cent and fell to 1.41 per cent during 1990–95 and then to 1.2 per cent during 1996–03. Despite controls and regulations on external trade of sugar, the absolute level of import has continuously increased during the latter half of the nineties, which could be explained by the fact that world price ruled at a low level after mid-nineties. High tariffs have been placed from early 2000 to control inflow of imports. It is found that variations in exports are explained more by stocks than by relative price. In contrast, imports are equally influenced by these two variables along with level of income and openness. The influence of tariffs is already captured through the price variable. The dummy that represents NTBs is found to be insignificant and is finally dropped.

To what extent have price incentives influenced area and yield under sugarcane? The analysis indicates that production of sugar, which is only 10 per cent of total sugarcane production, has been rising and so has the area. A declining trend has been observed during early nineties, which got recovered from 1996–97. Own price and lagged area turn out to be important factors in influencing acreage with elasticity estimated at 0.21 and 0.84, respectively. These along with competing crop price and relative yield explain almost 80 per cent of variations in total area under sugarcane. The yield of sugarcane is significantly influenced by rainfall (elasticity 0.20) and irrigation (elasticity 0.52). It is clear that irrigation stands out to be the most important factor.

FIGURE 6.3: *Sugarcane/Sugar: World and Domestic Prices, Exports, Imports, Area and Production*

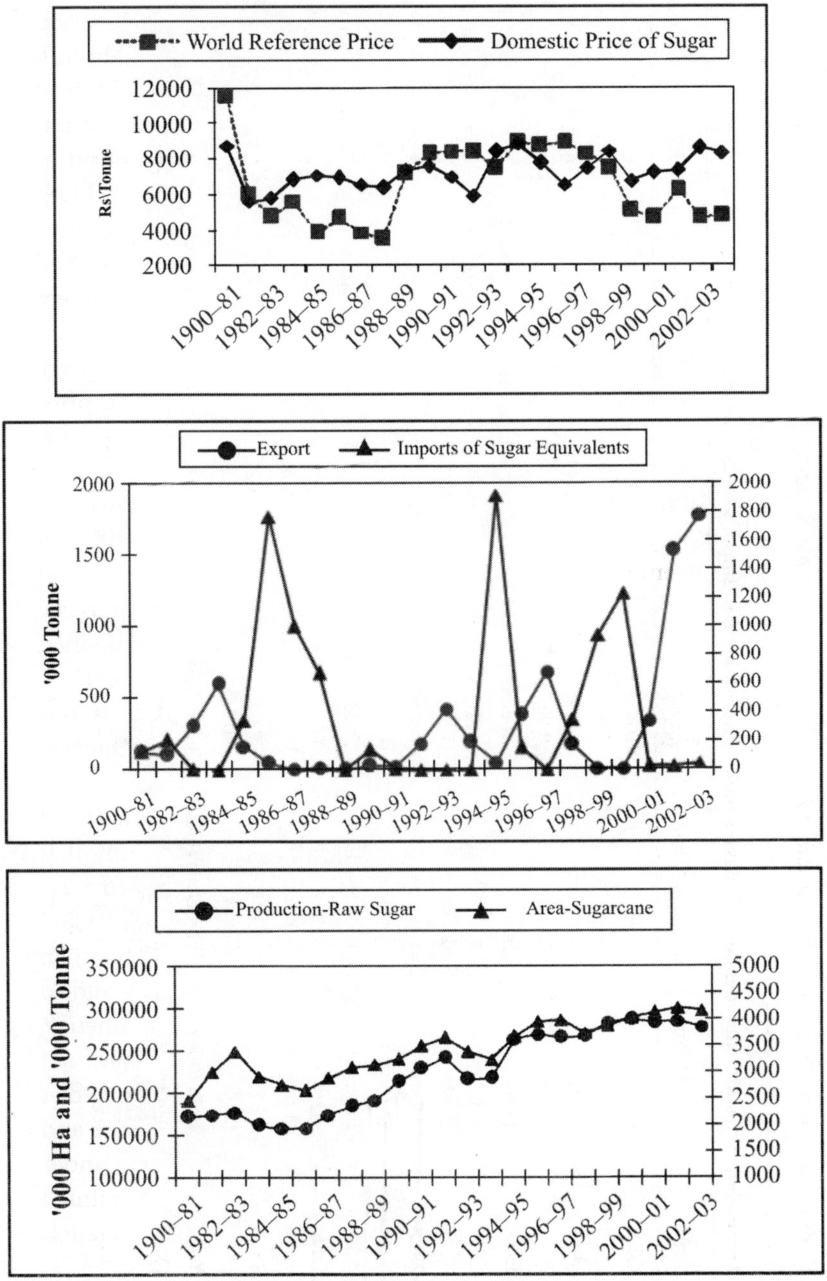

TABLE 6.3 *Sugar/Sugarcane: Results under Exportable and Importable Scenarios from 1980–81 to 2002–03 at 1993–94 Prices*

Dependent Variables/Independent Variables under Exportable and Importable Scenarios							
Price	*World Price*	*Support Price*	*Export*	*Production*	*Constant*	*R2*	*D-W*
OLS	0.14*** (1.71)	0.98* (2.51)	0.04*# (2.83)	–0.33 (–1.56)	5.96	0.61	2.40$
3SLS	0.03# (0.49)	0.79* (2.41)	0.01# (0.96)	–0.17# (–1.09)	6.00	0.25	1.27
Export	Pe/Pd	Stock	Openness (trade flow)	Lagged Export	Constant	R2	D-W
OLS	1.82***# (1.71)	1.61* (2.50)	0.42*** (1.94)	0.29 (1.24)	–8.92	0.69	1.98$
3SLS	2.87*# (2.79)	1.16***# (1.80)	0.38*** (1.87)	0.22 (0.77)	–4.46	0.57	1.73$
Area	Lagged Pd	Pc Rice-wheat	Yield/yieldc	Lagged Area	Constant	R2	D-W
OLS	0.21** (1.84)	–0.19# (–0.62)	0.059 (0.197)	0.84* (4.02)	0.82	0.79	1.49
3SLS	0.17** (2.02)	–0.17# (–0.84)	–0.04 (–0.18)	1.02* (7.19)	–0.13	0.73	1.32
Yield	Rain Index	Fert.Cons./GCA	GIA/Area	Technology	Constant	R2	D-W
OLS	0.20*** (1.79)	0.05 (1.24)	0.52** (2.07)	–	10.59	0.69	1.55
3SLS	0.20* (2.14)	–0.03 (–0.77)	0.80*# (6.77)	–	10.10	0.39	1.05

Cont'd...

Cont'd…

Dependent Variables/Independent Variables under Importable Scenario							
Price	World Price	Support Price	Lagged Import	Production	Constant	R2	D-W
OLS	0.13** (2.01)	1.16* (3.47)	0.02* (–2.93)	–0.18 (–1.19)	3.16	0.65	2.4$
3SLS	0.14* (3.39)	1.02* (5.20)	–0.01* (–3.47)	–0.03 (–0.38)	2.13	0.49	1.46$
Import	Pit/Pd	Stock	PDI	Openness (Trade flow)	Constant	R2	D-W
OLS	–6.29* (–2.39)	–5.78* (–4.07)	7.36* (3.12)	0.85*** (1.71)	–44.17	0.59	2.10
3SLS	–8.75* (–4.49)	–7.49* (–6.55)	8.44* (4.36)	0.58 (1.58)	–44.04	0.56	2.04
Area	Lagged Pd	PcRice-wheat	Yield/yieldc	Lagged Area	Constant	R2	D-W
3SLS	0.21* (2.48)	–0.04# (–0.28)	–0.39* (–2.25)	0.54* (4.12)	3.69	0.77	1.37
Yield	Rain Index	Fert./Cons.GCA	GIA/Area	Technology	Constant	R2	D-W
3SLS	0.22* (3.15)	0.04 (1.51)	0.38* (2.53)	0.35* (4.80)	10.59	0.83	1.31

Notes: Figures in parentheses are t-values. *,** and *** denote 1,5 and 10 per cent level of significance respectively. # denotes one year lag. $ specified using AR(1). The estimates are respective elasticities based on double log functional form. OLS estimates of area and yield equations remain same under the two scenarios.

Cotton

Table 6.4 presents results for cotton. Variations in its price are explained by world price, lagged exports and imports and procurement. The price elasticity is estimated to be 0.46 and 0.58 under the exportable and importable scenarios, respectively and that of exports, imports to be low at 0.09 and –0.03 and procurement at –0.10 and –0.19, respectively. Government administered price is not an important variable in determining the domestic price of cotton.

The dynamics of price incentives are also captured in the export and import demand functions. Before that, it is important to highlight that when economic reforms got initiated, the price of cotton lint was on a rising trend, which dropped in the subsequent years and then, recovered from 1997–98. As shown in Figure 6.4, compared with world reference price, domestic price of cotton lint has always been lower, which could be due to varietal differences. Like rice, NPC of cotton also reveals high competitiveness as relative domestic and external reference price has always been less than unity in most of the years. In this case, it is surprising to see that exports have not increased much, rather they have declined towards the end of nineties while imports have expanded enormously. The average fall in cotton export as percentage of production is almost 6 per cent from 9.02 during 1990–95 to 2.85 per cent during 1996–03, whereas import as percentage of production has increased from 1.4 per cent to 7.13 per cent during the same period. A decline in cotton exports could be due to the following: (i) decline in world price of cotton after 1996–97 due to which exports did not get a boost (ii) even if the commodity is price competitive, it loses its competitiveness due to high transportation and marketing costs. On import surge, one may note that India had placed tariffs on cotton at 40 per cent during 1997–98, reduced it to 25 per cent in 2000–01 and then finally to 5 per cent in the subsequent years, which is at its lowest level. This might have led to acceleration in imports. It is also noticed that even if a crop is competitive, it is still imported at one port or another due to freight advantage on that port, which results in a greater inflow of imports (Gulati, 2004).

Given a higher world price of cotton than the domestic price, one would expect export to positively respond to price incentives. The analysis reveals elasticity estimate of exports to relative price is positive and high at 2.15. Stocks and world income are also significant in explaining exports with the expected signs. The coefficient of time trend is negative, which is expected due to falling level of exports over time. Results on import function show imports to be negatively associated with

TABLE 6.4 *Cotton: Results under Exportable and Importable Scenarios from 1980–81 to 2002–03 at 1993–94 Prices*

Dependent Variables/Independent Variables under Exportable Scenario:									
Price	*World Price*	*Support Price*	*Lagged Export*	*Procurement*	*Production*	–	*Constant*	*R2*	*D-W*
OLS	0.46* (2.88)	–0.33 (–0.69)	0.09* (3.33)	–0.10*** (–1.88)	–0.05 (–0.35)	–	1.92	0.62	1.59
3SLS	0.29* (2.63)	0.13 (0.53)	0.09* (5.33)	–0.03 (–0.93)	–0.3 (–0.25)	–	5.88	0.58	1.47
Export	Pe/Pd	Stock	Lagged Export	Openness (share)	World Income	Trend	Constant	R2	D-W
OLS	2.15** (2.02)	2.71*# (2.70)	0.32 (1.34)	0.22 (0.17)	7.67* (2.31)	–0.66* (–2.82)	–112.97	0.58	1.77
3SLS	1.43*** (1.72)	2.63*# (3.40)	0.62 (3.61)	0.46 (0.43)	10.95* (4.19)	–0.88* (–4.77)	–155.22	0.53	1.71
Area	Lagged Pd	Rain Index	Pc Groundnut	GIA/Area	Yield/yieldc	Lagged Area	Constant	R2	D-W
OLS	0.12** (2.21)	0.22** (2.38)	–0.16*** (–1.83)	0.09***# (1.78)	–0.006# (–0.09)	0.73* (6.44)	1.81	0.86	1.84
3SLS	0.08* (2.62)	0.27* (5.05)	–0.16* (–3.29)	0.15*# (4.56)	–0.11*# (–2.94)	0.68* (8.01)	2.28	0.83	2.06
Yield	Rain Index	Fert.Cons./GCA	Technology	–	–	–	Constant	R2	D-W
OLS	0.35# (1.30)	0.25* (2.42)	0.96* (5.39)	–	–	–	5.48	0.66	2.42
3SLS	–0.06# (–0.30)	0.14*** (1.70)	0.99* (6.15)	–	–	–	7.12	0.59	2.07

Cont'd...

Cont'd...

Dependent Variables/Independent Variables under Importable Scenario:									
Price	World Price	Support Price	Lagged Import	Procurement	Production	–	Constant	R2	D-W
OLS	0.58* (4.61)	–0.37 (–0.72)	–0.03* (–2.44)	–0.19* (–3.10)	–0.04 (–0.24)	–	8.74	0.67	1.86$
3SLS	0.54* (6.05)	0.01 (0.03)	–0.02* (–2.83)	–0.15* (–3.65)	–0.03 (–0.32)	–	5.44	0.61	1.65
Import	Pit/Pd	Stock	PDI	Dummy (NTB)	–	–	Constant	R2	D-W
OLS	–1.02 (–0.34)	–4.84*** (–1.70)	7.99* (2.83)	–0.33 (–0.13)	–	–	–75.00	0.52	1.53
3SLS	1.41 (0.60)	–6.47*# (–2.95)	6.49* (2.82)	–2.77 (–1.45)	–	–	–44.30	0.46	1.46
Area	Lagged Pd	Rain Index	Pc Groundnut	GIA/Area	Yield/yieldc	Lagged Area	Constant	R2	D-W
3SLS	0.11* (2.73)	0.25* (3.15)	–0.14** (–1.94)	0.15 (3.2)	–0.0003 (–0.007)	0.76* (7.87)	1.17	0.83	1.83
Yield	Rain Index	Fert.Cons./GCA	Technology	–	–	–	Constant	R2	D-W
3SLS	0.25# (1.12)	0.21* (2.39)	0.92* (5.81)	–	–	–	5.76	0.65	2.27

Notes: Figures in parentheses are t-values. *,** and *** denote 1,5 and 10 per cent level of significance respectively. # denotes one year lag. $ specified using AR(1).. The estimates are respective elasticities based on double log functional form. OLS estimates of area and yield equations remain same under the two scenarios.

FIGURE 6.4 *Cotton: World and Domestic Prices, Exports, Imports, Area and Production*

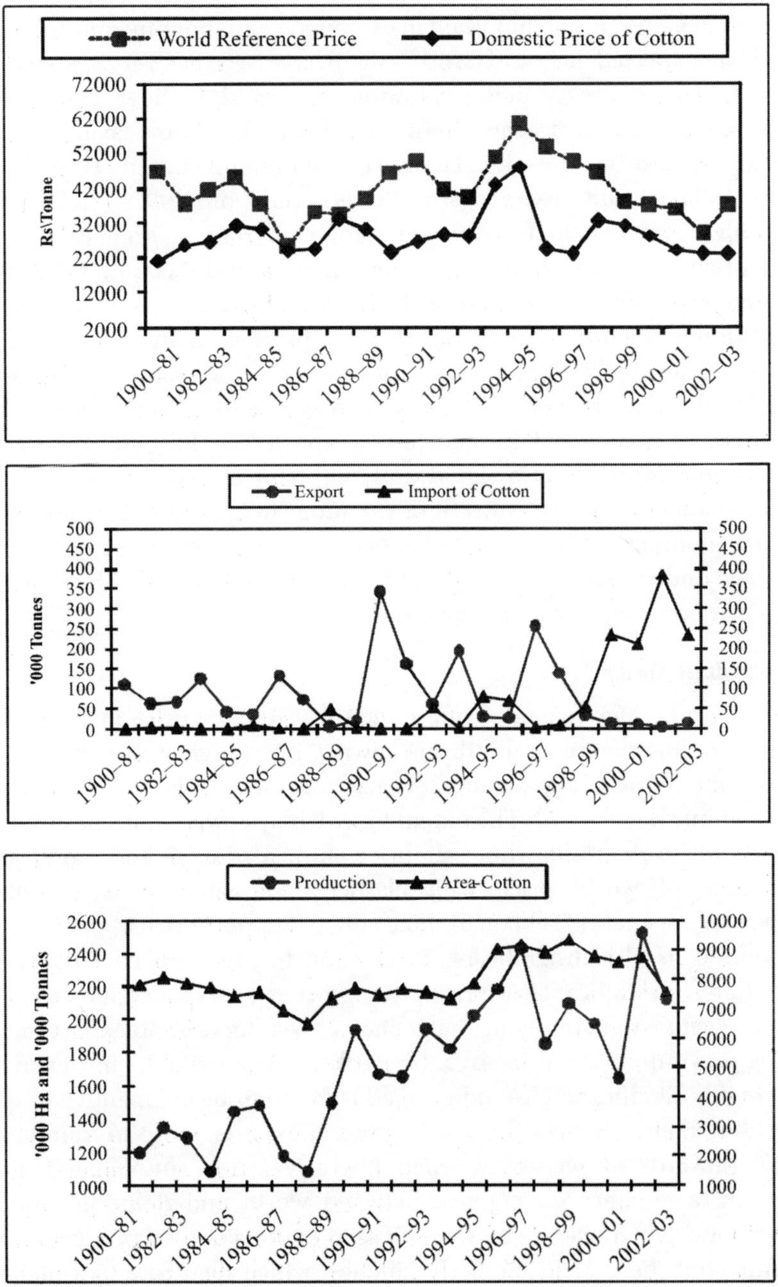

price incentives and also lack statistical significance. Stocks and income are significantly associated with imports. The coefficient of dummy, though negative, is not important in explaining variations in import. Same could be expected in case of tariffs as these have been at a very low level.

As far as acreage under cotton is concerned, it shows that unlike rice, wheat and sugarcane, there have been significant changes in it during the last two decades. The area under cotton started accelerating from 1993–94 and observed a declining trend from 1997–98. Analysis provides evidence in favour of a significant role of both price and non-price factors in explaining changes in area under cotton. Of all the factors, own price rather than profitability and price of competing crop (groundnut) are important factors showing price elasticity to be 0.12 and –0.16, respectively. Among non-price factors as a group, rainfall and irrigation dominate in explaining acreage with positive and high elasticity estimates at 0.22 and 0.09, respectively. Lagged area as an explanatory variable also significantly explains change in acreage. All these factors explain 86 per cent of variations in area and also indicate a greater dominance of non-price factors over price factors in influencing acreage under cotton. Finally, yield is found to be influenced by rainfall, fertilizer consumption and technology.

Groundnut Seed

The external reference price of groundnut seed, be it price in the major world trading centre or FOB, has always been higher than the price prevailing in the wholesale markets across India with large year to year fluctuations (Figure 6.5). The extent to which price variations have been passed on to domestic wholesale price show a positive and significant influence of world price with elasticity estimated at 0.38 under exportable scenario (Table 6.5). Like cotton, support price in the case of groundnut is also insignificant. Production has the expected negative sign but is insignificant. Surprisingly, export as an explanatory variable has a negative sign, implying that a one per cent increase in exports may bring down domestic price by 0.05 per cent. The variable, however, is not highly significant. Groundnut seed is found to be competitive in the world markets. That is why, acceleration in exports, more so from year 1995 onwards, is witnessed when liberal reforms got initiated and possibly a greater convergence between world and domestic prices could have taken place. The share of seed exports in total production is estimated to be 0.51 in the early nineties, which then rose to a higher

FIGURE 6.5 *Groundnut Seed: World and Domestic Prices, Exports, Area and Production*

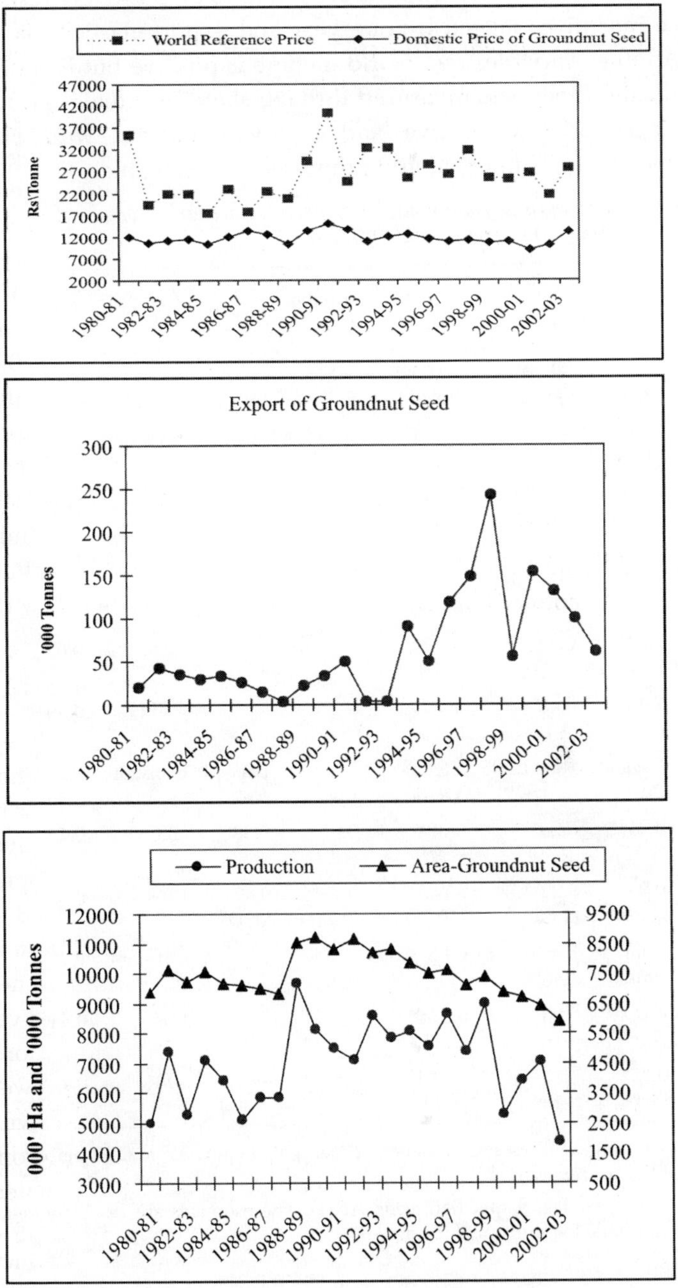

average level at 1.87 per cent in the latter half of the nineties and early 2000. From the estimates, exports are found to be positively responding to price incentives lagged by one year and export elasticity is high at 2.54. Another variable, viz., world income is positive but is statistically insignificant. Openness measured through share of India's agri-trade in world agri-trade is positive and highly significant with elasticity estimated at 3.06. Import of groundnut seed is negligible.

TABLE 6.5 *Groundnut: Results under Exportable Scenario from 1980–81 to 2002–03 at 1993–94 Prices*

Price	*World Price*	*Support Price*	*Export*	*Production*		*Constant*	*R2*	*D-W*
OLS I	0.38* (2.18)	–0.38 (–0.85)	–0.05** (–1.99)	–0.18 (–1.50)	–	10.73	0.43	2.05$
OLS II	0.26** (1.98)	–	–0.04 (–1.49)	–0.18 (–1.59)	–	8.48	0.41	1.89$
3SLS	0.36* (2.96)	–0.17 (–0.56)	–0.06* (–3.87)	–0.22* (–2.37)	–	9.51	0.39	2.1
Export	Lagged Pe/Pd	World Income	Openness (share)	–	–	Constant	R2	D-W
OLS	2.54* (2.63)	0.22 (0.44)	3.06* (3.70)	–	–	–0.67	0.63	1.86
3SLS	2.19* (2.79)	0.43 (1.12)	3.98* (5.66)	–	–	–3.11	0.59	1.70
Area	Lagged Pd	Rain Index	Yield/ Yieldc	Pc Jowar	Lagged Area	Constant	R2	D-W
OLS	0.21** (1.71)	0.29* (2.19)	0.09 (1.32)	0.07 (1.21)	0.58* (3.29)	–0.095	0.75	2.17
3SLS	0.23* (2.39)	0.22** (1.86)	–0.03 (–0.36)	0.12* (2.74)	0.42* (2.92)	1.02	0.69	1.9
Yield	Rain Index	Fert.Cons. /GCA	GIA/Area	–	–	Constant	R2	D-W
OLS	0.78* (2.23)	0.03 (0.33)	0.41#* (2.37)	–	–	4.06	0.51	2.3
3SLS	0.75* (3.32)	–0.14 (–1.59)	0.44#* (2.90)	–	–	3.74	0.42	2.02

Notes: Figures in parentheses are t-values. *,** and *** denote 1,5 and 10 per cent level of significance respectively.

# denotes one year lag. $ specified using AR(1). The estimates are respective elasticities based on double log functional form.

Has price incentive resulted in expansion of area and yield of groundnut seed? As is clear from Figure 6.5, acreage under seed started increasing from 1986 when technology mission programme on oilseeds was initiated. A favourable price structure and introduction of HYV helped to maintain area at a high level only for a few years. From the early nineties, it witnessed a downfall perhaps due to a greater demand for soyabean, sunflower and linseed. Acreage response function reveals own price along with rainfall and lagged area to have significant effects on area with expected positive signs and elasticities estimated at 0.21, 0.29 and 0.58 respectively. Of the two competing crops, viz., jowar and small millets, the price of jowar is positive but is insignificant. On variations in seed yield, results show it to be explained by rainfall (elasticity 0.78) and irrigation (0.41).

Soyabean Seed

The price of soyabean is available only for one state, viz., Madhya Pradesh, which is taken to represent the all-India price. Figure 6.6 depicts movements of domestic price and external reference price of soyabean seed, which became equal only during 1997 to 2001. They again diverged during 2002 and 2003 showing domestic price to be higher than the world price. Fluctuations in both the price series seem to be moving in the same direction indicating a greater price transmission. That is why, variations in world price are found to be statistically significant in explaining domestic price with the estimated value of the coefficient at 0.49 (Table 6.6). Like groundnut, changes in soyabean seed price are not explained by support price. Production has the expected negative sign and is significant in explaining variations in price with elasticity at 0.27. The sign of export coefficient is negative and insignificant. For all these years, soyabean seed had never been competitive in world markets and that is why, negligible exports and imports are reported. It is only from 1996–97 when world price fell, exports started picking up and reached its peak in the early 2000. An increase in exports can be explained more by openness through removal of trade restrictions than the relative prices. The coefficient of ratio of world and domestic price, though positive, is insignificant, indicating that seed exports may respond to price incentives. There is also scope for further acceleration in exports as it is likely to be price competitive and also export restrictions have been removed in recent years. The average export share of soyabean seed in total production has risen from 0.04 in the early nineties to 0.24 per cent during the late nineties and early 2000.

FIGURE 6.6 *Soyabean Seed: World and Domestic Prices, Exports, Area and Production*

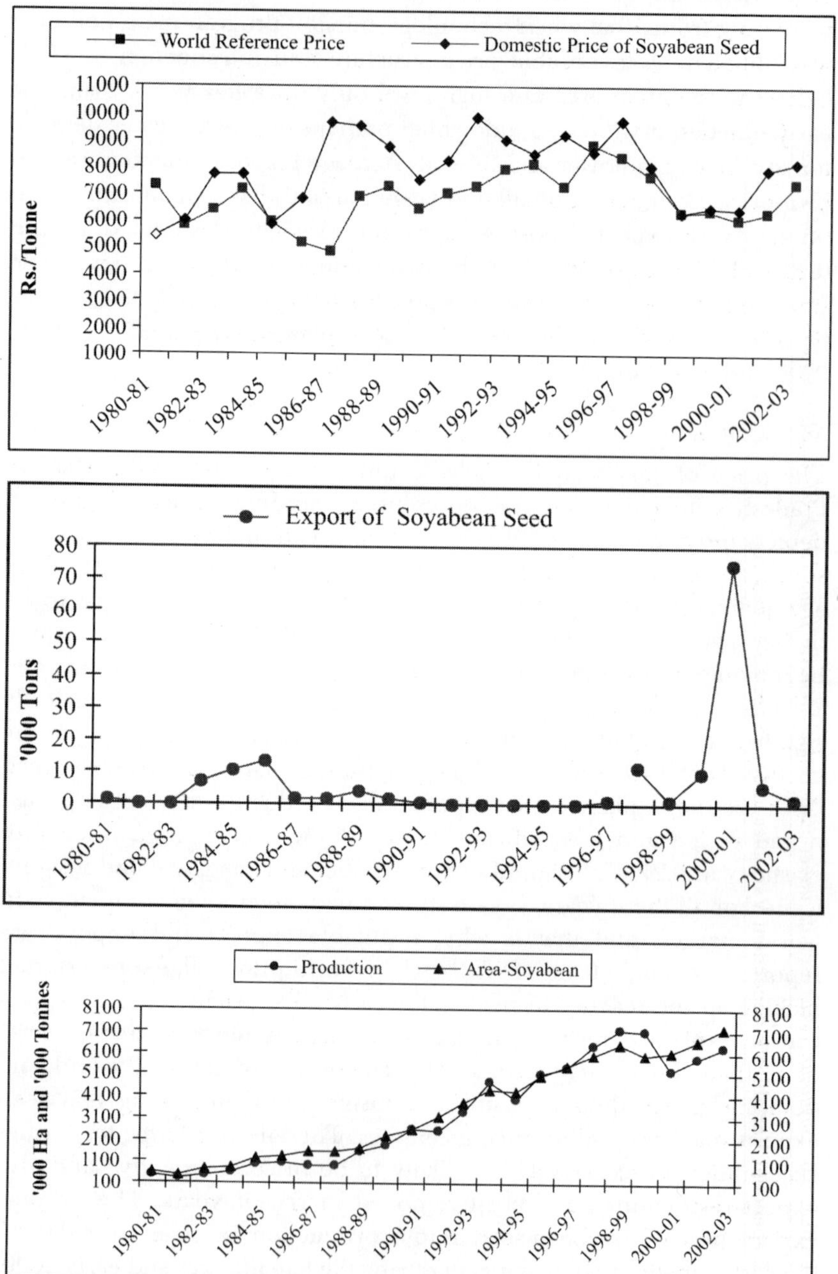

TABLE 6.6 *Soyabean Seed: Results under Exportable Scenario from 1980–81 to 2002–03 at 1993–94 Prices*

Dependent Variables/Independent Variables under Exportable Scenario

Price	*World Price*	*Support Price*	*Export*	*Production*	*Trend*	–	*Constant*	*R2*	*D-W*
OLS I	0.49***	–	–0.01	–0.27***	0.028	–	6.49	0.52	2.2$
	(1.87)		(–1.19)	(–1.81)	(1.34)				
II	0.36	–1.77	–0.02	–0.009	–	–	21.42	0.52	2.2$
	(1.25)	(–1.42)	(–1.64)	(–0.15)					
3SLS	0.39***	–1.94*	–0.01#	–0.010	–	–	22.34	0.42	1.71$
	(1.70)	(–2.23)	(–1.54)	(–0.03)					
Export	Pe/Pd	Openness (share)	Lagged Export	–	–	–	Constant	R2	D-W
OLS	0.64	6.84**	0.58*	–	–	–	1.28	0.59	1.69
	(0.15)	(2.07)	(3.48)						
3SLS	–5.37#	6.46*	0.51*	–	–	–	0.22	0.60	1.85
	(–1.22)	(2.43)	(3.51)						
Area	Lagged Pd/Ip	Rain Index	Yield/Yieldc	Pc Groundnut	RoadDensity	Lagged Area	Constant	R2	D-W
OLS I	0.72*^	0.83*#	0.22	–0.65**	2.01*	0.43*	–6.11	0.98	2.04
	(3.56)	(2.81)	(1.31)	(–2.11)	(2.46)	(2.90)			
OLS II	0.51***	0.54***#	0.21	–0.43	2.18**	0.44**	–7.78	0.98	1.96
	(1.83)	(1.7)	(0.96)	(–1.05)	(2.14)	(2.22)			
3SLS	0.63*	0.47**#	0.12	–0.32	2.12*	0.44*	–8.19	0.97	1.92
	(2.80)	(1.81)	(0.69)	(–1.02)	(2.65)	(2.79)			
Yield	Rain Index	Fert.Cons./GCA	Technology	–	–	–	Constant	R2	D-W
OLS	0.50***	0.11	1.01*#	–	–	–	5.80	0.62	2.06
	(1.75)	(0.98)	(5.13)						
3SLS	0.67*	0.02	0.95*#	–	–	–	4.72	0.69	2.14
	(3.29)	(0.31)	(6.23)						

Notes: Figures in parentheses are t-values. *,** and *** denote 1,5 and 10 per cent level of significance respectively. # denotes one year lag. ^ means no lag is specified. $ specified using AR(1). The estimates are respective elasticities based on double log functional form.

One can also see response to such incentives in terms of significant expansion in area and production of soyabean.

As seen from the graph, area and production of soyabean have drastically increased from 610 to 7,240 thousand ha and production from 440 to 6,379 thousand tonnes during 1980–81 to 2002–03. Madhya Pradesh is the major producer of this crop occupying nearly 72 per cent of area. Both area and yield expansion have been the prime factors responsible for an increasing level of production. From the area response function, it is evident that area elasticity with respect to lagged and current year's profitability is high at 0.51 and 0.72 and that with competing groundnut price is –0.65. Weather, road density (representing infrastructure) and lagged area are also influential in expanding area with elasticity estimated at 0.83, 2.01 and 0.43, respectively. These variables along with the price of competing crop and relative yield explain 98 per cent of variations in area under soyabean. Crop yield is also significantly explained by weather and technological factors.

Main Findings and Remarks

An attempt is made in this chapter to examine whether trade liberalization and macroeconomic policies impact agriculture and the magnitude of response of commodity price, trade, acreage and output to price incentives attributable to changes in macroeconomic and sector specific policies and other factors. For this, a structural econometric model consisting of a set of four behavioural equations and three identities is developed within a partial framework. The model is applied to individual commodities, separately under the exportable and importable scenarios and is estimated using OLS and 3SLS from 1980–81 to 2002–03.

The empirical results, though mixed across the selected crops reveal strong linkages among world price, exchange rate, trade, support price and agriculture. It emerges that barring wheat and rice, the wholesale price of cotton, sugar, groundnut and soyabean seeds are significantly explained by their respective world reference price. While a statistically insignificant coefficient of world wheat price is explained by lack of competitiveness of Indian wheat in the world markets, the same in case of rice could be due to the fact that not all states produce exportable rice and are hence, influenced by changes in world price and exchange rate. The findings also show that wholesale prices of cereals as well as sugar are highly influenced by their respective administered price. This tends to suggest that price policy, backed by procurement provides protection from an unexpected plunge in the world price. But it may dissuade full price transmission from world to domestic markets and could also bring imbalances in the latter, a point that has already been deliberated upon in Chapter 4.

The insignificance of exports/imports in determining the domestic price of cereals is explained by lagged relationship between production and exports of these commodities. A high production in year t is followed by an increase in exports in the subsequent period (year), which also happens to coincide with lower prices. In many instances, changes in domestic prices have influenced the decision to go for export and import rather than export/import being a lead factor in affecting domestic prices. If this kind of situation occurs, then the relationship between domestic price and exports turns out to be negative, which otherwise is expected to be positive. This aspect could be captured by setting appropriate lags and by using quarterly data rather than annual data.

Variations in exports are influenced by relative prices except for soyabean and to some extent for wheat and sugar primarily due to the higher domestic than world price. In the import function, relative price coefficient has the expected negative sign but is statistically significant only for wheat and sugar. In the case of rice and cotton, the relative prices are not important in explaining imports, which implies that imports may take place even if the external prices of these commodities are higher than their respective domestic prices. Besides relative prices, variations in exports and imports are explained by the availability of stocks with the government, level of income and openness to world trade. Quantitative controls and restrictions imposed through NTBs are found to be significant only for rice. From early 2000, NTBs have been removed on almost all the commodities and tariffs have been raised to control import surge of rice, wheat and sugar. Tariffs in cotton got reduced from 1996–97 after which a greater inflow of imports has been reported.

Finally, price incentives attributable to liberal policy changes explain changes in absolute area positively and significantly under each of the selected crops. Non-price factors, particularly rainfall and technology are equally important. Notably, area price elasticities varying from 0.09 to 0.72 in the short run and 0.14 to 1.31 in the long run, though not strictly comparable with the past estimates obtained under a closed trade regime, are fairly close to these. The area price elasticity estimated for selected crops is nearly 0.10 for both wheat and rice; 0.12 for cotton; 0.21 for both sugarcane and groundnut; and 0.51 for soyabean. In contrast, price elasticity estimated in different studies, summarized in Annexure Table 6.1 fall within a range of 0.01 to 0.18 for wheat; 0.02 to 0.17 for rice; –0.02 to 1.02 for sugarcane; 0.008 to 0.48 for cotton, and 0.03 to 0.39 for groundnut seed across various regions.

These results indicate that the impact of trade liberalization on agriculture is indeed encouraging but it has not made a considerable difference in changing the incentive structure, except for soyabean. Thus, the hypothesis that trade and macroeconomic policy changes have positively influenced the agricultural sector in India is accepted. However, the conjecture that crop area shifts have become more responsive to price factors than to non-price factors in a liberalized regime may not be accepted for all the selected crops. Further, except for soyabean, nothing definite can be said about the proposition that area price elasticity is positive and high for those crops whose prices are well integrated with world prices.

To some extent, these findings seem to go against the expectations highlighted in the literature regarding a significant change in the agricultural sector as a result of economic reforms. It is important to mention that these parameters may not be taken to reflect a complete impact of trade liberalization on agriculture as the analysis is partial, based on a few selected commodities. Also, a low supply response could be due to namely: (i) a good part of the sample period pertains to both pre- and post-reform periods; (ii) low market access of India's exports and high level of subsidies given to farmers in other countries; (iii) high volatility in world prices and little efforts to ensure stability in domestic prices of commodities other than of wheat, rice and sugar, (iv) inadequate technological advancement, irrigation and other infrastructure, and (v) partial nature of economic reforms such as adhocism in exports-imports, regulations and trade through government agencies. Trade in agricultural commodities was very strongly regulated and subject to QRs till as late as 1999. Even after 2002, quantitative restrictions and other NTBs have been re-imposed on cereals and other essential commodities. It is important to note that when trade is highly regulated through policy, then the impact of factors like international prices is captured partially. Nevertheless, the empirical model used and results obtained have enabled to evaluate the contribution of policies and other factors towards the performance of agriculture in a fairly open environment.

In what follows, the resilience of agriculture to the 'best and worst' situations is analysed based on exogenous impulses along with policy options that may counter their likely adverse effects in a market-driven economy.

Notes

1. As explained in Chapter 3, NTBs could be obtaining permits/license, quota/quantitative ceilings, minimum export price, standards, canalized and permitted through official agencies, etc. Though most of these barriers got removed from 1999–2000, but a few, such as obtaining export-import permits for essential commodities continue on grounds of health and food security.
2. The reason for the insignificance of variables when they should have been significant is explained by: (a) pure statistical reasons such as limited data set, a significant part of which relates to pre-reform period, (b) price data at all India level is representative of prices from 11 states in the selected wholesale markets, and (c) economic reasons.

7

Resilience of Indian Agriculture to Changes in Price and Macroeconomic Policies

Having evaluated that the performance of the agricultural sector in India is increasingly driven by factors such as: (i) an incentive structure based on its linkages with macroeconomic and sector-specific policies, (ii) world commodity price, and (iii) irrigation, infrastructure and technology; there is a case for examining the extent to which agriculture is resilient to changes in these factors in the post-reform period. The analysis assumes significance in understanding the relative importance of various factors impacting agriculture and proposing interventions to neutralize their adverse effects, if any so as to maintain an incentive structure. Counterfactual simulation experiments are carried out for the purpose based on the structural econometric model used in Chapter 6. Simulations are done by conceiving, 'what would happen if', for best and worst case scenarios wherein one time change or multiple changes are introduced in exogenous variables at a time and their impact on endogenous variables is examined. Accordingly, the sensitivity of agricultural prices, exports, imports, area and output to hypothetical changes in the exchange rate, tariffs, world price, support price and rainfall is examined. To begin with, the alternate scenarios of policy, price and natural factors that may positively or negatively influence the performance of the agricultural sector are presented. Simulation experiments are carried out separately for six selected commodities in the study. The next portion tests the efficacy of the structural model in carrying out the simulations. The model is validated by examining the difference between the actual and simulated (also called base-run equilibrium) values of endogenous variables. In the end, empirical findings along with policy options, which may counter the effects of unexpected shocks in a market-driven economy are outlined.

Alternate Scenarios for Simulation Experiments

In all, five alternate scenarios of change/shock are experimented upon with the objective to quantify the sensitivity of agriculture to changes in macro and sectoral policies and factors. The divergences introduced in the system are based on the maximum and minimum annual percentage changes in selected exogenous variables observed from 1991–92 to 2002–03.

Exchange Rate Fluctuations

India initiated a devaluation of its currency once during 1991 and then twice in 1992–93. Since then, the exchange rate is market driven and has an in-built mechanism that stabilizes its movements. From 1991–92 to 2002–03, the nominal exchange rate has shown a maximum yearly increase by 30 per cent and a minimum by 2 per cent. For simulation purposes, a hypothetical maximum and minimum change is introduced at a time in the structural model from the existing level during 2000–01, 2001–02 and 2002–03. Keeping in view the fact that exchange rate appreciated from 2003–04 with the result that the nominal rate came down from Rs 48.5 per dollar in 2002–03 to Rs 44 per dollar in 2005, another simulation experiment is done. The nominal exchange rate under it is allowed to appreciate annually by 5 per cent from its existing level.

Variations in Commodity Tariffs

The second experiment relates to alterations in commodity tariff. Of all the six commodities chosen, imports have taken place for rice, wheat, sugar and cotton. Tariffs have long been in place for sugar and cotton. For rice and wheat, tariffs have been imposed only from 2000–01 onwards. Except for rice, the tariff rates have been lower than the bound rates prescribed by the WTO, which indicates that there is further room for increasing import duties. For each commodity, two scenarios are generated. While an optimistic scenario represents the maximum increase in tariffs equal to WTO given bound rates, the pessimistic scenario focuses on a minimum or complete removal of tariffs, i.e., zero tariffs. The first scenario where the maximum tariffs are imposed also takes care of the impact of removal of NTBs. The estimated tariff equivalents of NTBs quantified in Chapter 3, fall within the range of 2 to 56 per cent across various commodities. Since the current tariff rates for wheat, cotton and sugar are well below the bound rate, imposition of a maximum tariff equal to bound rate under an optimistic scenario will account for the effects of NTBs on the level of imports. It is expected that a change in tariff policy will have a significant impact on the level of imports into the country.

World Price Volatility

Commodity prices are subject to fluctuations due to changing demand and supply conditions. Compared to domestic markets, fluctuations in commodity prices in world markets are higher. It has been argued in many studies that due to a greater integration of domestic markets with the world markets, price fluctuations in the latter would pass on to the former. An increase in world price may incentivize producers due to the price competitiveness of commodities and hence an increase in demand for exports. In contrast, a fall in world commodity price may have negative implications for the farm sector in terms of increasing imports. In a situation of highly volatile nature of world prices, producers need to take this facor into account in their area allocation and production decisions. The extent to which world price volatility may affect domestic price, area/production and external trade is studied by hypothetically raising world prices under the optimistic scenario and by lowering them under the pessimistic one. The maximum and minimum yearly percentage variations that have occurred in the world price of each commodity during the nineties and early 2000 are utilized for the purpose. Price variations fall within the maximum positive range of 25 to 35 per cent and a negative range of 20 to 45 per cent.

Changes in Minimum Support Price

Government fixes the support price of essential farm commodities and undertakes procurement of a few with a primary aim to provide incentives to producers to expand production by applying modern inputs/technology and bring stability in market price through open market sales. As analysed in Chapter 4, the wholesale prices of cereals in many states equal the level of the administered price, i.e., MSP tend to act as a floor price. The issue is highly debatable as many think this policy tends to be inflationary in nature, distort the process of market mechanism and brings demand-supply imbalances. The policy is also criticized due to its regional and crop bias as it acts as a floor price mainly in the case of wheat and rice that too in states where procurement operations are undertaken. Due to an opening up of domestic markets to external trade, opportunities to export cereals have been growing. Depending on price incentives and competitiveness, producers now have the option to sell either directly to state agencies or in the international markets. In view of these aspects, the degree of sensitivity of domestic prices, exports-imports and output as a result of changes in the support price is estimated.

The empirical estimates show MSP to be positive and significant in determining prices of only wheat, rice and sugar. For other selected crops, coefficients are insignificant with a positive or a negative sign, implying a weak or rather negligible association between MSP and domestic wholesale price. Given these findings, a simulation is undertaken only for wheat, rice and sugar. Changes in the system are introduced by increasing and decreasing the support price in accord with the maximum and minimum percentage change during 1991–92 to 2002–03, representing the best and worst situations. For wheat and rice, the maximum increase in MSP lies within the range of 8 to 20 per cent and falls between 5 to 8 per cent. For sugarcane, the maximum increase in support price is 8 per cent and the minimum is 1 per cent.

Variations in Rainfall

Despite advancements in major and minor irrigation works in the country, agriculture continues to be dependent on weather. A less than normal rainfall (index = 100) affects agricultural production and hence overall economic growth due to inter-sectoral demand and supply linkages. The extent to which rainfall affects area and production is studied under two scenarios. While the best one depicts above normal rainfall, the worst scenario depicts a below normal average rainfall, i.e., drought. The above normal rainfall is depicted at the maximum of 15 per cent during the last more than 10 years and the minimum is observed to be 20 per cent during 1987 and than during 2002, which happened to be drought years.

Validation of the Structural Model

Based on the above alternate hypothetical scenarios of exogenous impulses, simulation experiments are undertaken to demonstrate the performance of agriculture under situations that are different from the prevailing. Before introducing alterations in policy, price and natural variables, it is important to determine the effectiveness of the structural model in generating simulations and its ability to address "what would happen if" queries for proposing a policy change. The behavioural equations determined by the use of OLS and 3SLS in the preceding chapter show estimates to be by and large consistent. Simulations are performed on OLS estimates as the estimated parameters also show robustness based on t-test and other tests. The model is first validated by comparing the actual past and base run simulated values of endogenous variables for the period of investigation without introducing any change in the exogenous variables. A co-movement of actual and base-run values (also called equilibrium values) indicates that the error is low and unbiased, i.e., the model is fit for carrying out simulations or forecasts.

Annexure Figure 7.1 presents results of the validation exercise for one endogenous variable, viz., crop acreage. The graphical representation shows actual and simulated values of area under each crop from 1990–91 to 2002–03. The simulated values are representative of equilibrium values that are generated on the basis of actual time paths of exogenous variables and given time paths of factors relating to trade, exchange rate and world prices. The equilibrium-simulated values of endogenous variables are termed as 'base run' or 'reference run' values. By and large, these estimates show a negligible difference between the actual and simulated values of crop acreage. For other endogenous variables also, viz., domestic prices, exports, imports and yield, the two values are free from errors and biases, i.e., the model is able to closely track movements of endogenous variables. However, in the case of cotton, deviations between the actual and base run values of imports are identified in some years. Similarly, the simulated values of sugar exports and prices diverge from their actual historical values during the early 2000.

The statistical reasons for occurrence of errors can be explained by for example: (i) regression techniques used to determine the behavioural equations in the model have an inherent stochastic component that represents the random nature of variables, (ii) techniques used in constructing and solving the model, (iii) quite often when equations are determined simultaneously, the errors of individual variables multiply instead of adding up, (iv) dynamic method used to do simulations/forecasts could be a source of error because the present values of impact variables are generated on the basis of forecasted past values rather than the actual values of the past. Errors tend to be more compared to the static models (Bhattacharya and Kar, 2007). The economic reasons for various sources of error could be namely: (i) behavioural equations developed are based on theories with well developed market structures and hence may not explain conditions in the Indian context, (ii) mix of sample period pertaining to pre- and post-reform periods having year-to-year changes in tariff rates, NTBs and fixation of support price, (iii) imposition of internal trade barriers such as octroi and changes in inter-state/zonal restrictions on movement of essential commodities, which may distort prices. It is important to mention that these distortionary changes identified in some years cannot be quantified. However, broad economic variables in the model correctly elicit directional changes.

Exogenous Impulses and the Performance of Agriculture

After validation of the model, a maximum or a minimum variation in the exogenous variable at a given time is introduced to explain the behaviour and magnitude of its impact on endogenous variables. The maximum change represents an optimistic case and a minimum change or fall indicates a pessimistic situation or a shock. The impact of exogenous impulses on endogenous variables is measured by comparing changes in the base-run equilibrium values obtained through validation with equilibrium values generated under simulation. The exercise is done for each commodity separately from 2000–01 to 2002–03. The choice of period is based on the fact that macroeconomic policies had already been adopted by this time and also agriculture policy changes with respect to removal of NTBs and their replacement by tariffs was allowed to be implemented only from 2000–01. The empirical results, presented in Tables 7.1A–E show annual average percentage change in the base run and simulated values of endogenous variables from 2000–01 to 2001–2003. Then estimated percentage change in prices, exports, imports and acreage/production of selected commodities are shown under alternate scenarios. Tables 7.2A–F provide relative and total impact of various policy, price and natural factors on the performance indicators. It also gives the sum total of the annual average percentage change corresponding to various factors under optimistic and pessimistic scenarios.

Impact of Exchange Rate Fluctuations

Fluctuations in nominal exchange rate represent the first scenario, where depreciation of currency is postulated to be higher by maximum 30 per cent and minimum by 2 and lower by (appreciation) 5 per cent from the existing rate during 2000, 2001 and 2002. A depreciation of currency by 30 per cent raises the nominal exchange rate from Rs 44.92, 47.23 and 48.49 per dollar to Rs 58.39, 61.39 and 63.04, respectively during these three years. Similarly, a minimum change of 2 per cent increases it by Rs 45.82, 48.17 and 49.45, respectively. In contrast, an appreciation of currency by 5 per cent reduces nominal exchange rate to Rs 42.67, 44.87

TABLE 7.1A Impact of Exchange Rate Volatility

Annual Average % Change 2000–01 to 2002–03	*Maximum Variations:+30%*				*Minimum Variations: +2%*				*Minimum Variations: –5%*			
	Price	*Exports*	*Imports*	*Area/ Production*	*Price*	*Exports*	*Imports*	*Area/ Production*	*Price*	*Exports*	*Imports*	*Area/ Production*
Wheat	-1.53	172.89	-60.49	0.64	0.38	7.72	-15.63	0.89	0.95	-17.93	5.40	0.96
Rice:India	1.41	56.38	14.38	0.74	0.94	1.27	40.17	0.54	0.81	-10.82	48.81	0.58
Rice:Haryana	7.97	35.23	–	0.64	-0.58	-2.27	–	-0.05	-1.46	-5.65	–	-0.12
Sugar	2.99	91.81	-72.57	-0.51	-1.83	14.85	-9.24	-1.28	-3.20	-1.11	28.80	-1.51
Cotton	13.88	34.41	-10.12	1.20	0.46	3.83	-0.86	0.05	-3.16	-3.73	2.02	-0.29
Groundnut Seed	7.46	74.53	–	-2.22	0.39	6.86	–	-3.30	-1.59	-7.34	–	-3.61
Soyabean Seed	13.23	31.49	–	7.62	0.78	14.67	–	-0.83	-2.60	10.18	–	-3.18

and 46.07 per dollar from the existing level in the selected years. Results show that keeping other policy variables unchanged, a maximum variation in the exchange rate can augment exports and decline imports through change in the price structure. Across commodities, the impact of devaluation on annual percentage increase in domestic prices is positive in rice, cotton, sugar and oilseeds and negative in case of wheat. This is because the estimates show crop prices other than wheat to have responded positively and significantly to changes in the world price from 1980–81 to 2002–03 (Tables 6.1 to 6.6). It is also evident from the analysis that the response in case of rice is statistically insignificant at the national level. In order to demonstrate the sensitivity of rice to exogenous impulses, a case of one paddy cultivating state, viz. Haryana is taken up. Since data on external trade, NTBs, etc., is not available at the state level, estimates are generated using series at all-India, and thus may be taken with a caveat. The OLS estimates in Annexure Table 7.1 show variations in wholesale price of rice in Haryana to be positively and significantly explained by the world reference price during the study period.

Devaluation of the rupee results in an increase in domestic price from a minimum of 1.41 per cent (for rice) to a maximum 13.88 per cent (for cotton) per year. The impact of exchange rate variations is directly visible on the volume of exports-imports, which shows an annual average increase in exports by a minimum 31 per cent (in case of soyabean) and a maximum by more than 100 per cent (in case of wheat). This indicates that had India been more open to world trade during the eighties, average exports in a year would have been higher by 172 per cent in case of wheat, 30–56 per cent in case of soyabean seed, rice and cotton, 74 per cent in case of groundnut seed and 92 per cent in case of sugar. The impact of devaluation on imports is found to be negative except in rice. As far as impact of currency depreciation on area allocation is concerned, one may find an annual average percentage increase in area by 0.64 for wheat; 0.64 for rice in Haryana; 1.20 for cotton and 7.62 for soyabean. In case of groundnut and sugarcane, acreage shows a downfall by 2.22 and 0.51 per cent per year. The decline is expected due to the fact that crop area shifts are taking place at the all-India level and area under groundnut is found to be diversifying to other oilseed crops. The trend growth rate of area under groundnut has declined from 1.6 per cent during the eighties (1980–1990) to 1.4 per cent during the nineties (1991–2003). Similar is the case of sugarcane which shows a decline in the rate of growth rate in area over time. Estimates on supply response have also indicated that technological and irrigation factors play an equally important role in inducing area under a particular crop along with price incentives.

Compared to above optimistic scenario of high currency depreciation, a minimum depreciation of currency by 2 per cent and appreciation by 5 per cent again provide useful insights. Domestic price rises by maximum 3.20 per cent, which is less than what has been observed in the optimistic scenario. The situation also negatively affects crop area. Annual average commodity exports increase by 7.72, 14.85, 3.83 and 14.67 per cent in case of wheat, sugar, cotton and soyabean seed, respectively and decline by 2.27 per cent in case of rice. Exports tend to fall for all commodities under a scenario of currency appreciation by 5 per cent from the existing level. Only exceptional case is that of soyabean seed. Imports remain negative except for rice, which on an average rises by 40.17 per cent per year. In case of a severe shock to agriculture through appreciation of currency by 5 per cent, the average rate of imports increases significantly in case of rice by 48.8 per cent, sugar by 28.8 per cent and wheat and cotton by 5.4 and 2.02 per cent per year, respectively. Results show appreciation of currency to be negatively affecting domestic prices, exports and area and hence production of commercial crops, implying lack of resilience of the farm sector to this change. The impact is not severe on wheat and rice at the all-India level as world price movements do not influence the prices of these two crops significantly. However, it is found to be negatively affected at the state level.

Impact of Changes in Tariffs and Elimination of NTBs

Changes in tariffs and removal of NTBs represent the second simulation experiment to gauge the impact on performance of agriculture. The exercise is carried out only for rice, wheat, cotton and sugar as India hardly imports groundnut and soyabean seeds. For rice and wheat, tariffs were 0 till 1999–2000 and were imposed at 92 and 108 per cent during 2000–01. In the subsequent years, tariffs for these two commodities fell to 75 and 100 per cent. The prescribed WTO bound rates for wheat was 100 per cent and for rice within a range of 70–80 per cent. For commodities other than wheat and rice, tariffs were placed at 100 for sugar and at 25, 5, and 5 per cent for cotton during 2000, 2001 and 2002, respectively. The respective bound rates for these two commodities were 150 per cent each. Given these tariffs, two simulations have been carried out, first with maximum tariffs equal to bound rate and second with minimum or no (zero) tariffs. In the case of rice, maximum tariff is placed at 100 per cent in order to see its impact on imports. Zero tariffs may be treated as a shock as it may lead to a heavy inflow of imports into the domestic markets. An increase in tariff equal to bound rates also takes care of complete elimination of NTBs. The tariff equivalents of NTBs of commodities estimated in Chapter 3 vary between 3 to 14 per cent for cereals and 9 to 43 per cent for sugar during early 2000.

Assuming there is no change in the exchange rate and other exogenous and policy variables, the results given in Table 7.1B under the optimistic scenario of increase in tariff rates equal to WTO prescribed bound rates reveal an increase in domestic price of commodities. Import of wheat does not show an increase whereas that of rice increases by an average of 36.37 per cent per year. Sugar and cotton imports could be hard hit by an increase in tariff rate to 150 per cent from the existing level of 100 and 5 per cent. While average sugar imports may fall by 66.7 per cent per year, cotton imports fall by almost 29 per cent. A decline in cotton imports may negatively impinge upon growth of the textile industry, which has become increasingly dependent on import from other countries. As expected, the effect of increase in tariff rates though positive on domestic price may not be high enough to accelerate or decelerate growth in crop acreage and output except in the case of sugar and cotton.

TABLE 7.1B *Impact of Variations in Tariffs*

Annual Average % Change 2000–01 to 2002–03	*Maximum Variations: +100 to 150%*			*Minimum Variations: 0%*		
	Price	*Imports*	*Area/Production*	*Price*	*Imports*	*Area/Production*
Wheat	–1.72	–2.90	0.53	1.37	747.99	0.88
Rice:India	1.07	36.37	0.70	–0.24	144.10	0.54
Rice:Haryana	2.49	43.14	0.29	–16.61	362.25	–1.36
Sugar	4.12	–66.70	2.39	–12.70	2,955.10	–0.54
Cotton	61.76	–28.70	2.86	–6.86	3.28	–2.42

Note: Minimum variation for sugar is 40 per cent.

In a situation of shock induced by eliminating tariffs, the results reveal that had we not raised tariffs in case of wheat, rice and sugar from 2000, the impact would have been extensive in terms of surge in their imports and fall in domestic prices. The impact of reduction in tariffs on import of cotton is low at 3.3 per cent per year compared to the large increase in the volume of wheat, rice and sugar imports. The impact on prices of cotton, sugar and rice is negative and may decrease at an annual average rate of 6.86, 12.7 and 0.24 per cent respectively. Finally, of all the four crops, the area under rice in Haryana, sugarcane and cotton is found to be decelerating annually by 1.36, 0.54 and 2.42 per cent, respectively due to a tariff shock. Area under wheat and rice at the all-India level is resilient to tariff shock as average annual percentage change in area is estimated to be 0.88 and 0.54 per year, respectively. Acreage under paddy/rice in Haryana declines at an annual average rate of 1.36 per cent due to low price incentive attributable to a shock due to zero tariffs.

Impact of World Price Volatility

World prices of farm commodities are positive and significant in explaining variations in domestic prices of sugar, cotton and oilseeds. In the case of rice, the coefficient is positive at the all-India level and is positive and statistically significant at the state level. Simulations are done for cotton, sugar, groundnut, soyabean at the all-India level. For rice, the analysis is done at the all-India level as well as for Haryana. In the case of wheat, world price is not statistically important in explaining domestic price at the national and state level. Its impact is, therefore shown only on exports, imports and area. For each commodity, a maximum and a minimum yearly change in world price (in dollar) is calculated from 1991–92 to 2002–03. World price of commodities shows a maximum increase and a decline by 30 and 20 per cent in case of wheat; 35 and 20 per cent in case of rice; 35 and 35 per cent in case of sugar; 25 and 30 per cent in case of cotton; 30 and 45 per cent in case of groundnut seed and 25 and 25 per cent in case of soyabean seed. Simulations are done by increasing/decreasing the world price of these commodities during 2000–01, 2001–02 and 2002–03, respectively by their maximum/minimum percentage change in each year.

The results in Table 7.1C show that volatility on the higher side increases the average domestic price of commodities between −1.53 to 11.59 per cent per year. It does not seem to exert an inflationary pressure but needs continuous monitoring. Acceleration in exports is the highest for wheat and sugar at an average of 172 and 107 per cent followed by 74 per cent for groundnut seed, 67 per cent for rice and 28 per cent for cotton and soyabean. As expected, an increase in world price relative to domestic price brings level of imports downward and raises acreage/production of a crop. The annual average increase in area on account of high world price is estimated to be 0.75, 1.01, 0.64 and 6.2, respectively for rice, cotton, wheat and soyabean seed. Area under groundnut and sugarcane increased by 0.67 and 0.51 per cent only in

2002–03, showing on an average a decline. These results though not strictly comparable with the estimates given in the literature due to different methodology, assumptions and time period are yet similar in demonstrating directional changes in price, output and exports. Gulati and Kelly (1999) while simulating the impact of increase in domestic price in tune with international price anticipated percentage change in domestic price and supply of rice, wheat, cotton and sugarcane/sugar to be positive at 6.61 and 0.68 per cent for rice; 6.38 and 4.95 per cent for wheat; 4.5 and –0.73 per cent for sugarcane and 6.38 and 9.58 per cent for cotton, respectively from base level during 1993–94. Rice exports may increase to 3.6 million tonne and that of wheat to 5.1 million tonne, sugar to 0.34 million tonne and cotton to 0.55 million tonne under a scenario of alignment of domestic prices and world prices.

TABLE 7.1C *Impact of Volatility in World Commodity Price*

Annual Average % Change 2000–01 to 2002–03	*Maximum Variations:+25 to 35%*				*Minimum Variations: 20 to –45%*			
	Price	*Exports*	*Imports*	*Area/ Production*	*Price*	*Exports*	*Imports*	*Area/ Production*
Wheat	–1.53	172.83	–60.48	0.64	–0.83	–57.53	80.48	0.63
Rice:India	1.48	67.30	10.83	0.75	0.48	–34.45	71.94	0.63
Rice:Haryana	9.19	41.31	–6.13	0.73	–6.10	–22.23	127.42	–0.54
Sugar	3.76	107.77	–77.22	–0.38	–10.18	–55.36	737.70	–2.70
Cotton	11.59	28.90	–8.69	1.01	–17.27	–30.36	15.43	–1.70
Groundnut Seed	7.45	74.50	–	–2.22	–15.57	–68.58	–	–5.96
Soyabean Seed	11.12	28.60	–	6.20	–13.06	–3.49	–	–10.57

In contrast to the above optimistic scenario, the pessimistic one, represented by a fall in world commodity prices shows a negative impact on domestic prices, exports and area. The shock is predominant, and if occurs it would negatively affect exports of all commodities. The impact is also extensive in terms of import surge by nearly 700 per cent per year for sugar; more than 100 per cent for rice; 80 per cent for wheat and 15 per cent for cotton. A double increase in the inflow of import may badly affect the performance of agriculture in terms of area and production. Policies such as increase in tariff rates can be followed to counter this shock of excessive imports. It is important to mention that the impact of world price shock on area under wheat and rice at the all-India level may not be severe as these commodities are influenced more by their support price than by the movements in world prices. The impact of this shock on rice price and area is significant in Haryana and shows that on an average, price and area of rice/paddy would fall by 6.1 and 0.54 per cent, respectively every year. Based on these estimates, one can deduce that if the price of rice at the national level gets fully integrated with the world price, a shock in the latter due to fall in price would result in an annual average 0.54 per cent decline in acreage and hence production of rice/paddy.

Impact of Changes in MSP

The fourth simulation experiment postulates changes in the support price of commodities keeping all the other policy variables, viz., exchange rate, tariffs and world prices unchanged. The OLS estimates show the coefficient of support price to be positive and significant in explaining variations in the domestic price of wheat, rice and sugar only. Simulation experiments are, therefore, confined to these commodities only. The maximum and minimum (negative) variations observed in the support price of these three commodities during 1991–2003 are: +20 and –8 per cent for wheat and +8 and –5 per cent for rice and +8 and –1 per cent for sugarcane. Based on these, the level of MSP during 2000–01, 2001–02 and 2002–03 is changed by their respective maximum and minimum rates of variations. The MSP of wheat under an optimistic scenario for three years is Rs 4,701.35, Rs 4,621.12 and Rs 4,581.82 per tonne, respectively and the same under the pessimistic scenario is Rs 3,604.37, Rs 3,542.86 and Rs 3,512.73 per tonne, respectively. In the case of rice, the MSP varies between a maximum and minimum range of Rs 3,537.57 –3,111.75 per tonne in 2001, between Rs 3,555.28–3,127.33 per tonne in 2002 and between Rs 3,534.55–3,109.09 per tonne in 2003, respectively.

Results furnished in Table 7.1D reveal that agriculture is resilient to changes in the support price in terms of its impact on price, exports and area. With a 20 and 8 per cent increase in MSP of wheat and rice, their average domestic prices increase by a maximum 13 and 6 per cent per year, which indicate a not so elastic response of domestic prices to changes in MSP. Similarly, a fall in MSP by 8 and 5 per cent reduces domestic price by nearly 5 per cent per year for wheat and rice. Variations in the wholesale price of rice are found to be relatively elastic in Haryana consequent upon a hike in MSP. Besides change in prices, the annual average maximum increase in area under wheat and rice is also estimated at 2.45 and 1.29 per cent and a minimum at 0.21 and 0.06 per cent, respectively. Rice acreage in Haryana would fall annually by 0.96 if

MSP is reduced. Clearly, under an optimistic scenario of an increase in support price, acreage and hence production get a boost but exports decline on an average of 34 per cent in case of wheat; 10 per cent in case of rice and 2.67 per cent in case of sugar annually. Average imports for wheat, rice and sugar may rise annually by 7.87, 43.46 and 66.71 per cent per year, respectively. In contrast, a decline in the support price, if it occurs may bring down domestic price and raises average exports of wheat, rice and sugar by 21, 3.23 and 12 per cent per year, respectively but its effect on expected decline in imports is visible only in case of wheat and sugar. Sugar price and export would fall by an annual average rate of 3.15 and 12 per cent, respectively. Rice imports may continue to take place at an average rate of 42 per cent per year as under a situation of rise in MSP. This suggests that even if the domestic price of rice falls as a result of fall in MSP, it remains higher than the world price and hence augment imports. The effect of MSP shock on area and production goes against the expectation and shows an average yearly increase by 0.21 per cent in case of wheat and 0.06 per cent in case of rice. This indicates a resilience of the farm sector to a shock arising by fall in MSP at the aggregate level. However, at the disaggregate level, MSP shock can bring on an average, a 0.96 per cent fall in rice area every year. Similarly, Statutory Minimum Price (SMP) shock in the case of sugarcane may bring down allocation of area by 1.53 per cent every year. The impact of production is not found to be large as variations in the support price do not suggest a considerable change in the productivity.

TABLE 7.1D *Impact of Variations in MSP/SMP*

Annual Average % Change 2000–01 to 2002–03	*Maximum Variations:+8 and 20%*				*Minimum Variations: 5 and –8%*			
	Price	*Exports*	*Imports*	*Area/ Pro-duction*	*Price*	*Exports*	*Imports*	*Area/ Pro-duction*
Wheat	13.18	–34.40	7.87	2.45	–4.75	20.99	–16.25	0.21
Rice:India	5.99	–9.83	43.46	1.29	–3.48	3.23	41.94	0.06
Rice: Haryana	17.93	–17.91	62.16	1.46	–10.41	14.53	52.73	–0.96
Sugar	5.20	–2.67	66.71	0.07	–3.15	12.01	–6.38	–1.53

Impact of Rainfall Variations

In this scenario, the rainfall index is assumed to be the maximum (15% higher than normal) at 106.08, 106.9 and 91.31 and minimum (20 % below normal) at 73.8, 74.36 and 63.52 compared to the actual values of

92.25, 92.96 and 79.4, respectively during 2000, 2001 and 2002. Rainfall above normal is expected to increase production whereas a below normal rainfall represents drought conditions, which negatively affects output. Bhattacharya and Kar (2007) generated a pessimistic scenario of rainfall shock in their macro-econometric model. Results show a substantial fall in agricultural growth rate from 3.3 per cent to −1.7 per cent (151% change) in the short run and 2.6 to 2.0 per cent (23% change) in the long run. Drought may result in a 10 per cent decline in the overall growth of the economy due to strong spillover effects of farm sector onto industrial sector growth rates. The results of the simulation exercises in the present study estimate an average fall in area/production of selected crops between 2 to 12 per cent per year.

For each commodity, the results given in Table 7.1E indicate that area, yield and hence production rises as a result of good rainfall and vice versa. The annual average percentage change in area/production is the maximum for soyabean seed (6.41%), wheat (4.63%) followed by rice, cotton and groundnut seed (nearly 4%). In contrast, a rainfall shock adversely affects area and the magnitude of yearly average fall is 13 per cent for oilseeds, 7.47 per cent for cotton and almost 5 per cent for cereals, respectively. In both situations of good rainfall and drought, the prices of rice, sugar, cotton and oilseeds are negatively affected. Sugar acreage does not seem to be sensitive to drought conditions. An invisible impact of rainfall on cereals prices at all-India level could be due to fixation of MSP backed by procurement, which stabilizes the domestic prices of these commodities. Not much variation in the exports and imports of farm commodities is found as a result of changes in rainfall.

TABLE 7.1E *Impact of Variations in Rainfall*

Annual Average % Change 2000–01 to 2002–03	*Maximum Variations:+15 %*				*Minimum Variations: 20 %*			
	Price	*Exports*	*Imports*	*Area/ Production*	*Price*	*Exports*	*Imports*	*Area/ Production*
Wheat	0.54	–0.15	–10.23	4.63	0.54	–0.15	–10.23	–4.76
Rice:India	0.20	–2.25	42.53	4.30	0.20	–2.25	42.53	–5.15
Rice:Haryana	–16.76	–	–	1.35	–0.27	–	–	–2.03
Sugar	–2.22	10.16	–1.19	3.21	0.07	1.83	0.26	1.83
Cotton	–0.56	1.66	–0.07	4.92	–0.56	1.66	–0.07	–7.47
Groundnut Seed	–0.17	2.68	–	3.79	–0.17	2.68	–	–13.80
Soyabean Seed	–0.18	13.40	–	6.41	–0.18	13.40	–	–12.37

Summing up and Implications

This chapter primarily examines the extent to which performance of the agricultural sector is resilient in the face of disturbances caused by macro and sectoral policies, price and other exogenous factors. Counterfactual simulations are carried out for individual commodities in the post-reform period based on estimates obtained from the structural model. The key findings are summed up along with suggested change in policies that may counter the effects of unexpected shocks:

1. The performance of agriculture under an optimistic scenario of maximum devaluation and world price reveals that domestic price, exports and area/production would be higher by a maximum of 13.23, 172 and 7.62 per cent respectively per year than the existing level across the selected commodities. The same under a pessimistic scenario of shock due to currency appreciation and fall in the world commodity price reveals a maximum yearly downfall in price, exports and area by 17, 68 and 10 per cent respectively. The volume of imports under the two scenarios shows a maximum yearly decline by 77 per cent (optimistic situation) and increase by 737 per cent (pessimistic situation) in comparison to the existing level. Since exchange rate is now market determined, the agricultural sector can be resilient to adverse impacts arising out of currency appreciation. Import surge caused by currency appreciation and world price shocks can be handled by keeping a check on imports and imposing higher tariffs. Price stability in the domestic markets can also be maintained through storage as is done for wheat and rice (Chand, 2010). But this option may not work in view of a limited capacity in the country for storage of all commodities. A variable tariff policy must synchronize with price policy in terms of fixation of support price of commodities in accordance with conditions prevailing in the domestic and world markets.
2. Support price has a positive and significant influence only on prices of wheat, rice and sugar. Any change in support price may lead to a 18 per cent maximum increase in the domestic price under an optimistic scenario and 10 per cent decline under the pessimistic scenario. The impact of increase in the support price and hence domestic price is severe in terms of changes in the volume of external trade. While exports decline by a maximum 34 per cent per year, imports rise by a maximum 52 per cent annually. Compared to the optimistic scenario, the worst scenario of a decline in administered price and hence domestic price shall maintain the level of exports with slight variations but prevents imports of only

wheat and sugar. Rice imports continue to take place at an average rate of 42 per cent per year. Results suggest agricultural prices, exports and area to be sensitive to shocks in the support price. To some extent, the area under cereals appears to be resilient to changes in MSP at the national level. However, at the state level, the acreage under paddy would fall at an annual average rate of almost 1 per cent.

3. Under a maximum (high tariff) and negligible (low tariff) protection situation, a heavy inflow of imports may take place at a minimum of 36 per cent and a maximum more than 1,000 per cent per year. Average price would increase by 62 per cent per year under high tariffs and decrease by 16 per cent under zero (minimum) tariffs. Accordingly, the average imports fall by 66 per cent per year when tariffs are high and increase beyond limits when the tariffs are zero. The latter situation adversely affects area under sugarcane and cotton by an average annual rate of 0.54 and 2.42 per cent, respectively. The acreage under wheat and rice is resilient to low tariffs as both have increased by 0.88 and 0.54 per cent per year, respectively. The average fall in area under paddy/rice in Haryana is estimated to be 1.36 per cent per year. A flexible tariff rate policy is, therefore, desirable.
4. The impact of rainfall on agriculture is visible mainly on area put to cultivation and yield. While good rainfall results in an increase in acreage by maximum 6.4 per cent, drought conditions lead to a decline by maximum 13.8 per cent in a year except in the case of sugarcane. There is not much change in the level of prices, exports and imports. Shocks arising due to drought can be countered on its own as rainfall has a tendency to follow a cyclical pattern.
5. For each commodity, the sum total of each of the annual average percentage change corresponding to various factors under the scenarios shows changes in world price, exchange rate and tariffs to have stronger positive/negative effects on agriculture compared to rainfall and support price (Tables 7.2A-F). Rainfall shock has a significant impact on impeding growth in area and hence output. The only exceptional case is that of sugar/sugarcane, which shows resilience to drought. Furthermore, changes in support price have considerable impact on price of wheat and rice rather than on their trade and area. The movements in the world price and tariffs have fairly stronger and pervasive effects on both prices and trade, especially in case of cotton, sugar and oilseeds. On the whole, agricultural output and prices appear to be much more resilient to shocks compared to the exports and imports.

TABLE 7.2A *Wheat: Relative Impact of Changes in various Factors (Annual Average Percentage Change)*

	Exchange Rate	*Tariff Rate*	*World Price*	*Support Price*	*Rainfall*	*Total*
Optimistic Scenario						
Price	-1.53	-1.72	-1.53	13.18	0.54	8.93
Exports	172.89	-	172.83	-34.40	-0.15	311.18
Imports	-60.49	-2.90	-60.48	7.87	-10.23	-126.23
Area/Production	0.64	0.53	0.64	2.45	4.63	8.90
Pessimistic Scenario						
Price	0.95	1.37	-0.83	-4.75	0.54	-2.72
Exports	-17.93	-	-57.53	20.99	-0.15	-54.63
Imports	5.40	747.99	80.48	-16.25	-10.23	807.38
Area/Production	0.96	0.88	0.63	0.21	-4.76	-2.08

TABLE 7.2B *Rice: Relative Impact of Changes in various Factors (Annual Average Percentage Change)*

	Exchange Rate	*Tariff Rate*	*World Price*	*Support Price*	*Rainfall*	*Total*
India: Optimistic Scenario						
Price	1.41	1.07	1.48	5.99	0.20	10.16
Exports	56.38	-	67.30	-9.83	-2.25	111.59
Imports	14.38	36.37	10.83	43.46	42.53	147.56
Area/Production	0.74	0.70	0.75	1.29	4.30	7.78
Pessimistic Scenario						
Price	0.81	-0.24	0.48	-3.48	0.20	-2.22
Exports	-10.82	-	-34.45	3.23	-2.25	-44.29
Imports	48.81	144.10	71.94	41.94	42.53	349.32
Area/Production	0.58	0.54	0.63	0.06	-5.15	-3.34
Haryana: Optimistic Scenario						
Price	7.97	2.49	9.19	17.93	-16.76	20.82
Exports	35.23	-	41.31	-17.91	-	58.63
Imports	-	43.14	-6.13	62.16	-	99.18
Area/Production	0.64	0.29	0.73	1.46	1.35	4.47
Pessimistic Scenario						
Price	-1.46	-16.61	-6.10	-10.41	-0.27	-34.85
Exports	-5.65	-	-22.23	14.53	-	-13.36
Imports	-	362.25	127.42	52.73	-	542.39
Area/Production	-0.12	-1.36	-0.54	-0.96	-2.03	-5.02

TABLE 7.2C *Sugar/Sugarcane: Relative Impact of Changes in various Factors (Annual Average Percentage Change)*

	Exchange Rate	*Tariff Rate*	*World Price*	*Support Price*	*Rainfall*	*Total*
Optimistic Scenario						
Price	2.99	4.12	3.76	5.20	–2.22	13.85
Exports	91.81	–	107.77	–2.67	10.16	207.07
Imports	–72.57	–66.70	–77.22	66.71	–1.19	–150.96
Area/Production	–0.51	2.39	–0.38	0.07	3.21	4.78
Pessimistic Scenario						
Price	–3.20	–12.70	–10.18	–3.15	0.07	–29.16
Exports	–1.11	–	–55.36	12.01	1.83	–42.63
Imports	28.80	2,955.10	737.70	–6.38	0.26	3,715.48
Area/ Production	–1.51	–0.54	–2.70	–1.53	1.83	–4.44

TABLE 7.2D *Cotton: Relative Impact of Changes in various Factors (Annual Average Percentage Change)*

	Exchange Rate	*Tariff Rate*	*World Price*	*Support Price*	*Rainfall*	*Total*
Optimistic Scenario						
Price	13.88	61.76	11.59	–	–0.56	86.67
Exports	34.41	–	28.90	–	1.66	64.97
Imports	–10.12	–28.70	–8.69	–	–0.07	–47.58
Area/ Production	1.20	2.86	1.01	–	4.92	9.98
Pessimistic Scenario					–	
Price	–3.16	–6.86	–17.27	–	–0.56	–27.85
Exports	–3.73	–	–30.36	–	1.66	–32.42
Imports	2.02	3.28	15.43	–	–0.07	20.66
Area/ Production	–0.29	–2.42	–1.70	–	–7.47	–11.87

TABLE 7.2E *Groundnut Seed: Relative Impact of Changes in Various Factors (Annual Average Percentage Change)*

	Exchange Rate	*Tariff Rate*	*World Price*	*Support Price*	*Rainfall*	*Total*
Optimistic Scenario						
Price	7.46	–	7.45	–	–0.17	14.74
Exports	74.53	–	74.50	–	2.68	151.70
Imports	–	–		–	–	–
Area/Production	–2.22	–	–2.22	–	3.79	–0.65
Pessimistic Scenario						
Price	–1.59	–	–15.57	–	–0.17	–17.34
Exports	–7.34	–	–68.58	–	2.68	–73.24
Imports	–	–	–	–	–	–
Area/Production	–3.61	–	–5.96	–	–13.80	–23.37

TABLE 7.2F *Soyabean Seed: Relative Impact of Changes in various Factors (Annual Average Percentage Change)*

	Exchange Rate	*Tariff Rate*	*World Price*	*Support Price*	*Rainfall*	*Total*
Optimistic Scenario						
Price	13.23	–	11.12	–	–0.18	24.17
Exports	31.49	–	28.60	–	13.40	73.49
Imports	–	–	–	–	–	–
Area/Production	7.62	–	6.20	–	6.41	20.23
Pessimistic Scenario						
Price	–2.60	–	–13.06	–	–0.18	–15.84
Exports	10.18	–	–3.49	–	13.40	20.10
Imports	–	–	–	–	–	–
Area/Production	–3.18	–	–10.57	–	–12.37	–26.11

To wind up, the analysis based on selected cereals and commercial crops indicates variations in the policy, price and natural factors to have strong bearing on the performance of agriculture. Shocks caused by a fall in the world price, tariffs and currency appreciation are more pervasive than support price and rainfall in changing the incentive structure, exports, imports and area and production. Effects of such shocks on land allocation and production can be countered by following a flexible tariff structure. A situation of drought can be moderated by increasing public investment in irrigation. Further, the impact of shocks arising due to various policy variables, though significant in bringing down commodity prices, do not result in changes in area, especially in the case of wheat and rice. The only exception is that in case of drought it brings down the acreage of these two crops. Clearly, there are tradeoffs involved. For instance, a hike in support price may increase domestic price and area but it may not lead to higher exports. Finally, results vary across the selected crops. Commercial crops are more vulnerable to shocks compared to cereals. This is because commercial crops are relatively more responsive to price incentives arising out of a liberal exchange rate and trade policies and openness of domestic markets to international trade. On the other hand, wheat and rice though open to external trade and somewhat responsive to price incentives, are backed by support price and procurement, which provide a cushion against external shocks caused by an unexpected plunge in the world price. Overall results indicate though these vary across crops that the agricultural sector in India is quite sensitive to shocks. However, due to macro, trade and price policy measures, commodity prices and output tend to be much more resilient to various shocks compared to the exports and imports. Appropriate and timely adjustments in tariffs together with changes in support price may help to counter the adverse effects of exogenous impulses, maintain price stability and an incentive structure in a market-driven economy.

8

Conclusions and Policy Implications

Issues Explored

With the inception of Structural Adjustment Programme (SAP), the agricultural sector in many developing countries has begun to be viewed in a larger macroeconomic policy framework and is being looked upon as a source of income growth in its own right. The programme, based on an open economy model of the neo-classical, supported a greater integration of domestic economy with the world economy for higher economic growth and technological advancements. Noticeably, the 'anti-agriculture bias' was manifested through a policy orientation of an overvalued exchange rate, restrictive trade policy and high industrial protection identified in the classical 'industry-led growth' model. This was to be obliterated by currency devaluation, reduction in tariffs, elimination of trade restrictions and initiation of liberal farm price and marketing policies. Initiation of macro- and sector-specific policies is expected to change the incentive structure in favour of agriculture through increase/decrease in price of exportable/importable relative to the world price. A favourable price structure for agriculture along with the emergence of well-functioning markets would accelerate production, private investment, exports, and thereby result in higher rates of agriculture and economic growth in the long run. This vision envisaged the agricultural sector in the developing countries to increasingly face global markets for taking land allocation and production decisions in favour of crops that are competitive and have export demand.

How do macroeconomic and sector-specific policies affect relative prices and hence producers' incentives for higher production and growth? What is the magnitude of response of agriculture to liberalization in these policies? Literature in this respect, available mainly for the developed and Sub-Saharan African countries, provides evidence in favour of strong theoretical and empirical links between macroeconomic (trade, exchange rate, fiscal), farm price and marketing policies and the agricultural sector. The interactions that have been studied mainly through price effects reveal that following the economic reforms, the terms of trade indeed became favourable to agriculture in many developing countries and the price transmission from world to domestic markets also improved. However, the impact of liberal policies on growth in production and trade, though positive, is found to be mixed across countries.

It has also been realized that the linkages in the chain from trade liberalization to export and output response are not simple as envisaged in the theory and put into practice within the multilateral trading rules under the AOA. Further, despite considerable changes in the nature and structure of external trade, several developing countries have not been able to gain as much as was expected from trade liberalization. It could be explained by a falling trend in the world prices since 1997–98, which adversely affected trade in many commodities of their interest. The opportunities might have also been affected due to various factors and policies, some of which intend to protect farmers' income while others aim to maintain price stability, food security and self-sufficiency and regional equalities. Yet another factor relates to differing goals of the developed and the developing countries, and hence their interests, which may also cause distortions in the world trade. In such situations, agriculture and trade policies that are being followed internally come in direct conflict with the external trade policy. All this may not only impede a quicker and higher transmission of world prices to domestic producers but may also adversely affect production incentives and agricultural growth.

Recognizing these factors and also considerable differences in the opinions of the developed and developing countries on various issues that confront agriculture, the WTO members tried to streamline multilateral trading rules as per the UR AOA. Proposals on certain exemptions to agriculture of the developing nations, placement of subsidies into different boxes, formulation of a food security box, special and differential treatment to agriculture on grounds of food security and livelihood needs, etc., were also discussed in various rounds. While some of these proposals were agreed upon in the July Package 2004, agreement on several others that aimed at providing a level playing field to developing countries and reducing protection and farm subsidies by developed nations could not materialize. After several rounds of negotiations, the trade talks finally broke down on July 29, 2008. Meanwhile, realignments have taken place among member countries culminating in various positions represented by several groups of countries. One positive fallout is the emergence of bilateral and regional trade agreements that might help countries to gain from trade.

Clearly, such developments have not only exposed agriculture in the developing countries to greater openness but have also made apparent that any change in the broader policies will have a significant influence on their macroeconomic and agricultural policies. The present study in the Indian context delineate reforms in the macroeconomic and sectoral policies that influence producers' incentives and their impact on the performance of agriculture in a free trade regime. The main issues that have been explored are namely:

1. To what extent has the agricultural sector opened up to external trade during the nineties and early 2000 relative to that in the past?
2. Has the magnitude of price transmission across state-level agricultural markets and from international markets towards the domestic ones improved in the years following economic reforms?
3. How have cropping patterns changed temporally and spatially during the period from seventies to 2000 and what is the magnitude of crop diversification?
4. What is the acreage response of major crops with respect to price (world price, individual and competing crop price, input price), policies (tariffs, exchange rate, minimum support price) and non-price factors (irrigation, weather, technology)?
5. Are agricultural prices, exports, imports, area and output resilient to extreme divergences in the exogenous macroeconomic policies and factors, viz., tariffs, exchange rate, world price, minimum support price and rainfall?
6. What is the relative importance of macro policies and factors impacting agriculture, and are price and tariff policies more powerful instruments than the exchange rate in neutralizing the adverse effects of shocks arising in an open economy and maintaining an incentive structure?

The investigations are carried out at the all-India and state-level, separately for six important tradable commodities, viz., wheat, rice, cotton, sugar, groundnut and soyabean seeds. The choice of crops is based on their increasing share in the external trade and likely changes in their prices and output in due course. The analyses cover a time span of more than two decades from 1980–81 to 2002–03, broadly representing the pre-reform period from 1980 to 1991 and post-reform period from 1992 to 2003. Both descriptive statistics and time series empirical models, viz., OLS, 3SLS, cointegration and error correction approach and structural econometric model are employed to test the proposed hypotheses. Counterfactual simulations are carried out from 2000–01 to 2002–03 under alternate scenarios of policies, price and other exogenous factors. The data is collected mainly from secondary sources and information given in reports (published and unpublished) brought out by various ministries.

Main Findings

At the outset, a detailed review of studies on the response of Indian agriculture to policy changes during the pre- and post-liberalization periods is undertaken. In Chapter 2, the focus is primarily on gauging improvement in spatial price transmission and supply response along with methodologies used to test the response. While literature abounds on price transmission in the domestic markets, only a handful of studies have been done to analyse linkages between domestic and world prices. The findings reveal considerable improvement in price transmission of many commodities within the domestic markets along with a positive supply response to the incentive structure and other factors. Some of the research gaps and pertinent issues regarding the movement of domestic and world prices, crop area shifts and their response to free market prices and broader policies in a market-driven economy are identified. On methodological front, significant refinements in the existing techniques along with development of new empirical models have been observed over the period. Accordingly, Chapter 3 takes up the first issue: what is the magnitude of openness of Indian agriculture to world trade? It begins with delineation of principal features of trade, price and marketing policies as they relate to major commodities and reforms undertaken. The analysis carried out from 1980–81 to 2002–03 reveals that liberalization in agricultural trade gained momentum only after the implementation of the UR AOA during 1994–95. Since then, substantial reduction in the tariff rates of commodities along with removal of many NTBs and controls on trade have been observed. From 2001, tariffs are fixed keeping in view the bound rate and are sufficiently high to restrain imports. For commodities like pulses, cotton and edible oils, applied tariffs are fixed below the bound rate so as to allow imports. Notwithstanding these liberal changes, protection is still given to essential commodities, which is somewhat permissible under the WTO provisions and is also considered to be desirable in view of food security concerns, world price volatility, import surge, poverty alleviation and livelihood needs. The tariff equivalents of NTBs that can be applied to maintain the same level of imports is estimated within a range of 2 to 55 per cent across commodities.

The analysis further reveals that India's agricultural trade policy is well aligned with the three major provisions of the AOA, viz., market access, domestic support and export competition. Despite imposition of NTBs, the agricultural sector has become more open relative to the past scenario. The import penetration rate of select commodities has increased and so has the share of agri-trade in NDPA, which doubled from 5.01 per cent during the early nineties to 10.48 per cent during early 2000. However, the share of exports in agricultural GDP, which showed a remarkable increase during the nineties, has become stable in the recent period and the share of imports has continued to accelerate. This can be a major cause of concern, more so when the rate of growth of area, production and yield of principal crops has also been decelerating. Another disquieting feature is that while India's external trade policy does not face discipline as a result of the UR AOA tenets, internal trade in many commodities continues to be inflicted with stringent regulations and controls under the price, institutional and legislative set-up. Compliance between the two, though not mandatory under the WTO provisions, can be effective for avoiding any constraining factors reforming external trade and progressing towards integration of domestic agriculture with the world agriculture.

To what extent have reforms and a greater openness of agriculture led to a quicker and higher price transmission between world and domestic markets? This issue is analysed empirically by estimating the magnitude of price integration that has taken place across the state-level markets and from world to domestic ones. The analysis is undertaken for six major commodities based on monthly prices in international and state-level wholesale markets from 1980–81 to 2002–03. The bifurcation of the period into pre- and post-reform is based on structural breaks identified in the relative price series. ADF and Johansen multivariate cointegration and error correction approaches are used for the purpose.

Results provide evidence in favour of an improvement in the long-run transmission of prices of wheat, rice, sugar and groundnut seed in the post-reform period with a larger set of states in India to be integrated with each other. For cotton and soyabean seed, price integration in domestic markets is non-existent in the years following reforms. Results are not satisfactory for states other than the major crop-producing states. Findings on the magnitude of price transmission between the world and domestic markets are akin to those obtained across the domestic markets. Integration is identified only in those states which hold a higher share of crop output, which is expected as the major crop-producing states can only generate surplus for exports. Of all the selected commodities, wheat, rice and groundnut seed markets are found to be better integrated with world markets compared to sugar, cotton and soyabean seeds markets in the post-reform period.

Compared to the long-run analysis, which indicates that the produce is transferred from one market to another in accordance with price changes and arbitrage through trade bind their prices together; the short-run dynamics reveals prices to have considerably drifted apart in all the markets. The estimated values of the error term, though negative and significant, are low during both time periods which implies that the previous period's disequilibrium in prices is corrected at a slower pace with a time lag of 2–3 weeks in a month. Nevertheless, the speed of convergence towards the long-run path resulting from price shocks is found to be somewhat quicker in the post-reform period for all the commodities except groundnut seed.

To some extent, these results validate the findings obtained in many other developing countries on the subject namely, that a complete pass through of domestic and world prices has not yet transpired in many commodities and regions, which is explained by various factors and policies. Some of these in the Indian context could be for example: (i) high volatility in international prices and variations in the exchange rate, (ii) lack of competitiveness of commodities, (iii) delay in dissemination of information across markets, transport and infrastructural bottlenecks, (iv) the structure of export-import market is dominated by a few players whose interest seems to lie more in the movement of domestic prices, and are, thus reluctant to import when the situation demands as it would reduce prices and hence their margin in country's market, (v) partial openness to external trade and adhocism in the trade policy, (vi) no settlement on issues raised by several developing countries concerning rules on market access, high level of subsidies and income support by the developed nations, which often result in a large gap in commodity prices, (vii) price and legislative controls and regulations on essential commodities and also on private trade, which also signify lack of compatibility between internal and external trade regime.

The analysis further shows that there exist fewer variations along the long-run adjustment path for wheat and rice and to some extent for sugar as compared to cotton and oilseeds. The test of price variability also substantiates that prices in most of the states, particularly those of wheat and rice are more stable compared to those in several other states and in the global markets. As highlighted in the literature, this phenomenon could be attributable to price policy, which helps absorb price shocks and bring stability, particularly in states that make a significant contribution to the central pool. Empirical result validates this point as a higher degree of integration of wheat and rice is identified mainly among the wholesale markets in Andhra Pradesh, Haryana, Punjab, Tamil Nadu and Karnataka where government agencies actively undertake procurement operations at pre-announced prices. A co-movement of wholesale and minimum support price of wheat and rice is identified in these states, which apparently sets the trend in the market for prices to wander and stabilize and hence creates complexity in terms of comprehending price transmission in an empirical model. In comparison, in states like Bihar, Orissa and Kerala, where procurement of cereals is not effective, their prices tend to follow the forces of demand and supply and often fall when the produce reaches the market. Empirical exercise confirms absence of price convergence in these states. This in a way indicates that price policy has not been effective in appropriately targeting the regions for regular supply of food, and protecting consumers from price volatility. A deeper probe into this aspect further divulges that a higher and improved integration, identified between domestic and world wheat and rice markets in the post-reform period was driven primarily by a policy of support price than by liberal trade policy and multilateral trading rules. Again, an integrated relationship was visible only in those state-level markets where government undertakes procurement at pre-announced prices.

The upshot of the analysis is that following economic reforms, price policy has been successful in providing remunerative prices to wheat-rice growers in line with increase in the world price, supporting them in a situation of fall in the world price by not allowing a roll back in MSP and achieving price stability. Nonetheless, it seems to have inhibited a free play of the market mechanism in providing signals to producers for good allocation of resources. For commodities other than cereals, the forces of demand and supply operate at large because their guaranteed prices are not backed by procurement. Also, the prices of non-food commodities tend to be more volatile as compared to those of cereals and there is hardly any effort to bring stability in these prices.

The next issue that is taken up relates to cropping pattern changes, magnitude of crop diversification and the response of area shifts to price incentives manifested in liberal macroeconomic and sectoral policies. A temporal and spatial analysis of cropping pattern reveals changes in area in favour of wheat, paddy, oilseeds, cotton and sugarcane up to the eighties and towards paddy, sugarcane, fruits-vegetables, fibres, plantations, condiments and spices during the nineties and early 2000. While acreage under wheat and paddy has expanded solely at the cost of coarse cereals and pulses, commercial crops have benefited both from area shifts and fresh land brought under cultivation. While absolute area under cereals shows a marginal increase, their relative share in GCA has declined from 60.86 per cent to 52.61 per cent over a period of more than three decades. A considerable change in the structure and composition of oilseeds is also observed. As a result, traditional oilseeds have been losing their area share to new ones, viz., soyabean, safflower and sunflower. Another significant trend is that while an initial spurt occurred in the absolute acreage of oilseeds from 17.9 million ha during early seventies to 23.8 million ha during 2000 and in relative terms from 10.8 to 13.01 per cent over this period; this has subsided. Probably, the positive impacts of a favourable price policy, the Technology Mission programme and restricted trade policy observed during the eighties and in some years during the nineties have faded away.

The state-level picture provides mixed results. While a dominance of wheat-paddy in gross cropped area is visible in all the states, cultivation of commercial crops has become more prominent in the western, central and southern parts, than in the northern states. Further, slight locational shifts have also been identified during the nineties for example: in the case of paddy to almost all the states; cotton shift from Punjab, Karnataka and Tamil Nadu to Andhra Pradesh, Gujarat and Rajasthan and in the case of sugarcane from Uttar Pradesh to Karnataka, Andhra Pradesh, Tamil Nadu and Maharashtra. Madhya Pradesh and Rajasthan have emerged as the major states in oilseed production. Consequent upon these trends, an increased level of specialization towards cereals, sugarcane, fruits-vegetables, plantation and fodder crops and diversification within pulses and fibres over time is found. For oilseeds the trend indicates an increasing tilt towards diversification till the end of eighties and specialization during the nineties and early 2000. This could be explained by changes in the area and composition of oilseeds during the nineties; the period marked by globalization and liberalization of agriculture. Non-foodgrains as a whole have witnessed diversification from the mid-nineties.

Overall, the analysis indicates that diversification has been taking place in India but at a slower pace. The northern states and West Bengal have experienced a fall in diversity in the cropping pattern over time due to a dominance of the wheat-paddy rotation under the influence of price policy. The declining diversity has far-reaching implications in terms of overuse of natural resources, ecological and income risks. In contrast, a good number of south-western states are slowly heading towards an increasing diversity. The most disturbing feature of specialization in cereals and also diversification towards non-food crops is that it has not led to any significant improvement in their rate of growth in area, output and productivity. This finding is somewhat contrary to what has been observed in the post-green revolution period, especially during the period from 1981–82 to 1991–92 when the annual rate of growth in crop output and productivity rose significantly to a higher level compared to that from 1968–69 to 1981–82.

To what extent are crop area changes responsive to price incentives stemming from liberal macro, trade and price policies compared to non-price supply side factors? Is acreage response positive and high for those crops whose prices are well integrated with the world prices? These questions are addressed in Chapter 6 with the help of a structural econometric model. The model is developed on the basis of a priori theoretical links of macroeconomic policies and factors to the agricultural sector through world price, exchange rate, trade (tariff and non-tariff barriers), support price, procurement and technology, etc. It represents a simultaneous equation system of four behavioural equations and three identities and is applied to individual commodities, separately under the exportable and importable scenarios from 1980–81 to 2002–03. The equations are estimated individually as well as simultaneously applying OLS and 3SLS.

Broad findings indicate that except for wheat and rice, the domestic wholesale prices of cotton, sugar, groundnut and soyabean seeds are significantly explained by their respective world reference price. While a statistically insignificant coefficient of world wheat price is explained by lack of competitiveness of Indian wheat in global markets, the same in the case of rice could be due to the fact that not all the states produce exportable rice and are hence, influenced by changes in world price and exchange rate. Also, variations in prices of cereals as well as sugar are explained more by their respective administered price than the world price. One inference that can be drawn is that price policy, backed by procurement provides protection from an unexpected plunge in the world price. Nevertheless, it may dissuade full price transmission from world to domestic markets and could also bring imbalances in the latter, a point that has already been deliberated upon above. The insignificance of exports/imports in determining wholesale prices of cereals is explained by the lagged relationship between production and exports of these commodities. A high production in year t is followed by an increase in exports in the subsequent period (year), which also happens to coincide with lower prices. In many instances, domestic prices have influenced the decision to go for export and import rather than export/import being a lead factor in affecting domestic prices. If this kind of situation occurs, then the relationship between domestic price and exports turns out to be negative, which otherwise is expected to be positive.

Variations in exports are influenced by relative prices except for soyabean and to some extent for wheat and sugar primarily due to higher domestic price than the world price. In the import function, the relative price coefficient has the expected negative sign but is statistically significant only for wheat and sugar. In the case of rice and cotton, the relative prices are not important in explaining imports, which implies that imports may take place even if the external prices of these commodities are higher than their respective domestic prices. Besides relative prices, variations in exports and imports are explained by availability of stocks with the government, level of income and openness to world trade. Quantitative controls and restrictions imposed through NTBs are found to be significant only for rice. From early 2000, NTBs have been removed on almost all the commodities and tariffs have been raised to control the import surge of rice, wheat and sugar. Tariffs in cotton were reduced from 1996–97 after which a greater inflow of imports has been reported.

Finally, the price incentives attributable to liberal policy measures positively and significantly explain changes in absolute area under each of the selected crops. Non-price factors, particularly rainfall and technology are equally important. Notably, area price elasticities varying from 0.09 to 0.72 in the short run and 0.14 to 1.31 in the long run, though not strictly comparable with the past estimates obtained under a closed trade regime, are fairly close to these. The area price elasticity for selected crops is estimated to be nearly 0.10 for both wheat and rice; 0.12 for cotton; 0.21 for both sugarcane and groundnut; and 0.51 for soyabean. In contrast, estimates on price elasticity in different studies fall within a range of 0.01 to 0.18 for wheat; 0.02 to 0.17 for rice; –0.02 to 1.02 for sugarcane; 0.008 to 0.48 for cotton, and 0.03 to 0.39 for groundnut seed across various regions.

Clearly, trade liberalization and macroeconomic policy reforms have positively influenced the agricultural sector in India. However, the hypothesis that acreage has become relatively more responsive to price factors than non-price factors in a liberalized regime may not be accepted for all the selected crops. Further, except for soyabean, nothing definite can be said about the conjecture that area price elasticity is positive and high for those crops whose prices are well integrated with the world prices. A low supply response could be attributable to for example: (i) a good part of the sample period pertains to both pre- and post-reform periods; (ii) low market access of India's exports and high level of subsidies given to farmers in other countries; (iii) high volatility in world prices and little efforts to ensure stability in the domestic prices of commodities other than wheat, rice and sugar, (iv) inadequate technological advancement, irrigation and other infrastructure, and (v) partial nature of economic reforms and government intervention in export-import of many commodities. Agricultural trade was strongly regulated and subject to QRs till as late as 1999. Even after 2002, quantitative restrictions and other NTBs have been re-imposed on cereals and other essential commodities. Notably, when trade is highly regulated through policy, then the impact of factors like international prices is captured partially.

Given a positive response of export, import and crop acreage to price incentives arising out of a liberal exchange rate, trade policies, price and other factors, the last two issues raised in the study are as follows: what would happen to price and production incentives if world price reaches a low level or exchange rate becomes highly volatile or tariffs get changed or MSP is abolished or rainfall becomes erratic? What policy measures can be initiated to neutralize the adverse effects of shocks that may arise in a free trade economy and maintain producer's incentives? The answers to these questions are sought by carrying out simulation experiments based on estimates obtained from the structural model. Simulations are done by conceiving 'what would happen if' best and worst scenarios wherein one time change or multiple changes are introduced in the relevant exogenous variables at a time and their impact on endogenous variables (price, exports, imports, area and output) is examined. For each commodity, the base-run equilibrium values of endogenous variables are compared with their respective simulated values to assess the degree of resilience of agriculture to unexpected changes.

Broad findings reveal that under an optimistic scenario of maximum change in world price and devaluation, domestic prices, exports and area/production across the selected commodities would be higher by a maximum of 14, 172 and 7.62 per cent, respectively per year than the existing level. An increase in export does not seem to exert inflationary pressure on domestic price but the situation needs to be monitored continuously. The same under a pessimistic scenario of shock due to currency appreciation and fall in the world commodity price reveals a maximum yearly downfall in price, exports and area by 17, 68 and 10 per cent, respectively. The volume of imports under these two scenarios shows a maximum decline by 77 per cent (optimistic situation) and increase by 737 per cent per year (pessimistic situation) than the existing level.

Second, support price has a positive and significant influence on domestic prices of only wheat, rice and sugar. Any change in the support price may lead to a maximum 18 per cent increase in price under an optimistic scenario and 10 per cent decline under the pessimistic scenario. The impact of increase in the support price and hence domestic price is severe in terms of changes in the volume of external trade. While exports decline by a maximum 34 per cent per year, imports rise by a maximum 52 per cent annually. Compared to the optimistic scenario, the worst scenario of a decline in administered price and hence domestic price shall maintain the level of exports with slight variations but prevents imports of only wheat and sugar. Rice imports continue to take place at an average rate of 42 per cent per year. Results suggest agricultural prices, exports and area to be sensitive to shocks in the support price. To some extent, area under cereals appears to be resilient to changes in MSP at the national level. However, at the state level, acreage under paddy would fall at an average annual rate of almost 1 per cent.

Third, under a maximum (high tariff)/negligible (low tariff) protection situation, a heavy inflow of imports of wheat-rice may take place at minimum 36 per cent/maximum more than 1,000 per cent per year. Average commodity price would increase by 62 per cent per year under high tariffs and decrease by 16 per cent under zero (minimum) tariffs. Accordingly, imports fall by 66 per cent when tariffs are high and increase beyond limits when tariffs are zero. The latter situation adversely affects area under sugarcane and cotton by an annual average rate of 0.54 and 2.42 per cent, respectively. Acreage under wheat and rice is resilient to low tariffs as both have increased by 0.88 and 0.54 per cent per year, respectively. Average fall in area under rice in Haryana is estimated to be 1.36 per cent per year. Fourth, the impact of rainfall on agriculture is visible mainly on area put to cultivation and yield. While good rainfall results in an increase in acreage by maximum 6.4 per cent, drought conditions lead to a decline by maximum 13.8 per cent in a year except in the case of sugarcane. There is not much change in the level of prices, exports and imports.

Fifth, for each commodity, the sum total of each of the annual average percentage changes corresponding to various factors under the scenarios shows that changes in world price, exchange rate and tariffs have stronger effects (positive and negative) on agriculture compared to rainfall and support price. Rainfall shock has a significant impact on impeding growth in area and hence output. Only exception here is that of sugar/sugarcane, which shows resilience to drought. Further, changes in support price have a considerable impact on price of wheat and rice rather than on their trade and area. Movements in the world price and tariffs have fairly stronger and pervasive effects on both prices and trade, especially in the case of cotton, sugar and oilseeds. On the whole, agricultural output and prices appear to be much more resilient to shocks compared to the exports and imports.

In short, results indicate that shocks caused by a likely fall in the world price, tariffs and currency appreciation are somewhat more pervasive than support price and rainfall in changing the incentive structure, exports, imports and area and production. The impact of shocks arising due to various policy variables though significant in bringing down prices, do not result in changes in area, especially in case of wheat and rice. An exceptional case is that of drought that brings down acreage of these two crops. Clearly, there are tradeoffs involved. For instance, a hike in support price may increase domestic price and area but it may not lead to higher exports. Furthermore, commercial crops are more vulnerable to shocks compared to cereals. This is because commercial crops are comparatively more responsive to price incentives arising out of a liberal exchange rate and trade policies and openness of domestic markets to international trade. On the other hand, wheat and rice, though open to external trade and somewhat responsive to price incentives, are backed by support price and procurement, which provide a cushion against external shocks caused by an unexpected plunge in the world price. On the whole, results indicate that the agricultural sector in India is quite sensitive to shocks. Nonetheless, due to macro, trade and price policy measures, the prices and output tend to be much more resilient to various shocks compared to the exports and imports.

Inferences Drawn and Implications for Policy Interventions

The major inference that can be drawn from the above findings is that the response of Indian agriculture to trade liberalization is indeed encouraging but it has not made a considerable difference in changing the incentive structure, integrating domestic markets with global markets and influencing acreage. To some extent, this seems to go against the expectations highlighted in the literature regarding a significant upturn in agriculture following economic reforms. Another important finding that has emerged is that macroeconomic and agricultural policies that are in place have made agriculture fairly resilient to shocks and other critical phases experienced in the global economy.

It is important to mention that the findings obtained in this study should not be taken to reflect a complete impact of globalization and liberalization on agriculture because the analysis is carried out in a partial framework based on six tradable commodities with a focus mainly on supply side factors. Besides, the empirical model pertains to both pre- and post-reform periods. Yet another equally important aspect is that international trade in agriculture has not been fully liberalized as both developed and developing countries provide protection to their agriculture on grounds of several trade and non-trade issues. Notwithstanding these, the analysis undertaken has enabled a study of the linkages in the chain from trade liberalization to agricultural prices, exports, imports, acreage and output response and an evaluation of the contribution of policies towards the performance of agriculture, though at a disaggregate level. A quantification of the impact of untoward situations or shocks on agriculture, which may arise in a free trade regime have important implications for policy interventions, howsoever provisional. Some of these are elicited below and are meant only to be suggestive.

Recognizing that the progress of agriculture towards greater openness is still partial, one policy implication is that reforms in the external trade as well as in domestic trade, marketing, price and legislative policies must go hand in hand. These need to be supplemented by appropriate developments in markets and institutions. The second policy issue that has been brought out relates to producers incentives and market efficiency. The results lend support to the hypothesis of market integration across several state-level markets and also international markets in the long run but there exist considerable lags in the short run, which need to be bridged. At the broader level, the relationship between world and domestic prices may encounter either of the two situations. First, is that of volatility when world commodity prices are at an extreme high and a rising trend in prices is greater than the domestic prices, thus negating perfect convergence. This is because if domestic price is higher than the corresponding support price, then there is some pressure to equate the two so that price fluctuations are not passed on to the producers and consumers. Second, when world commodity prices are lower than the domestic prices, integration may not happen on its own but may come through trade, provided high tariffs are not imposed. In both these situations, protectionist policies such as price and trade are generally followed, particularly for cereals, to ensure price stability and to offset the market power of intermediaries involved in trade. Clearly, the process of price transmission is far from complete and also appears to be asymmetric.

In this regard, timely and appropriate interventions in price and marketing policies are required. There is hardly any transparency in the manner in which commodity prices are fixed in the regulated markets. Quite often, local traders form cartels leading to lower price realization by farmers. Lack of adequate facilities of grading, storage, processing and infrastructure add to the woes of producers. The legislative amendments in the ECA and APMC Act need to be reviewed from time to time along with the existing multiple tax structure, licensing requirements and restrictions on the movement of essential commodities in some states. Amendments suggested in the model APMC Act, 2003 look promising in reducing regulations and encouraging competition through contract farming and development of private agricultural markets and investment. However, the progress on this front is tardy and much more remains to be accomplished. It is high time that market intelligence services should get enhanced along with dissemination of information about prices and infrastructure services across the state-level regulated markets. These measures would further liberalize agricultural markets, integrate prices, incentivise producers to increase investment and production and reap the benefits of market liberalization.

Another interrelated aspect is an increasing exposure of agricultural prices to high volatility inherent in the global prices and exchange rate. Since exchange rate is now market determined, the agricultural sector can be resilient to adverse impacts arising out of currency appreciation. Maintaining price stability in a situation of high fluctuations in prices globally is a difficult task that needs attention. Literature suggests that monetary policy may not be very successful in containing food inflation. One option is to provide guaranteed prices to all the crops in all the regions and undertake procurement as the situation demands.

Maintaining price stability through storage as is done for wheat and rice may not help in view of a limited capacity in the country for storage of all commodities. Other measures could be crop insurance and futures trading. The latter, however requires liberalization in the legislation that inhibits private traders to stock goods beyond a certain limit and reforms in the existing multiple tax structure along with setting up of a regulatory framework on futures trading.

Results drawn in the study indicate the possibility of maintaining high tariffs in a situation of fall in the world price and a consequent likely decrease in domestic price and import surge. This policy applied in the case of wheat, rice and sugar from 2000–01 has been successful in preventing their imports into the country. For commodities other than these, a hike in the tariff without exceeding the WTO prescribed bound rate is possible. The tariff rate can be fixed on the basis of the difference between the lowest level of world reference price and the highest level of domestic price that is expected. A flexible tariff policy has to be complemented with reforms in price policy. Given the fact that producers respond to price incentives, the policy has to be redesigned in such a way that the MSP of a commodity is fixed fairly above its cost of production but is not so high as to distort the market.[1] Further, the level of prices should be maintained for both producers and consumers without being biased towards certain crops and regions and is also cost effective for the government. The manifold objectives through price policy may be achieved by fixing support price on the basis of price bands having upper and lower limits. While setting the price, the movement of international price has to be taken into account along with the prevailing situations in the domestic and world markets. A continuous monitoring of prices would also address the tradeoffs identified between an increase in the support price and the resultant hike in domestic price and hence fall in exports.

Another policy issue that emerges from the study relates to variability in the exports and imports of farm commodities. As analysed, India has already introduced liberalized export policies through a reduction in the number of commodities subject to state trading, removal of minimum export price and availability of credit. Implementation of these measures along with a higher and increasing trend in the world prices led to an almost doubling up of export up to the mid-nineties. However, a decelerating trend in the world prices from the year 1996 reversed the trend and made the country attractive for imports.[2] Simulation results reveal that trade in a liberalized economy cannot be insulated from the impact of changes in the global prices. For all the selected commodities, exports and imports are found to be quite sensitive to shocks, which necessitate adequate incentives and protective measures against fluctuations in the global prices.

It may not be possible for India to protect domestic production through subsidy or direct income support though in some years budgetary subsidy was given to enable export of surplus wheat and rice. In a situation of higher domestic price relative to world price, appropriate adjustments in the support price (mentioned above) may be initiated to encourage exports. Provision of monetary support as is done in the case of plantation crops can be tried for food and non-food crops as well.[3] Results further suggest that an import surge caused by world price shocks and currency appreciation may be handled by keeping a check on imports and imposing higher tariff rates. However, recent experience shows that high tariffs have failed to dissuade import of some of the commodities. One way that has already been followed is to undertake trade through STEs and impose NTBs on grounds of food security. Such measures are dealt with externally at a broader level under the auspices of the WTO. Since trade through STEs has not been properly attended to in the GATT, India should try to enhance their efficiency and closely monitor whether STEs facilitate or distort trade so that their functioning is compatible with the WTO provisions. Similar is the case of high tariffs and QRs that are used to restrict trade of essential commodities through SSM and hence need constant vigilance for negotiations. India, along with many other developing countries, has already submitted proposals for negotiations on issues related to trade through STEs, Special Safeguard Mechanism to protect agriculture from imports, exemption of 'special products' that will not be subject to market access commitments and so on. Agreements on these proposals are on hold for now but, once agreed upon, are expected to reduce distortions in agricultural trade and regulate imports and exports.

The fifth policy implication concerns drought. The situation can be countered on its own as rainfall has a tendency to follow a cyclical pattern. Nevertheless, a less than normal rainfall situation can be compensated for by increasing public investment in irrigation. The central government has already accelerated public investment in agriculture during the 11th Five-Year Plan which needs to be maintained. Lastly, it is evident from the findings that crop area shift and hence output are positively influenced by an incentive structure along with non-price technological and infrastructural factors. This calls for initiation of an investment strategy that promotes intensification of agriculture, aiming at higher output levels by adopting latest technologies and modern inputs, investment in irrigation, roads, markets, infrastructure and post-harvest marketing. Such investments may avert stagnation in growth in farm productivity, reduce cost of production and increase returns, encourage diversification towards market oriented crops and stimulate private investment.

To wind up, the empirical results reinforce a considerable scope in maintaining producers' incentives, accelerating output and competitiveness of the agricultural sector in a free trade regime. However, there are several challenges that agriculture faces in a new environment, which needs to be addressed by pursuing reforms in trade, price and marketing policies together with other complementary measures.

Notes

1. Some of the distortionary effects of MSP of wheat and rice above the market clearing level reported in the literature are imbalances in the demand and supply and hence piling up of stocks, export subsidy to clear excessive stocks, low demand for exports due to higher domestic price relative to world price, little contribution to poverty reduction and food security.
2. The average agri-exports witnessed a decline from \$5,557 million during the beginning of the WTO (1995–98) to \$5,087 million in the post-WTO period (1999–2002). The average agri-imports accelerated from \$2,711 million to \$3,699 million during the same period.
3. Government has announced establishment of a price stabilization fund from April 2003 under which growers of tea, coffee, rubber and tobacco are compensated in the event of fall in commodity prices below a certain level and in case prices rise, they have to contribute to the fund.

Annexures

Annexure 4.1: Wholesale Markets Selected from each State and World Reference Price

Crop/State	*Wholesale Market in India/Global Trading Centre*
Wheat	
Bihar	Patna
Gujarat	Rajkot
Haryana	Karnal
Madhya Pradesh	Indore
Punjab	Amritsar
Rajasthan	Jaipur
Uttar Pradesh	Kanpur
Karnataka	Bangalore
Delhi	Delhi
World	No. 1, US Hard Red Winter, FOB Gulf of Mexico
Rice	
Andhra Pradesh	Hyderabad
Haryana	Karnal
Karnataka	Bangalore
Kerala	Thiruvanthapurum
Maharashtra	Mumbai
Orissa	Bhubaneshwar
Tamil Nadu	Chennai
West Bengal	Kolkatta

Cont'd...

Cont'd...

Bihar	Patna
Gujarat	Rajkot
Uttar Pradesh	Kanpur
World	Thailand (Bangkok) 5 per cent broken FOB
Sugar	
Uttar Pradesh	Hapur
Bihar	Patna
Punjab	Jullandhar
Maharashtra	Mumbai
Andhra Pradesh	Anakapalli
Tamil Nadu	Chennai
Karnataka	Bangalore
World	Brazil, FOB Caribbean Port ISA Prices of Sugar
Cotton Lint	
Maharashtra	Mumbai
Tamil Nadu	Tirupur
World	Cotton Outlook A Index, CIF Liverpool
Groundnut Seed	
Andhra Pradesh	Nandyal
Gujarat	Rajkot
Maharashtra	Mumbai
Tamil Nadu	Chennai
Uttar Pradesh	Kanpur
World	US Runners 40/50, CIF Rotterdam
Soyabean Seed	
Madhya Pradesh	Dewas
Uttar Pradesh	Haldwani
World	US No. 2 Yellow, CIF Rotterdam

Annexure 6.1: Supply Response Models: Methodological Approaches and Application in Indian Agriculture

The main objective of this note is to review empirical models that have been employed to examine the acreage/supply response in Indian agriculture, refinements in these over time and research gaps. Broadly, the studies have used analytical models to examine the determinants of output and in some cases analyse factor (input) demand for total agriculture and for individual crop, both at the national and regional level. The review here is confined to supply response at the commodity level at aggregate and disaggregate levels. Accordingly, the studies are classified into the type of model used for estimation of area price elasticity and treatment of price, natural, technological and policy variables. At the outset, the salient features of various models used to study commodity-specific response and empirical evidences in the Indian context are examined. The second section summarizes main findings that have originated from the application of models, and research gaps. The last part concludes by offering remarks on the choice of the model.

Methodological Approaches on Acreage (Supply) Response

The methodologies that have been employed to estimate the supply response function fall under two broad categories, viz., partial equilibrium analysis and general equilibrium analysis. Literature reveals significant advancements that have taken place in both the approaches. But the partial equilibrium approaches have shown a greater dominance in their application in the Indian context. The discussion in this note is, therefore, limited to models evolved under partial analysis. Some of these models are: (a) Nerlovian Adaptive Expectation Model, (b) Profit Function Approach, (c) Multinomial Logit Model, (d) Time Series and/or Cross Section Econometric Models, (e) Other Approaches, viz. Production Function and Normative Programming. Of all these partial equilibrium approaches, Nerlove's work on adaptive expectation has continued to dominate and strengthen the specification of supply models in agriculture. These models rest on the theoretical premise that farmers act as profit maximizers and adjust their crop acreage and output to changes in crop prices or relative profitability. In what follows, the basic features of supply models, advancements in these over time and their application in some of the crop-specific studies in Indian agriculture are presented. This review is based on published literature as also from Narayana (1989), Chand (1991), and Kohli Singhal (1996).

The Nerlovian Model

Nerlove (1958) developed a dynamic partial adjustment model based on the concept of adaptive expectation consists of three equations:

$A_t^D = a_o + a_1 P_t^e + a_2 Z_t + U_t$ (Desired Acreage) (1)

$P_t^e = P_{t-1}^e + B(P_{t-1}\ P_{t-1}^e)$ (Adaptive Expectation) (2)

$A_t = A_{t-1} + r(A_t^D - \dot{A}_{t-1})$ (Partial Adjustment) (3)

Where

At = Actual area under cultivation at time t;

A_t^D = Desired area to be put under cultivation at time t;

P_t = Actual Price of output at time t;

P_t^e = Expected price at time t;

Z_t = Other exogenous factors that affect supply at time t; and

U_t = random disturbance or error in period t.

B and r are termed the expectation and adjustment coefficients, respectively. The expectation or the adaptation coefficient indicates how fast the expectations change. The above model is an acreage response model and a similar model on output response can also be constructed. However, the area planted under a crop is considered to be a better representation of planned production as the area that is to be allocated is under the farmer's control. The model assumes that farmers adjust crop area (output supply) continuously over time and base their decision on expectations of future price of the crop. The actual change in supply is only a proportion of the desired change as farmers are not able to change factors of production in the short run. The expected future price is taken to be the weighted moving average of normal price in the previous years with greater weights being attached to more recent years. In many cases, last year's price is taken to represent the current year's price. Koyck's distributed lag and polynomial lags are the most commonly used in this approach. The equations can be solved through estimation of reduced form by ordinary least squares.

This model has been extensively applied in India since its inception. Among many, Krishna (1963) and Herdt (1970) were pioneers in applying the Nerlovian model to estimate supply response of individual crops or aggregate agriculture. They reported both short-run and long-run estimates of elasticity by specifying the relevant price and non-price factors that determine farmer's decision regarding acreage to be put under a crop and output to be produced. Other important contributors to supply analysis based on the Nerlovian model and its variants include Kaul and Sidhu (1971), Nowshirwani (1968), Parikh (1972), Maji, Jha and Venkataramanan (1971), Cummings (1975), Narayana and Parikh (1979 and 1981), Ghosh and Neogi (1995), and Naik and Jain (1999). In almost all these studies, the price factors, deflated either by consumer price index or price index of all commodities were represented by absolute prices, relative output price, input prices. The non-price factors were represented by relative yield, irrigated area, and weather lagged by one year. An increase in price is expected to provide incentive to the farmer to produce more. Whereas an increase in the price of input as well as price of competing (alternative) crop is a disincentive to produce more of the main crop.

An important contribution on the subject is by Askari and Cummings (1977) who provided a comprehensive review of the application of Nerlovian model in several studies done in various states and districts for different time periods. The authors found Indian agriculture to be responsive to price incentives and rewards accruing to cash crops and cereals in the markets. Technological factors equally play an important role in influencing acreage decisions. However, marked variations in the short run and long run area and supply elasticities with respect to price and non-price factors were identified across the crops and states. The short-run supply elasticities varied from 0.02 to 0.14 for rice, from 0.02 to 0.93 for wheat and from 0.14 to 0.89 for groundnut. However, estimates obtained from most of the studies are not comparable because of variation in the models used, different time periods and locational differences. Further, results vary on account of usage of price and non-price variables.

The authors while deliberating upon elasticity estimates of price and irrigation/technology pointed out the usefulness of the adaptive expectation model in making projections. They further highlighted its simple procedures and flexibility in developing dynamic specifications and minimization of specification errors that often accumulate over successive estimation stages. Some of the limitations or difficulties that are encountered in the application of this kind of model were identified. These include the lack of the theoretical base for the concept of expected nominal price, difficulty in appropriate usage of price variable to reflect crop profitability, no explicit treatment of technological variables, absence of farmer's response to risk factors, choice of deflators for price variable and number of lags to be used. In many studies, distributed lags are taken to capture price expectation. However, the lag length would vary across crops depending upon whether the crop is an annual or a perennial crop. Further, the components of Zt that specify non-price factors are not defined appropriately. The Nerlove model specifies weather and time trend, broadly taken to explain non-price variables, which are not adequate to explain farmer's choice of a crop. On econometric estimation, it was pointed that estimation of the reduced form by OLS in the adaptive expectations model leads to inconsistent estimates due to a correlation of error term with the lagged endogenous variable. Also, exclusion of other variables, mainly non-price such as population density, income level, literacy, risk/shocks, etc., may bring omitted variable bias in the results.

Realizing these limitations, several modifications were made in the original model with respect to exogenous Z_t variables. In many studies, exogenous variables that are generally included such as farm size, technology, farm income levels, rainfall, government policy variables, and variability of yield (representing risk) were correctly specified. Other important developments that have taken place relate to namely, (a) explicit treatment of risk in supply response, (b) inclusion of support price, subsidies and other government policies in the model, (c) appropriate lag structure, and (d) refinements of expectation models as to price, yield and returns. Maji, Jha and Venkataramanan (1971) while studying price responsiveness of wheat, maize and paddy in Punjab from 1948 to 1965 used standard deviation of price over the preceding three years as a measure of risk aversion. The inclusion of risk variable resulted in a substantial decline in the coefficient of lagged acreage. Similarly, in the case of paddy and groundnut in Punjab, Kaul and Sidhu (1971) found the coefficient of variation and standard deviation of productivity to be better measures of farmers, risk aversion than price or yield variances. These significantly affected the short-run and long-run elasticity of acreage response.

For the recent period, Naik and Jain (1999) applied the partial adjustment model to estimate the extent of influence of price (own and competing) and non-price factors, viz., yield and risk on acreage of major cash crops at the national and state levels from 1975–76 to 1995–96 and at the district level from 1975–76 to 1992–93. Results showed short- and long-term own price elasticities of area under cotton, jute, soyabean, oilseeds, pepper, coffee and castor seeds to be positive and low in most of the states. Overall, the extent of change in acreage of commodities varies from state to state depending on the direction and magnitude of changes in the factors, trade opportunities that India has in world markets and productivity and competitiveness of crops.

An important development in the original Nerlovian model relates to expectations of prices in the dynamic supply response model. It is argued that land allocation decisions and hence actual supply depend on how farmers make expectations about future prices or returns. The Nerlovian partial adjustment with adaptive expectations simply presumes that farmers have a notion of a normal price which they keep on revising on the basis of their past experiences and errors that produce a dynamic process of price formation. This aspect along with the sensitivity of expectations and adjustment coefficients estimated values to omission of variables in the model have been questioned. An important contribution in this regard is that the expectation in each period differs from the realized price by a random disturbance. And farmers take into account not only the past prices but also the disturbances while forming expectations, which lead to the Auto Regressive Integrated Moving Average (ARIMA) process. The specification of price in this regard is:

$$P_t^{*}=P_{t-}\ W_t=a_1P_{t-1}+a_2P_{t-2}+A_3P_{t-3}+\ldots\ldots u_t+b_1W_{t-1}+b_2W_{t-2}+b_3W_{t-3}+\ldots\ldots,$$

Where W_t indicates the random disturbance term with usual statistical properties and represents deviations between expected and realized prices. The approach is criticized on grounds that, (a) the dynamics of equilibrium price depends on different exogenous specifications of price expectation formations, which involve only past trends, and (b) price expectations are not informed predictions as these ignore information on current policy effects.

In order to take note of these factors, Muth (1961) developed a Rational Expectation Hypothesis (REH) that explains farmer expectations concerning prices to be formed on the basis of the structure of the economic system. The policy changes are incorporated into the model so that variations in the price expectations take note of the effects of policies. That is, price expectations are dependent not only on the basis of supply side factors alone but also on the basis of demand side and policy factors operating in an economy. And these together form rational expectations. The rational expectation hypothesis of Muth essentially equates two distinct concepts, viz., farmers subjective psychological expectations of variables and mathematical conditional expectations of those variables, i.e., $X_t^e = E(X_t/I_{t-1})$, where X_t^e is the subjective expectation and X_t/I_{t-1}

is the mathematical expectation of X at time t and I is the information available. The REH is widely acceptable as it allows for uncertainty as to price and yield of various crops and applies to both exogenous and endogenous variables. A simple model of agricultural market is explained as:

$Q_t^D = -bP_t + eY_t + u_t$ (Demand) (1)

$Q_t^S = cP_t^e + fW_t + v_t$ (Supply) (2)

$Q_t^D = Q_t^S$

$E(P_t) = P_t^e$,

Where QD and QS are the quantities demanded and supplied, P is price and e stands for expected value, Y is income; W is weather or irrigation, t is time, U_t and V_t are the disturbance terms with mean zero and serially uncorrelated. Equilibrium in the market implies:

$-bP_t + y_t^e + u_t = cP_t^e + fW_t + v_t$ -(3)

Taking conditional expectations and using REH to get expected price as a function of expected values of exogenous variables income and irrigation and the structural parameters that derive the model. This is in contrast to adaptive expectations where the expected price depends only on an arbitrarily defined expectation coefficient.

$P_t^e = (eY_t^e - f(W_t^e)/(c+b)$

Putting back the expected price variable in the supply equation, supply then becomes a function of expected values of exogenous variables as follows.

$Q_t^S = f(Y_t^e, W_t^e, W_t)$.

The supply and demand equations in the REH model can be solved by using three stage least squares or full information least square methods. It is evident that the rational expectations are related more to endogenous variables of the system than to exogenous variables like rainfall which is not affected by expectations. Further as pointed out in the literature, past experiences certainly matter in the formulation of expectations and also not all markets adjust with equal quickness as envisaged under the REH. Nowshirvani (1968) nullified some of the objections against REH by corresponding expected price to adaptive expectations with its price expectation coefficient being a function of the parameters of demand and supply functions. Yet another development with respect to the process of expectations is that in case exogenous (policy) variables, viz., income and irrigation or variables that represent their transformation are stationary then these could be modelled as ARIMA process. The expectations thus generated are termed as Quasi-Rational Expectations (QRE) with certain assumptions on the distribution of parameters.

The empirical formulations of ARIMA and REH models have been carried out by Narayana and Parikh (1981). The authors applied the ARIMA process in the crop revenue expectation functions. While appraising the approach they stated that compared to adaptive expectations, it takes into account past realizations as well as the extent to which expectations were off the mark using appropriate weights. They further argued that expectations about prices must reflect a secular trend in relative prices and revenues. In such situations, it is reasonable to assume that farmers observe the level of prices and revenues over time and are also aware of any random shocks to which variables have been subjected. The expected price, thus adequately account for this process of movement and occasional random shocks. Ghosh and Neogi (1995) also applied REH for studying the Indian foodgrain market using different factors from demand as well as supply sides, such as income levels, government stocks, imports and public foodgrain policy measures that influence commodity prices. The authors arrived at positive estimates of supply elasticity separately for rice and wheat from 1964–65 to 1989–90.

Profit Function Approach

Unlike Nerlovian model that considers single equation approach to estimate the area and output response of individual crops, the profit function approach rests upon simultaneous application of output supply and factor (input) demand equations. The approach is based on the following assumptions: (a) farmers are profit maximizing agents, (b) farmers are price takers in both output and variable input markets, (c) farmers are technically efficient, and (d) their production function is concave in variable inputs, i.e., there exists one to one correspondence between the set of concave production functions and the set of convex profit functions. This implies that every concave production function has a dual, which is convex profit function and vice versa. Based on the duality theorem, a system of output supply and input demand equations can be derived from the profit function. The specified function is:

$A(P,w) = [\max_{y,x} P'y\text{-}w'x\text{: } (x,y) \text{ ,} J \text{ }],$

Where P is a vector of M output prices, w is a vector of N input prices, y is a vector of M output quantities, x is a vector of N input quantities and J is a closed, bounded, smooth and strictly convex production possibility set. Based on Hotelling's (1932) or Shephard's (1953) lemma, the Marshallian vectors of output supply and input demand [y(P,w) and x(P,w) can be obtained from A(P,w) by differentiation with respect to P and w.

The estimation procedure of profit function is based on joint estimation or profit or supply function and factor demand function using Zellner's Seemingly Unrelated Regression Estimation (SURE). The model can be specified using either the Cobb Douglas form of profit function or Translog, Normalized Quadratic and Generalized Leontief profit functions. The Cobb Douglas specification suffers from limitations which are listed with proofs in Chand (1991). Some of these are for example: (i) own price elasticity of factor demand is always elastic, (ii) variables are considered complementary to each other with no possibility of substitution, and (iii) the effect of change in fixed factors is same on demand functions for all inputs. Realizing these problems, Sidhu and Baanante (1981), Bapna, Binswanger and Quizon (1981) and Chand (1991) laid a greater emphasis on the use of other profit functions.

Sidhu and Baanante (1981) estimated normalized restricted translog profit function and the corresponding system of derived demand with Zellner's method of generalized least squares based on cross section data on wheat from Punjab. The authors specified restricted estimates of translog function and compared this with the restricted estimates of the Cobb Douglas form. Wheat output supply elasticity to its price in the latter case was 0.63 and in the former case, to be 0.78. Input demand elasticities were also more consistent in the former case than in the latter. The translog function also allowed flexibility, which enabled exogenous variables to produce different impacts across input demand functions of labour, fertilizer and animal power. Similarly, Bapna, Binswanger and Quizon (1981) estimated the system of output supply and factor demand equations for semi-arid and tropical regions in India. In all, 93 districts from various states were grouped and data were obtained for the years 1955–56 to 1973–74. Various crops were also grouped into superior cereals, coarse cereals, pulses, oilseeds and other crops. Two functional forms of profit function, viz., normalized quadratic and generalized Leontief were specified. Results indicated the supply elasticity of wheat and rice at 0.33 and 0.37, while fertilizer demand elasticity ranged between –0.62 to –0.90. Normalized quadratic function was considered better than the generalized leontief profit function in the study. Chand (1991) studied supply response in the context of price policy of major crops, viz., wheat, gram, paddy and cotton in the Punjab region. Using the normalized quadratic profit function, the author simultaneously estimated output supply and factor demand equations based on farm level cross-sectional data for the period 1977–1979. Results indicated that factor prices negatively affect output supply, i.e., output decreases with increase in normalized prices of variable inputs.

Notably, these studies have made a strong case for the simultaneous estimation of output supply and factor demand equations based on profit function than that of single equation approach. Within that, application of the Cobb Douglas formulation of profit function is given less preference compared to other types of functional forms, viz., translog, normalized quadratic and generalized Leontief. The results derived with the use of these techniques are considered to have provided better and consistent estimates compared to the Cobb Douglas form. Despite consistency and efficiency in the estimates as well as the advantage of estimating multiple output supply responses, the profit function approach is found to suffer from several theoretical, econometric and data problems. Some of these relate to the assumption of fully developed capitalist markets for all inputs and outputs, existence of competitive markets with fully developed infrastructure and perfect information and knowledge of technology and prices. These assumptions may not hold true in many developing countries including India. Furthermore, the model does not specify time lags that distinguish between short-run and long-run responses and also fails to capture the effects of certain non-price factors like rural market development, irrigation and roads. On econometric and data quirks, the approach is silent as to the number of variable inputs to be included, limitation of degree of product and input dis-aggregation, choice of an appropriate functional form and problems in measurement of fixed inputs like land and input (labour) prices, non-availability of data on many variables.

Multinomial Logit Model

The multinomial logit model is employed to study area allocation among alternative crops. The area shares that are allocated to crops are limited dependent variables because by definition the sum of shares equals one. These shares can be interpreted as probabilities. The model can be explained for two crops as follows. Let P be the probability that farmers cultivate rice and hence 1-P the probability that they grow some other crop. A linear model can be specified to identify the determinants of P:

$P = a + b_1r_1 + b_2r_2 + c_1A_1 + c_2A_2$,

where r_1 and r_2 are the net revenues from the two competing crops. A_1 and A_2 are total irrigated area and annual rainfall in the region. While right hand side variables can take arbitrary values, left hand side Probability P appears to be a constraint to the interval from zero to one. This problem can be solved by replacing P with a suitable variable as:

$[(P/1\text{-}P)] = e^{\alpha}\Pi_i(r_i)^{\beta i}\Pi j(A_j)^{\gamma i}$ or the logarithmic form as

$\ln[(P/1\text{-}P)] = \alpha+\Sigma_i\beta_i\ln(r_i) + \Sigma_i\gamma_i\ln(A_j)$

The left-hand variable in the equation is similar to the logit function and corresponds to the probability that rice is cultivated. Since more than two crops are grown on a piece of land, a system of linear logit functions, i.e., multinomial logit model has to be specified. The linear logit model produces a highly non-linear system. This is because all the variables and disturbances affect all equations through the denominator even when restrictions are placed on some of the fits. This can be estimated by transforming the model so that each equation shares a common term. Theil (1971) proposed to take the ratio of one equation to another and a cancellation of the common terms. The log of this ratio produces an equation, which is linear in parameters.

$\ln(w_i/w_h) = (\alpha i - \alpha i) + \Sigma j(\beta_{ij} - \beta ih)\, x_j + (u_i - u_h)$

This approach suffers from limitations that its coefficient cannot be interpreted directly as elasticities. Also, one needs to satisfy two conditions if the definition of total area and the percentage share of crops in that hold namely: One, same crops compete for the given area year after year, and two, the crops identified do not compete with any other crop for area.

Kumar and Rosegrant (1993) developed a model that is based on a linear version of the multinomial logistic function to study the area allocation among crops. The share of total crop area allocated to each crop is taken to be a function of expected crop revenues per hectare and quasi-fixed inputs.

$\ln(w_i/w^*) = a_i + \Sigma_j b_{ij}\ln(r_j) + \Sigma j c_{il}\ln(A_l) + u_i$,

Where $\ln(w^*) = \Sigma w_{ji}\ln w_i$, w_i are individual crop shares, w_{ii} is the average share of the ith crop, w* is the weighted geometric mean of the crop area shares, r_j is the jth expected net crop revenue, and A_l is the lth type of total land in the cropping system (total irrigated area and total rainfed area). The transformed share of total area allocated to each crop is a function of the normalized expected net crop revenues, total irrigated area and total rainfed area. The expected net crop revenue of the nth crop is used as a deflator to normalize expected net crop revenues. The elasticities of area shares in response to expected net revenue are given by:

$E^{rj}_{wi} = b_{ij} - \Sigma^{n}_{k=1} w_{ii} b_{ik}$

$E^{rn}_{wi} = -\Sigma^{n-1}_{j=1} E^{rj}_{wi}$ (i=1,.....,n;j=1..........,n–1).

Similarly, the elasticities of area share with respect to quasi-fixed variables can be found. The elasticities give the area response equation as:

$\Delta w_i = \Sigma n_{j=1} E^{rj}_{wi} \Delta r_j + \Sigma^{m}_{l=1} E^{Al}_{wi} \Delta A_l$

Where Δdenotes rate f change since $\Delta w_i = \Delta A_l - \Delta A$,

$\Delta A_i = \Sigma n_{j=1} E^{rj}_{wi} \Delta r_j + \Sigma^{m}_{l=1} E^{al}_{wi} \Delta A_l + \Delta A.$

Now, $\Delta A = \Sigma \delta l \, \Delta A_l$, where $*_I$ is the share of the lth type of land in the total cultivated area. Therefore,

$\Sigma A_i = {}^{n}_{j=1} E^{rj}_{wi} \Delta r_j + \Sigma m_{i=1} (E^{al}_{wi} + \delta_l) \Delta A_l.$

This implies that area elasticity with respect to expected net revenue and type of land are:

$E^{rj}_{Ai} = E^{rj}_{wi}$ (I,j = 1,....n)

$E^{al}_{ai} = (E^{al}_{wi} + \delta_l)$ (I=1,......n;l=1,......m).

In another study, Kumar (1998 and 2001) applied this dynamic supply response model for estimation of area response of rice, sorghum, pearl millet and maize crops. The all-India estimates were arrived at from 1970–71 to 1988–89 on the basis of time series cross sectional input output data using four blocks of supply system (quasi-fixed inputs, area allocation, choice of techniques and yield and input determination) in block recursive mode. The area share of the crop system was made a function of expected crop revenue, normalized returns to maize, irrigated and rainfed area in the crop system, lagged dependent variable and dummy variables for regions. Zellner's generalized least squares technique corrected for correlation and heteroscedasticity in the disturbance terms was applied in the model. The model of area allocation was derived with a multinomial logistic function.

Time Series and/or Cross Section Econometric Models

Time series models and time series-cross section pooled models are employed to estimate acreage/supply response of both aggregate and individual crops. Some of the important developments that have taken place in these models over time are outlined below.

Time Series Models

Time series models generally are grouped under econometric models such as the ordinary least squares, simultaneous equation models and cointegration and error correction models. The Nerlovian lagged adjustment model or further extensions of it discussed above can be incorporated into the time series models.

To recall, the actual model and its variants involve a one-stage procedure and directly regress crop area or production on prices and other relevant explanatory variables based on future price expectations and/or adjustment costs. In contrast, time series econometric models such as simultaneous equation model and cointegration and error correction mechanism can be used for direct estimation of price and non-price factors in a single or multi-equation framework. The simultaneous equation model may be called a structural model as it enables an explanation of the behaviour of sector-specific variables and their linkages with other sectors in the economy. The main advantage of this direct approach is that besides relative prices one can include the weather index and time trend in the supply equation to represent weather and technology. For instance, Krishna and Raychaudhuri (1980) while examining the effects of price movements on wheat and rice output in India took other shifter variables in the equations. The estimated supply equations for the period 1957–1970 are as follows:

$$Q_{tR} = f(PR_{t-1}/IPR_t, RN_t, QR_{t-1})$$

$$Q_{tW} = f(PW_{t-1}/IPW_t, V_{t-1}),$$

Where Q_{tR} referred to all India output of rice, PR_{t-1} wholesale price index lagged by six months, RN_t rainfall index, and IPR_t, index of input prices used for rice. Similarly for wheat, V_{t-1} referred to the ratio of irrigated area under wheat to total lagged one year area under wheat. The results arrived at using the linear function revealed short-run price elasticity to be 0.45 and longrun price elasticity to be 0.85 for rice. For wheat, output elasticity with respect to output-input price ratio was 0.59 and with respect to irrigation 0.81.

There are several issues in the application of direct estimation of output response based on time series econometric techniques. The main limitation is that data on different output and input prices move more or less in the same direction, which results in multicollinearity among the explanatory variables. At times, the problem of auto-correlated error term in the regression model is also encountered. Some of the other difficulties relate to selection of correct area, output and price variables and deflators (consumer price, index, input prices or other crop prices) used in formulating price responses. Inconsistent estimate based on reduced form of OLS is also an issue to be dealt with. Yet another difficulty lies in the use of OLS method, which assumes data to be stationary. It is argued that most of the time series economic variables tend to be non-stationary, i.e., their mean and variance are not constant. Therefore, an application of OLS in the case of non-stationary data may result in spurious regressions (Granger and Newbold, 1974). This shortcoming it is suggested can be dealt with by using recent time series approaches based on co-integration, viz. Augmented Dickey Fuller and/or Johansen Maximum Likelihood Tests.

The Johansen test is considered to be better than other cointegration approaches as it addresses the endogeneity and simultaneity problems being faced in other methods. The approach is developed in a structural vector autoregressive (VAR) model that enables an examination of the co-movement of set of economic variables and measure their long-run and short-run effects in a bivariate as well as multivariate framework. The structural relationships are specified among a set of variables to find out how these variables adjust to deviations from long-run equilibrium relationships using the system of equations in a vector error correction model.

As far as application of these models in the estimation of supply response in agriculture is concerned, there are not many studies in India. A few attempts have been made in other countries by Mckay, Morrissey and Vaillant (1997 and 1998) to examine the response of individual crops to prices using cointegration analysis. In India, the approach is employed by Deb (2005) for estimating aggregate supply response. Literature however abounds in empirical estimation of OLS and other econometric techniques. Some of the well-known studies that have employed OLS/reduced form based on the Nerlovian framework are already quoted above. A few more that have used a simultaneous equation framework to arrive at crop area/supply response estimates are by Krishna and Chibber (1983) for wheat, Gulati (1987) for wheat and rice, and Sharma, Ghosh and Kumar (2001) for wheat. In these studies, behavioural equations with respect to output, foodgrain stocks, imports, sales through public distribution system, demand for consumption and many more are specified. The results on price series, output elasticity with respect to price and other variables are arrived at using OLS, its reduced form and FIML methods.

Over time improvements have been made in the estimation procedures of traditional time series models. Nevertheless, new models have assumed added significance as cointegration combined with the error correction models gives consistent estimates of both long-run and short-run elasticities. Also, the dynamics of supply are explained directly in the cointegration approaches, which in the partial adjustment model are based on certain assumptions with respect to the process of price expectation. The latter hypothesizes that farmers while making land allocation decisions move closer to their equilibrium position by some fraction each year. In contrast, the dynamics of adjustment is intrinsically embodied in the theory of cointegration, which is revealed by the same order of integration of the variables. The Granger representation theorem states that variables are cointegrated (1,1) and the residuals of the cointegrating regression are of order I(0), then, there exists an ECM describing an equilibrium relationship.

Time Series-Cross Section Models

Compared to time series models, pooled time series-cross section models are known for enhancing the statistical degrees of freedom and improving the efficiency of estimates along with an estimation of effects associated with a particular dimension of the data set. These models can be categorized as for example, (i) fixed effects model and (ii) random effects (error component) model. The fixed effects model isolates the cross-sectional unit specific and/or the time period specific effects in a behavioural relationship. It allows the intercept term to vary across N cross sectional units and/or across the T time periods. These (N-1) + (T-1) dummy variables can be introduced and the OLS estimation technique can be applied. However, when economic relationships under investigation are of dynamic nature, the dummy variables stand invalid as they take cross sectional and/or time effects to be constant parameters. In contrast, the random effects model treat individual effects as random variables. A typical random effects model can be explained as:

$Y_{it} = x_{1it}\,\beta 1 + \ldots\ldots x_{kit}\beta_k + u_{it},$

Where i=1,.....N farms observed over t = 1,.....T time periods. The disturbance term u_{it} is decomposed into two or three components as $u_{it} = \mu i + \lambda_t + v_{it}$ where μ_i, λ_t and v_{it} denote the individual, time specific and the observation specific effects (errors). These equations can be written in a matrix form as $y = X\beta + u$, where y and u are TNx1 vectors, X is a TNxk matrix and β is a Kx1 vector.

In case the lagged value of the dependent variable are not included in the explanatory variables and the variance covariance matrix of the residuals is known, then the maximum likelihood estimation technique yield consistent, asymptotically normal and efficient estimates. When the matrix is unknown, a two-stage estimation procedure proposed by Zellner can be applied. The only problem with this method is that it may yield biased coefficient estimates. This is because it ignores the possibility of a correlation between the random error associated with each cross sectional unit and other regressors. Another limitation that in fact applies to time series-cross section models is that they fail to capture the simultaneity between output supply and input demand decisions. Other problems identified in such models relate to invalid results due to inclusion of lagged dependent variables, non-standardized tests to check the presence of serial auto correlation in the model and inadequate tests for their correction (Bapna, 1977). Nevertheless these models are of significant use when a sample of observations is drawn from a large population and inferences regarding the population are to be obtained.

Application of the fixed effect model is done in Gulati and Kelly (1999). The authors have studied the price and crop acreage responses across 23 crop zones in the SAT region in India over time from 1970 to 1990. The elasticities of crop area changes are estimated with respect to various price and non-price factors. The factors broadly fall under the profit and consumption equations specified in the model for each district and each crop grown in these regions. The model that is specified is as follows:

$A^i_{jt} = b_{oj} + \Sigma\, b_k X^i_{kjt} + e_{jt},$

Where i refers to the ith crop. The differences in the intercept value for each of the districts in the region were expected due to unique district-specific characteristics. Here b_{oj} is treated as a fixed parameter that varies across districts, X_{kjt} are relevant variables. Since usage of lagged dependent variable in time series-cross section models produce biased estimates of various components of error term, such variables were not used in the model. Profit and consumption related equations in the model were solved using the log linear functional form to obtain acreage elasticities. The likely impacts of changes in prices on production, consumption, welfare and growth are analysed using a multi-market model at the all-India level. The broad results revealed a positive but low supply response to own price (profit-related factors) as well as competing crops. However, the importance of price factors along with non-price factors varied from crop to crop and from zone to zone.

Other Approaches: Production Function and Linear Programming

Literature reveals production function and normative programming approaches which can be employed to estimate the supply response function. Supply response is derived indirectly from an empirically estimated production function. The underlying assumption is that the profit-maximizing farmer knows both the product and factor prices and seeks to maximize profit or other goals subject to technology and economic environment or prices. The results are constructed input demands and output supplies, which are expressed as a function of prices and technology. This approach is not used much as the derived estimates of parameters are sensitive to specification of the production function. The linear programming approach to model acreage allocation among crops, which is relatively less employed than other models discussed above is similar. There is hardly any study done in the Indian context that has used this approach. Shumway and Chang (1977) study for Californian agriculture can be referred to for application of programming techniques.

Main Findings and Research Gaps

The main findings that can be drawn from the literature survey on methodological approaches on acreage/supply response models and their applications in Indian agriculture are as follows.

First, the Nerlovian partial adjustment model has dominated the supply response studies in India. While applying the model, researchers have introduced several modifications and refinements with respect to formation of price expectations and inclusion of variables other than price in the original model. Literature also highlights development of some variants of the Nerlove model along with other supply response models such as profit function, time series-cross section models and multinomial logit model. Application of these models has ranged from complete supply-demand analysis of agriculture to crop-specific estimates of area and supply elasticity and their projections both at the all-India and regional levels. Undoubtedly, these models suffer from certain limitations and shortcomings related to econometric problems such as lag length to be specified, choice of an appropriate functional form, assumptions made, measurement of fixed inputs and their prices, multicollinearity and non-availability of data on many variables. However, some attempts have been made in the studies to overcome some of the limitations by using alternate estimation procedures.

Second, the application of supply response models is based on the premise that farmers seek to maximize profits, which suggests that farmer's land allocation and production decisions depend on changes in crop prices through their effect on relative crop profitability. Undoubtedly, other factors both from the supply and demand sides also play an important role in influencing such decisions. The effect of these factors on farm supply has been incorporated in the models and is captured through specification of technology, infrastructure, weather, policy variables like support price and income. Deficiency in any of these factors may wipe out the positive effect of price on farm acreage/output. Third, evidence on the estimates on elasticity of individual area/output to price and non-price factors arrived at using different models reveals area/output expansion responds to price incentives. The long run price elasticity is found to be higher than the short run. Fourth, the estimated crop area/output price elasticities are not strictly comparable due to varying assumptions made under each of the models, time period covered, diverse agro-climatic conditions across the regions and inclusion of several price and non-price variables. Finally, the approaches that have been developed vary in price, income and trade policies, primarily to explore their impact as also that of government programmes, input cost, technology, export and import needs on land allocation and output decisions.

The observations and findings obtained from a review of supply response models make apparent that these models are applied under certain assumptions related to price and non-price effects of variables, objectives and hypotheses at hand, availability of data on chosen variables, regional dimensions, limitations of the model and so on. It may be argued that these factors, if not adequately dealt with can affect the elasticity estimates and hence fail to capture the exact magnitude of relationship that exists between output and price and non-price variables. For instance, in many studies, the relevant variables have been omitted which might have biased the results. Further, most of the studies have not dealt with the simultaneity bias that originates when price and supply/area are simultaneously determined. Failure to check the endogeneity of price and other explanatory variables can produce inconsistent estimates. It is, therefore, essential to perform exogeneity tests such as Hausman exogeneity test before running the model. Similarly, studies where OLS has been used have not provided any evidence on the stationarity of time series variables.

Another important aspect which has not been dealt with in the literature on supply response in India is the likely asymmetries in output in response to price changes. In almost all the studies, the absolute value of acreage or output is modeled to show that a price increase or decrease results in a similar change in output. In other words, agricultural supply is taken to be symmetric or reversible, as a downfall in price will bring back the supply to its original level. It is argued that the fixed assets purchased and/or technology introduced when prices were high are not disposed off when prices are low, which implies that a change in price (high or low) may not bring a similar change in the output (Mamingi, 1996). This irreversible or asymmetric response implies that when prices decline, the rate of decline in the output is less than the increase in output when prices rise.

Evidence on the application of supply response models in India has not addressed this issue. One reason could be that the quantification of price increase and price decrease and partition of data series separately into rising and falling prices is not straightforward. A few attempts that have been made in studying asymmetric area/output response to price changes relate to studies done in Sub-Saharan Africa, United States and Bangladesh for cocoa, onion and sugarcane crops. The results based on asymmetric approach reveal crop area to be responsive more to the rising price than to the falling price (Mamingi, 1996).

Yet another issue that has remained unaddressed in the extant literature on supply response in India is the role of macroeconomic policies and other conditions that may influence agricultural prices. Theoretically, trade, exchange rate, monetary and fiscal policies influence prices (incentives) and hence output through change in tariffs and non-tariff barriers, devaluation of currency, interest rate and budget deficit/surplus. Changes in any of these policies affect the general price level, terms of trade between rural and urban as well as between sectors, investment, income and output. Following liberalization, the role of exchange rate and trade policies is considered to be relatively more important in influencing agricultural area and output. Currency devaluation, lowering of tariffs and NTBs induce producer incentives as they increase the price of tradeable goods relative to non-tradeable goods, improve the competitiveness of produce in foreign markets and lead to higher exports and growth. The models on supply response have taken real producer price as an explanatory variable, which indeed subsumes the effects of exchange rate. However, the direct effects of exchange rate and tariffs in changing the incentive structure and their linkage with real prices and output have not been incorporated in many studies. Inclusion of such policy variables along with other factors operating at the global level would not only explain the exact movements in the real producer price but also provide firm and consistent estimates of impacts on the farm sector.

Choice of Supply Response Model

Having reviewed the salient features of supply response models, econometric and other limitations associated with their application, determinants of individual crop acreage/supply and gaps in the literature, it is pertinent to focus on the choice of appropriate model. One may find that of all the partial equilibrium models on supply response to changes in prices/returns, the Nerlovian partial adjustment model has a greater dominance in the literature. The model is simple to estimate and is considered useful in short-term forecasting of aggregate as well as commodity-specific farm output. Certain refinements with respect to process of expectations, treatment of risk, inclusion of government policy variables, etc., have also been made in the original model. As a result of these improvements, several variants of the original model such as the ARIMA model, rational expectation hypothesis and quasi expectation hypothesis have evolved over time. Despite these developments, the model suffers from one major limitation and that is it assumes both quantities of inputs and their prices to be determined exogenously. In reality, production and input demand decisions are considered to be made simultaneously. In this situation, the policy effects on crop supply are difficult to capture. In contrast, other supply response models such as the multinomial logit model and profit function approaches fulfil these gaps by analysing long-term changes in the cropping pattern. The profit function approach assumes added significance as it analyses the interdependencies that exist between output supply and input demand so as to achieve both technical and allocative efficiency. Also, it captures the impact of various policies on input use and evaluates the productivity and equity impact of technological and policy changes. The main advantage of the multinomial model, which is absent in other approaches, is that it ensures that the share of crop areas in gross cropped area sums to one. The limitations that are identified with the use of these models are that multinomial assumes the same crop to compete for area year after year and the profit function requires a highly dis-aggregate data set.

Time series-cross section econometric models, which comprise fixed effects and random effects/error component models are considered to be highly useful in studying individual cross-sectional unit effects. These models also enhance degrees of freedom and improve efficiency of the estimates while forecasting. However, they do not ensure the crop area shares to be equal to one as is assumed in the multinomial logit model. Also, unlike the profit function approach, they tend to ignore the simultaneity that exists between output supply and input demand decisions. Compared to these the simultaneous equation and cointegration and error correction models have acquired greater attention over time. These models can also incorporate the Nerlovian framework and its variants and provide direct estimates of crop supply response to price and non-price variables. The main difficulties that are encountered in these models are multicollinearity among the explanatory variables, auto-correlated error term and non-stationarity of data. In fact, some of these problems can be corrected by appropriately specifying the variables in the model and improving estimation procedures, correcting the stationarity problem associated with the use of OLS by applying cointegration approaches. Two such widely used cointegration techniques are the Augmented Dickey Fuller Test and the Johansen maximum likelihood approach, which analyse non-stationary data to avoid spurious regressions and also obtain consistent estimates. Of the two, the Johansen test is considered to be better than the traditional models as it gives consistent estimates of both long-run and short-run elasticities and explains directly the dynamics of supply without making any assumption on process of price expectation as is done in the partial adjustment model based on the reduced form of OLS.

In sum, the choice of analytical model ultimately depends upon the objectives and issues that are at hand, level of disaggregation required and availability of data. When the purpose of the study is simply to estimate the crop acreage or output elasticities in a particular region, the Nerlovian formulation based on time series econometric model is the most suitable approach. However, if the objective is extended to analyse the policy effects on the individual crop production decision and their predictive performance in the selected areas, then the profit function and time series techniques would serve the purpose. Obviously, each model has to be used with caution depending upon the questions raised by the researcher and limitations associated with their use. Also, to the extent possible it is important to address the omitted variable bias, simultaneity of variables, stationarity of time series data and asymmetry in the supply response to change in price. One may sum up in the words of Nerlove and Bachman (1960) that the various approaches are complementary rather than competitive.

Annexure 6.2: Identification and Selection of Variables in the Structural Model and Data Sources

The variables that affect farm commodity prices in the domestic markets, exports, imports and crop acreage have been identified on the basis of theoretical relationships. Only those variables that appear to have relatively more influence on acreage decisions are selected in the analysis. The choice of variables is also influenced by availability of times series data from 1980–81 to 2002–03. An explanation of each variable taken in the structural model along with its source of data is outlined below.

Endogenous or Impact Variables

Own Price of Individual Commodity

Farm commodity price is collected at three levels, (i) at the time of harvest called the farm harvest price, (ii) when the commodity reaches the wholesale markets for distribution called wholesale price and (iii) retail/consumer price. The produce is mostly sold immediately after harvest and one should ideally take farm harvest price to capture the response of farm area/output to price. However, time series data on farm harvest price, collected at the district level and aggregate state level is missing in many states for many commodities. Therefore, the wholesale prices, which pertain to selected major markets operating in several districts in each of the states, are taken. For each commodity, the annual wholesale price in one major market is chosen to represent state-level data. The markets for which price data is taken are listed in Annexure 4.1. For all-India analysis, two options were tried namely: (i) using commodity-wise wholesale price data available in index form at the national level and (ii) taking annual state level average wholesale price of a commodity weighted by production. Both series were taken as per crop year and converted into real prices at base 1993–94 using the wholesale price index of all commodities. The average wholesale price yielded better results and was retained for the analysis. The sources of wholesale price data are *Report of the Commission on Agricultural Costs and Prices* (CACP) and Agriculture Prices in India, Ministry of Agriculture, GOI.

Export/Import

Data on annual export and import of commodities at eight and six digit HS system level is given in *Monthly Statistics of Foreign Trade*, DGCI&S, Kolkata and Food and Agriculture Organization website: www.fao.org.

Crop Acreage

Area that is put to crop cultivation in a year is taken as a dependent variable in the model. In many studies, relative crop area, i.e., share of a crop acreage in GCA is taken as an appropriate variable. This is because it captures the substitution effect when both crops show a rise in their absolute areas in response to an increase in GCA, but their relative areas may show opposite signs (Gulati and Kelly, 1999). However, the relative area doesn't capture direct elasticity for acreage. Since one of the objectives in this study is to estimate elasticity of area to price/profit, crop acreage in absolute terms is only used. Data on area under a crop is taken from Agricultural Statistics at a Glance, Ministry of Agriculture, GOI.

Exogenous and/or Policy Variables

Exchange Rate

This is given in Rs/US $ in nominal terms and the series is extracted from the *Report on Currency and Finance*, RBI from 1980–81 to 2002–03.

Trade Policy Variables

Two variables, viz., tariff and non-tariff barriers are taken to capture the effect of trade policy on domestic commodity prices. Tariff rate (import duty) for each commodity during the nineties is extracted from Custom Tariff Reports, Arun Goyal. From 1980–81 to 1989–90, these are noted down from *Custom Tariff Reports*, Ministry of Finance, GOI. The documents publish the standard rate of duty and preferential rate for commodities at 6 and 8 digit levels. In case of cereals, import duty is 0 from 1980 to 1998. These documents also list NTBs that are applicable to each commodity every year. A commodity-wise inventory of NTBs that have been placed on selected commodities over time is prepared. Major NTBs that are identified are quantitative restrictions, import permits, licensing, export restrictions through export quota, minimum export price by the government and trading through state agencies. Though the number of NTBs has been reduced significantly during the last two decades but some restrictions on imports continue. An index is prepared to represent NTBs and serves as an explanatory variable. Interestingly, each of the selected commodities in the study is identified with one or the other NTBs and the import coverage ratio index equal 0. Therefore, the effect of NTBs on import/export is captured through a dummy variable '0 and 1'. The value is given '1' from 1980–81 to 1998–99 and '0' in the subsequent years. This is because most of the restrictions on external trade of farm commodities had got removed from the year 1999 and were replaced by tariffs under the WTO commitments.

Export/Import Price (World Commodity Price)

Data on export (fob) and import (cif) price is difficult to find. In many studies, unit value index, i.e., ratio of value of imports/exports to quantity imported/exported are used. But it is difficult to identify the effect of unit value index on variation in the domestic price. Therefore, world reference prices of commodities that are available for major global trading centres in the international markets are taken to represent import/export price. This is a limitation of the study. Time series data is used in absolute terms to determine domestic commodity price and in relative terms (world price/domestic price) to analyse the influence on the external trade (export/import). The nominal world prices, available in dollar terms are converted into domestic currency using exchange rate and are deflated by wholesale price index for all commodities at base 1993. Data on international commodity prices is taken from *International Financial Statistics* of the IMF.

Minimum Support Price

Data on minimum support price is extracted from Agricultural Statistics at a Glance, Ministry of Agriculture from 1980–81 and 2002–03. The series given in nominal terms in Rs/tonne are converted into real price using wholesale price index of all commodities at base 1993 published in *CACP Reports.*

Commodity Stock/Procurement by Central and State Agencies:

Many commodities such as wheat, paddy (rice), cotton lint and oilseeds are procured by the government. Their stocks are maintained by FCI, CCI and NAFED. For each commodity, data on procurement done in each state and stocks maintained at all India are obtained. Time series data on stocks of oilseeds are not available and procurement operations by the NAFED are occasional. For commodities other than groundnut and soybean seeds, data on procurement and stocks are taken from Agricultural Statistics at a Glance and Bulletin on Food Statistics, Ministry of Agriculture.

Exogenous and Supply Side Variables

Own/Relative Price

Own price of a commodity is employed both as an endogenous and an exogenous variable in the model. It is employed as an exogenous variable in the acreage response function equation to examine the price effect/incentives on land allocation to a specific crop. Besides using own price in absolute terms, the price effect is also tested using two alternate variables in the acreage equation. First, the model is run by using relative own price to competing crop price and then using relative own price to input price. Own price of a commodity is expected to have a positive influence on area/output. Whereas competing crop price and input price are negatively related to area under a crop, particularly in fertilizer intensive crops such as wheat and paddy. The influence of relative price is expected to be positive on acreage under a crop unless increase in competing crop price/input price is higher than own crop price. In the final run, the ratio of output to input price is mainly used, which broadly represents profitability. In some cases, equations have been tried with own commodity price also. Both current year and one-year lag prices/profitability are used to see the response of area to current price or lagged price in forming expectations.

All these variables are used in real terms in the model. Also, the variables are tried either in the current year or are appropriately lagged. Fertilizer price weighted by consumption is taken to represent input price. The sources of data are *Reports of the CACP and Agriculture Prices in India*, GOI.

Input Price

This variable is used in the acreage response equation to determine the effect of change in input price on area. An increase in input price is negatively related to area under a crop. The variable in the equation is represented by fertilizer price. Data is given separately for N, P and K at all India. The nominal price of each fertilizer is weighted by its consumption and is deflated by wholesale price index of all commodities at base 1993–94. Data on price and consumption of NPK has been sourced *Fertilizer Statistics.*

Production: Data on production in each of the states and at the all India level is published annually in the CMIE and Agricultural Statistics at a Glance, Ministry of Agriculture.

Income

Among many other factors, the level of income or economic growth determines imports into a country. An attempt has been made to capture the effect of income on imports through personal disposable income and/or net GDP. The nominal data on these variables is obtained from *National Accounts Statistics* (NAS), Central Statistical Organization. Of the two variables, personal disposable income has given a reasonably good fit and positively explains the level of imports. The series, given in Rs crore at nominal price are deflated by GDP deflator at 1993–94 price, given in NAS.

Irrigation

The effect of irrigation on crop acreage is captured by absolute gross irrigated area under a crop or as ratio to gross cropped area. The impact of irrigation is expected to be positive on area except in regions where dry land crops are grown. Often, crop yield captures the effect of irrigation because yield is usually higher if the new area that is brought under cultivation is irrigated. Against this, water intensive crops that are already irrigated do not display yield expansion as a result of an increase in irrigated area. Both own yield and gross irrigated area under a crop are taken as separate variables in the equation to represent technology and irrigation. These variables are interrelated and are expected to positively influence absolute area under a crop. A high correlation between gross irrigated area and own yield is also expected. Data on gross irrigated area under each of the crops is extracted from *Fertilizer Statistics* and *Statistical Abstract of India* (various years).

Rainfall

Data on annual and monthly rainfall is given for rain gauge stations located across the regions/states in the *Statistical Abstract of India*, CSO. There may be more than one rain gauge station in each region/state. In this study, monthly data for each of the stations located in the states are taken and are averaged to arrive at state-level and national-level rainfall. Both actual and normal rainfall data are taken to prepare the rainfall index. Three rainfall indexes are prepared one, on an annual basis, two, for the months of June-July-August-September, and, three, for the months of October-November-December. While the second is expected to positively influence cultivation of kharif crops, viz., rice and maize grown immediately during/after the arrival of monsoons, the third index is likely to raise the yield and output of rabi crops (wheat and mustard) sown during the months of October and November. For each crop, these alternate indexes are tried. The annual rainfall index and June-July-August-September rainfall index yield similar results and are chosen.

Technology

The effect of technological change on area/output is captured by irrigation ratio. This variable is also taken separately and is proxied by the following: (i) yield of crop under consideration, (ii) ratio of own crop yield to competing crop yield, and (iii) area under high yielding varieties (HYV). All these variables are expected to positively influence crop acreage, especially commercial crops and represent technological change. In case the competing crop yield is taken as a separate variable, it is expected to bear a negative sign. This is because an increase in the yield of a competing crop is likely to bring down the area under the crop considered. Both current and one-year lagged yield, yield ratio and area under HYV are tried in the model. The area under HYV is correlated with gross irrigated area and was dropped in the final-run model. The source of data on crop yield is Agricultural Statistics at a Glance, GOI.

Infrastructure

Literature on area response studies consider road density, number of markets and rural electrification as key infrastructural variables that determine changes in land to be put under a specific crop. Of these three variables, time series data on road density is readily available. The data is extracted from *CMIE Publications.*

Risk

Risk is used as an explanatory variable and is expected to negatively influence the area under a crop. This variable is represented either by variations in the price or by variations in the yield. In both cases, it is estimated by a squared deviation of difference between actual and expected price or crop yield. The expected crop price/yield is taken to be three years moving average.

World GDP (Income)

This variable is used to capture variations in commodity exports from India to world markets. An increase in the level of world income is expected to increase exports and hence bears a positive sign. Data on world GDP at real prices has been taken from the *World Development Indicators*, World Bank.

India's Share of Agriculture Trade in World Agriculture Trade

Time series data on share of India's external trade or exports in world trade/exports is available in the FAO website. This variable is taken to capture the openness of Indian agriculture to international trade of farm commodities and is likely to bear a positive sign due to significant changes in the policies.

Ratio of Agriculture Trade to GDP Agriculture

The ratio of agricultural trade to GDP agriculture in India is again taken to represent the extent of openness of agriculture to world trade. It is expected to have a positive effect on exports from the country and imports into the country. Data is taken from the *FAO website and NAS*, CSO.

Annexure Tables and Figure

ANNEXURE TABLE 4.1A *Wheat: State-wise Augmented Dickey Fuller Test for Unit Root in the Pre- and Post-reform Periods*

Series in Log	*Levels*			*First Difference*		
	Constant Only	*Constant and Time Trend*	*No of Lags*	*Constant Only*	*Constant and Time Trend*	*No of Lags*
			Sample: 1980 April to 1991 March			
Gujarat	–2.02	–3.36***	1	–8.62*	–8.59*	1
Haryana	–1.54	–1.42	12	–5.11*	–5.17*	10
Karnataka	–0.895	–2.45	1	–8.16*	–8.14*	1
Madhya Pr.	–1.41	–2.66	4	–9.54*	–9.49*	2
Rajasthan	–1.35	–2.58	1	–8.55*	–8.54*	1
Uttar Pr.	–0.295	–2.69	9	–6.44*	–6.46*	8
Delhi	–1.15	–3.44**	3	–8.36*	–8.33*	2
Bihar	–1.49	–2.92	3	–9.34*	–9.29*	2
Punjab	–1.86	–2.71	1	–7.92*	–7.89*	1
World	–1.30	–2.28	9	–3.60**	–3.57**	8
			Sample: 1991 April to 2003: March			
Gujarat	–2.42	–4.00**	1	–9.87*	–9.87*	1
Haryana	–1.43	–1.33	12	–3.42**	–3.47**	12
Karnataka	–2.43	–3.13	4	–8.53*	–8.57*	1
Madhya Pr.	–1.97	–4.14**	2	–8.79*	–8.82*	1
Rajasthan	–0.77	–2.12	9	–6.96*	–6.93*	8
Uttar Pr.	–1.43	–2.95	12	–3.39**	–3.39**	10
Delhi	–0.78	–2.66	12	–4.68*	–4.66*	10
Bihar	–1.75	–2.70	6	–5.95*	–5.96*	5
Punjab	–1.44	–0.48	9	–7.36*	–7.51*	8
World	–2.57	–2.86	3	–5.72*	–5.74*	2

ANNEXURE TABLE 4.1B *Rice: State-wise Augmented Dickey Fuller Test for Unit Root in the Pre- and Post-reform Periods*

Series in Log	*Levels*			*First Difference*		
	Constant Only	*Constant and Time Trend*	*No of Lags*	*Constant Only*	*Constant and Time Trend*	*No of Lags*
Sample: 1980 October to 1991 September						
Andhra Pr.	–1.10	–3.13	5	–9.78*	–9.78*	2
Haryana	–.785	–1.50	1	–8.06*	–8.05*	1
Karnataka	–1.19	–3.13	4	–6.47*	–6.44*	3
Kerala	–0.42	–2.01	11	–5.42*	–5.32*	10
Maharashtra	–.88	–3.48**	1	–9.28*	–9.25	1
Orissa	–2.33	–3.11	10	–5.73*	–5.70	6
Tamil Nadu	–0.36	–3.09	11	–4.70*	–4.72	10
West Bengal	–0.78	–2.76	12	–6.54*	–6.48	8
Bihar	–1.67	–2.86	3	–6.83*	–6.78*	2
Gujarat	–0.77	–2.56	1	–8.15*	–8.13*	1
Madhya Pr.	–0.41	–2.56	3	–7.36*	–7.35*	2
Uttar Pr.	–1.98	–3.03	1	–8.13*	–8.10*	1
World	–0.092	–1.34	1	–6.09*	- 5.64*	2
Sample: 1991 October to 2002 September						
Andhra Pr.	–0.389	–2.84	12	–4.19*	–4.14*	12
Haryana	–2.09	–3.02	3	–7.36*	–7.39*	3
Karnataka	–2.29	–2.29	2	–8.45*	–8.62*	
Kerala	–2.44	–1.22	6	–4.53*	–4.86*	2
Maharashtra	–0.117	–3.57**	7	–6.20*	–6.17*	6
Orissa	–1.92	–1.28	3	–8.04*	–8.13*	1
Tamil Nadu	–1.70	–1.89	7	–7.11*	–7.21*	6
West Bengal	–1.43	–1.08	6	–5.08*	–5.22*	5
Bihar	–2.39	–2.22	1	–9.30*	–9.38*	1
Gujarat	–1.49	–0.095	3	–8.52*	–8.97*	2
Madhya Pr.	–0.22	–3.73**	4	–6.19*	–6.19*	3
Uttar Pr.	–0.99	–2.20	10	–5.21*	–5.23*	10
World	–2.50	–2.41	2	–6.65*	–6.67*	1

ANNEXURE TABLE 4.1C *Sugar: State-wise Augmented Dickey Fuller Test for Unit Root in the Pre- and Post-reform Periods*

Series in Log	*Levels*			*First Difference*		
	Constant Only	*Constant and Time Trend*	*No of Lags*	*Constant Only*	*Constant and Time Trend*	*No of Lags*
Sample: 1980 October to 1991 September						
Uttar Pr.	–0.36	–3.02	12	–6.46*	–6.64*	10
Bihar	–1.118	–3.51**	1	–8.40*	–8.40*	1
Punjab	–0.131	–2.85	8	–8.37*	–8.51*	7
Maharashtra	–0.13	–3.61**	7	–6.59*	–6.76*	6
Andhra Pr.	–0.96	–3.75**	7	–7.05*	–7.18*	6
Tamil Nadu	–2.13	–3.54**	2	–8.49*	–8.45*	1
Karnataka	–1.72	–2.82	2	–8.90*	–8.91*	1
World	–0.61	–2.21	11	–4.28*	–4.80*	10
Sample: 1991 October to 2001 September						
Uttar Pr.	–2.82	–3.06	11	–2.98**	–3.15***	11
Bihar	–2.17	–2.00	8	–6.49*	–6.59*	7
Punjab	–2.20	–3.13	1	–8.43*	–8.41*	1
Maharashtra	–2.54	–2.46	1	–5.96*	–5.96*	1
Andhra Pr.	–2.57	–3.01	6	–6.62*	–6.65*	5
Tamil Nadu	–2.50	–2.76	4	–6.88*	–6.90*	3
Karnataka	–2.55	–2.66	1	–8.53*	–8.62*	1
World	–1.67	–1.66	9	–4.47*	–4.47*	8

ANNEXURE TABLE 4.1D *Cotton: State-wise Augmented Dickey Fuller Test for Unit Root in the Pre- and Post-reform Periods*

Series in Log	*Levels*			*First Difference*		
	Constant Only	*Constant and Time Trend*	*No of Lags*	*Constant Only*	*Constant and Time Trend*	*No of Lags*
Sample: 1982 October to 1990 September						
Maharashtra	–2.30	–2.38	1	–7.31*	–7.28*	1
Tamil Nadu	–1.08	–1.90	1	–7.16*	–7.12*	1
World	–1.21	–1.75	1	–5.50*	–5.59*	1
Sample: 1990 October to 1998 September						
Maharashtra	–1.86	–1.79	1	–6.40*	–6.42*	1
Tamil Nadu	–1.14	–2.21	1	–8.69*	–8.64*	1
World	–1.61	–2.11	1	–5.18*	–5.19*	1

ANNEXURE TABLE 4.1E *Groundnut Seed: State-wise Augmented Dickey Fuller Test for Unit Root in the Pre- and Post-reform Periods*

Series in Log	*Levels*			*First Difference*		
	Constant Only	*Constant and Time Trend*	*No of Lags*	*Constant Only*	*Constant and Time Trend*	*No of Lags*
Sample: 1980 November to 1992 October						
Andhra Pr.	–0.69	–2.88	3	–8.83*	–8.81*	2
Gujarat	–1.60	–3.31***	1	–8.90*	–8.87*	1
Maharashtra	–0.97	–2.71	1	–9.12*	–9.09*	1
Tamil Nadu	–0.83	–2.87	3	–9.49*	–9.46*	2
Uttar Pr.	–0.60	–2.84	1	–8.02*	–8.03*	1
World	–1.91	–3.82**	1	–7.37*	–7.43*	1
Sample: 1992 November to 2003 October						
Andhra Pr.	–2.21	–2.89	6	–6.08*	–6.07*	6
Gujarat	–2.61***	–3.65**	1	–9.45*	–9.43*	1
Maharashtra	–0.77	–2.33	5	–6.53*	–6.47*	4
Tamil Nadu	–2.30	–3.39**	1	–8.03*	–7.91*	1
Uttar Pr.	–2.50	–2.22	2	–12.27*	–12.42*	1
World	–3.41*	–3.87*	1	–7.68*	–7.50*	1

ANNEXURE TABLE 4.1F *Soyabean Seed: State-wise Augmented Dickey Fuller Test for Unit Root in the Pre- and Post-reform Periods*

Series in Log	*Levels*			*First Difference*		
	Constant Only	*Constant and Time Trend*	*No of Lags*	*Constant Only*	*Constant and Time Trend*	*No of Lags*
	Sample: 1982 November to 1995 October					
Madhya Pr.	–0.98	–3.13	1	–9.21*	–9.19*	1
Uttar Pr.	–1.18	–3.14	1	–8.63*	–8.61*	1
World	–0.68	–2.40	2	–8.16*	–8.14*	1
	Sample: 1995: November to 1999: October					
Madhya Pr.	–1.39	–1.93	1	–6.00*	–6.07*	1
Uttar Pr.	–1.70	–3.05	1	–4.73*	–4.93*	1
World	–1.03	–2.92	2	–6.56*	–6.52*	1

Notes: *, **, and *** denote significance at 1 per cent, 5 per cent and 10 per cent levels, respectively. Critical values of ADF statistics with constant are –3.48, –2.88, –2.58 and with constant and trend are –4.05, –3.45 and –3.15 at 1, 5 and 10 per cent levels of significance, respectively. The same at first difference with constant are –3.85, –3.04,–2.66 and with constant and trend are –4.67, –3.73 and –3.308 at 1, 5 and 10 per cent levels of significance, respectively. The optimum lag length is determined by Akaike Information Criterion (AIC).

ANNEXURE TABLE 4.2 *Normalized Cointegrating Coefficients obtained from Cointegration and Error Correction Model*

Crop/States	*Domestic Wholesale Markets*	*Domestic and World Markets*	*Domestic Wholesale Markets*	*Domestic and World Markets*
Wheat	**Sample: 1980 April to 1991 March**		**Sample: 1991 April to 2003 March**	
Constant	–	–	–	–0.01
Punjab	–	–	–	–
Haryana	–12.39 (20.16)	–1.57 (0.90)	1.17 (0.14)	1.09 (0.15)
Karnataka	–0.29 (1.21)	1.18 (0.38)	–0.08 (0.09)	–0.09 (0.09)
Rajasthan	8.51 (12.62)	0.85 (0.38)	–0.70 (0.16)	–0.84 (0.18)
Uttar Pradesh	5.19 (8.21)	–0.14 (0.40)	0.53 (0.17)	0.76 (0.19)
World	–	0.68 (0.20)	0.35 (0.44)	0.08 (0.05)
Rice	**Sample: 1980 October to 1991 September**		**Sample: 1991 October to 2002 September**	
Constant	–	2.851	4.03	4.06

Cont'd...

Cont'd…

Andhra Pradesh	–	–	–	–
Karnataka	–0.22 (0.32)	–0.180 (0.104)	–0.15 (0.14)	–
Kerala	1.50 (0.46)	0.679 (0.089)	–	–
Orissa	0.13 (0.19)	–	–	–
Tamil Nadu	–0.18 (0.20)	–0.160 (0.062)	–0.77 (0.24)	–0.80 (0.23)
West Bengal	–0.22 (0.29)	–	0.34 (0.15)	
Haryana	–	–	0.65 (0.21)	0.86 (0.23)
Uttar Pradesh	–	–	0.05 (0.16)	0.14 (0.16)
World	–	0.042 (0.025)	–	–0.09 (0.06)
Sugar	**Sample: 1980 October to 1991 September**		**Sample: 1991 October to 2001 September**	
Constant	–0.41	–0.45 (0.32)	1.83	8.43
Uttar Pradesh	–		–	–
Punjab	0.90 (0.07)	0.91 (0.07)	0.16 (0.33)	–0.57 (1.54)
Karnataka	0.18 (0.05)	0.19 (0.06)	–0.10 (0.46)	–1.43 (2.26)
Tamil Nadu	–		1.64 (0.61)	7.30 (7.60)
Bihar	–		1.13 (0.43)	3.62 (3.79)
Andhra Pradesh	–		–2.24 (0.85)	–11.02 (11.80)
World	–	–0.01 (0.03)		1.28 (1.53)
Cotton	**Sample: 1982 October to 1990 September**		**Sample: 1994 October to 1998 September**	
Constant	2.136 (0.978)		–59.48	54.58
Maharashtra	–		–	–
Tamil Nadu	0.529 (0.212)	1.426 (0.216)	13.92 (6.74)	2.70 (1.56)
World	–	–0.435 (0.218)	–	9.51 (3.08)
Groundnut Seed	**Sample: 1980 November to 1992 October**		**Sample: 1992 November to 2003 October**	
Constant	0.38 (0.11)	–	0.50 (1.18)	–4.19
Andhra Pradesh	–	–	–	–
Tamil Nadu	–0.84 (0.50)	–	–	–
Uttar Pradesh	0.80 (0.11)	–	0.89 (0.26)	1.13 (0.34)
World	–	–		0.79 (0.29)
Soyabean Seed	**Sample: 1982 November to 1991 October**		**Sample: 1995 November to 1999 October**	
Constant	0.42 (0.47)	0.823 (0.534)	0.182 (1.013)	63.00
Madhya Pradesh	–	–	–	–
Uttar Pradesh	0.91 (0.10)	0.984 (0.108)	0.957 (0.218)	–6.90 (11.28)
World	–	–0.163 (0.095)	–	20.79 (30.49)

Note: Figures in parentheses are the standard errors.

ANNEXURE TABLE 4.3A.1 *Wheat – Reduced Form VECM in Domestic Markets: 1980 April to 1991 March*

Series in Log	*D(Punjab)*	*D(Haryana)*	*D(Karnataka)*	*D(Rajasthan)*	*D(Uttar Pr.)*	*D(Gujarat)*
ECM	–0.26*	–0.38*	–0.13*	–0.26*	–0.22*	–0.16*
	(–3.42)	(–2.43)	(–2.12)	(–2.67)	(–2.36)	(–2.55)
D(Punjab(–1))	–0.162	–0.03	–0.140	–0.183	–0.085	0.035
	(–1.58)	(–0.43)	(–1.87)	(–1.72)	(–0.94)	(0.36)
D(Punjab(–2))	0.142	0.088	–0.044	0.115	0.056	0.240
	(1.43)	(1.04)	(–0.61)	(1.12)	(0.64)	(2.56)
D(Haryana(–1))	0.183	–0.175	0.088	–0.156	0.030	–0.078
	(1.035)	(–1.16)	(0.68)	(–0.84)	(0.19)	(–0.46)
D(Haryana(–2))	0.047	–0.157	–0.031	–0.159	–0.108	–0.057
	(0.30)	(–1.20)	(–0.28)	(–0.99)	(–0.79)	(–0.39)
D(Karnataka(–1))	–0.159	–0.190	–0.139	–0.298	–0.040	–0.063
	(–1.15)	(–1.614)	(–1.38)	(–2.06)	(–0.32)	(–0.48)
D(Karnataka(–2))	–0.009	0.0002	0.052	–0.132	0.180	0.118
	(–0.06)	(0.002)	(0.54)	(–0.96)	(1.53)	(0.94)
D(Rajasthan(–1))	–0.049	–0.007	0.047	–0.128	–0.047	0.169
	(–0.46)	(–0.07)	(0.60)	(–1.14)	(–0.49)	(1.66)
D(Rajasthan(–2))	–0.157	–0.123	–0.056	0.082	–0.159	0.073
	(–1.65)	(–1.518)	(–0.80)	(0.82)	(–1.87)	(0.81)
D(Uttar Pr.(–1))	–0.001	0.134	–0.066	0.166	–0.003	–0.093
	(–0.01)	(1.136)	(–0.65)	(1.14)	(–0.03)	(–0.70)
D(Uttar Pr.(–2))	–0.111	0.008	–0.023	0.015	0.187	–0.171
	(–0.85)	(0.07)	(–0.25)	(0.11)	(1.62)	(–1.39)
D(Gujarat(–1))	0.272	0.279	0.171	0.297	0.116	0.038
	(2.55)	(3.07)	(2.20)	(2.67)	(1.22)	(0.38)
D(GujaratJ(–2))	0.154	0.172	0.086	0.310	–0.002	0.013
	(1.42)	(1.873)	(1.10)	(2.76)	(–0.029)	(0.127)
R-squared	0.277	0.260	0.221	0.275	0.195	0.171
Adj. R-squared	0.181	0.161	0.118	0.178	0.088	0.06
Sum sq resids	0.502	0.365	0.267	0.54	0.399	0.452
S.E. equation	0.066	0.056	0.048	0.06	0.059	0.06
F-statistic	2.88	2.649	2.149	2.858	1.832	1.56
Log likelihood	174.76	195.35	215.37	169.49	189.58	181.5
Akaike AIC	–2.46	–2.78	–3.09	–2.37	–2.69	–2.56
Schwarz SC	–2.10	–2.426	–2.73	–2.025	–2.33	–2.212

Notes: Figures in parentheses denote t values. D denotes first difference.

ANNEXURE TABLE 4.3A.2 *Wheat – Reduced Form VECM in Domestic Markets: 1991 April to 2003 March*

Series in Log	*D(Punjab)*	*D(Haryana)*	*D(Karnataka)*	*D(Rajasthan)*	*D(Uttar Pr.)*	*D(Gujarat)*
ECM	–0.44*	–0.37*	–0.27*	–0.41*	–0.38*	–0.39*
	(–4.40)	(–2.89)	(–4.31)	(–3.74)	(–3.63)	(–3.88)
D(Punjab(–1))	0.054	–0.184	–0.071	0.059	0.042	0.094
	(0.53)	(–1.86)	(–0.67)	(0.62)	(0.407)	(0.74)
D(Punjab(–2))	0.059	–0.042	–0.165	–0.040	0.070	–0.095
	(0.69)	(–0.51)	(–1.86)	(–0.51)	(0.81)	(–0.90)
D(Haryana(–1))	–0.228	–0.077	–0.211	–0.003	–0.058	–0.506
	(–1.69)	(–0.59)	(–1.50)	(–0.03)	(–0.42)	(–3.03)
D(Haryana(–2))	–0.247	–0.086	–0.219	–0.208	–0.171	–0.137
	(–2.02)	(–0.72)	(–1.73)	(–1.83)	(–1.38)	(–0.91)
D(Karnataka(–1))	–0.056	0.0004	–0.054	–0.017	0.016	0.153
	(–0.69)	(0.005)	(–0.64)	(–0.23)	(0.20)	(1.51)
D(Karnataka(–2))	0.027	–0.041	–0.0008	–0.113	–0.014	0.128
	(0.34)	(–0.54)	(–0.01)	(–1.53)	(–0.18)	(1.30)
D(Rajasthan(–1))	0.050	0.15	0.199	0.018	0.100	–0.174
	(0.42)	(1.28)	(1.59)	(0.167)	(0.82)	(–1.16)
D(Rajasthan(–2))	0.051	0.112	0.155	0.067	0.003	–0.067
	(0.52)	(1.18)	(1.53)	(0.74)	(0.03)	(–0.55)
D(Uttar Pr.(–1))	0.249	0.32	0.078	–0.085	–0.035	0.162
	(1.99)	(2.64)	(0.60)	(–0.73)	(–0.27)	(1.05)
D(Uttar Pr.(–2))	0.191	0.161	0.281	0.144	0.092	0.117
	(1.76)	(1.53)	(2.49)	(1.42)	(0.83)	(0.86)
D(Gujarat(–1))	0.17	0.153	–0.204	0.023	0.067	–0.219
	(1.97)	(1.83)	(–2.27)	(0.28)	(0.77)	(–2.04)
D(Gujarat(–2))	0.065	0.098	–0.036	–0.014	0.069	–0.044
	(0.86)	(1.33)	(–0.46)	(–0.20)	(0.89)	(–0.46)
R-squared	0.32	0.274	0.29	0.24	0.22	0.33
Adj. R-squared	0.24	0.187	0.206	0.154	0.131	0.25
Sum sq resids	0.432	0.404	0.464	0.37	0.446	0.66
S.E. equation	0.058	0.056	0.060	0.054	0.05	0.072
F-statistic	4.00	3.157	3.43	2.70	2.41	4.27
Log likelihood	207.87	212.6	202.87	218.29	205.7	177.68
Akaike AIC	–2.72	–2.78	–2.65	–2.86	–2.69	–2.29
Schwarz SC	–2.38	–2.45	–2.316	–2.53	–2.35	–1.95

Notes: Figures in parentheses denote t values. D denotes first difference.

ANNEXURE TABLE 4.3A.3 *Wheat – Reduced Form VECM in Domestic and World Markets: 1980 April to 1991 March*

Series in Log	*D(Punjab)*	*D(Haryana)*	*D(Karnataka)*	*D(Rajasthan)*	*D(Uttar Pr.)*	*D(World)*	*D(Gujarat)*
ECM	–0.08*	–0.34*	–0.13*	–0.02	–0.13	–0.04*	–0.10**
	(–2.42)	(–3.18)	(–2.31)	(–0.26)	(–1.62)	(–2.74)	(–1.93)
D(Punjab(–1))	–0.26	–0.001912	–0.114	–0.212	–0.096	0.014	0.003
	(–2.72)	(–0.02)	(–1.65)	(–2.02)	(–1.12)	(0.25)	(0.03)
D(Punjab(–2))	0.102	0.111	–0.015	0.087	0.049	–0.073	0.22
	(1.018)	(1.37)	(–0.22)	(0.81)	(0.56)	(–1.21)	(2.43)
D(Haryana(–1))	0.415	–0.26	0.045	0.012	0.077	–0.031	0.045
	(2.56)	(–1.99)	(0.40)	(0.07)	(0.54)	(–0.32)	(0.30)
D(Haryana(–2))	0.186	–0.197	–0.056	–0.045	–0.092	–0.005	0.03
	(1.24)	(–1.63)	(–0.53)	(–0.28)	(–0.70)	(–0.05)	(0.24)
D(Karnataka(–1))	–0.237	–0.217	–0.121	–0.335	–0.036	0.108	–0.05
	(–1.66)	(–1.89)	(–1.21)	(–2.21)	(–0.29)	(1.26)	(–0.44)
D(Karnataka(–2))	–0.046	–0.026	0.087	–0.187	0.175	0.141	0.126
	(–0.33)	(–0.24)	(0.91)	(–1.29)	(1.46)	(1.717)	(1.00)
D(Rajasthan(–1))	–0.014	0.005	0.073	–0.26	–0.013	–0.038	0.130
	(–0.14)	(0.05)	(0.99)	(–2.33)	(–0.14)	(–0.60)	(1.34)
D(Rajasthan(–2))	–0.113	–0.108	–0.068	0.024	–0.127	–0.073	0.044
	(–1.17)	(–1.38)	(–1.00)	(0.24)	(–1.50)	(–1.25)	(0.49)
D(Uttar Pr.(–1))	–0.08	0.198	–0.131	0.215	–0.007	–0.052	–0.142
	(–0.55)	(1.68)	(–1.27)	(1.39)	(–0.06)	(–0.59)	(–1.05)
D(Uttar Pr.(–2))	–0.125	0.059	–0.048	0.066	0.175	–0.009	–0.170
	(–0.93)	(0.55)	(–0.51)	(0.46)	(1.49)	(–0.116)	(–1.38)
D(World(–1))	0.081	0.210	–0.021	0.023	–0.153	0.122	0.024
	(0.52)	(1.67)	(–0.194)	(0.14)	(–1.12)	(1.30)	(0.167)
D(World(–2))	–0.051	0.065	–0.240	0.008	0.083	0.073	–0.221
	(–0.31)	(0.49)	(–2.09)	(0.05)	(0.58)	(0.75)	(–1.47)
D(Gujarat(–1))	0.344	0.292	0.180	0.231	0.140	0.026	0.0005
	(3.25)	(3.42)	(2.42)	(2.06)	(1.512)	(0.40)	(0.005)
D(Gujarat(–2))	0.209	0.180	0.078	0.251	0.034	–0.099	–0.035
	(1.92)	(2.05)	(1.02)	(2.17)	(0.36)	(–1.51)	(–0.35)
R-squared	0.23	0.299	0.23	0.203	0.179	0.157	0.168
Adj. R-squared	0.132	0.206	0.134	0.097	0.070	0.045	0.058
Sum sq resids	0.532	0.345	0.263	0.599	0.407	0.191	0.454
S.E. equation	0.068	0.055	0.048	0.072	0.060	0.041	0.063
F-statistic	2.307	3.22	2.320	1.926	1.648	1.40	1.53
Log likelihood	171.0	198.87	216.50	163.43	188.30	237.07	181.3
Akaike AIC	–2.40	–2.83	–3.108	–2.28	–2.67	–3.42	–2.56
Schwarz SC	–2.04	–2.48	–2.75	–1.93	–2.316	–3.07	–2.20

Notes: Figures in parentheses denote t values. D denotes first difference.

ANNEXURE TABLE 4.3A.4 *Wheat – Reduced Form VECM in Domestic and World Markets: 1991 April to 2003 March*

Series in Log	*D(Punjab)*	*D(Haryana)*	*D(Karnataka)*	*D(Rajasthan)*	*D(Uttar Pr.)*	*D(World)*	*D(Gujarat)*
ECM	–0.34*	–0.35*	–0.28*	–0.42*	–0.41*	–0.062*	–0.48*
	(–4.08)	(–3.19)	(–4.97)	(–4.19)	(–3.66)	(–2.67)	(–5.31)
D(Punjab(–1))	–0.012	–0.158	–0.047	–0.007	–0.034	0.008	0.109
	(–0.14)	(–1.92)	(–0.53)	(–0.10)	(–0.404)	(0.113)	(1.105)
D(Haryana(–1))	–0.073	–0.005	–0.063	0.135	0.037	0.07	–0.406
	(–0.61)	(–0.04)	(–0.51)	(1.25)	(0.31)	(0.642)	(–2.93)
D(Karnataka(–1))	–0.056	0.055	–0.016	0.052	0.045	–0.038	0.139
	(–0.68)	(0.70)	(–0.19)	(0.70)	(0.55)	(–0.51)	(1.47)
D(Rajasthan(–1))	0.032	0.182	0.156	–0.054	0.102	0.120	–0.125
	(0.32)	(1.92)	(1.53)	(–0.60)	(1.04)	(1.328)	(–1.08)
D(Uttar Pr.(–1))	0.164	0.216	–0.088	–0.137	–0.030	–0.07	–0.007
	(1.49)	(2.03)	(–0.78)	(–1.37)	(–0.279)	(–0.69)	(–0.06)
D(World(–1))	–0.052	–0.107	0.018	0.071	0.0001	0.168	–0.055
	(–0.56)	(–1.20)	(0.19)	(0.83)	(0.001)	(1.96)	(–0.50)
D(Gujarat(–1))	0.172	0.133	–0.159	0.07	0.064	0.042	–0.163
	(2.37)	(1.90)	(–2.12)	(1.13)	(0.88)	(0.63)	(–1.92)
R-squared	0.27	0.22	0.24	0.23	0.191	0.16	0.37
Adj. R-squared	0.212	0.156	0.178	0.165	0.122	0.098	0.32
Sum sq resides	0.465	0.433	0.49	0.38	0.468	0.39	0.63
S.E. equation	0.059	0.057	0.06	0.05	0.06	0.055	0.069
F-statistic	4.45	3.37	3.78	3.54	2.79	2.39	7.16
Log likelihood	204.63	209.64	199.8	217.51	204.18	216.12	182.70
Akaike AIC	–2.71	–2.78	–2.64	–2.89	–2.7	–2.87	–2.40
Schwarz SC	–2.46	–2.53	–2.39	–2.64	–2.45	–2.62	–2.15

Notes: Figures in parentheses denote t values. D denotes first difference.

ANNEXURE TABLE 4.3B.1 *Rice – Reduced Form VECM in Domestic Markets: 1980 October to 1991 September*

Series in log	*D(Andhra Pr.)*	*D(Karnataka)*	*D(Kerala)*	*D(Orissa)*	*D(Tamilnadu)*	*D(West Bengal)*	*D(Maharashtra)*
ECM	–0.35*	–0.33*	–0.37*	–0.18*	–0.27*	–0.23*	–0.20*
	(–4.72)	(–3.98)	(–5.40)	(–3.47)	(–3.40)	(–3.26)	(–2.36)
D(Andhra Pr.(–1))	–0.129	–0.021	–0.162	–0.055	0.0008	–0.11	0.01
	(–1.48)	(–0.19)	(–1.45)	(–0.619)	(0.006)	(–1.04)	(0.14)
D(Karnataka(–1))	–0.05	–0.06	0.062	0.07	0.192	0.120	0.0007
	(–0.71)	(–0.65)	(0.64)	(0.964)	(1.67)	(1.31)	(0.009)
D(Kerala(–1))	–0.080	–0.02	0.112	–0.069	–0.074	–0.152	0.036
	(–1.127)	(–0.28)	(1.23)	(–0.94)	(–0.687)	(–1.75)	(0.484)
D(Orissa(–1))	0.062	–0.011	–0.028	0.125	–0.131	0.42	–0.015
	(0.815)	(–0.107)	(–0.26)	(1.415)	(–1.00)	(4.02)	(–0.175)
D(Tamilnadu(–1))	–0.0009	0.017	0.082	0.052	–0.0100	0.103	0.024
	(–0.015)	(0.21)	(1.00)	(0.78)	(–0.10)	(1.31)	(0.36)
D(West Bengal(–1))	–0.11	0.118	0.084	0.086	0.048	–0.126	0.074
	(–1.58)	(1.32)	(0.91)	(1.15)	(0.44)	(–1.43)	(0.97)
D(Maharashtra(–1))	0.03	0.096	0.090	0.064	0.108	0.157	–0.11
	(0.34)	(0.793)	(0.72)	(0.63)	(0.71)	(1.30)	(–1.06)
R-squared	0.25	0.243	0.26	0.20	0.186	0.30	0.128
Adj. R-squared	0.182	0.17	0.201	0.126	0.11	0.236	0.047
Sum sq resids	0.24	0.36	0.396	0.25	0.56	0.36	0.268
S.E. equation	0.045	0.055	0.057	0.046	0.069	0.055	0.047
F-statistic	3.61	3.44	3.96	2.69	2.45	4.62	1.583
Log likelihood	223.89	196.75	192.07	219.67	168.66	197.86	217.33
Akaike AIC	–3.25	–2.84	–2.77	–3.19	–2.41	–2.85	–3.15
Schwarz SC	–2.99	–2.57	–2.50	–2.93	–2.145	–2.59	–2.89

Notes: Figures in parentheses denote t values. D denotes first difference.

ANNEXURE TABLE 4.3B.2 *Rice – Reduced Form VECM in Domestic Markets: 1991 October to 2002 September*

Series in Log	*D(Andhra Pr.)*	*D(Tamil-nadu)*	*D(Karna-taka)*	*D(West Bengal)*	*D(Har-yana)*	*D(Uttar Pr.)*	*D(Maha-rashtra)*
ECM	–0.46*	–0.35*	–0.17*	–0.14*	–0.25*	–0.32*	–0.30*
	(–5.32)	(–4.14)	(–3.42)	(–2.93)	(–3.10)	(–4.25)	(–4.71)
D(Andhra Pr.(–1))	–0.046	0.066	0.042	–0.099	–0.032	0.029	–0.062
	(–0.53)	(1.12)	(0.56)	(–1.49)	(–0.476)	(0.408)	(–1.130)
D(Tamil-nadu(–1))	0.176	–0.173	0.021	–0.089	0.006	–0.100	–0.068
	(1.26)	(–1.86)	(0.18)	(–0.85)	(0.061)	(–0.877)	(–0.789)
D(Karna-taka(–1))	0.077	0.013	–0.075	0.131	0.118	0.197	0.006
	(0.74)	(0.195)	(–0.86)	(1.68)	(1.474)	(2.296)	(0.104)
D(West Bengal(–1))	–0.14	0.136	–0.048	–0.027	0.124	–0.020	–0.044
	(–1.16)	(1.68)	(–0.47)	(–0.305)	(1.317)	(–0.207)	(–0.585)
D(Haryana(–1))	–0.20	–0.038	0.23	0.026	–0.083	0.120	–0.027
	(–1.55)	(–0.44)	(2.17)	(0.272)	(–0.830)	(1.122)	(–0.339)
D(Uttar Pr.(–1))	–0.190	–0.0005	–0.095	0.006	–0.046	–0.050	0.001
	(–1.70)	(–0.007)	(–1.01)	(0.082)	(–0.537)	(–0.542)	(0.017)
D(Mahara-shtra(–1))	0.19	–0.077	–0.058	0.078	0.094	–0.071	0.073
	(1.35)	(–0.79)	(–0.47)	(0.720)	(0.842)	(–0.594)	(0.812)
R-squared	0.31	0.27	0.163	0.156	0.18	0.231	0.265
Adj. R-squared	0.243	0.204	0.086	0.077	0.103	0.159	0.197
Sum sq resids	0.58	0.259	0.41	0.327	0.347	0.397	0.226
S.E. equation	0.07	0.046	0.059	0.052	0.054	0.058	0.043
F-statistic	4.76	4.02	2.10	1.99	2.35	3.22	3.88
Log likelihood	167.20	219.65	189.46	204.43	200.54	191.8874	228.41
Akaike AIC	–2.38	–3.194	–2.73	–2.96	–2.90	–2.76	–3.32
Schwarz SC	–2.123	–2.93	–2.46	–2.69	–2.63	–2.502	–3.06

Notes: Figures in parentheses denote t values. D denotes first difference.

ANNEXURE TABLE 4.3B.3 *Rice – Reduced Form VECM in Domestic and World Markets: 1980 October to 1991 September*

Series in Log	*D(Andhra Pr.)*	*D(Karna-taka)*	*D(Kerala)*	*D(Tamil-nadu)*	*D(World)*	*D(Maha-rashtra)*
ECM	–0.64*	–0.43*	–0.49*	–0.30*	–0.00098	–0.010
	(–5.48)	(–4.74)	(–5.20)	(–3.40)	(–0.073)	(–0.19)
D(Andhra Pr.(–1))	0.029	0.123	–0.349	–0.047	–0.041	0.022
	(0.28)	(0.88)	(–2.36)	(–0.26)	(–0.33)	(0.185)
D(Andhra Pr.(–2))	0.030	0.049	–0.113	–0.069	0.016	–0.059
	(0.34)	(0.41)	(–0.89)	(–0.46)	(0.155)	(–0.57)
D(Karna-taka(–1))	–0.048	0.020	0.1123	0.215	0.058	0.115
	(–0.63)	(0.198)	(1.04)	(1.70)	(0.65)	(1.302)
D(Karna-taka(–2))	–0.026	0.096	0.134	0.108	–0.052	0.067
	(–0.38)	(1.049)	(1.378)	(0.936)	(–0.644)	(0.82)
D(Kerala(–1))	–0.115	–0.1044	0.165	–0.075	0.0419	–0.0011
	(–1.66)	(–1.12)	(1.68)	(–0.64)	(0.51)	(–0.01)
D(Kerala(–2))	–0.014	–0.206	0.155	0.110	–0.074	0.059
	(–0.20)	(–2.28)	(1.62)	(0.97)	(–0.93)	(0.74)
D(Tamil-nadu(–1))	0.063	0.084	0.078	–0.014	0.053	0.118
	(1.008)	(1.00)	(0.88)	(–0.14)	(0.71)	(1.604)
D(Tamil-nadu(–2))	–0.0002	0.040	0.050	0.028	0.035	0.013
	(–0.003)	(0.525)	(0.62)	(0.29)	(0.528)	(0.197)
D(World(–1))	0.032	0.050	0.029	0.122	0.378	0.037
	(0.407)	(0.46)	(0.25)	(0.90)	(3.97)	(0.39)
D(World(–2))	0.053	–0.222	0.040	0.146	–0.016	–0.075
	(0.65)	(–2.05)	(0.34)	(1.07)	(–0.16)	(–0.78)
D(Maha-rashtra(–1))	0.0040	0.057	0.090	0.155	0.086	–0.270
	(0.045)	(0.48)	(0.71)	(1.033)	(0.816)	(–2.56)
D(Maha-rashtra(–2))	–0.041	–0.109	–0.114	–0.040	0.153	–0.256
	(–0.47)	(–0.95)	(–0.94)	(–0.28)	(1.51)	(–2.54)
Constant	0.0025	0.0009	0.0006	0.0008	–0.0001	0.0019
	(0.70)	(0.18)	(0.12)	(0.135)	(–0.033)	(0.46)

Cont'd...

Cont'd...

R-squared	0.354	0.295	0.280	0.227	0.217	0.140
Adj. R-squared	0.262	0.194	0.178	0.116	0.105	0.017
Sum sq resids	0.190	0.343	0.385	0.539	0.26	0.26
S.E. equation	0.041	0.055	0.058	0.069	0.048	0.048
F-statistic	3.84	2.93	2.73	2.05	1.94	1.143
Log likelihood	237.32	199.35	191.90	170.22	215.75	216.05
Akaike AIC	–3.41	–2.82	–2.71	–2.37	–3.081	–3.086
Schwarz SC	–3.03	–2.45	–2.33	–1.99	–2.70	–2.70

Notes: Figures in parentheses denote t values. D denotes first difference.

ANNEXURE TABLE 4.3B.4 *Rice – Reduced Form VECM in Domestic and World Markets: 1991 October to 2002 September*

Series in Log	*D(Andhra Pr.)*	*D(Tamil-nadu)*	*D(Har-yana)*	*D(Uttar Pr.)*	*D(World)*	*D(Maha-rashtra)*
ECM	–0.44*	–0.36*	–0.135*	–0.35*	–0.006	–0.28*
	(–5.20)	(–4.93)	(–2.05)	(–4.67)	(–0.39)	(–4.14)
D(Andhra Pr.(–1))	–0.056	0.074	–0.041	0.030	0.051	–0.061
	(–0.63)	(1.26)	(–0.58)	(0.42)	(0.78)	(–1.09)
D(Tamil Nadu(–1))	0.174	–0.184	0.0013	–0.075	0.027	–0.055
	(1.29)	(–2.06)	(0.012)	(–0.69)	(0.27)	(–0.65)
D(Haryana(–1))	–0.28	–0.030	–0.156	0.090	–0.088	–0.046
	(–2.27)	(–0.37)	(–1.59)	(0.90)	(–0.97)	(–0.58)
D(Uttar Pr.(–1))	–0.146	0.011	0.0064	–0.049	–0.053	0.011
	(–1.31)	(0.15)	(0.072)	(–0.54)	(–0.64)	(0.155)
D(World(–1))	–0.01	–0.062	0.020	0.098	0.309	–0.095
	(–0.08)	(–0.79)	(0.21)	(1.02)	(3.53)	(–1.25)
D(Maharashtra(–1))	0.22	–0.11	0.012	–0.126	–0.204	0.111
	(1.53)	(–1.18)	(0.104)	(–1.05)	(–1.85)	(1.17)
R-squared	0.29	0.271	0.11	0.252	0.225	0.218
Adj. R-squared	0.240	0.216	0.045	0.196	0.167	0.159
Sum sq resids	0.592	0.259	0.376	0.386	0.323	0.241
S.E. equation	0.070	0.046	0.056	0.056	0.051	0.044
F-statistic	5.547	4.96	1.68	4.49	3.88	3.72
Log likelihood	165.9	219.5	195.36	193.69	205.30	224.36
Akaike AIC	–2.39	–3.22	–2.85	–2.82	–3.00	–3.29
Schwarz SC	–2.17	–3.00	–2.63	–2.60	–2.78	–3.07

Notes: Figures in parentheses denote t values. D denotes first difference.

ANNEXURE TABLE 4.3C.1 *Sugar – Reduced Form VECM in Domestic Markets: 1980 October to 1991 September*

Series in Log	*D(Uttar Pr.)*	*D(Punjab)*	*D(Karnataka)*	*D(Tamilnadu)*	*D(Bihar)*	*D(Maharashtra*	*D(Andhra Pr.)*
ECM	–0.70*	–0.057	–0.019	–0.036*	–0.097*	–0.074*	–0.40*
	(–4.67)	(–0.83)	(–1.17)	(–2.41)	(–2.51)	(–2.30)	(–2.89)
D(Uttar Pr.(–1))	0.048	0.065	0.0008	–0.021	–0.148	0.082	0.043
	(0.391)	(0.62)	(0.007)	(–0.22)	(–1.66)	(1.06)	(0.377)
D(Punjab(–1))	–0.158	–0.341	0.021	0.004	0.132	–0.055	–0.137
	(–1.22)	(–3.14)	(0.19)	(0.04)	(1.43)	(–0.69)	(–1.15)
D(Karnataka(–1))	–0.133	0.065	–0.158	0.028	–0.032	0.162	0.089
	(–1.26)	(0.73)	(–1.75)	(0.34)	(–0.42)	(2.48)	(0.91)
D(Tamil Nadu(–1))	0.133	0.128	0.142	–0.06	0.026	0.041	0.047
	(1.05)	(1.20)	(1.312)	(–0.70)	(0.29)	(0.53)	(0.40)
D(Bihar(–1))	–0.12	0.180	0.078	0.158	–0.18	–0.08	0.113
	(–1.02)	(1.74)	(0.75)	(1.66)	(–2.06)	(–1.16)	(1.01)
D(Maharashtra(–1))	–0.028	0.044	–0.093	–0.118	0.115	–0.17	–0.191
	(–0.19)	(0.35)	(–0.73)	(–1.02)	(1.08)	(–1.84)	(–1.38)
D(Andhra Pr.(–1))	–0.01	–0.025	–0.047	0.06	0.053	–0.021	–0.083
	(–0.07)	(–0.23)	(–0.436)	(0.63)	(0.58)	(–0.26)	(–0.704)
R-squared	0.255	0.14	0.09	0.16	0.144	0.158	0.203
Adj. R-squared	0.20	0.08	0.03	0.10	0.088	0.103	0.151
Sum sq resids	1.80	1.28	1.31	1.09	0.927	0.69	1.534
S.E. equation	0.122	0.10	0.10	0.094	0.087	0.07	0.112
F-statistic	5.18	2.50	1.58	2.88	2.56	2.85	3.86
Log likelihood	93.61	115.6	114.2	126.30	136.78	155.7	104.07
Akaike AIC	–1.30	–1.64	–1.61	–1.804	–1.96	–2.25	–1.46
Schwarz SC	–1.10	–1.44	–1.42	–1.606	–1.76	–2.05	–1.264

Notes: Figures in parentheses denote t values. D denotes first difference.

ANNEXURE TABLE 4.3C.2 *Sugar – Reduced Form VECM in Domestic Markets: 1991 October to 2001 September*

Series in Log	*D(Uttar Pr.)*	*D(Punjab)*	*D(Karnataka)*	*D(Tamilnadu)*	*D(Bihar)*	*D(Andhra Pr.)*
ECM	–0.37*	–0.17*	–0.34*	–0.36*	–0.417*	–0.37*
	(–3.96)	(–2.59)	(–3.51)	(–3.94)	(–5.23)	(–3.99)
D(Uttar Pr.(–1))	0.255	0.178	–0.100	–0.062	0.031	0.074
	(2.22)	(2.85)	(–1.39)	(–0.75)	(0.38)	(0.89)
D(Punjab(–1))	–0.012	–0.043	–0.010	–0.093	0.054	0.116
	(–0.07)	(–0.47)	(–0.10)	(–0.78)	(0.46)	(0.96)
D(Karnataka(–1))	–0.134	–0.006	–0.103	–0.087	0.074	–0.250
	(–0.84)	(–0.059)	(–0.99)	(–0.73)	(0.62)	(–2.35)
D(Tamil Nadu(–1))	0.161	0.173	0.041	–0.094	–0.031	–0.077
	(1.22)	(2.09)	(0.48)	(–0.96)	(–0.32)	(–0.89)
D(Bihar(–1))	0.027	0.047	0.035	0.156	–0.010	0.086
	(0.21)	(0.58)	(0.43)	(1.64)	(–0.11)	(1.02)
D(Andhra Pr.(–1))	–0.185	–0.008	–0.071	–0.388	0.024	–0.121
	(–1.23)	(–0.085)	(–0.73)	(–3.46)	(0.22)	(–1.21)
R-squared	0.20	0.195	0.26	0.324	0.27	0.306
Adj. R-squared	0.127	0.119	0.198	0.26	0.20	0.241
Sum sq resids	1.47	0.58	0.63	0.83	0.79	0.65
S.E. equation	0.117	0.07	0.07	0.088	0.08	0.078
F-statistic	2.71	2.59	3.89	5.13	4.03	4.72
Log likelihood	90.91	145.18	140.8	124.9	127.7	139.0
Akaike AIC	–1.35	–2.27	–2.20	–1.93	–1.97	–2.16
Schwarz SC	–1.09	–2.01	–1.94	–1.67	–1.72	–1.91

Notes: Figures in parentheses denote t values. D denotes first difference.

ANNEXURE TABLE 4.3C.3 *Sugar – Reduced Form VECM in Domestic and World Markets: 1980 October to 1991 September*

Series in Log	*D(Uttar Pr.)*	*D(Punjab)*	*D(Karnataka)*	*D(Tamilnadu)*	*D (Bihar)*	*D(Maharashtra)*	*D (Andhra Pr.)*	*D (World)*
ECM	–0.64*	–0.41*	–0.09*	–0.003	–0.27*	–0.34*	–0.198**	–0.046
	(–4.02)	(–3.45)	(–3.38)	(–0.08)	(–4.01)	(–5.30)	(–1.98)	(–1.02)
D(Uttar Pr.(–1))	0.028	0.006	–0.048	–0.053	–0.089	0.045	0.025	–0.051
	(0.21)	(0.05)	(–0.44)	(–0.52)	(–1.00)	(0.62)	(0.21)	(–0.212)
D(Punjab(–1))	–0.090	–0.166	0.078	0.082	–0.024	–0.067	–0.114	–0.74
	(–0.62)	(–1.44)	(0.65)	(0.73)	(–0.24)	(–0.82)	(–0.86)	(–2.65)
D(Karnataka(–1))	–0.151	0.048	–0.146	0.046	–0.013	0.173	0.06	0.076
	(–1.45)	(0.57)	(–1.67)	(0.56)	(–0.18)	(2.91)	(0.63)	(0.37)
D(Tamilnadu(–1))	0.176	0.146	0.078	–0.110	–0.009	–0.022	0.075	0.255
	(1.38)	(1.44)	(0.74)	(–1.11)	(–0.10)	(–0.319)	(0.648)	(1.03)
D(Bihar(–1))	–0.180	0.03	0.031	0.101	–0.086	–0.07	0.085	0.227
	(–1.37)	(0.37)	(0.294)	(0.99)	(–0.95)	(–1.00)	(0.70)	(0.87)
D(Maharashtra(–1))	–0.037	0.065	0.008	–0.086	0.153	–0.071	–0.17	–0.355
	(–0.24)	(0.53)	(0.06)	(–0.72)	(1.45)	(–0.82)	(–1.21)	(–1.17)
D(Andhra Pr.(–1))	–0.108	–0.052	–0.071	0.167	0.06	–0.092	–0.22	0.351
	(–0.87)	(–0.53)	(–0.70)	(1.74)	(0.78)	(–1.32)	(–1.97)	(1.46)
D(World(–1))	0.063	0.083	0.024	–0.004	–0.006	–0.002	0.07	–0.26
	(1.35)	(2.25)	(0.622)	(–0.12)	(–0.216)	(–0.10)	(1.66)	(–2.94)
R-squared	0.254	0.238	0.15	0.159	0.207	0.30	0.213	0.196
Adj. R-squared	0.192	0.174	0.08	0.089	0.141	0.245	0.147	0.128
Sum sq resids	1.80	1.140	1.23	1.090	0.85	0.573	1.51	6.812
S.E. equation	0.123	0.097	0.10	0.09	0.084	0.069	0.112	0.239
F-statistic	4.06	3.72	2.13	2.26	3.12	5.20	3.23	2.91
Log likelihood	93.5	123.37	118.4	126.28	141.77	168.03	104.90	7.21
Akaike AIC	–1.27	–1.72	–1.65	–1.77	–2.01	–2.41	–1.44	0.058
Schwarz SC	–1.02	–1.48	–1.41	–1.53	–1.76	–2.17	–1.20	0.301

Notes: Figures in parentheses denote t values. D denotes first difference.

ANNEXURE TABLE 4.3C.4 *Sugar – Reduced Form VECM in Domestic and World Markets: 1991 October to 2001 September*

Series in Log	*D(Uttar Pr.)*	*D(Punjab)*	*D(Karnataka)*	*D(Tamilnadu)*	*D(Bihar)*	*D(Andhra Pr.)*	*D(World)*
ECM	–0.302*	–0.14*	–0.209*	–0.33*	–0.429*	–0.403*	0.014
	(–3.39)	(–2.25)	(–2.56)	(–4.77)	(–5.59)	(–4.20)	(0.58)
D(Uttar Pr.(–1))	0.094	0.120	–0.099	–0.139	–0.112	–0.074	0.009
	(0.86)	(1.77)	(–1.39)	(–1.74)	(–1.44)	(–1.05)	(0.09)
D(Punjab(–1))	–0.038	–0.046	0.147	–0.037	–0.121	0.128	0.17
	(–0.24)	(–0.48)	(1.45)	(–0.33)	(–1.09)	(1.26)	(1.165)
D(Karnataka(–1))	–0.274	–0.002	–0.146	–0.072	0.016	–0.272	0.040
	(–1.71)	(–0.02)	(–1.41)	(–0.61)	(0.145)	(–2.62)	(0.26)
D(Tamilnadu(–1))	0.304	0.144	0.129	–0.108	–0.001	–0.061	–0.20
	(2.44)	(1.877)	(1.59)	(–1.195)	(–0.02)	(–0.74)	(–1.69)
D(Bihar(–1))	–0.068	0.076	–0.021	0.161	–0.029	0.064	–0.108
	(–0.55)	(0.99)	(–0.27)	(1.77)	(–0.32)	(0.79)	(–0.915)
D(Andhra Pr.(–1))	–0.173	–0.025	–0.057	–0.410	0.025	–0.091	0.128
	(–1.13)	(–0.26)	(–0.57)	(–3.67)	(0.23)	(–0.92)	(0.88)
D(World(–1))	0.109	–0.038	0.075	0.112	0.005	–0.071	–0.49
	(1.216)	(–0.69)	(1.29)	(1.71)	(0.08)	(–1.21)	(–5.81)
R-squared	0.16	0.194	0.248	0.33	0.29	0.309	0.278
Adj. R-squared	0.09	0.119	0.177	0.27	0.22	0.242	0.211
Sum sq resids	1.54	0.59	0.651	0.82	0.77	0.651	1.391
S.E. equation	0.120	0.07	0.078	0.08	0.085	0.078	0.113
F-statistic	2.16	2.58	3.53	5.33	4.38	4.78	4.131
Log likelihood	88.44	145.15	139.34	125.6	129.14	139.27	94.60
Akaike AIC	–1.312	–2.27	–2.17	–1.943	–2.00	–2.17	–1.41
Schwarz SC	–1.054	–2.01	–1.91	–1.68	–1.74	–1.91	–1.15

Notes: Figures in parentheses denote t values. D denotes first difference.

ANNEXURE TABLE 4.3D.1 *Cotton – Reduced Form VECM in Domestic Markets: 1982 October to 1990 September*

Series in Log	*D(Maharashtra)*	*D(Tamil Nadu)*
ECM	–0.181*	0.029
	(–3.70)	(1.06)
D(Maharashtra(–1))	0.085	0.111
	(0.84)	(1.046)
D(Maharashtra(–2))	0.0125	–0.010
	(0.123)	(–0.09)
D(Tamil Nadu(–1))	–0.190	–0.096
	(–1.80)	(–0.85)
D(Tamil Nadu(–2))	–0.17	–0.034
	(–1.61)	(–0.30)
R-squared	0.141	0.023
Adj. R-squared	0.102	–0.020
Sum sq resides	0.392	0.447
S.E. equation	0.066	0.071
F-statistic	3.63	0.540
Log likelihood	122.26	116.19
Akaike AIC	–2.521	–2.39
Schwarz SC	–2.38	–2.25

Notes: Figures in parentheses denote t values. D denotes first difference.

ANNEXURE TABLE 4.3D.2 *Cotton – Reduced Form VECM in Domestic and World Markets: 1982 October to 1990 September*

Series in Log	*D(Maharashtra)*	*D(Tamil Nadu)*	*D(World)*
ECM	–0.125*	–0.034	–0.034*
	(–3.43)	(–0.63)	(–2.99)
D(Maharashtra(–1))	0.045	0.080	–0.118
	(0.443)	(0.75)	(–1.61)
D(Maharashtra(–2))	–0.037	–0.007	0.055
	(–0.36)	(–0.064)	(0.74)
D(Tamil Nadu(–1))	–0.203	–0.045	–0.048
	(–1.84)	(–0.39)	(–0.61)
D(Tamil Nadu(–2))	–0.179	0.015	–0.178
	(–1.63)	(0.13)	(–2.26)
D(World(–1))	0.002	0.231	0.385
	(0.015)	(1.54)	(3.74)

Cont'd...

Cont'd...

D(World(–2))	–0.064	–0.026	–0.060
	(–0.44)	(–0.177)	(–0.57)
R-squared	0.129	0.041	0.269
Adj. R-squared	0.068	–0.025	0.218
Sum sq resids	0.398	0.439	0.207
S.E. equation	0.068	0.07	0.049
F-statistic	2.12	0.62	5.287
Log likelihood	121.5	117.04	152.0
Akaike AIC	–2.46	–2.36	–3.11
Schwarz SC	–2.27	–2.17	–2.92

Notes: Figures in parentheses denote t values. D denotes first difference.

ANNEXURE TABLE 4.3D.3 *Cotton – Reduced Form VECM in Domestic and World Markets: 1994 October to 1998 September*

Series in Log	*D(Maharashtra)*	*D(Tamil Nadu)*	*D(World)*
ECM	0.025	–0.095	–0.524*
	(0.59)	(–1.60)	(–4.02)
D(Maharashtra(–1))	–0.076	0.0004	–0.039
	(–0.42)	(0.004)	(–0.665)
D(Maharashtra(–2))	0.133	–0.084	–0.066
	(0.75)	(–0.92)	(–1.165)
D(Maharashtra(–3))	–0.055	–0.066	0.025
	(–0.31)	(–0.72)	(0.44)
D(Tamil Nadu(–1))	0.241	0.013	0.135
	(0.721)	(0.077)	(1.251)
D(Tamil Nadu(–2))	0.299	0.170	0.180
	(0.88)	(0.95)	(1.633)
D(Tamil Nadu(–3))	0.093	0.077	0.080
	(0.27)	(0.42)	(0.714)
D(World(–1))	–0.488	0.461	0.270
	(–1.14)	(2.07)	(1.954)
D(World(–2))	0.079	–0.045	0.168
	(0.18)	(–0.197)	(1.177)
D(World(–3))	0.428	0.116	0.007
	(1.00)	(0.519)	(0.050)

Cont'd...

Cont'd...

Constant	–0.010	–0.0007	–0.004
	(–0.58)	(–0.078)	(–0.82)
R-squared	0.112	0.181	0.411
Adj. R-squared	–0.156	–0.066	0.233
Sum sq resids	0.461	0.126	0.048
S.E. equation	0.118	0.061	0.038
F-statistic	0.417	0.731	2.308
Log likelihood	37.81	66.26	87.20
Akaike AIC	–1.218	–2.511	–3.46
Schwarz SC	–0.772	–2.06	–3.01

Notes: Figures in parentheses denote t values. D denotes first difference.

ANNEXURE TABLE 4.3E.1 *Groundnut Seed – Reduced Form VECM in Domestic Markets: 1980 November to 1992 October*

Series in log	*D(Andhra Pr.)*	*D(Uttar Pr.)*	*D(Gujarat)*	*D(Tamil Nadu)*
ECM	–0.210**	–0.233*	–0.425*	–0.263*
	(–1.75)	(–6.10)	(3.10)	(2.12)
D(Andhra Pr.(–1))	–0.202	–0.347	–0.20	–0.081
	(–1.70)	(–3.45)	(–1.48)	(–0.66)
D(Uttar Pr.(–1))	–0.017	–0.029	0.031	0.060
	(–0.205)	(–0.399)	(0.31)	(0.677)
D(Gujarat(–1))	–0.035	–0.050	–0.124	0.099
	(–0.43)	(–0.73)	(–1.34)	(1.179)
D(Tamil Nadu(–1))	0.267	0.345	0.520	0.05
	(2.30)	(3.49)	(3.92)	(0.43)
R-squared	0.105	0.272	0.145	0.051
Adj. R-squared	0.07	0.245	0.114	0.016
Sum sq resids	0.93	0.672	1.213	0.997
S.E. equation	0.08	0.070	0.09	0.085
F-statistic	3.21	10.18	4.64	1.46
Log likelihood	155.32	178.54	136.61	150.5
Akaike AIC	–2.10	–2.43	–1.83	–2.03
Schwarz SC	–1.97	–2.30	–1.71	–1.91

Notes: Figures in parentheses denote t values. D denotes first difference.

ANNEXURE TABLE 4.3E.2 *Groundnut Seed – Reduced Form VECM in Domestic Markets: 1992 November to 2003 October*

Series in log	*D(Andhra Pr.)*	*D(Uttar Pr.)*	*D(Gujarat)*	*D(Tamil Nadu)*
ECM	–0.186*	–0.038	–0.205*	–0.160
	(–3.03)	(–1.09)	(–3.50)	(–1.57)
D(Andhra Pr.(–1))	–0.034	–0.147	0.152	–0.074
	(–0.35)	(–1.84)	(1.47)	(–0.60)
D(Uttar Pr.(–1))	–0.116	–0.191	–0.083	–0.034
	(–1.09)	(–2.17)	(–0.73)	(–0.255)
D(Gujarat(–1))	0.082	–0.037	–0.120	0.015
	(0.98)	(–0.54)	(–1.35)	(0.15)
D(Tamil Nadu(–1))	–0.006	0.281	0.029	–0.244
	(–0.06)	(3.83)	(0.30)	(–2.16)
R-squared	0.098	0.192	0.16	0.119
Adj. R-squared	0.069	0.166	0.133	0.09
Sum sq resides	0.505	0.342	0.57	0.80
S.E. equation	0.06	0.05	0.067	0.080
F-statistic	3.42	7.43	5.95	4.24
Log likelihood	176.2	201.5	168.37	145.87
Akaike AIC	–2.63	–3.02	–2.513	–2.167
Schwarz SC	–2.52	–2.91	–2.40	–2.05

Notes: Figures in parentheses denote t values. D denotes first difference.

ANNEXURE TABLE 4.3E.3 *Groundnut Seed – Reduced Form VECM in Domestic and World Markets: 1980 November to 1992 October*

Series in Log	*D(Andhra Pr.)*	*D(Tamil Nadu)*	*D(Uttar Pr.)*	*D(Gujarat)*	*D(World)*
ECM	–0.224*	–0.082	–0.27*	–0.24*	–0.01
	(–2.24)	(–1.36)	(–5.39)	(–3.41)	(–1.11)
D(Andhra Pr.(–1))	–0.22	–0.092	–0.331	–0.234	–0.290
	(–2.07)	(–0.83)	(–3.35)	(–1.85)	(–1.75)
D(Tamil Nadu(–1))	0.19	–0.135	0.280	0.47	0.269
	(1.89)	(–1.30)	(2.99)	(3.97)	(1.72)
D(Uttar Pr.(–1))	–0.014	0.051	–0.043	0.030	0.078
	(–0.18)	(0.605)	(–0.56)	(0.31)	(0.60)
D(Gujarat(–1))	–0.04	0.084	–0.058	–0.037	–0.020
	(–0.53)	(1.07)	(–0.83)	(–0.409)	(–0.172)

Cont'd...

Cont'd...

D(World(–1))	–0.106	–0.055	0.11	0.079	0.227
	(–1.94)	(–0.98)	(2.17)	(1.21)	(2.66)
R-squared	0.160	0.072	0.272	0.196	0.07
Adj. R-squared	0.123	0.031	0.240	0.161	0.029
Sum sq resids	0.719	0.766	0.62	1.01	1.73
S.E. equation	0.072	0.075	0.067	0.086	0.11
F-statistic	4.31	1.75	8.43	5.51	1.71
Log likelihood	173.76	169.27	184.19	149.03	111.19
Akaike AIC	–2.348	–2.28	–2.49	–2.00	–1.46
Schwarz SC	–2.20	–2.13	–2.35	–1.85	–1.32

Notes: Figures in parentheses denote t values. D denotes first difference.

ANNEXURE TABLE 4.3E.4 *Groundnut Seed – Reduced Form VECM in Domestic and World Markets: 1992 November to 2003 October*

Series in log	*D(Andhra Pr.)*	*D(Uttar Pr.)*	*D(Gujarat)*	*D(Tamil Nadu)*	*D(World)*
ECM	–0.32*	–0.057	–0.55*	–0.184	–0.04
	(–4.05)	(–1.25)	(–5.36)	(–1.64)	(–1.37)
D(Andhra Pr.(–1))	0.02	–0.173	0.049	–0.065	0.044
	(0.21)	(–2.06)	(0.48)	(–0.50)	(0.433)
D(Uttar Pr.(–1))	–0.169	–0.187	–0.120	–0.028	–0.032
	(–1.62)	(–2.06)	(–1.09)	(–0.20)	(–0.295)
D(Gujarat(–1))	0.06	–0.010	0.016	0.007	–0.011
	(0.77)	(–0.13)	(0.17)	(0.063)	(–0.12)
D(Tamil Nadu(–1))	0.018	0.269	–0.051	–0.234	0.037
	(0.21)	(3.53)	(–0.55)	(–2.00)	(0.40)
D(World(–1))	–0.25	–0.021	0.064	–0.089	0.217
	(–3.02)	(–0.29)	(0.72)	(–0.79)	(2.43)
R-squared	0.20	0.199	0.259	0.126	0.087
Adj. R-squared	0.163	0.160	0.22	0.084	0.042
Sum sq resids	0.447	0.339	0.50	0.800	0.502
S.E. equation	0.060	0.052	0.06	0.080	0.063
F-statistic	5.20	5.09	7.17	2.973	1.96
Log likelihood	184.20	202.1	176.5	146.40	176.6
Akaike AIC	–2.72	–3.00	–2.60	–2.14	–2.60
Schwarz SC	–2.57	–2.84	–2.45	–1.99	–2.45

Notes: Figures in parentheses denote t values. D denotes first difference.

ANNEXURE TABLE 4.3F.1 *Soyabean Seed – Reduced Form VECM in Domestic Markets: 1982 November to 1991 October*

Series in Log	*D(Madhya Pradesh)*	*D(Uttar Pradesh)*
ECM	–0.111	–0.292*
	(–1.15)	(–4.25)
D(Madhya Pradesh(–1))	–0.211	–0.020
	(–1.87)	(–0.23)
D(Uttar Pradesh(–1))	–0.021	0.063
	(–0.18)	(0.69)
R-squared	0.089	0.187
Adj. R-squared	0.072	0.171
Sum sq resids	0.771	0.473
S.E. equation	0.08	0.067
F-statistic	5.08	11.89
Log likelihood	110.49	136.3
Akaike AIC	–2.028	–2.51
Schwarz SC	–1.952	–2.44

Notes: Figures in parentheses denote t values. D denotes first difference.

ANNEXURE TABLE 4.3F.2 *Soyabean Seed – Reduced Form VECM in Domestic and World Markets: 1982 November to 1991 October*

Series in Log	*D(Madhya Pradesh)*	*D(Uttar Pradesh)*	*D(World)*
ECM	–0.127	–0.314*	–0.012
	(–1.31)	(–4.18)	(–1.29)
D(Madhya Pr.(–1))	–0.20	–0.0160	–0.015
	(–1.79)	(–0.18)	(–0.23)
D(Uttar Pr.(–1))	–0.038	0.088	0.0007
	(–0.32)	(0.93)	(0.010)
D(World(–1))	–0.024	–0.062	0.276
	(–0.15)	(–0.506)	(2.91)
R-squared	0.093	0.186	0.098
Adj. R-squared	0.066	0.162	0.07
Sum sq resids	0.768	0.474	0.27
S.E. equation	0.08	0.068	0.05
F-statistic	3.50	7.80	3.70
Log likelihood	110.70	136.31	165.06
Akaike AIC	–2.01	–2.49	–3.03
Schwarz SC	–1.91	–2.39	–2.93

Notes: Figures in parentheses denote t values. D denotes first difference.

ANNEXURE TABLE 4.3F.3 *Soyabean Seed – Reduced Form VECM in Domestic and World Markets: 1995 November to 1999 October*

Series in Log	*D(Madhya Pradesh)*	*D(Uttar Pradesh)*	*D(World)*
ECM	0.033*	–0.095	–0.72*
	(2.40)	(–1.11)	(–3.91)
D(Madhya Pr.(–1))	–0.196	0.214	0.025
	(–1.25)	(1.54)	(0.25)
D(Uttar Pr.(–1))	–0.094	0.222	–0.003
	(–0.53)	(1.41)	(–0.03)
D(World(–1))	0.578	–0.25	0.266
	(2.10)	(–1.04)	(1.55)
Constant	–0.00075	–0.005	–0.005
	(–0.06)	(–0.55)	(–0.80)
R-squared	0.148	0.109	0.291
Adj. R-squared	0.065	0.022	0.222
Sum sq resids	0.23	0.180	0.091
S.E. equation	0.075	0.066	0.047
F-statistic	1.78	1.26	4.216
Log likelihood	56.49	62.16	77.91
Akaike AIC	–2.23	–2.48	–3.17
Schwarz SC	–2.04	–2.28	–2.97

Notes: Figures in parentheses denote t values. D denotes first difference.

ANNEXURE TABLE 6.1 *Summary Chart of Crop-Specific Estimates of Area/Supply Elasticity in India*

Crop/Author	*Location/Response*	*Elasticity*		*Time Period*
		Short Run	*Long Run*	
Wheat				
Chand (1991)	Punjab/Supply	0.18	–	1977–80
Kumar (1998,2001)	All India/Area	0.063	0.229	1975–96
Gulati and Kelly (1999)	SAT/Area	No Effect		1970–90
Sharma, Ghosh and Kumar (2001)	All India/Supply	0.13	0.30	1973–97
Bhalla and Singh (1996)	Punjab/Supply	0.01	0.02	1980–94
Present Study	All India/Area	0.10	0.15	1980–03
Rice				
Chand (1991)	Punjab/Supply	0.132	–	1977–80
Kumar (1998,2001)	All India/Area	0.019	0.119	1975–96
Gulati and Kelly (1999)	SAT/Area	0.06–0.17		1970–90
Bhalla and Singh (1996)	Punjab/Supply	0.15	0.42	1980–94
Present Study	All India/Area	0.09	0.14	1980–03
Sugarcane				
Bhalla and Singh (1996)	Punjab/Supply	0.12	0.14	1980–94
Gulati and Kelly (1999)	SAT/Area	–0.02–0.23	–	1970–90
Naik and Jain (1999)	Uttar Pr./Area	0.47	1.57	1975–96
	Maharashtra/Area	1.02	3.29	1975–96
	All India/Area	0.27	0.90	1975–96
Present Study	All India/Area	0.21	1.31	1980–03
Cotton				
Chand (1991)	Punjab/Supply	0.008	–	1977–80
Bhalla and Singh (1996)	Punjab/Supply	0.05	0.07	1980–94
Gulati and Kelly (1999)	SAT/Area	0.27–0.93	–	1970–90
Naik and Jain (1999)	Maharashtra/Area	0.29	1.71	1975–96
	Tamil Nadu/Area	0.48	0.73	1975–96
	All India/Area	0.20	0.32	1975–96
Present Study	All India/Area	0.12	0.44	1980–03
Groundnut Seed				
Kapila (1982)	Andhra Pr/Area	0.11–0.80	0.35–0.99	1962–75
Naik and Jain (1999)	Andhra Pr/Area	0.39	2.39	1975–96
	All India/Area	0.033	0.093	1975–96
Present Study	All India/Area	0.21	0.50	1980–03
Soyabean Seed				
Present Study	All India/Area	0.51	1.26	1980–03

Note: Long-run area/supply price elasticity is computed by dividing the estimated price/profitability coefficient by one minus the coefficient of lagged dependent variable, i.e., area/output.

ANNEXURE TABLE 7.1 *Rice-Haryana: OLS Results under Exportable and Importable Scenarios from 1980–81 to 2002–03 at 1993–94 Prices*

Dependent Variables/Independent Variables under Exportable Scenario									
Price	World Price	Support Price	Export	Production			Constant	R2	D-W
	0.43*# (3.61)	2.15* (3.46)	0.003 (0.09)	–0.34*** (–1.76)	–	–	–9.82	0.75	1.59$
Export	Pe/Pd	Stock	World Income	Open-ness (share)	–	–	Constant	R2	D-W
	1.85*# (4.19)	0.59*** (1.81)	1.16* (3.14)	2.59* (4.49)	–	–	–14.8	0.87	1.27
Area	Lagged Pd/Ip	Rain Index	Yield/Yieldc	Pc Maize	Yield Risk	Lagged Area	Constant	R2	D-W
	0.18** (2.22)	0.17* (4.17)	–0.27* (–3.04)	–0.48*# (–2.81)	–0.01 (–1.53)	0.52* (3.85)	6.61	0.96	1.63
Yield	Rain Index	Yield/Yieldc	Technology	–	–	–	Constant	R2	D-W
	0.08** (1.89)	0.32* (3.31)	0.79* (2.91)	–	–	–	8.12	0.42	1.95$
Dependent Variables/Independent Variables under Importable Scenario									
Price	World Price	Support Price	Import	Procurement	Productio n	–	Constant	R2	D-W
	0.28**# (1.95)	1.22** (1.82)	0.004 (0.44)	–0.04 (–0.49)	–0.02 (–0.10)	–	–3.28	0.53	1.07
Import	Pit/Pd	Stock	Dummy (NTB)	Lagged Import	–	–	Constant	R2	D-W
	–0.54# (–0.27)	–4.65* (–4.06)	–2.34*** (1.71)	0.36* (2.44)	–	–	45.9	0.72	1.82

Note: Data on rice exports-imports and variable used to capture openness of agriculture are at the country level.

ANNEXURE FIGURE 7.1 *Validation of Area under Selected Crops from 1990–91 to 2002–03*

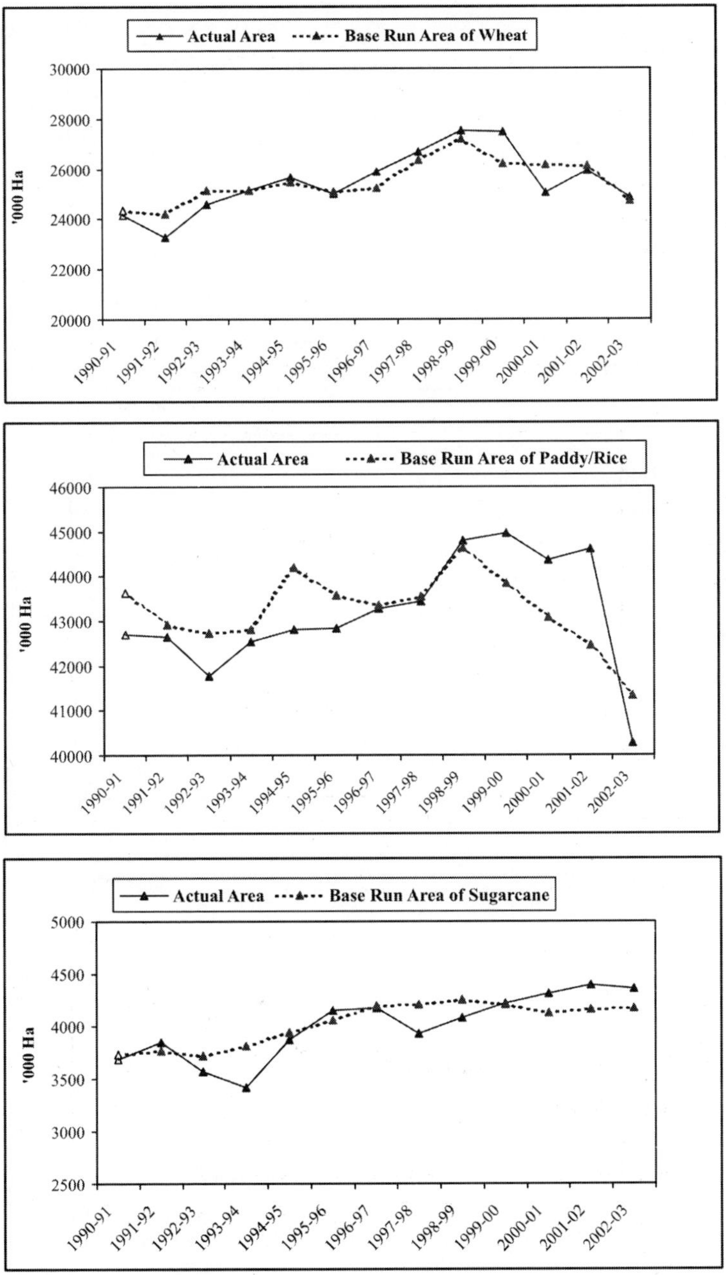

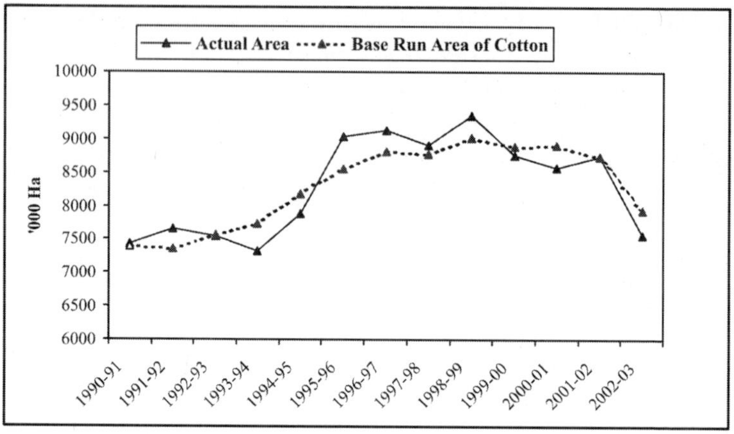
Actual Area
Base Run Area of Cotton
10000
9500
9000
8500
8000
7500
7000
6500
6000
'000 Ha
1990-91
1991-92
1992-93
1993-94
1994-95
1995-96
1996-97
1997-98
1998-99
1999-00
2000-01
2001-02
2002-03

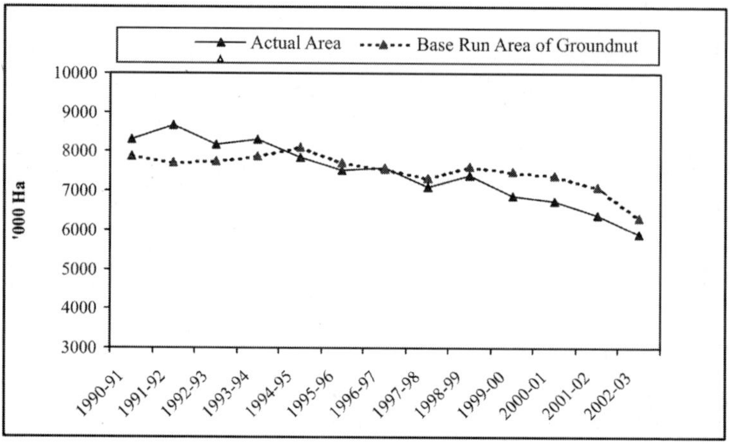
Actual Area
Base Run Area of Groundnut
10000
9000
8000
7000
6000
5000
4000
3000
'000 Ha
1990-91
1991-92
1992-93
1993-94
1994-95
1995-96
1996-97
1997-98
1998-99
1999-00
2000-01
2001-02
2002-03

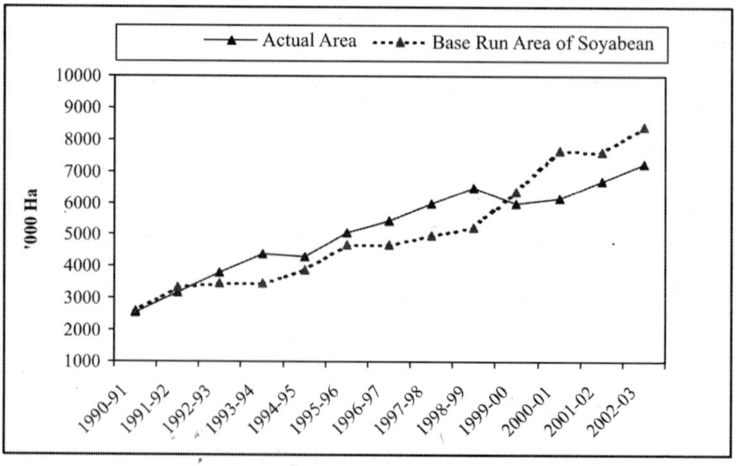
Actual Area
Base Run Area of Soyabean
10000
9000
8000
7000
6000
5000
4000
3000
2000
1000
'000 Ha
1990-91
1991-92
1992-93
1993-94
1994-95
1995-96
1996-97
1997-98
1998-99
1999-00
2000-01
2001-02
2002-03

References

Acharya, S.S. (2001), 'Domestic Agricultural Marketing Policies, Incentives and Integration', in S.S. Acharya and D.P. Chaudhri (eds.) *Indian Agricultural Policy at the Crossroads*, Jaipur: Rawat Publications.

Ackerman, Karen Z. and Praveen M. Dixit (1999), *An Introduction to State Trading in Agriculture,* Market and Trade Economic Division, Economic Research Service, US Department of Agriculture, Report No. 783.

Aradhyula, S.V. (1987), 'Rational Expectations and Policy Modelling: The Case of Wheat in India', *Journal of Policy Modelling*, 9 (4), Winter.

Ardeni, P.G. (1989), 'Does the Law of One Price really hold for Commodity Prices', *American Journal of Agricultural Economics*, 66: pp. 661–69.

Asche, F., H. Bremnes and C.R. Wessells (1999), 'Product Aggregation, Market Integration and Relationships between Prices: An Application to World Salmon Markets', *American Journal of Agricultural Economics*, 81, August: pp. 568–581.

Askari, H. and J.T. Cummings (1976), *Agricultural Supply Response: A Survey of Econometric Evidence,* New York: Praeger Publishers.

——. (1977), 'Estimating Agricultural Supply Response with the Nerlove Model: A Survey', *International Economic Review*, 18(2): pp. 257–92.

Baffes, J. (1991), 'Some Further Evidence on Law of One Price: The Law of One Price Still Holds', *American Journal of Agricultural Economics*, 68: pp. 1,264–1,273.

Baffes, J. and B. Gardener (2003), 'The Transmission of World Commodity Prices to Domestic Markets under Policy Reforms in Developing Countries', *Journal of Policy Reform*, 6(3): pp. 159–80.

Balassa, B. (1986), 'Policy Responses to Exogenous Shocks in Developing Countries', Papers and Proceedings of the Ninety-eighth Annual Meeting of the American Economic Association, *The American Economic Review*, 76(2), May.

Bapna, S.L. (1981), *Aggregate Supply Response of Crops in a Developing Region,* New Delhi: Sultan Chand and Sons.

—— . (1977), 'Estimation of Supply Functions for Semi-Arid Tropical Crops: Methodology and Some Results', Presented at the 7th Annual Conference of the Indian Econometric Society, 19–21 December, Centre for Development Studies, Trivandrum.

Bapna, S.L., H.P. Binswanger, and J.B. Quizon (1981), 'System of Output Supply and Factor Demand Equations for the Semi-Arid Tropical India', Studies in Employment and Rural Development No. 73, I.B.R.D. Washington, DC.

Barret, C.B. and J.R. Li (2002), 'Distinguishing between Equilibrium and Integration in Spatial Price Analysis', *American Journal of Agricultural Economics,* 84(2), May: pp. 292–307.

Bathla, Seema (2009), 'Market Integration of Agricultural Commodities: An Analysis of Selected Cereals, Oilseeds and Horticultural Crops', Report Submitted to IASRI, New Delhi as part of the V-PAGe Project of NAIP being carried out at IASRI.

—— . (2009), 'Macro Economic Policies and Agriculture Supply Response in India: A Commodity Level Analysis', *Indian Economic Journal,* 57(2), July–September.

—— . (2008), 'Agriculture Reforms and Market Integration: A Spatial Analysis of Food and Non-food Commodities', *Journal of Social and Economic Development,* 10(2).

—— . (2008), 'Regional Dimensions of Inter-crop Diversification in India: Implications for Production and Productivity Growth', *Agriculture Situation in India,* 64(12), March.

—— . (2006), 'Trade Policy Reforms and Openness of Indian Agriculture: Analysis at the Commodity Level', *South Asia Economic Journal,* 7(1).

—— . (2004), 'Agriculture Market Intervention Policies: Trends and Implications in a New Regime', *Occasional Paper No. 34,* NABARD, Mumbai.

Bautista, R.M. and A. Valdes (eds.) (1993), *The Bias against Agriculture: Trade and Macroeconomic Policies in Developing Countries,* Institute for Contemporary Studies, San Fransisco.

Bhalla, G.S. (eds.) (1994), *Economic Liberalization and Indian Agriculture,* New Delhi: Institute for Studies in Industrial Development.

—— . (2004), *Globalization and Indian Agriculture, Millennium Study on the State of Indian Farmer,* New Delhi: Academic Foundation.

Bhalla, G.S. and Gurmail Singh (1996), *Impact of GATT on Punjab Agriculture,* Institute for Development and Communication Monograph Series II, Chandigarh.

Bhatia, S. (1991), *Agricultural Price Policy and Production in India,* Bhubaneshwar: Konark Publishers.

Bhattacharya, B.B. and Sabyasachi Kar (2007), *Macroeconomic Reforms, Growth and Stability*, New Delhi: Oxford University Press.

Binswanger, Hans P. (1989), 'The Policy Response of Agriculture', Proceedings of the World Bank Annual Conference on Development Economics, Supplement to the *World Bank Economic Review:* pp. 231–58.

Binswanger, Hans P., Shahihdur Khandekar and Mark Rosenzweig (1989), 'How Infrastructure and Financial Institutions affect Agricultural Output and Investment in India', *World Bank Policy, Planning and Research Working Paper 163*, Washington D.C.

Blyn, Goerge (1973), 'Price Series Correlation as a measure of Market Integration', *Indian Journal of Agricultural Economics,* 28: pp. 56–59.

Bond, Marian E. (1983), 'Agricultural Responses to Prices in Sub-Saharan Africa', *International Monetary Fund Staff Paper,* 30(4): pp. 703–26.

Brown, R.L., J. Durbin and J.M. Evans (1975), 'Technique for Testing the Constancy of Regression Relationships Over Time', *Journal of Royal Statistical Society*, 37.

Cardenas, M. (1994), 'Stabilization and Redistribution of Coffee Revenues: A Political Economy Model of Commodity Marketing Boards', *Journal of Development Economics*, 44: pp. 351–80.

Carol, Alexander and John Wyeth (1994), 'Cointegration and Market Integration: The Indonesian Rice Markets', *The Journal of Development Studies*, 30 (2): pp. 303–328.

Chakravarty, S. (1973), 'Reflections on the Growth Process in the Indian Economy', in *Writings on Development*, New Delhi: Oxford University Press.

Chambers, R.G. and R.E. Just (1981), 'Interrelationships between Money Instruments and Agricultural Commodity Trade', *American Journal of Agricultural Economics,* 63: pp. 934–941.

Chandrasekhar, C.P. and Jayati Ghosh (2002), *The Market that Failed: A Decade of Neo-Liberal Reforms in India*, New Delhi: Leftword Books.

Chand, Ramesh (2010), 'Understanding the Nature and Causes of Food Inflation', *Economic and Political Weekly*, March 21: XLV (26/27), February.

—. (2009), 'The Wheat Market: Distortions caused by Government Interventions', *Economic and Political Weekly*, March 21: XLIV (12): pp. 4,146.

—. (2001), 'Wheat Exports: Little Gain', *Economic and Political Weekly*, June 23–29: XXXVI (25): pp. 2,226–2,228.

—. (1991), *Agricultural Development Price Policy and Marketed Surplus in India,* New Delhi: Concept Publishing Company.

Chand, Ramesh and Dayanatha Jha (2001), 'Trade Liberalization, Agricultural Prices and Net Social Welfare', in S.S. Acharya and D.P. Chaudhari (eds.) *Indian Agricultural Policy at the Crossroads*. Jaipur: Rawat Publications.

Chand, Ramesh and Seema Bathla (2005), 'WTO Agriculture Negotiations and South Asian Countries: Concerns, Viewpoints and Consensus', *South Asia Economic Journal*, 6(1): pp. 1–22.

Chibber, Ajay (1988), 'Raising Agricultural Output: Price and Non-price Factors', *Finance and Development*, 25(2): pp. 591–605.

Clark, C. (1951), *The Conditions of Economic Progress*. London: Macmillan.

Cleaver, K.M. (1988), 'Agricultural Policy Reform and Structural Adjustment in Sub-Saharan Africa: Results to Date', World Bank Africa Department I, Washington DC.

Cummings, J.T. (1975), 'The Supply Responsiveness of Indian Farmers in the Post Independence Period', *Indian Journal of Agricultural Economics*, 30(1): pp. 25–41.

Cummings, Ralph W.J. (1967), *Pricing Efficiency in the Indian Wheat Market,* New Delhi: Impex.

De Janvry, A. and K. Subbarao (1986), *Agricultural Price Policy and Income Distribution in India,* New Delhi: Oxford University Press.

Deardorff, A. and R.Stern (1999), *Measurement of Non-tariff Barriers*, Ann Arbor: University of Michigan Press.

Deb, Surajit (2005), 'Terms of Trade and Supply Response in Indian Agriculture: Analysis in a Cointegration Framework', *Indian Economic Review*, XXXX(1), January-June.

Deshpande, R.S. (2008), 'Price Policy and Minimum Support Prices in a changing Agricultural Economy', in S.K. Bhaumik (ed.), *Reforming Indian Agriculture: Towards Employment Generation and Poverty Reduction,* New Delhi: Sage Publications.

Diaz-Bonilla E. and Sherman Robinson (2010), 'Macroeconomics, Macrosectoral Policies, and Agriculture in Developing Countries', in Prabhu Pingali and Robert Evenson (ed.), *Handbook of Agricultural Economics*, Vol. 4, North Holland: Elsevier BV.

Edward, S. (1988), *Exchange Rate Misalignment in Developing Countries. Baltimore:* Johns Hopkins Press for the World Bank.

Eicher, Carl. K. and John M. Staaz (eds.) (1984) *Agricultural Development in the Third World*, Baltimose and London: The John Hopkins University Press.

Engle, R.F. and B.S. Yoo (1987), 'Forecasting and Testing in Co-integrated System', *Journal of Econometrics*, 35: pp. 143–159.

Engle, R.F. and C.W.J. Granger (1987), 'Co-integration and Error-Correction: Representation, Estimation and Testing', *Econometrica*, 55: pp. 251–276.

Epstein, T.S. (1962), *Economic Development and Social Change in South India*, Manchester: Manchester University Press.

Fei, J.C.H. and G. Ranis (1964), *Development of the Labour Surplus Economy, Theory and Policy*, Illinois: Homewood: Irwin Publishing Company.

Ganesh-Kumar, A., Ashok Gulati and Ralph Cummings Jr. (2009), 'Reforming Food Grains Management: Achieving Food Security and Cost Effectiveness', in Surjit Singh and V. Ratna Reddy (eds.), *Changing Contours of Asian Agriculture; Policies, Performance and Challenges*, New Delhi: Academic Foundation.

Ghosh, Nilabja and Chiranjib Neogi (1995), 'Supply Response of Foodgrains and Policy Actions: A Model with Rational Expectations Hypothesis', *Indian Journal of Agricultural Economics*, L(2), April June: pp. 135–152.

Giles, Mohan, Ed Brown, Bob Milward and Alfred B. Zack-Williams (2000), *Structural Adjustment: Theory, Practice and Impacts*, New York: Routledge.

Goldin, Ian and Odin Knudsen (eds.) (1990), *Agricultural Trade Liberalization: Implications for Developing Countries*. OECD, Paris.

Golleti, Francesco and Suresh Babu (1994), 'Market Liberalization and Integration of Maize Markets in Malawi', *Agricultural Economics*, 11: pp. 311–324.

Goodwin, Barry K. and Ted. C. Schroeder (1991), 'Co-integration Tests and Spatial Price Linkages in Regional Cattle Markets', *American Journal of Agricultural Economics*, 73: pp. 452–464.

Government of India (2000–01) and (2002–03), Economic Survey, Economic Division, Ministry of Finance.

——. (2002), Long Run Grain Policy, Abhijit Sen Committee Report, Department of Consumer Affairs, Food and Public Distribution, New Delhi.

——. (various issues), Agricultural Statistics at a Glance, Directorate of Economics and Statistics, Department of Agriculture and Cooperation, Ministry of Agriculture, New Delhi, Various Issues from 1980 to 2003.

——. (various issues), Agriculture Prices in India, Department of Agriculture and Cooperation, Ministry of Agriculture, New Delhi, Various Issues from 1980 to 2003.

——. (various issues), Custom Tariff of India, Ministry of Finance, Various Issues from 1980 to 2000.

——. (various issues), Economic Survey, Ministry of Finance, New Delhi, Various Issues from 1980 to 2003.

——., Import and Export Policy, April 1997-March 2002, ITC (HS) Classifications of Export and Import Items, Ministry of Commerce.

——. Monthly Statistics of Foreign Trade of India, Vol. I and II, Annual Number, Ministry of Commerce.

——. (various issues), Reports of the Commission on Agricultural Costs and Prices, Department of Agriculture and Cooperation, Ministry of Agriculture, New Delhi, Various Issues from 1980 to 2003.

——. (Various issues), Fertiliser Statistics, the Fertiliser Association of India, New Delhi.

——. (Various issues), National Accounts Statistics, Central Statistical organisation, New Delhi, Various Issues from 1980 to 2003.

Goyal, Arun (Various Issues) Custom Tariff, New Delhi: Academy of Business Studies.

Granger, C.W.J. (1986), 'Developments in the Study of Cointegrated Economic Variables', *Oxford Bulletin of Economics and Statistics*, 48: pp. 213–228.

Granger, C.W.J. and P. Newbold (1974), 'Spurious Regression in Econometrics', *Journal of Econometrics*, 2: pp. 111–120.

Greenaway, D. and C. Milner (1993), *Trade and Industrial Policy in Developing Countries: A Manual for Policy Analysis*, London: Macmillan.

Greene, William H. (1990), *Econometric Analysis,* New York: Macmillan Publishing Company.

Grimwade, N. (2004), 'The GATT, the Doha Round and the Developing Countries', in Homi Katrack and Roger Strange (eds.), *The WTO and Developing Countries*, Basingstoke: Palgrave Macmillan.

Gulati, Ashok (1987), *Agricultural Price Policy in India: An Econometric Approach*, New Delhi: Concept Publishing Company.

——. (1998), 'Liberalizing Indian Agriculture', in Bibek Debroy and Partha Shah (eds.), *Agenda for Change: Action Plan for the Economy*, No. 1, Centre for Civil Society, Rajiv Gandhi Institute for Contemporary Studies, March.

——. (2004), 'Trade Policies, Incentives, Investment and Institutions in Indian Agriculture', in India's Economic and Social Development: National and International Perspective', International Conference in Honour of Prof. C.H. Hanumantha Rao, 16–17 November, Administrative Staff College of India, Hyderabad and Centre for Economic and Social Studies, Hyderabad.

Gulati, Ashok and Gary Pursell (1992), *Trade Policy Incentives and Resource Allocation in Indian Agriculture,* Mimeo, World Bank.

Gulati, Ashok, Rajesh Mehta and Sudha Narayanan (1999), 'From Marrakesh to Seattle: Indian Agriculture in a Globalizing World', *Economic and Political Weekly*, October 2–8: XXXIV(40): pp. 2931–2942.

Gulati, Ashok, Setu Kahkonen and Pradeep Sharma (2000), 'The Food Corporation of India: Successes and Failures in Indian Marketing', in Setu Kahkonen and Anthony Lanyi (eds.) *Institutions, Incentives and Economic Reforms in India,* New Delhi: Sage Publications.

Gulati, Ashok and Sudha Narayanan (2003), *Subsidy Syndrome in Indian Agriculture,* New Delhi: Oxford University Press.

Gulati, Ashok and Tim Kelly (1999), *Trade Liberalization and Indian Agriculture,* New Delhi: Oxford University Press.

Gupta, R.P. (1973), *Agricultural Prices in a Backward Economy,* New Delhi: National Publishing House.

Gupta, S.C. and A. Majid (1965), *Producers' Response to Changes in Price and Marketing Policies: A Case Study of Sugarcane and Paddy in Uttar Pradesh,* London: Asia Publishing House.

Harris, B. (1979), 'There is Method in my Madness: or is it vice versa? Measuring Agricultural Market Performance', *Food Research Institute,* 17(2): pp. 197–218.

Hazell, P. et al. (1990), 'The Relationship between World Price Instability and the Prices Farmers Receive in Developing Countries', *Journal of Agricultural Economics,* 41: pp. 227–243.

Herdt, R.W. (1970), 'A Disaggregated Approach to Agricultural Supply', *American Journal of Agricultural Economics,* 52(4): pp. 512–20.

Heytens, P. (1986), 'Testing Market Integration', *Food Research Institute Studies,* 20: pp. 25–41.

Hirchman, A. (1958), *The Strategy of Economic Development,* New Haven Conn. USA: Yale University Press.

Hoda, Anwarul and Ashok Gulati (2007), WTO Negotiations on Agriculture and Developing Countries, New Delhi: Oxford University Press.

Hoekman, Mernard M. and Michel M. Kostecki (2001), *The Political Economy of the World Trading System: The WTO and Beyond,* Second Edition, New York: Oxford University Press.

Hotelling, H. (1932), 'Edgeworth's Taxation paradox and the Nature of Demand and Supply Functions', *Journal of Political Economics,* 40(5): pp. 577–616.

In, F. and T. Mount (1994), *Dynamic Macroeconomic Linkages to the Agricultural Sector,* Newcastle upon Tyne, UK: Athenaeum Press.

Ingco, D. Merlinda and Tonia Kandiero (2003), 'Introduction', in Merlinda D. Ingco (eds.) *Agriculture, Trade and WTO in South Asia,* Washington DC: World Bank. pp. 1–37.

International Monetary Fund, International Financial Statistics, Washington, Various Issues from 1980 to 2003.

Jayasuriya, Sisira, Jae H. Kim and Parmod Kumar (2007), 'International and Internal Market Integration in Indian Agriculture: A Study of the Indian Rice Market', Paper/poster prepared for presentation at the 106th seminar of the EAAE – Pro-poor Development in Low Income Countries, Food, Agriculture, Trade, and Environment, 25–27 October 2007 – Montpellier, France.

Jha, Raghbendra, K.V. Bhanumurthy and Anurag Sharma (2005), Market Integration in Wholesale Rice Markets in India. ASARC Working Paper 2005–03, Australian National University, Australian South Asia Research Centre.

Jha, Raghbendra, K.V. Bhanumurthy, Hari K. Nagarajan and Ashok K. Seth (1997), *Market Integration in Indian Agriculture.* No. 269, Indira Gandhi Institute of Development Research, Mumbai.

Johansen, S. (1988), 'Statistical Analysis of Cointegration Vectors', *Journal of Economic Dynamics and Control*, 12: pp. 231.54.

Johansen, S. and Katrina Juselius (1990), 'Maximum Likelihood Estimation and Inference of Cointegration with Applications to Demand for Money', *Oxford Bulletin of Economics and Statistics*, 52: pp. 169–210.

Johnston, B.F. (1970), 'Agriculture and Structural Transformation in Development Countries: A Survey of Research', *Journal of Economic Literature*, 3: pp. 369–404.

Johnston, B.F. and J.W. Mellor (1961), 'The Role of Agriculture in Economic Development', *American Economic Review*, 78(4): pp. 566–593.

Jorgenson, D.W. (1961), 'The Development of a Dual Economy', *The Economic Journal*, 71 (2): pp. 309–34.

Joshi P.K., Ashok Gulati and Ralph Cummings (eds.) (2007), *Agricultural Diversification and Small Holders in South Asia*, New Delhi: Academic Foundation.

Kaabia, Monia Ben and Jose M. Gil (2000), 'Short and Long-run Effects of Macroeconomic Variables on the Spanish Agricultural Sector', *European Review of Agricultural Economics*, 27 (4): pp. 449–471.

Kalirajan, Kaliappa and Shashanka Bhide (2003*), A Disequilibrium Macroeconometric Model for the Indian Economy*, England: Ashgate Publishing Ltd.

Kapila, Uma (1982), *Oilseeds Economy of India: A Case of Groundnut*, New Delhi: Agricole Publishing Academy.

Kaul, J.L. and D.S. Sidhu (1971), 'Acreage Response to Prices for Major Crops in Punjab-An Econometric Analysis', *Indian Journal of Agricultural Economics*, 26(4): pp. 427–434.

Kohli, Singhal Deepali (1996), 'Supply Response in Agriculture: A Review of Methodologies', *Working Paper No. 63*, National Council of Applied Economic Research, New Delhi.

Krishna, Jai and M.S. Rao (1967), 'Dynamics of Acreage for Wheat in Uttar Pradesh – A Study in Supply Response', *Indian Journal of Agricultural Economics*, XXII, January-March: pp. 37–52.

Krishna, Raj (1963), 'Farm Supply Response in India-Pakistan: A Case Study of the Punjab Region', *The Economic Journal*, 73, September: pp. 478–487

——. and Ajay Chibber (1983), 'Policy Modelling of a Dual Grain Market: The Case of Wheat in India', *Research Report No. 38*, IFPRI Washington D.C.

Krishna, Raj and G.S. Raychaudhuri (1980), 'Some Aspects of Wheat and Rice Price Policy in India', *The World Bank Staff Working Paper No. 381*, World Bank, Washington D.C.

Krivonos, Ekaterina (2004), 'The Impact of Coffee Market Reforms on Producer Prices and Price Transmission', *Policy Research Working Paper 3358*, The World Bank Development Research Group Trade Team, July.

Krueger, Anne. O. (1984), 'Trade Policies in developing Countries', in R.W. Jones and P.B. Kennen (eds.), *Handbook of International Economics 1*, Holland: Elsevier Science Publishers. pp. 519–66

Krueger, A.O., M. Schiff and A. Valdes (1988), 'Agricultural Incentives in Developing Countries: Measuring the Effect of Sectoral and Economy wide Policies', *World Bank Economic Review*, 2(3).

Kumar, Praduman (2001), 'Agricultural Performance and Productivity,' in S.S. Acharya and D.P. Chaudhri (eds.) *Indian Agricultural Policy at the Crossroads*, Jaipur: Rawat Publications.

——. (1998), 'Food Demand and Supply Projections for India', *Agricultural Economics Policy Paper 98–01*, Indian Agricultural Research Institute, New Delhi.

Kumar, Praduman and Mark W. Rosegrant (1993), 'Dynamic Supply Response of Rice and other Major Food Crops in India', Paper Presented at the International Conference on Projections and Policy Implications of Medium and Long Term Rice Supply and Demand, IRRI, Manila (Phillippines), April 14–16.

Kumar, Pramod (2007), *Farm Size and Marketing Efficiency: Pre- and Post-Liberalization*, New Delhi: Concept Publishing Company.

Kumar, Pramod and R.K. Sharma (2003), 'Price Integration and Pricing Efficiency at the Farm Level: A Study of Paddy in Haryana', *Indian Journal of Agricultural Economics*, 58(2): pp. 201–217.

Kuznets, Simon (1955), 'Economic Growth and Income Inequality', *American Economic Review*, 45 (1): pp. 1–28.

——. (1966), *Modern Economic Growth: Rate, Structure and Spread.* New Haven: Yale University Press.

Lassaad, Lachaal and Abner W. Womack (1998), 'Impact of Trade and Macroeconomic Linkages on Canadian Agriculture', *American Journal of Agricultural Economics*, 80, August: pp. 534–542.

Lele, Uma J. (1967), 'Market Integration: A Study of Sorghum Prices in Western India', *Indian Journal of Farm Economics*,49: pp. 147–59.

—. (1971), *Foodgrain Marketing in India: Private Performance and Public Policy.* Ithaca: Cornell University Press.

Lewis, W.A. (1955), *The Theory of Economic Growth.* Homewood, IL: Irwin.

Mackinnon, J.G. (1990), Critical Values for Cointegration Tests, Department of Economics, Queen's University, Canada, Mimeo.

Madhavan, M.C. (1972), 'Acreage Responses of Indian Farmers: A Case Study of Tamil Nadu', *Indian Journal of Agricultural Economics*, 27(1). pp. 67–85.

Maji, C.C., D. Jha and L.S. Venkataramanan (1971), 'Dynamic Supply and Demand Models for better Estimations and Projections: An Econometric Study for Major Foodgrains in the Punjab Region', *Indian Journal of Agricultural Economics*, 26, 1: pp. 21–34.

Mamingi, Nlandu (1996), 'How Prices and Macroeconomic Policies affect Agricultural Supply and Environment', *Policy Research Working Paper No. 1,645*, The World Bank Policy Research Department Environment, Infrastructure and Agriculture Division, September.

McKay, Andrew, Oliver Morrissey and Charlotte Vaillant (1998), 'Aggregate Export and Food Crop Supply Response in Tanzania', *DFID-TERP: Credit Discussion Paper No. 4*, Centre for Research in Economic Development and International Trade.

— (1997), 'Trade Liberalization and Agricultural Supply Response: Issues and Some Lessons', *European Journal of Development Research*, 9(2), December: pp. 129–147.

Meerman, Jacob (1997), *Reforming Agriculture: The World Bank Goes to Market.* World Bank.

Mehta, Rajesh (1997), 'Trade Policy Reforms during 1991–92 to 1995–96: Impact on India's External Trade', *Economic and Political Weekly*, XXXII(15): pp. 779–84.

Mellor, John W. (1966), *The Economics of Agricultural Development.* Ithaca: Cornell University Press.

Meyer, Jochen and Stephan von Cramon-Taubadel (2004), 'Asymmetric Price Transmission: A Survey', *Journal of Agriculture Economics*, 55(3), pp. 581–611.

Misra S.N. and M. Govinda Rao (2003), 'Trade Policy, Agricultural Growth and Rural Poor', *Economic and Political Weekly*, October 25–31, XXXVIII(43): pp. 4,588–4,603.

Monke, Eric and Todd Petzel (1984), 'Market Integration: An Application to International Trade in Cotton', *American Journal of Agricultural Economic, 66(4):* pp. 481–487.

Mundlak, Yair and Donald F. Larson (1992), 'On the Transmission of World Agricultural Prices', *The World Bank Economic Review*, 6 (2): pp. 394–422.

Muth, J.F. (1961), 'Rational Expectations and the Theory of Price Movements', *Econometrica,* 29(3): pp. 315–335.

Mydral, G. (1968), *Asian Drama: An Enquiry into the Poverty of Nations,* New York: Twentieth Century Fund.

Naik, Gopal and S.K. Jain (1999), 'Growth, Stability and Acreage Response of Agricultural Crops: Likely Impact of WTO Regime', in Samar K. Datta and Satish Y. Deodhar (eds.), *Implications of WTO Agreements for Indian Agriculture.* Indian Institute of Management, Ahmedabad.

Naik, Gopal and V.P.S. Arora (1986), 'Marketing Pattern and Pricing Efficiency in Indian Arecanut Market', *Indian Journal of Agricultural Economics,* 41(2): pp. 172–182.

Narayana, N.S.S. (1989), 'Production Decisions and Farm Supply Response to Policy Changes: A Review of Theoretical and Empirical Issues', International Conference on Methods of Planning and Policy Analysis for Mixed Economies, Indira Gandhi Institute of Development Research, Mumbai.

Narayana, N.S.S. and K.S. Parikh (1979), 'Agricultural Planning and Policy in Draft Sixth Plan: Will Farmers fulfil Planners' Expectations?' *Economic and Political Weekly,* August, XIV(30–32).

——. (1981), *Estimation of Farm Supply Response and Acreage Allocation: A Case Study of Indian Agriculture,* Luxemburg: International Institute for Applied Systems Analysis.

Narayana, N.S.S., K.S. Parikh and T.N. Srinivasan (1987), 'Policies and Impacts: An Analysis with a General Equilibrium Model for India', *Discussion Paper No. 3,* Indira Gandhi Institute of Development Research, Mumbai.

Narayana, N.S.S. and M. Shah (1984), 'Farm Supply Response in Kenya: Acreage Allocation Model', *European Review of Agricultural Economics,* 11(1): pp. 85–105.

Narian, D. (1965), *Impact of Price Movements on Areas under Selected Crops in India,* London: Cambridge University Press.

Nayyar, Deepak and Abhijit Sen (1994), 'International Trade and the Agricultural Sector in India', *Economic and Political Weekly,* XXIV (20), May 14: pp. 1187–1203.

Nerlove, Marc (1958), *Dynamics of Supply: Estimation of Farmers' Response to Price.* Baltimore: Johns Hopkins University Press.

Nerlove, M. and K.L. Bachman (1960), 'The Analysis of Changes in Agricultural Supply: Problems and Approaches', *Journal of Farm Economics,* August, LII(3): pp. 531–554.

Norton, Roger D. (2004), *Agricultural Development Policy Concepts and Experiences.* Food and Agricultural Organization of the United Nations: John Wiley and Sons Ltd.

Nowshirvani, Wahid (1968), 'Agricultural Supply in India: Some Theoretical and Empirical Studies', Ph.D. Dissertation, MIT.

Osterwald, Lenum (1992), 'A Note with Quantiles of the Asymptotic Distribution of the Maximum Likelihood Cointegration Rank Statistics', *Oxford Bulletin of Economics and Statistics*, 54: 461–71.

Oyejide, T.A. (1993), 'The Oil Boom, Macroeconomic Policies and Nigerian Agriculture: Analysis of a 'Dutch Disease' Phenomenon' in R.M. Bautista and A. Valdes (eds.), *The Bias against Agriculture: Trade and Macroeconomic Policies in Developing Countries*, Washington: ICEG and IFPRI.

Palaskas, T.B. and Harriss-White B. (1993), 'Testing Market Integration: New Approaches with Case Material from West Bengal Food Economy', *Journal of Development Studies*, 30:1–57.

Pandey, Mihir (1999), '*Trade Liberalization: Non-tariff Barriers in India*', Report Submitted to the Ministry of Finance, Government of India.

Parikh, A. (1972), 'Market Responsiveness of Peasant Cultivators: Some Evidence from Pre-war India', *Journal of Development Studies*, 8: pp. 289–306.

Patnaik, Utsa (1996), 'Export-Oriented Agriculture and Food Security in Developing Countries and India', 31 (35/37), Special No. (September), pp. 2,429–2,433.

Peltzman, S. (2000), 'Prices Rise Faster than they Fall', *Journal of Political Economy*, 108(3), pp. 466–502.

Preobrazhensky, E. (1965), *The New Economics*, Oxford: Clarendon Press.

Quizon, J. and H. Binswanger (1986), 'Modelling the Impact of Agricultural Growth and Government Policy on Income Distribution in India', *World Bank Economic Review*,1: pp. 103–48.

Rao, C.H. Hanumantha and Hans Linnemann (eds.) (1996), *Economic Reforms and Poverty Alleviation in India,* Indo-Dutch Studies on Development Alternatives–17, New Delhi: Sage Publications.

Rashid, Shahidur (2004) 'Spatial Integration of Maize Markets in Post-Liberalized Uganda', MTID Discussion Paper No. 71, International Food Policy Research Institute, 2033 K Street, NW Washington, D.C.

Rausser, G.C., J.A. Chalfant, H.A. Love and K.G. Stamoulis (1986), 'Macroeconomic Linkages, Taxes and Subsidies in the US Agricultural Sector', *American Journal of Agricultural Economics*, 56, February: pp. 1–14.

Ravallion, M. (1986), 'Testing Market Integration', *American Journal of Agricultural Economics*, 68(1): pp. 102–109.

Rivera-Gonzalez, Gloria and Steven M. Helfand (2001), 'The Extent, Pattern and Degree of Market Integration: A Multivariate Approach for the Brazilian Rice Market', *American Journal of Agricultural Economics*, 83 (3): pp. 576–592.

Saleth, Maria R. (1999), *Shift in Cropping Pattern from Cereals to Non Cereals*, Report, Institute of Economic Growth, September.

Sawant, S. (1972), *Supply Behaviour in Agriculture: An Econometric Analysis,* Mumbai: Himalaya Publishing House.

Sawant, S.D. and C.V. Achuthan (1995), 'Agricultural Growth Across Crops and Regions: Emerging Trends and Patterns', *Economic and Political Weekly,* XXX(12), March 25, Review of Agriculture: pp. A2–A13.

Schiff, M. and A. Valdes (1992*), The Plundering of Agriculture in Developing Countries,* World Bank Washington D.C.

—. (1998), 'Agriculture and the Macroeconomy' in B. Gardener and G. Rausser (eds.), *Handbook of Agricultural Economics,* Elsevier Science.

Schiff, S. and C. Montenegro (1995), 'Aggregate Agricultural Supply Response in Developing Countries: A Survey of Selected Issues', *World Bank Policy Research Working Paper No. 1,485.*

Schuh, G. Edward (1974), 'The Exchange Rate and US Agriculture, *American Journal of Agricultural Economics,* February, 56: pp. 1–13.

Schultz, T.W. (1964), *Transforming Traditional Agriculture,* New Haven: Yale University Press.

Sharma, Anil, Nilabja Ghosh and Pramod Kumar (2001), *A Policy Model for Open Market Operations of Wheat,* National Council of Applied Economic Research, New Delhi.

Shephard, R.W. (1953), *Cost of Production Functions.* Princeton: Princeton University Press.

Shumway, R. and A.A. Chang (1977), 'Linear Programming versus Positively Estimated Supply Functions: An Empirical and Methodological Critique', *American Journal of Agricultural Economics,* 59(1): pp. 344–357.

Sidhu, S.S. and Carlos A. Baanante (1981), 'Estimating Farm level Input Demand and Wheat Supply in the Indian Punjab using a Translog Profit Function', *American Journal of Agricultural Economics,* 63(2): pp. 237–246.

Singh, Gurdev and S.R. Asokan (2001), 'Impact of WTO on Indian (edible) Oilseeds Sector', in Samar K. Datta and Satish Y. Deodhar (eds.), *Implications of WTO Agreements for Indian Agriculture,* New Delhi: Oxford and IBH Publishing Co. Pvt. Ltd. pp. 687–712.

Sinharoy, Saikat and Sanjith R. Nair (1994), 'International Trade and Pepper Price Variations: A Cointegration Approach', *Indian Journal of Agricultural Economics,* 49 (3), July-September: pp. 417–425.

Storm, Servaas (1993), *Macro-economic considerations in the Choice of an Agricultural Policy: A Study into Sectoral Interdependence with reference to India,* Amsterdam: Thesis Publishers.

— (1997), 'The Unfinished Agenda: Indian Agriculture under the Structural Reforms', *The Journal of International Trade and Economic Development,* 6 (2): pp. 249–286.

Subbarao, K. (1978), *Rice Marketing System and Compulsory Levies in Andhra Pradesh – A Study of Public Intervention in Foodgrains Marketing*, New Delhi: Allied Publishers Pvt. Ltd.

Teyers, R. and K. Anderson (1992), *Disarray in World Food Markets: A Quantitative Assessment,* New York: Cambridge University Press.

Theil, Henri (1971), *Principles of Econometrics,* New York: John Wiley and Sons.

Timmer, P.C. (1974), 'A Model of Rice Marketing Margins in Indonesia, *Food Research Institute Studies*, 13 (2): pp. 145–167.

Wilson, Edgar J. (2001), 'Testing Agricultural Market Integration: Further Conceptual and Empirical Considerations Using Indian Wholesale Prices' in S.S. Acharya and D.P. Chaudhari (eds.), *Indian Agricultural Policy at the Crossroads*, Jaipur: Rawat Publications.

Wobst, Peter (2001), *Structural Adjustment and Intersectoral Shifts in Tanzania: A Computable General Equilibrium Model*, Washington: IFPRI.

World Bank. (1999), *Indian Foodgrain Marketing Policies: Reforming to Meet Food Security Needs,* Vol. 1 and II, Report No. 18329-IN, April 17.

—. (2002), *Global Economics Prospects and the Developing Countries 2002: Making Trade Work for the World's Poor.* Washington, DC: World Bank.

WTO (1998), *Trade Policy Review: India 1998*, Geneva.

—. (2001), Agriculture Negotiations Backgrounder; The Issues, and Where We Are Now. http://www.wto.org/english/tratop_e/agric_e/nogoti_e.htm, March 21.

Zanias, G.P. (1993), 'Testing for Integration in European Community Agricultural Product Markets', *Journal of Agricultural Economics*, 44: pp. 418–427.

Index